THE EAR

To the Time of Gregory the Great

BY

JOSEF A. JUNGMANN, S.J.

Translated by Francis A. Brunner, C.SS.R.

DARTON, LONGMAN & TODD

LONDON

DARTON, LONGMAN & TODD LTD
89 LILLIE ROAD
LONDON SW6 1VD

The Early Liturgy was first published in 1959 by the University of Notre Dame Press as one of the titles in its series of Liturgical Studies. This edition first published in 1960, reprinted in 1963, 1966, 1972, 1976 and 1980

IMPRIMI POTEST: Very Reverend John N. McCormick, C.S.S.R. *Provincial*, St. Louis Province, March 28th, 1959. IMPRIMI POTEST: Theodore J. Mehling, C.S.C., *Provincial*. NIHIL OBSTAT: William Havey, C.S.C., *Censor Deputatus*. IMPRIMATUR: ✠ Leo A. Pursly, D.D., LL.D., Bishop of Fort Wayne, April 2nd, 1959.

ISBN 0 232 48394 9

Printed in Great Britain by litho at
The Anchor Press Ltd and bound by
Wm Brendon & Son Ltd both of
Tiptree, Essex

Preface

These lectures, which I gave at Notre Dame in the summer of 1949, were not originally intended for publication. But the Editor of the University of Notre Dame Liturgical Series asked me to present them in book form in order to include in this series an introduction into the oldest and most important period in the history of the liturgy.

The carrying out of this task is due chiefly to the efforts of Rev. Francis A. Brunner, C.SS.R., to whom we are also indebted for the translation of *Missarum Sollemnia* (*The Mass of the Roman Rite*). He has improved the language of the lectures, supplemented the references to available English literature, added a summary here and there, as well as made occasional additions to the text itself. For this work the reader may be grateful. It goes without saying that I myself have included any important contributions from the intervening nine years of liturgical-historical research which would serve to shed further light on a particular point.

These lectures, by their very nature, are comprehensive in scope and necessarily deal with many subjects which I have treated more thoroughly in other works. For this book is not intended as a guide to scientific research in the field of liturgical history, but rather as an introduction into the manner of worship in the early Church. It is my hope that it will serve to deepen the reader's understanding of his own worship, as well as to present possible suggestions and aids to those engaged in pastoral work.

JOSEF A. JUNGMANN, S.J.

Innsbruck, March, 1958

Contents

1. Introduction: History, the Present and the Future 1

SECTION I. THE PRIMITIVE CHURCH

2. The Church as a Worshipping Community 10
3. Sunday and Easter in the Primitive Church 19
4. The Breaking of Bread: The Oldest Form of Eucharistic Service 29
5. The Celebration of the Eucharist in the Writings of the Apologists 39

SECTION II. THE THIRD CENTURY

6. The Eucharistic Liturgy of the Third Century 52
7. Baptism and Preparation for Baptism 74
8. The Apostles' Creed 87
9. Daily Devotions of the Early Christians 97
10. The Defense Against Gnosticism 109

SECTION III. THE AGE OF CONSTANTINE

11. The Impact of Paganism on Christian Worship 122
12. Pagan and Christian Mysteries 152

13. The Role of the Liturgy in the Transformation of Pagan Society 164
14. The Veneration of the Martyrs 175
15. Christological Disputes and Their Influence on the Liturgy 188

Section IV. Developments since the Fourth Century

16. Ecclesiastical and Linguistic Provinces 200
17. The Oriental Liturgies 210
18. The Latin Liturgies 227

Section V. The Roman Liturgy Before Gregory the Great

19. Baptism and Penance 240
20. The Easter Cycle 253
21. The Christmas Cycle 266
22. The Daily Office 278
23. The Roman Mass Before Gregory the Great 288

Index 309

CHAPTER ONE

Introduction: History, the Present and the Future

THE liturgy in the early Church to the time of Gregory the Great—this is our subject. But first we need to discuss some preliminary questions. Why, for instance, should we be concerned about the history of liturgy? Is it really worth our while to spend so much time in trying to learn how divine services were conducted long ago, when we have our own present-day problems and should surely be more concerned with the future than the past?

The answer, certainly, must be obvious. History furnishes us with valuable hints that help us deal with the very issues we are facing to-day. We cannot properly evaluate or properly solve the problems of the present and the future unless and until we study the past. And the more involved and profound these problems, the more thorough must be our search into history. This is particularly true in the field of liturgy, for here history must help us to recognize what we actually possess as an inheritance from the past. As our late Holy Father, Pope Pius XII, said so pointedly in his encyclical letter *Mediator Dei:*

> Assuredly it is a wise and most laudable thing to return in spirit and affection to the sources of the sacred liturgy. For research in this field of study, by tracing it back to its origins, contributes valuable assistance toward a more thorough and careful investigation of the significance of feast-days, and of the meaning of the texts and sacred ceremonies employed on their occasion.[1]

1. *Mediator Dei,* Nov. 20, 1947. Vatican Library translation (N.C.W.C. pamphlet), par. 62.

True, some subjects in the vast area of world history no longer have any bearing on the present; we study them only because our natural curiosity impels us to try to learn how things were in days gone by. Thus, for example, we dig into royal Egyptian tombs in order to throw light on the story of the tenth or the twentieth dynasty. But what happened at that time has no effect on the present, nor does it aid us to a better understanding of a present-day situation.

With the history of the liturgy, however, it is quite different. Here research has a very practical bearing on the present. The liturgy of the Catholic Church is an edifice in which we are still living today, and in essentials it is the same building in which Christians were already living ten or fifteen or even eighteen and more centuries ago. In the course of all these centuries, the structure has become more and more complicated, with constant remodelings and additions, and so the plan of the building has been obscured—so much so that we may no longer feel quite at home in it because we no longer understand it.

Hence we must look up the building plans, for these will tell us what the architects of old really wanted, and if we grasp their intentions we shall learn to appreciate much that the building contains and even to esteem it more highly. And if we should have the opportunity to make changes in the structure or to adapt it to the needs of our own people, we will then do so in such a way that, where possible, nothing of the precious heritage of the past is lost.

Thus to a great extent we can apply to the history of the liturgy what Cardinal Newman said about another department of history:

> . . . the history of the past ends in the present; and the present is our scene of trial; and to behave ourselves towards its various phenomena duly and religiously, we must understand them; and to understand them, we must have recourse to those past events which led to them. Thus the present is a text and the past its interpretation.[2]

We are going to deal, therefore, with that period of liturgical history which surpasses all others in importance because it is concerned with the basic outlines, the very ground-plan of the structure, namely the period up to Gregory the Great.

Liturgical history today has become a science possessing an extensive literature and already giving evidence of momentous results. This is true particularly of the history of primitive liturgy; indeed it is precisely in this field that research has been carried out for the last hundred years, and to good effect. A scientific history

2. J. H. Card. Newman, "Reformation of the XIth Century," in *Essays Critical and Historical*, 10th ed., vol. II (London, 1890), 250.

of liturgy had existed since the sixteenth century, connected originally with the so-called Reformation. The attacks which Luther and the other Reformers launched against the Church's worship, against the Mass and the Sacraments, put the Church on the defensive. Libraries were searched and ancient manuscripts sought out. The most important texts were published in printed form with accompanying commentaries. All this resulted in a defense that was truly brilliant—a defense of the Church and her dogmas and her worship. After all, defense—apologetics—was the prime purpose of this liturgical study.

It was in this era that the principal sources for liturgical history in the West were made known: the Roman and Gallican sacramentaries, edited first by Pamelius and Giuseppe Bianchini and later by Mabillon and Muratori; the most important Roman *ordines,* published by Hittorp and again later by Mabillon; and an array of texts, especially from the Middle Ages, issued through the activity of the Benedictines of St. Maur. On the other hand, very little could be done at that time to shed light on the history of the primitive liturgy. Isolated texts, it is true, were preserved, excerpts from the writings of the great Fathers of the Church—Augustine and Ambrose and Jerome and Leo the Great and, later, the Greek Fathers. But no one was in a position to visualize, in more than a very sketchy way, the liturgy as it was celebrated in early times, or the way in which the texts were actually used. And thus things remained up to the nineteenth century.

Even today our knowledge remains defective in many details, the simple reason being that our sources do not furnish a clue to these matters. Those were days of fervor; people lived Christian lives and prayed in Christian fashion. But not much was written down. This is especially true in matters liturgical; there was no real need to put things in writing; the living practice sufficed. In fact practically no written texts were used in ancient times, even by the priest at the altar; only a little, then, was actually written down.

For the past hundred years, however, our knowledge of the primitive liturgy has made marked progress in all essentials. This development is connected first of all with the advance made during the nineteenth century in Biblical and patristic studies. It is associated also with the controversies regarding the historical foundations of Christianity. When a David Friedrich Strauss claimed that Christianity is, in its entirety, a product of myths, when even the historical existence of Jesus Christ was questioned, it was high time to examine with renewed effort the existing source materials—the writings of the New Testament as well as the writings and monuments of subsequent decades and centuries.

With G. B. Rossi, systematic excavations of the catacombs were undertaken; their inscriptions and paintings began to convey their message to us, telling us many surprising things about the life of the first Christian generations. Dust-covered volumes in the libraries of oriental monasteries were made accessible. From the sands of the Egyptian desert, papyrus rolls and papyrus fragments were brought to light. All these investigations and discoveries enriched our knowledge of the liturgical life of those early days, while an ever increasing number of scholars labored to exploit these results and to make them bear fruit.

The very character of liturgical science was thereby greatly altered. Whereas during the period of the Reformation and the centuries that followed, the study of the liturgy bore an apologetic character, now a very new and different interest came to the fore. Today we no longer need to defend the Catholic liturgy against attacks, since our adversaries no longer direct their assaults against liturgy and worship but against the very foundations of Christianity itself. Our task is simply to study the liturgy of the first Christian centuries because it is something worthy of our study. This is especially the case with regard to the most ancient forms which reach back to the primitive Church and perhaps even to the age of the apostles. What the liturgy looked like at the very beginning would certainly be worth our knowing.

This study of the early beginnings of the liturgy was undertaken with considerable vigor a little more than half a century ago. At that time—1889—L. Duchesne published the first edition of his book, *Les origines du culte chrétien*. A little later, in 1906, F. Cabrol conducted his conferences on *Les origines liturgiques*.

Without doubt, the discovery of the origins of our worship holds a special attraction—much like the philologist's desire to find the original text of an ancient work. In matters liturgical, however, a knowledge of the original text, or the original form used in the primitive Church, while of considerable value, is not our only interest. Nowadays we no longer expend such efforts as did scholars fifty years ago to reestablish the original text from the documents that have come down to us. For we now realize that other forms, which developed in the years that followed, also proceeded from the life of the Church. In the same way as the original, or at least in a similar way, they are derived from the inspiration and activity of the Holy Spirit. They tell us of the manner in which those later generations prayed and worshipped, and what they added to the primitive forms out of their own resources. And also, they form the links of a chain connecting our present-day worship with the life and worship of the primitive Church. All the links in that chain are important, for only when we possess them all do we have a complete explanation of the present-day form of our divine worship. But it remains true that the first links are the more important, for they determined the course that succeeding forms were to take.

At this point, we might find it both interesting and useful to review the literary sources that are now available for a study of early times—first, those that were known before the middle of the nineteenth century, and then, those added since about 1870.

The most important of the liturgical sources made known at the earlier period are the following:

(1) Justin, the philosopher and martyr, who wrote his first *Apology* about 155 A.D. This contains, in chapters 65–67, some precious information about divine service.

(2) The *Apostolic Constitutions.* This is a work which is basically fictitious, purporting to present the decrees which Pope Clement I received from the apostles. Consisting of eight books, it contains many liturgical regulations, and gives a complete Mass formulary in the final book; this formulary is therefore often called the "Clementine liturgy." In the sixteenth century, scholars still believed that they really possessed a work of Pope Clement I, and even F. Probst, writing in about 1870 concerning the liturgy of the third century, places the Clementine liturgy in the second century. In Migne's great *Patrologia Graeca* also, the *Constitutiones Apostolorum* are found in the first volume. But it has been common knowledge for quite some time that this is a work of the late fourth century. Even so the Clementine formulary is important for us, because in it we do possess an oriental form of the liturgy of the fourth century.

(3) The *Mystagogic Catecheses* of Jerusalem, likewise of the fourth century. These catechetical instructions have come down to us along with the catecheses delivered by St. Cyril of Jerusalem about the year 347. Although the *Mystagogic Catecheses* are generally cited as written by Cyril, they are probably not his, but of a somewhat later date, about 400. These instructions are called "mystagogic" because they were intended for the newly baptized;

they served to acquaint them with the sacraments or "mysteries." These *Mystagogic Catecheses* include an explanation of the Mass that is very valuable for our purposes.

(4) Ambrose, *De Sacramentis*. This, too, is a series of catechetical instructions for the newly baptized; they were given by St. Ambrose about 390 and written down in shorthand by one of his audience. In these, again, a lengthy portion deals with Holy Mass, and a section of the Canon is actually quoted. (Most of us are probably familiar with part of this work; up to 1955, it was read in the Roman Breviary during the octave of Corpus Christi.) Eighty years ago, these were all the known sources of the primitive Christian liturgy, aside from the parenthetical observations found here and there in the writings of the Fathers.

To these sources, various new and important discoveries have now been added:

(1) The *Didache*, or *Teaching of the Twelve Apostles*, from the beginning of the second century. It was discovered in 1873 by an oriental bishop, Philotheos Bryennios. In the ninth and tenth chapters of the *Didache* are found the well-known eucharistic prayers, but the precise place and meaning of these prayers is not very clear.

(2) The *Traditio Apostolica* of Hippolytus of Rome, written about the year 215. This work gives us a very clear picture of the Church's liturgical life; it also contains the oldest text of the *canon missae*. Later we shall have occasion to discuss this work thoroughly and be able to glean from it much valuable information.

(3) The *Euchologion* of Serapion. Serapion of Thmuis was a friend of St. Athanasius; he died about 360. The *Euchologion* or "Prayerbook" was discovered by a Russian scholar, Dmitrijewsky, in a monastery on Mount Athos. It contains thirty prayers meant for use in public worship; amongst them is a complete text of the *anaphora*, that is, the Canon of the Mass.

(4) *Peregrinatio Aetheriae*. This is a description of a pilgrimage made about the year 400 to the Holy Land—*ad loca sancta;* it is the work of a nun whose name was probably Aetheria and who was a native of Gaul. It was discovered in 1887 by an Italian scholar, Gamurrini. It contains a lengthy description of the church services then in use in Jerusalem, namely the daily service and the canonical hours, and the Sunday service; the services of Holy Week are detailed with special clarity.

(5) The *Catecheses* of Theodore, Bishop of Mopsuestia in Cilicia, who died in 428. This work was discovered and published

in 1932 by Mingana in Syriac and English. These, too, are catechetical instructions for the newly-baptized, and contain a thorough and detailed explanation of Baptism and the Mass, much like the *Catecheses* of Jerusalem and those of St. Ambrose of Milan.

(6) And finally the *Testamentum Domini Nostri Jesu Christi*, which was discovered by the Syrian Patriarch Rahmani in 1899 and published by him in Syriac and Latin. This is a work of the fifth century. It is related to the *Constitutiones Apostolorum* and contains some important liturgical texts.

We can add to these sources also various papyri rescued from the desert sands of Egypt which contain valuable liturgical texts from Christian antiquity. Of these the papyrus of Dêr-Balyzeh is especially famous; it also contains a section from the prayers of the Mass.

A considerable number of new sources has thus become available to us. And, as we can well imagine, the picture previously drawn of the primitive Christian liturgy has thereby been altered. Now we can compose a description that is both more accurate and more detailed than was previously possible. As a result, many of the older descriptions of the ancient Christian liturgy have today only a very limited value. Thus, for example, F. Probst from 1870 to 1895 published a series of volumes on the liturgy of the first three centuries, on the liturgy of the fourth century, etc. Much of his material he gathered from scattered remarks of the Fathers, and in this regard his work is still valuable. But as a description of the actual liturgy of the period, his work must today be regarded as quite incomplete.

The principal sources which are available to us today were assembled and published by Johannes Quasten (now professor at the Catholic University of America, in Washington, D.C.), in his volume *Monumenta eucharistica et liturgica vetustissima* of the series *Florilegium Patristicum* (Bonn, 1937).

Our knowledge of the liturgy of this early period is not, of course, complete. Much remains obscure and will probably always remain obscure. But we do possess sufficient information to throw light on the essential elements of worship, sufficient information even to present a somewhat detailed description of the liturgy of the Catholic Church in those early formative years, and to help us understand how the Christians in the age of persecution, in the epoch of Constantine, and in the years of the first barbarian invasions, paid their homage to God. Our present task, then, is to study the liturgy of these early centuries with a view both to gaining knowledge for ourselves and to applying that knowledge, where possible, to the liturgical problems of the present time and those we can foresee in the years to come. History is a precious corrective of mere speculation, of subjective hypotheses. True knowledge of our present liturgy is knowledge based on the solid rock of historical facts; it is by studying the past that we can best learn how to shape the future.

Section I

THE PRIMITIVE CHURCH

CHAPTER TWO

The Church as a Worshipping Community

THAT Christianity should be endowed even from the very beginning with a rich liturgical life is not something simply to be taken for granted. Liturgy implies a communal life, and a communal life that is solidly organized, to which the individual must adapt himself without question. Jesus' teaching, however, is aimed primarily at making the individual independent, separating him from external concerns and considerations, teaching him the proper control of his own emotions and senses. Our Lord Himself quotes the phrase: "I desire mercy and not sacrifice." Again He says: "When you pray go into your chamber and close the door and pray to your Father in secret, and the Father who sees in secret will reward you." The whole Sermon on the Mount is permeated with ideas of this kind.

Liturgy in the sense of a grand and solemn service of God existed in Christ's time in the temple of Jerusalem. Priests and Levites were at hand to carry out the services according to a designated plan. On great feasts, the high priest appeared to perform his service with the greatest dignity. Day after day prayers and sacrifices were offered up; every prescription of the law was fulfilled in minutest detail. We see how even on Good Friday the Jews were careful not to enter the Praetorium of the pagan Pilate, "so that they might not be defiled, but might be able to eat the passover" (John 18:28); in other words, that they might be able to carry out the liturgy properly.

Our Lord did not oppose this cult of the Old Testament as it took place in the temple. In fact, He Himself went to the temple for the great festivals. But He also clearly announced that this cult was not to endure much longer, and that the worship of the New Law was to be of a different kind and endowed with a different spirit. St. John has preserved for us, in his fourth chapter, a conversation in which our Lord expressed His own views with regard to this cardinal question of the liturgy. The Samaritan woman at Jacob's well poses the question whether one is bound to adore in Jerusalem or on Garizim. The answer she receives is: Neither here nor there; "but a time is coming, in fact, it is now here, when true worshipers will worship the Father in spirit and in truth. Such are the worshipers the Father demands. God is spirit, and his worshipers must worship in spirit and in truth" (John 4:21–24). The same thought is found in St. Paul's letter to the Romans (12:1); he demands of the faithful a spiritual service, the offering of their bodies to God as a living, holy and pleasing sacrifice. They should keep themselves undefiled by the world's way of life and should endeavor to do, according to God's will, what is good and acceptable and perfect. That should be their consecration, that should be their sacrifice.

The opposition between this new concept of worship and the concept of liturgy held by the Jews appears in the clearest light in the history of St. Stephen. The accusation brought against him was that "this man is never tired of uttering insults against the holy place and the law. We have heard him say that the Nazarene, Jesus, will destroy this place, and will alter the traditions which Moses handed down to us" (Acts 6:13 f.). Indeed even Stephen's own defence is climaxed with the words: "It was Solomon who built a house for God. Yet we are not to think that the most High dwells in temples made by men's hands; the prophet says: Heaven is my throne, and earth is the footstool under my feet" (Acts 7:47 ff.). Stephen the Protomartyr shed his blood for the concept that the liturgy of the Old Testament and the cult connected with the Temple at Jerusalem had to cease and that a new sort of worship which is inward and spiritual must take its place.

Now the new worship was indeed a spiritual sort; it was worship "in spirit and in truth." For it was worship paid God by men who were moved by the Holy Spirit. Yet its inwardness was not to debar all outward expression. This worship was not to consist exclusively in the individual's private prayer; it was not to be inimical to liturgy. For our Lord did not only reveal doctrine, He founded a Church, a visible Church, a Church with visible men as leaders to guide the Church in His name, a Church into which entrance was to be gained by the visible sign of Baptism, a Church whose members would gather together visibly in a communal meal, whose members were to honor God in common. He had established a new liturgy, the liturgy of the New Testament.

Christ our Lord had indeed prayed on the mountain alone, in solitude, but He also prayed along with His apostles. At the last supper, at the paschal meal, He had sung with them the great *Hallel;* "after the hymn"—*hymno dicto,* as the evangelist puts it—He went with them to the Mount of Olives. Precisely by the institution of the Eucharist at the Last Supper He created that center of unity around which they were to assemble for common prayer and common sacrifice, for the liturgy of the new and eternal Testament. Incipient Christianity actually stressed the importance of always gathering at stated hours for common worship. Ignatius of Antioch especially impressed this very strongly on the faithful, as we gather from his letters. He hopes that the Ephesians will "come together in common, one and all without exception in charity, in one faith and in Jesus Christ," so that they might break together the one bread, the food of immortality, with their bishop and the presbyterium.[1] To the Christians of Smyrna he writes:

> Let that Eucharist be held valid which is offered by the bishop or by one to whom the bishop has committed this charge. Wherever the bishop appears, there let the people be; as wherever Jesus Christ is, there is the Catholic Church.[2]

Gregory Dix, the Anglican monk, in his book, *The Shape of the Liturgy* (2nd ed., Westminster, 1945), has a fine chapter on the pre-Nicene background of the liturgy. In this work he shows definitely with what firmness the early Christians held to their common worship, and this in spite of persecution.[3] It was precisely their attendance at worship which constituted their great crime in the eyes of the pagan state. Anyone and everyone could *believe* what he pleased, but that the Christians should shun the official state worship in favor of their own cult—that was the reason for the persecution. This hostile attitude towards the special Christian gatherings was aggravated by the numerous and wide-spread calumnies of which these gatherings became the object: Christians

1. Ignatius of Antioch, *Ephesians,* 20, 2.
2. Ignatius of Antioch, *Smyrnaeans,* 8, 1.
3. Gregory Dix, *The Shape of the Liturgy* (2nd ed., Westminster, 1945), 141–155, esp. 151 ff.

held forbidden and secret meetings, where they had meals at which human flesh was eaten and infants' blood was drunk. Nevertheless the Christians held fast to their assemblies, even though they could have prayed at home and (as we shall see later in detail) even though they received the Eucharist in their own dwellings. Every Sunday they went to celebrate the Eucharist in common, though this endangered their lives. Even at this early period, the Christians must have had the same thought that was expressed by the martyrs of Abitina during the Diocletian persecution: We cannot survive without the Eucharist: *Sine Dominico (esse) non possumus*. The Eucharistic celebration cannot be superseded: *Intermitti Dominicum non potest.*

Now let us examine the divine worship of the primitive Church in greater detail, first as to the place where it was held, then as to time, and lastly as to contents.

Where would the Christians of this early period assemble for divine worship? The first answer to this question is given in the New Testament. The Christians living in Jerusalem at first frequented the temple, but this was not Christian worship as such. For the truly Christian celebration, they assembled in their homes. They celebrated the "breaking of bread" κατ' οἶκον, at this house or that (Acts 2:46). Not κατ' οἴκους, in each single house, but κατ' οἶκον, in various homes suitable for the purpose, in which there was a ὑπερῷον, a *coenaculum* as the Vulgate puts it, that is, a large dining room—for the meal was the principal object of the gathering.

We find much the same thing true of the gatherings at Corinth and Troas. And Rome, too; St. Paul sends greetings to "the gathering" in the house of Prisca and Aquila. At Colossae, Philemon is the patron of a congregation. In the early Church, this was the only possible solution to the problem of finding a place for liturgical celebrations: well-to-do Christians who possessed suitable rooms put them at the disposal of the Church. Christian archeology long ago established the fact that in Rome we still have a great number of old churches bearing the names of Christians who had dwellings in that particular locality and put them at the service of the Christian community during the first centuries: S. Clemente, S. Cecilia, S. Pudenziana and others. In some cases the "Saint" was added to the name only at a much later date, on the false assumption that the *titulus* enshrined the resting place of a martyr of that name.

Thus the Church became a guest in the house of a Clement, a

Cecilia, a Pudens. But naturally such an arrangement could not be suitable permanently. All sorts of conditions had to be considered; and in case of a change of ownership there was always the possibility that the successor would not be as well disposed as his predecessor had been. The Church was, therefore, forced to look for property of her own, and in many instances, no doubt, as in the case of the Roman establishments mentioned, this was made possible through some generous will or grant. At any rate, about the year 200 the Church in many places had become the owner of her own buildings. In this era, however, the Church still lived in constant uncertainty; were a persecution to break out afresh anywhere, all such properties could be taken away, for the Church could hardly be said to enjoy any legal rights. But periods of persecution did not last forever. In fact, until the time of the Emperor Decius the persecutions were limited as to place, and confined to certain localities where perhaps the intolerance of an angry mob or the whim of some capricious governor provoked them. In general, peace reigned. After Decius, too, there were decades of comparative tranquillity. It is in regard to this period that Eusebius [4] relates the case where a lawsuit over a certain building was decided in favor of a Christian community. Paul of Samosata, Bishop of Antioch, had become a heretic and was therefore deposed; but he did not want to leave the "house of the Church" where, obviously, he had his lodgings. The matter was brought before the Emperor Aurelian (272) and decided in favor of those who were in communion with the Bishop of the Christians in Italy (that is, the Catholic Church). The Church, therefore, even before Constantine, was temporarily recognized as a corporation that could acquire property.

What we have already said answers to some extent the question we have posed, what the places of worship in the first centuries looked like. We must exclude the romantic idea which is still sometimes proposed in popular writings, that the early Christians held their religious meetings in the dark chambers of the catacombs. The catacombs—which, for the most part, are found only in Rome and Italy—were, as we know, both for Christians and pagans the underground places of burial. They were laid out generally in the form of long corridors which widened out at certain points into a so-called *cubiculum*. But even these *cubicula* were of modest dimensions, as every Roman pilgrim has discovered; the largest of them could perhaps hold a hundred people, but hardly more. They

4. Eusebius, *Hist. Eccl.*, VII, 30.

therefore certainly could not be considered as ordinary places of worship for a community, since they did not meet the requirements of a large gathering. Only burial services, Masses for the dead, and such, could be held there, where a small group, perhaps the relatives alone, would take part.

For congregational service, a larger place, a hall, or perhaps even an open plaza, was necessary. The houses of the Roman nobility generally had such a room as the Christian community required; and it was houses of this sort that were first utilized for Sunday services. In such residences the *atrium* was especially suitable for the purpose. This was a courtyard at the very entrance, covered for the most part except in the center where the *impluvium,* or basin, stood. Opposite the entrance and opening onto the *atrium* was a small room, the so-called *tablinum,* used as a living room, reception room, work room, where the household gods, the *lares* and *penates,* were kept. Behind this, often in wings, were the real living quarters. If divine services were to be held in such a residence, a large crowd of people could easily find a place in the *atrium* and the clergy in the *tablinum,* and here too an altar table could be erected that would be visible to all.

As it happens, we are not forced to conjecture all this. In 1930 at Dura-Europos in Mesopotamia, excavations unearthed for the first time the ruins of a Christian church building dating from the age before Constantine. The building gives conclusive evidence of having originally been a dwelling which was remodeled into a regular church about the year 232. The main room was a large rectangular hall. The only feature of which one could be certain from the remains was a little platform, the place for the bishop. Of the altar no trace could be found; apparently it was still only an ordinary table, as we can also conclude from other sources.[5]

In the church buildings of the ancient Church, there were naturally other rooms besides the large main hall. We get a fairly complete idea of them from a report regarding the confiscation of a church during the Diocletian persecution—the Christian church at Cirta in North Africa. The protocol of this confiscatory action has been preserved.[6] The church is described as *domus in qua Christiani conveniebant*—the house in which the Christians conducted their assemblies. The imperial officials had demanded the books, but these had already been transported to safety. Bookcases in the library were found empty. Then an inventory was taken,

5. A. Lassus, art. *"Syrie":* DACL, XV (1953), 1861–1865.
6. PL, 8:730–732; cf. Dix, *op. cit.,* 24 f.

and the officials confiscated two golden chalices, six silver chalices, a large number of torches, candelabra and oil lamps that served to illuminate the building. In the dining room or refectory were found six casks and six earthen vessels; and, further, a great store of shoes and clothes—for example, eighty-two ladies' tunics, thirty-eight cloaks or mantles, sixty pairs of shoes—obviously stock destined for charity.

The house of a Christian community of that early period of the Church, therefore, hardly differed externally from any other house. There were living quarters, used by the clergy. There were rooms for storage. There was a library. But above all there was a large hall where the community gathered for worship. On this latter point we must concentrate still more closely, for it is essential to a proper understanding of the peculiar nature of the Christian church and the Christian liturgy.

The Christian church—the Christian place of worship, I mean—differs and differed fundamentally from the pagan temple of antiquity. The Christian church is constructed for *community meetings,* whereas the pagan temple—whether that of early Babylon, or the temple built by Greek and Roman civilizations—was essentially intended as a *dwelling of the deity*. The pagan temple was meant to be a worthy place for the idol or the sacred stone or whatever else was to be venerated there. For this a small narrow *cella* was sufficient. The rest was merely outward structure, ornament and show. At most, there might be lodgings for the priests and a room where the sacrifices were performed. But since the sacrifice was a rite performed by a priesthood, it was not necessary that others take part in it. In pagan antiquity there was no form of worship for which it was essential that a praying community be gathered together. This necessity is to be found only in the religions of revelation. In the Old Testament, there was at least a fore-court for the people as part of the temple structure; and the synagogue was a gathering-place of the Israelites for reading and prayer. But it is only in the Christian religion, in the religion of the New Testament, that the idea is fully developed. In other religions the place of worship is the main thing; the gathering of the community is at best accidental. In the Christian religion it is the assembled community, the gathering of the congregation, that is the main thing. Hence the place of worship had to be constructed, as a matter of principle, with the community in view.

This peculiarity is deeply founded in the very essence of the Christian religion. Here again that fundamental inwardness and spirituality, of which we made mention at the start of this chapter, is revealed. This is characteristic of Christianity. Not the holy place, not the lifeless walls, not the gold and silver of its decoration are the primary things. No, it is rather the holy community, the *plebs sancta,* the gathering of the new people of God who worship the Father in spirit and in truth. "You are the temple of the living God" (II Cor. 6:16). The external structure is in a certain sense only the shadow of that internal structure built *ex vivis et electis lapidibus.* Therefore the oldest name for the Christian house of God is "house of the *ecclesia,*" οἶκος τῆς ἐκκλησίας, and it is from this phrase that the later simpler name is derived: *ecclesia*—gathering, congregation. In English, too, the same name is employed both for the Christian community and for the building in which the community gathers: "church."

Christians of this early period in the Church's history were fully conscious of this fundamental difference between the church-buildings of the Catholic community and the places of worship erected by pagans. Hence Minucius Felix could make the blunt claim: "We have no shrines and altars" (that is, what we have is something far different from the buildings you build for your gods).[7]

This brings us to another point that was very dear to the primitive Church and which is basic for a proper understanding of the Christian liturgy. The Catholic Church, as a gathering or society of all the faithful, is aware of possessing a priestly character. The faithful who, through Baptism, are joined to Christ, form (to use St. Peter's words) a spiritual fabric, a holy priesthood, to offer up that spiritual sacrifice which God accepts through our Lord; or (as we read in the Apocalypse) they have been made a royal race of priests, priests of God, priests of Christ.

That does not mean that all the faithful enjoy the same rights or that all have the power to consecrate which is given only to those who receive the presbyterate. But it does express a very important fact, the fact that the assembly of the faithful, because it is joined to Christ, enjoys a nearness to God and can therefore glorify God in a way impossible to the priests of the ancient pagan peoples and even to the priests of the Chosen People of the Old Testament—though, indeed, they sought to glorify Him perfectly. I am sure it was not a mere accident that the primitive Church did not apply the term ἱερεύς ("priest") to either bishop or presbyter. It was applied in the first place to Christ: He is *the* priest, the high-priest eternal. The whole Epistle to the Hebrews deals with this subject.

7. Minucius Felix, *Octavius,* c. 32, 1.

Then in the second place, they applied the term to the assembly of Christians in so far as they are associated with Christ and can glorify God with Him and through Him. And it was only in the third instance that the term was also applied to bishops and priests, that the words ἱερεύς and *sacerdos* were used of Christian ministers of the altar; for the ἐπίσκοπος and πρεσβύτερος of the new order of salvation occupied an altogether different position from that of the pagan priest or even the priest of the Old Testament. Among the pagans and even in the Old Covenant, the ἱερεύς was someone who himself, in his own name or at the command of the community, acted as mediator with the deity. Such a possibility does not exist in the New Covenant. For there is only one mediator between God and man, Jesus Christ, and all others are merely His instruments, able to act not in their own name but only in His. The term ἱερεύς was therefore applicable only to Christ and to the whole communion of the faithful, the holy Church, in so far as it is joined to Christ. It was not till after the distinctly Christian connotations of the terms had been thoroughly sifted and assimilated that they were gradually applied in a more general way, without fear of misunderstanding.

It might be of interest to note that both in the Latin and in the Germanic languages, the term more generally in use even at present is a term coined by Christianity itself: priest, Priester (Germ.), prêtre (French), prete (Italian), etc. are all derived from the Christian term *presbyteros*. We have even gone a step further, and now employ this terminology for the pagan "priesthood," for the "priesthood" of the Old Law, and even for the priesthood of Christ and of the faithful, to which, from the very beginning, the expression ἱερεύς, *sacerdos,* had been applied without hesitation.

The Christian community is therefore a priestly community. It is a *plebs sancta,* the holy people of God, and its most beautiful and most sacred task is to glorify God in its cult, to worship the Father "in spirit and in truth." But—it must be added—when doing this, when assembling for worship, it is not an unregulated and formless mass, a crowd in which all are equal. Rather it then appears in the fullest sense as an organism, a living body in which a distinction and difference exists between head and members. We heard St. Ignatius of Antioch state that the leader of the assembly is the bishop or one whom he commissions. Only to the bishop has full authority been given. This is the reason for the dictum: Only where the bishop is should the people be assembled—just as only where Jesus Christ is can we find the Catholic Church.

CHAPTER THREE

Sunday and Easter in the Primitive Church

THE new spirit of Christian worship manifested itself in the nascent Church, not only in the place, but also in the time chosen for worship. Although the time division long traditional in the Orient, the seven-day week, was naturally retained, still, even during the first century, it was no longer the Sabbath which was stressed within the week, but the Sunday. In the cycle of the year, the Easter festival was also retained but it was given an entirely new content, and, to emphasize this new meaning, it was transferred to the corresponding Sunday.

One point to note is that the Evangelists who otherwise never indicate the day of the week on which an event took place (unless they are calling attention to a dispute about the Sabbath), nevertheless remark with particular care that the Lord's resurrection took place "on the the first day of the week," *in prima sabbati.* The same day is strikingly stressed in St. Paul's activity, in two passages. The first passage is in the first Epistle to the Christians at Corinth; therein, among other matters, he invites them to make a collection for the poor brethren of the faith in Jerusalem; this collection should take place "on the first day of the week" (I Cor. 16:2). Hence they were meeting on the first day of the week, namely on Sunday. Again, on his third missionary journey, St. Paul came to Troas and remained there for a week, as the Acts tell us. Then the departure is mentioned, and is introduced by the following phrase:

"And on the first day of the week, when we were assembled to break bread" (Acts 20:7).

From these indications, we have to conclude that already in the 'fifties, at least in the Pauline communities, Sunday was observed, if not as the only day, then at least as the principal day, on which the breaking of bread, that is the Christian worship, took place. This day is then called, in the language of the Jewish milieu, "the first day of the week."

The Jewish week started with our Sunday and finished with the Sabbath. The Sabbath, recalling the first chapter of Genesis, was the day of rest, the day on which God Himself rested from the work of His creation. The Jewish Christians, of course, at first continued to observe the Sabbath with its law of rest and its meetings in the synagogue for Bible reading and prayer. But more important for them was the new commemorative day, the Sunday. This was not simply the weekly holiday postponed for one day; the Sunday was something quite distinctive, with an entirely new meaning and an entirely new character, and therefore it soon received a new name. Whereas the weekdays continued to be simply enumerated, one after the other (second, third day of the week), the new commemorative day received its own particular name, and this as early as the close of the first century. It was called the "day of the Lord," *κυριακή*. St. John says in the beginning of the Apocalypse: "I was in the spirit on the Lord's day" (Apoc. 1:10); and a little later the *Didache* (14, 1) says quite unmistakably: "meet on the Lord's day, break the bread and celebrate the Eucharist."

This new name is important, and its importance consists fundamentally in the meaning attached to the word "Lord." What is the meaning of "the Lord's day"? Although the word occurs also in the Old Testament, where it signifies the day on which God will come in judgment, this is surely not its meaning here. In fact God is not meant at all, but Christ. By the designation "Lord," St. Paul as a rule means Christ, unless he is simply quoting a passage from the Septuagint. And it was in this way that the word was employed in subsequent centuries. Even the *Kyrie eleison* of our present liturgy of the Mass originally conveyed the same sense as the *Christe eleison; κύριος* means Christ.

The word *Kyrios* was, then, fraught with meaning. We notice this in St. Peter's sermon on Pentecost (Acts 2:36). The apostle has just announced Christ's resurrection from the dead and that "He has claimed from his Father His promise to bestow the Holy Spirit" upon His disciples, as has just been accomplished; "from this, then, let it be known to all Israel that God has made him both Lord and Christ, this Jesus whom you crucified." Through His resurrection, through His glorification, Christ became, in the word's fullest sense, the Lord, *κύριος*, the head of His Church. In this were revealed His divine power and His regal greatness. "The Lord's day," *κυριακὴ ἡμέρα*, is therefore equivalent to "Christ's day." It is the same with the term *κυριακὸν δεῖπνον*, the Lord's meal, the Lord's supper, that is, the meal instituted by Christ.

There is another meaning embodied in the term "the Lord's day," a meaning it certainly possessed in the second century, but perhaps not as yet in the New Testament (although Deissmann assumes it did). This is its significance in opposition to the current emperor worship. Since the end of the first century, *κύριος*, *dominus,* was applied more and more as a distinctive name to the Roman emperor, making of him a divine being. Earlier emperors did not dare to assume such a title; Nero was the first to do so. Domitian had himself called "Lord and god"—*κύριος καὶ θεός*. From then on, the name *κύριος* became the favorite title of the emperors. In particular the adjective *κυριακός* is found in the later Greek vocabulary only with the meaning "imperial": for instance, *κυριακαὶ Ψῆφοι* = imperial finances, imperial treasury. If, then, a day of the week was called *κυριακὴ ἡμέρα*, it was almost equivalent to calling a month *Augustus: mensis augusti* = imperial month. So *κυριακὴ ἡμέρα* is the day of *our* Kyrios, our king, the day on which our "Lord" celebrated His triumph, His resurrection. "The Lord's day" is therefore a proud, imposing name, and a profession of faith.

The name was soon adapted to the Latin language: *dominica.* As early as Tertullian and Cyprian, it is the ordinary name for Sunday. And the Romance languages, as all of us know, have retained it to this day: *domenica, domingo, dimanche.*

Let us now take a look at the other names for Sunday to be found in ancient Christian usage. As we can easily understand, various names were tried for what amounted to something quite new, quite novel. But it is precisely in these attempts that we learn the ideas connected with the thing itself. The basic idea which, as we found, underlies the name *κυριακή*, *dominica,* is directly expressed also in a name which became customary among the Greeks, but only at a later time, since the fourth century. They called it the "day of the resurrection," *ἀναστάσιμος ἡμέρα.* We Christians observe the Sunday because on this day Christ completed His work and celebrated His triumph in the resurrection. The name is still in use today among the Russians: (*wosskressenije* = *ἀνάστασις*, resurrection);

and in the West, too, we can find texts up to the time of the Carolingian period, in which the term *dies resurrectionis* stands for Sunday. But, as already mentioned, these terms appeared only at a later time.

In the primitive Church, however, a favorite name for Sunday was "the eighth day." This name is linked with the enumeration of the weekdays customary among the Jews, of which we already made mention: the first day, the second day, the third day of the week, and so on; Sunday in Jewish reckoning was the first day, *prima sabbati.*

The Christians adopted the Jewish enumeration for the remaining days: in Latin we still say: *feria II, feria III* and so on. (The word *feria,* by the way, has here, as already in Tertullian, not the original meaning of "holiday," but simply of a periodically recurring day). But we do not say, *feria I;* in fact (except, of course, in the very first decades of Christianity), this term was never used. Why not?

The Christians wanted to avoid the notion that the week closed with the Sabbath, hence that the Sabbath is the climax of the week. The Sabbath and the whole order of the Old Testament have been vanquished and superseded by the Sunday and by the saving order of the New Testament. God created the world in six days and rested on the Sabbath. But it was on a Sunday that He continued the work, bringing it to its close. On a Sunday He constructed the new creation. Thus, if the count is continued, Sunday becomes the eighth day, *dies octava, ὀγδόη ἡμέρα.* The Fathers were so familiar with this idea that almost invariably in their commentaries, whenever they encountered the number eight in the scriptures, they saw in it a symbol of the Sunday, of the resurrection and of the world's renewal through Christ. This is already the case in the second century. On the eighth day after birth, circumcision was to be given; eight persons were in Noe's ark; there are eight verses in each strophe of Psalm 118—for Christian writers, all these were references to the day of the resurrection and the redemption in the New Covenant. The *Commune plurimorum Martyrum* of the Roman Breviary includes a homily by St. Ambrose in which the Milanese bishop explains the eight beatitudes. In the number eight, he naturally finds a mystic meaning: *ille* [Matthew] *in illis octo mysticum numerum reseravit.* Then he suggests reasons why eight is a number with special significance: *Pro octava enim multi inscribuntur Psalmi*—the familiar heading of some of the psalms, probably a reference to music. And an even more obscure quotation: *et mandatum ac-*

cipis octo illis partem dare—from Ecclesiastes (11:2) is made to suggest that eight has a deep meaning. Finally Ambrose adduces a more profound and more pertinent reason: the number eight signifies the completion and fulfillment of our hope—*spei nostrae octava perfectio est, octava summa virtutum est.* The number eight denotes perfection, completeness. It had an eschatological connotation.

And so Christian antiquity quite emphatically considered Sunday not as the beginning of the week, but as its end—a week-end in a very profound sense. But because the Jewish terminology had become customary, with Monday the second day, Tuesday the third, these numbers were retained; but at the same time they counted beyond the sabbath and Sunday became the eighth day. It is significant, however, that amongst the new peoples who accepted Christianity during the course of the Middle Ages—like the Slavic and Baltic peoples, and also the Hungarians—a new mode of counting was introduced, with Monday as the first day, Tuesday the second, and so forth. This terminology is preserved in the Slavic and Baltic countries to this day; in Lithuanian, for instance, Monday is *Pirmadienis* (first day); in Hungarian Monday is *Hétfö* (head of the week).

There is still another name for Sunday that we should mention—the name we employ in English and the other Germanic languages: Sunday, *Sonntag*. Of course the name is obviously not a Christian one. The Teutonic nations appear to have adopted the names of the week, as they did the division of time itself into the seven-day period, from the Romans; but they changed the names to corresponding Teutonic ones. "Sun-day" is the equivalent of the Latin *dies solis*. This was a name already used by the pagan Greeks and Romans, and also employed by the early Christians. When St. Justin (c. 150) wanted to describe the Sunday service, he started out, "On the day named after the sun"—*τῇ τοῦ ἡλίου καλουμήνῃ ἡμέρᾳ* [1] Christians were not in favor of the name, yet did not reject it entirely, because they saw the possibility of giving it a Christian connotation. Already as early as the second century—as we shall have occasion to discuss later—Christians were accustomed to call Christ their "sun," especially in reference to His resurrection. Like the sun setting in the evening, Christ descended into Limbo; like the sun (according to ancient conceptions) traversing during the night the dark region beneath the earth, Christ visited the just in the realm of the dead; and, like the sun rising again in the morn-

1. St. Justin, *First Apology*, c. 67.

ing with renewed splendor, Christ rose again on the third day with a glorified body, making that day truly a day of the sun. Good Friday was, therefore, the day of the sun's setting, so to speak, and Easter Sunday was the day of the sunrise. Again Sunday appears as the last day of the Christian week, its culmination, its crown.

This stressing of Sunday as the crowning day of the week must also be linked with the desire, already manifested in the earliest age of Christianity, to give not merely the Sunday but also the whole week a religious consecration. Even as early as the *Didache,* there is mention of a weekly fast, a custom already followed by the Jews. But different days were fixed for the Christian fast: "Your fasting should not coincide with that of the hypocrites; they fast on the second day and the fifth; but you should fast on the fourth and on the sixth (that is, counting in the older Jewish fashion, on Wednesday and Friday)." [2] It is plain why Christians should select Friday as a day of fasting: it was the day commemorating the Lord's passion, the day on which "the Bridegroom was taken away from them." Similarly the Wednesday fasting was also associated with the Lord's passion. Following a hint in the account of the Savior's last days (Matt. 26:2), Wednesday was regarded as the day on which Judas betrayed Jesus; [3] we still speak of "Spy Wednesday." It, too, was therefore a day of fasting. In ancient Christendom, these two days, Wednesday and Friday, were often called *dies stationis,* stational fast days—a name which in this connection signifies something like "days of (military) service." [4]

Christ's passion and resurrection form, therefore, week by week, the object of Christian commemoration; for both together constitute, in the eyes of the primitive Church, the work of salvation. We are inclined nowadays, according to the more precise terminology of our theology, to place the work of salvation more onesidedly in the passion and death, because the passion and death of Christ are the *causa efficiens meritoria* of salvation. This is quite correct. But the primitive Church thought more in images; she added to the passion and the battle also the victory of the Lord. We can perhaps express it in this way: she added to the *causa efficiens* the *causa exemplaris.* For only in the resurrection does what the Lord gained for us become visible; the glorified body of the risen Lord is the archetype, the pattern of the new life which the Lord wanted to bestow upon all. Hence the Church, though

2. *Didache,* 8, 1.
3. *Didasc.,* V, 17, 7 f.
4. Chr. Mohrmann, "Statio," *Vigiliae christianae,* 7 (1953), 221–245.

not forgetting the passion of Christ, did not make the day of Christ's passion the weekly commemoration day, but the Sunday, the day of victory and completion. And so it has continued in the Catholic Church till now.

Something similar holds true also of Easter. Easter is to the course of the year exactly what Sunday is to the course of the week: it is the great festival of salvation, the feast which was gradually extended into an entire cycle. And here, too, the objects of the celebration are the two aspects of the work of salvation: the passion and the resurrection.

Easter, like the Sunday, was already celebrated in the primitive Church. In the Sacred Scriptures of the New Testament, it is true, we find only vague traces of it: but in the second century it is considered everywhere, both in the East and in the West, as a feast derived from apostolic tradition. Up to the fourth century, it was the only feast which was celebrated by the whole Church. That Easter originated from apostolic tradition is also seen from the fact that the date of the Easter festival was fixed according to the Jewish calendar.

Even in the Old Testament, Easter was the feast par excellence; it was the feast commemorating the liberation from Egypt and the journey to the promised land. God so directed events in the history of salvation that the Redemption of the world by our Lord in the New Testament was seen as the fulfillment of what was prefigured in the Old Testament even to the days on which it occurred. There, liberation from the slavery of Pharaoh; here, liberation from the slavery of Satan; there, setting out to the promised land; here, the opening up of the eternal kingdom of God. The only question was whether, in fixing the date of Easter, the calendar of the Jews should be followed unconditionally, or whether here too a certain emancipation should take place.

This was one of the questions that most agitated the Church during the second century. It is fundamentally an echo of the argument in which St. Paul had been the great protagonist: to what extent was the law of the Old Testament still valid? The communities in Asia Minor had the tradition (and they appealed to the authority of the apostles John and Philip) that Easter should always be celebrated with the Passover of the Jews: namely on the 14th of the month of Nisan. On the 14th of Nisan Christ had died, at the same hour in which the paschal lambs were slaughtered in the Temple. Hence they wanted to keep to this day and thus express what St. Paul had announced (I Cor. 5:7): "For Christ, our passover, has been sacrificed." This party was called the *Quartodecimans* because they wanted to celebrate Easter on the *quartodecima die* of Nisan.

In the West, however, and especially in Rome, there was the tradition that Easter must always be celebrated on a Sunday, on that Sunday namely which follows after the 14th of Nisan. Hence the main emphasis had been put on the fact that the principal theme of the Easter feast was the Lord's resurrection, which had taken place on a Sunday. There was no difference of principle, for in Asia Minor also, after celebrating the death of the Lord they celebrated His resurrection, and they celebrated it, as elsewhere, throughout the whole period of the seven weeks of Pentecost. It was a difference of emphasis; but the difference was enough to give rise to a heated controversy, the so-called Easter controversy. Already Bishop Polycarp of Smyrna, during his stay in Rome in the year 154, negotiated with Pope Anicetus about it, but without avail. Under Pope Victor I, it nearly came to a schism, but St. Irenaeus, by his intervention, saved the unity of the church.

The Roman solution finally was acknowledged everywhere, even in Asia Minor; accordingly Easter was always to be celebrated on the Sunday after the 14th of Nisan of the Jews. The connection with the calendar of the Jews, therefore, remained. This was not very convenient, because the Jewish calendar was constructed quite differently from the western, the Julian calendar. The Jews counted according to lunar months. With every new moon a new month began; in the middle of the month there was the full moon. But as the twelve lunar months are not sufficient to fill up the whole year, the Jews added from time to time another month, the intercalary month. But with these intercalary months they proceeded very arbitrarily; the Jews were bad astronomers. Thus the question arose whether Christians should observe all these arbitrary proceedings of the Jews, or whether they should compute the time of the Easter festival on their own. By the third century, the latter choice had been made. But then within the Church various methods of computation developed. The council of Nicaea (325) attempted to establish uniformity: it did not succeed completely. But the council did order the bishop of Alexandria, the city of scholars, to have the correct date astronomically calculated every year and then to make it known to the whole of Christendom. This had to be done early in the year so that the date of Easter and of the beginning of Lent could be announced to the faithful in good time. The result was that this announcement was made on Epiphany. After the gospel the deacon ascended the ambo and sang the announcement in a solemn tone. So it was in the Middle Ages. In the *Pontificale Romanum* we still have the rubric for it: in the third part, under the title: *De publicatione festorum*. Nowadays, of course, it no longer matters; the announcement is only a reminder of olden days. I do not know whether it is still observed today in any cathedral.

How was Easter celebrated in the primitive Church? Just as the work of salvation contained two realities: the passion and the victory in the resurrection, so the Easter festival also had a twofold content, or more correctly, two phases: The Christian pasch began on Good Friday and closed with the Easter Sunday. The first part of the celebration consisted in penance and mourning, the second in great festive rejoicing with the Risen Lord. The main solemnity took place during the night between Holy Saturday and Easter Sunday. This was the real Pasch. Here occurred the denouement, the turning point in the holy drama, the transition from mourning to joy (*pascha* means: transition).[5]

With the celebration of the Eucharist in the early morning of Easter Sunday the period of Pentecostal joy began, and lasted, as the name implies, for fifty days. During this time the Christians were to realize: we are saved, we belong to Christ; we should be giving ourselves up to a life of Christian joy as the children of God. During this time the otherwise customary fast days were omitted. No fasting, was the rule. During this time, too, they did not kneel for prayers of petition, as they otherwise did, but prayed standing. This practice was also followed on Sundays. They prayed standing in order to express their conviction that they had arisen with Christ. "He who has risen, stands," thus a later writing explains this old Christian practice.[6] A last remnant of this custom is still extant at present: the Marian antiphon at the end of the office, which is as a rule said kneeling, is said standing during the whole of Easter time, and on Sundays beginning with Saturday evening. Even now the people in Germanic countries stand while they say the *Angelus* on Sundays, and the *Regina coeli* during Easter time. This is, therefore, a commemoration of the resurrection, and a very venerable one.

The preparation for the feast was also emphasized. In general, two fast-days each week were usual. Obviously they were observed with particular fervor before Easter. After that, perhaps as early as

5. O. Casel, "Art und Sinn der ältesten christlichen Osterfeier," *Jahrbuch für Liturgiewissenschaft*, 12 (1938) 1–78; E. Dekkers, *Tertullianus en de geschiedenes der Liturgie* (Brussels, 1947), 147–156.

6. *Const. Ap.* VII, 44, 1.

the second century, it became customary to keep Holy Week as an uninterrupted series of fast-days. Even earlier, it had become the custom to spend the last days of Holy Week in strict fasting, the time, namely, during which our Lord had been in the power of death. The Lord had predicted that His disciples would fast during the days in which the Bridegroom was separated from them. This prophecy they wanted to fulfill. But how long was the Bridegroom separated from His people? Calculations were made and the result obtained was this: from the moment the Lord gave up His spirit to the hour of His resurrection was forty hours. Thus those who felt healthy and strong passed these forty hours in complete fasting, without any food, in prayer and a penitential spirit.[7] This was the earliest form in which the devotion of the Forty Hours was held.

Later on, during the Middle Ages (as Fr. Thurston described in detail), there developed first the custom of watching before the holy sepulchre, and then later, of watching before the body of Christ exposed in the sepulchre for adoration. This custom is still in existence, though severed from its origin: it is the Forty Hours' devotion before the Blessed Sacrament exposed. Its origin lies in the penitential fervor with which the faithful of the primitive Church prepared themselves for Easter, and their desire to partake in the humiliation and passion of our Lord before His triumphal resurrection.

7. Eusebius, *Hist. Eccl.,* V, 24.

CHAPTER FOUR

The Breaking of Bread: The Oldest Form of Eucharistic Service

As EVERYONE knows beyond even the shadow of doubt, the most important, the essential part of the primitive Christian liturgy was the Eucharistic celebration, that rite, namely, which had been instituted by our Lord on the eve of His passion. The Christians in Jerusalem, it is true, in the early days still went to the Temple and the synagogue. But what they celebrated among themselves as Christians was the Eucharist.

In the oldest sources, this celebration is called "The Breaking of (the) Bread"; "(The faithful) continued steadfastly in the teaching of the apostles and in the communion of the breaking of the bread and in the prayers." (Acts 2:42). "And continuing daily with one accord in the Temple, and breaking bread in their houses, they took their food with gladness" (2:46). At Troas the faithful are gathered with Paul "for the breaking of bread" (20:7). The expression is obscure, perhaps purposely so, but it is explained by St. Paul's words: "Is not the bread that we break a participation in Christ's body?" (I Cor. 10:16). So it is at least probable that in these other expressions also the sacramental bread is meant.

The term "breaking of bread" seems clearly to indicate a *meal,* although nowhere is there evidence that in profane speech the expression "breaking bread" ever meant "having a meal." The term forms a link with the Last Supper, where our Lord took bread, broke it, and gave it to His disciples as His own body, and where He commissioned them to repeat what He Himself had done.

Now naturally we come to a question that has always aroused great interest: What did the celebration of the Eucharist look like during the time of the apostles? What was the first shape and form of the Mass?

Unfortunately this is a question to which we cannot give a definite answer. Only a few accounts of such celebrations have been preserved, and we are therefore reduced to putting two and two together and establishing inferences from a later date. Yet there are a number of details which we can settle with a high degree of probability.

The oldest celebration of the Eucharist took the form of a meal, at least in some places and at least for a few decades. Proof for this is offered by St. Paul's first Epistle to the Corinthians, in the section concerning the Lord's Supper. At least at Corinth the celebration was associated with a regular meal, for St. Paul takes such an arrangement for granted and makes no effort to upset it; his only concern is to put a stop to abuses. So it is probable that in other apostolic congregations as well, even in that of Jerusalem, this association with a meal existed. This probability grows with the following consideration. After our Lord's resurrection we find the apostles assembled almost always on the occasion of a meal; a common table seems to have drawn them together. In any case, the common repast was the opportunity afforded for renewing their memorial of the Lord. This is all the more apparent when we remember that in Jewish thought, and in the conception of our Lord's parables, the meal had an eminently *symbolic* significance. A favorite image of messianic splendor was the festive meal. St. Luke records the comment of one of our Lord's audience: "Hearing this, one of his fellow-guests said to him: Blessed is the man who shall feast in the kingdom of God." [1] And our Lord endorsed this picture, for He compared the kingdom of heaven to a great supper. It is striking how often the Gospels make mention of a meal, beginning with the marriage feast at Cana. So the apostles must have felt bound to preserve, if possible, the framework of a meal as the Lord had done at the institution of the Eucharist.

Now what did this meal look like?

The opinion has been expressed—and even in modern times has had its advocates—that it must be taken for granted that the Apostles fulfilled the commission of Christ by keeping as close as

1. Luke 14:15–24.

possible to the procedures followed at the Last Supper. It is an almost universal belief that the Last Supper was a *paschal meal*. And since we have a fairly accurate description of what a paschal meal looked like in the time of Christ,[2] we should know fairly well what the earliest shape of the Mass was like. The oldest form of the Mass would have been the rite of the paschal meal, and our only further problem would be to determine how the new sacramental action was combined with the old rite.

Unfortunately this assumption, that the apostles merely repeated the rite of the paschal meal, is not tenable, and that for several reasons. Not only was this rite too complicated for frequent repetition, but according to Jewish laws, to which the apostles at first strictly adhered, this rite was absolutely not permissible except at the paschal meal.

However the Jews did have another meal ritual that was furnished with a certain religious solemnity and consecration, namely the *Sabbath meal*. This was employed by individual families on Friday nights to inaugurate the Sabbath. Since it was customary to invite guests to participate in this Sabbath meal, the ritual employed could also be used on other occasions when friends met together. Such a meeting of friends was called a *chaburah;* hence the meal was known as the *chaburah meal*. The ritual of the Sabbath meal was quite suited to being combined with the Eucharistic celebration, all the more so because in it were to be found those same practices which our Lord in all probability used on the occasion of the institution of the Sacrament.

Among all the accounts of the Last Supper, the greatest agreement is to be found between St. Luke and St. Paul; St. Matthew and St. Mark present a slightly different record. Particularly striking in the Luke-Paul chronicle is the remark inserted before the words pronounced over the chalice, a little phrase which we continue to use at every Mass at the consecration of the chalice: *Simili modo postquam coenatum est*. According to this account, then, our Lord consecrated and distributed the chalice *after* the meal. Obviously, therefore, the consecration of the bread took place *before* the meal.

This leads us to a further observation. Both at the paschal meal and at the Sabbath meal, the custom of breaking bread was the first item on the program. The father of the house took a piece of bread, spoke over it a short prayer of blessing, broke it and distributed the pieces to the guests at table. The blessing he pro-

2. H. L. Strack and P. Billerbeck, *Kommentar zum Neuen Testament aus Talmud und Midrasch*, IV (Munich, 1928), 41–76.

nounced was worded as follows: "Praised be Yahweh, our God, the king of the world, who brings the bread forth from the earth." This little ceremony was certainly a very beautiful way of expressing the unity and fellowship that was to exist among the guests of the house.

It is quite likely that our Lord took the occasion of this ceremonial breaking of bread to give His apostles His own immolated body under the form of bread. He changed the words of the blessing which accompanied the action and gave the whole ceremony a new meaning and a new content.

Now what about the chalice, the cup of consecration? The ritual of the paschal meal demanded that at four different times during the meal the cups were to be filled and drunk. Of particular import, however, was the third cup, the so-called cup of blessing: *ποτήριον εὐλογίας*. It was this cup of blessing that was filled directly after the meal was finished. Then the father of the family had to take the cup, lift it up a little, and thus pronounce the prayer of thanksgiving. This prayer of thanksgiving was the proper and solemn saying of "grace." By it God was thanked not only for meat and drink but also for all the benefits He had bestowed upon His people, for the liberation from Egypt, for the beautiful and extensive land He had given them, for the covenant into which He had entered with His chosen ones and for the law He had delivered to them. It is, therefore, very probable that "after the meal" our Lord employed this cup, this third cup, for saying His prayer of thanksgiving and for giving His apostles His precious blood under the species of wine.

Both the ritual of the breaking of bread at the beginning of the meal and the cup of blessing after the meal were a part not only of the paschal meal but also of the Sabbath meal. So it is at least very probable that the apostles associated the commemoration of the Lord, in the manner mentioned, with the Sabbath meal—at the beginning the consecration and distribution of the bread, and at the end the consecration and distribution of the chalice. Of late, many Catholic exegetes have espoused this view, among others Father Hanssens, S.J., professor of liturgy at the Gregorian University at Rome; he has published several articles advocating this opinion and demonstrating that there are no theological objections to it.[3] We must add at once, however, that this form of the Eucharistic celebration cannot have lasted very long. It is worthy of note that

3. J. M. Hanssens, S.J., *Institutiones liturgicae de ritibus orientalibus,* II (Rome, 1930), 407–418.

neither Matthew nor Mark stress the *postquam coenatum est* of the Luke-Paul report. Apparently the evangelists leave out of their account whatever they think irrelevant to their actual practice in renewing the Last Supper. They therefore report almost nothing of the complicated ritual of the paschal meal, because that rite was not a consideration in the actual Eucharistic celebration by their Christian community. In other words, it would seem that in the communities where these two evangelists were working, the two consecrations were no longer separated by a meal. They were joined and placed together either before or after the meal—both methods seem to have been in use, to judge from the evidence. The blessings over the bread and the chalice were contracted into one solemn prayer of thanksgiving, expanded from the form originally employed over the chalice alone. Thus the consecrations were conducted under one blessing. Finally the meal itself was dropped, and thus the outlines of our present-day Mass liturgy appear.

Gregory Dix puts the matter as follows.[4] Originally, he says, the celebration of the Eucharist comprised a scheme of seven different actions; at the Last Supper our Lord (1) took bread, (2) gave thanks over it, (3) broke it, and (4) distributed it, saying certain words; later (5) He took a cup of wine, (6) gave thanks over it, and (7) handed it to His disciples, again saying certain words. We are so accustomed (Dix continues) to the liturgical shape of the Eucharist as we know it that we do not instantly appreciate the fact that it is not based in actual practice on this seven-action scheme, but on a somewhat drastic modification of it. With absolute unanimity, the liturgical tradition reduces these seven actions to four: (1) the offertory: bread and wine are "taken" together and together are placed on the altar; (2) the prayer of thanksgiving: the presiding official "gives thanks to God" over bread and wine together; (3) the fraction: the bread is "broken"; and (4) the communion: bread and wine are "distributed" together. Obviously such a rearrangement—if such it is—implies a selection of certain essential features and the discarding or fusing of others. Such a selection and rearrangement, Dix thinks, could have been carried out only in a community which enjoyed great authority and which was well and accurately acquainted with the Jewish meal ritual; otherwise the new arrangement would not have been taken up by others. He is, therefore, inclined to fix the locale of this change in Rome; but he adds, as he must, that all this is mere

4. Gregory Dix, *The Shape of the Liturgy* (Westminster, 1945), 48.

speculation.[5] Once this new form was shaped, it was but a short step to the absolute elimination of the meal, for the meal was now only loosely connected with the sacramental celebration; either it preceded or followed it. Furthermore, as the Christian communities grew, there was a proportionate increase in the practical difficulties connected with the serving of a meal. Even in small communities like that at Corinth, St. Paul was forced to investigate and to decry the abuses that so easily crept in. It will repay us, then, to study what actually happened at Corinth (I Cor. 11:17–34).

What happened at Corinth? What abuse or abuses was St. Paul trying to correct? At such an assembly as St. Paul describes, the proper procedure would have been for the well-to-do members of the community to bring provisions for the common meal and share them with all the others. The Corinthians, however, had begun to divide themselves into distinct groups, relatives with relatives, friends with friends, thus destroying the symbolical beauty of the fraternal banquet. Moreover, instead of spreading out the food in common, each group consumed its own provisions with a selfishness at once offensive and shocking. Those who arrived first sat down at once to eat, without waiting for the congregation to gather, and turned the religious feast into a sort of picnic that often ended in drunkenness. They hardly paid any attention to the beginning of the celebration, when the president began the prayers at his table and when he took the bread and broke it. Finally, when the meal was to follow, there was nothing to eat because the poor had not brought anything along. "You shame the poor," St. Paul states, and energetically condemns the abuses.

But the meal itself St. Paul does not attack, nor question its rightness; in fact he even calls the whole celebration by the one common term "the Lord's Supper"—*κυριακὸν δεῖπνον*. This expression seems to describe not only the Eucharistic celebration, but the sacramental celebration and the meal together, the whole liturgical festival.

Nevertheless, this linking together of Eucharist and meal cannot have lasted long, at least not for the regular celebrations of the community. In special cases, however, this primitive practice seems to have been retained for several centuries. Take the case of Maundy Thursday. Even in St. Augustine's time, it was the custom, not only in North Africa but also elsewhere in both eastern and western Churches, to take supper at home before going to church to celebrate Mass and go to Communion. Thus the attempt was

5. *op. cit.*, 101 f.

made to imitate the proceedings of the Last Supper on the first Maundy Thursday. Traces of this practice are to be found even centuries later.[6]

Another instance which concerns the communal celebration, where at least a relic of the ancient meal was retained even longer, was the Mass celebrated after solemn Baptism, in particular the Mass on Easter. The *Church Order* of Hippolytus [7] reports a curious custom in regard to this Mass celebration. At this Mass, the neophytes received Holy Communion for the first time. This was done as follows: First they received the Body of the Lord; then, before receiving the precious Blood, they were presented first with a chalice containing milk and honey, then with one containing water. Only afterwards did they receive the Eucharistic chalice. Thus, between the Communion of the bread and the Communion of the chalice, there was interposed what might be considered at least a faint indication of the ancient meal. Milk and honey are the food of the newly born: *quasimodo geniti infantes.* Moreover they are the signs of the Promised Land. Water (as is expressly pointed out in the document) is a reference to the interior cleansing that took place at Baptism. This custom at the Communion of the newly-baptized was still observed in Rome about the year 215; but it must have disappeared after the third century. However the blessing of milk and honey at Easter was still preserved in many missals of the Middle Ages even as late as the fourteenth century.

Besides the community celebration on Sundays, conducted in the large community hall, there was for a long time also a more private form of celebration in private homes when the family had occasion for a special celebration and a bishop or priest could be invited. These are the beginnings of our private Mass. It seems quite probable that here too the connection with a meal was preserved for a longer time, although we have no clear proofs for this contention. Certainly a celebration of this sort, with only a small group present, did not present the technical difficulties encountered in having a large banquet linked to the community celebration of Mass. It seems likely that in the famous prayers preserved in the ninth and tenth chapters of the *Didache* (written about the year 100) we possess remnants of such a domestic celebration. The prayers almost certainly refer to a material meal, not to the Eucharist; such is the common opinion of present-day

6. L. Eisenhofer, *Handbuch der kath. Liturgik,* II (Freiburg, 1933), 304.
7. Gregory Dix, *The Apostolic Tradition of St. Hippolytus of Rome* (London, 1937), 40–42.

exegetes. Only the short sentences that appear at the end point more clearly to the Eucharistic celebration. Let us study these prayers.

(c. 9) First, in connection with the cup, 'We give Thee thanks, Our Father, for the holy vine of David Thy Son, which Thou hast made known to us through Jesus Thy Son; to Thee be glory forever.' And in connection with the breaking of bread, 'We give Thee thanks, Our Father, for the life and knowledge which Thou hast revealed to us through Jesus Thy Son; to Thee be glory forever. As this broken bread was scattered upon the mountain tops and after being harvested was made one, so let Thy Church be gathered together from the ends of the earth into Thy kingdom, for Thine is the glory and the power through Jesus Christ forever.' But let no one eat or drink of the Eucharist with you except those baptized in the name of the Lord, for it was in reference to this that the Lord said: 'Do not give that which is holy to dogs.'

(c. 10) But after it has been completed, give thanks in the following way: 'We thank Thee, holy Father, for Thy holy name which Thou hast caused to dwell in our hearts, and for the knowledge and faith and immortality, which Thou hast made known to us through Jesus Thy Son; to Thee be glory forever. Thou, Lord Almighty, hast created all things for Thy name's sake and hast given food and drink to men for their refreshment, so that they might render thanks to Thee; but upon us Thou hast bestowed spiritual food and drink, and life everlasting through Thy Son. For all things we render Thee thanks, because Thou art mighty; to Thee be glory forever. Remember, O Lord, Thy Church, deliver it from all evil and make it perfect in Thy love and gather it from the four winds, sanctified for Thy kingdom, which Thou hast prepared for it; for Thine is the power and the glory forever. Let grace come, and let this world pass away. Hosanna to the God of David. If anyone is holy, let him come; if anyone is not, let him repent. Marantha. Amen.' [8]

We are led to consider these prayers as referring immediately not to the Eucharistic celebration but to a meal for the following reasons. First of all, because the chalice is put first. This is something we find nowhere in the whole history of the Mass. All the accounts of the New Testament also place the bread first. Secondly there is a phrase at the beginning of chapter 10 that can hardly be referred to the Eucharist. The translation presented above is ambiguous, but the original Greek must be interpreted "after having had your fill" or "after having had enough": μετὰ δὲ τὸ ἐμπλησθῆναι. Such an expression is possible only if a meal properly so-called has preceded. To be sure, the Postcommunion prayer of the Roman Mass does sometimes use the word *Repleti*. . . . But there is a

8. Trans., F. C. Glimm, in *The Apostolic Fathers* (The Fathers of the Church; New York, 1947), 178–180.

great difference between an expression used in a poetically fashioned oration and one in the very prosaic context of a rubric. Besides there is no mention of the words of institution; this may have been done on purpose, however, because the celebrant would know them by heart.

And now a short remark about the words of institution. The Gospels furnish us with a noteworthy indication that the words of institution or consecration formed part of the Eucharistic celebration in the first century. For they reproduce an account of the Last Supper and its proceedings based, at least in part, not on recollections of what actually occurred but on methods of actually reproducing that recollection, of performing what the Lord had commanded them to do in imitation of His own act. Let us try to demonstrate this.

As all of us know, the accounts presented by the three evangelists Matthew, Mark and Luke, and by St. Paul differ widely in many particulars. Not even the words which our Lord pronounced over the bread and wine are reproduced in the same form. And, besides, the oldest extant texts of the Mass present the account in still different forms. What can be the reason for this diversity? It seems that this diversity can best be explained by supposing that the varying Biblical texts represent, not so many hazy recollections of what our Lord said at the Last Supper, but the actual liturgical usages of the primitive Christian communities, each shaping and developing its own redaction of the tradition. To this opinion we have been moved also by the observation that, in St. Luke and in St. Paul, the little remark "after the meal" is introduced before the consecration of the chalice, while in the other two acounts this is missing. This, too, as we explained above, is in all likelihood the result of actual practice and not of two varying traditions regarding our Lord's own procedure. If this is true, as we believe it is, then the New Testament accounts of the Last Supper disclose the first glimmerings of the liturgical life of the Christian communities of the first century.

This liturgical life, as we know, was as yet but little bound by definite regulations, however much it was kept together through a common tradition. Hence the customs of each community could vary considerably. And so it was also possible that even within a short time important changes could take place, not (of course) in doctrine, but in practice. The great change which occurred in liturgical practice, the greatest perhaps in the whole course of the history of the Mass, was the abandonment of the meal as a setting for the Mass. With the gradual enrichment of the prayer of thanksgiving and, at the same time, the continual growth of the convert communities which became too large for a domestic table-gathering, the supper character of the Christian assembly could and did disappear, and the celebration became in truth a Eucharistic celebration. This change had occurred already by the end of the first century.

This change brought in its train great alterations in the outward shape of the celebration. The tables disappeared from the room, all except the one at which the bishop or the presbyter presided. The dining room broadened into a hall large enough to hold the whole congregation, a hall with its focal point the single table which now was more emphatically the "Lord's table," the *mensa Domini*—the altar. The participants no longer reclined or sat at supper; they became the *circumstantes*, standing in worship before God. And the ideal—already mentioned by St. Ignatius at the beginning of the second century—was for all to gather for one common Eucharist.

Thus the Eucharist became the basic form and shape of the Mass-liturgy. Discarded were the terms "breaking of bread" and "the Lord's meal." The prayer of thanksgiving, into which the solemn words of consecration were inserted, gave its name not only to the celebration but to the gift offered therein. Both are simply called "The Eucharist."

CHAPTER FIVE

The Celebration of the Eucharist in the Writings of the Apologists

SINCE the beginning of the second century, the name for the celebration of Mass generally found in the Greek writers is "Eucharistia." Ignatius of Antioch uses this name. So does the *Didache*, not only in the prayers, where the meaning might be doubtful, but also in a passage where express mention is made of the Sunday service (c. 14): "On the Lord's day (κατὰ κυριακὴν δὲ κυρίου) meet and break bread and offer the Eucharist (εὐχαριστήσατε), after having first confessed your offences, so that your sacrifice may be pure." Here the old term "to break bread" is employed side by side with the new term "Eucharist" or "thanksgiving." Moreover the action is called a sacrifice. The Gnostic writings of the second century, especially the apocryphal Acts of the Apostles, employ the same term "Eucharistia." And the name was soon used as well for the celebration itself as for the sacrament originating in the celebration. By the end of the century, the Greek term "Eucharistia" is to be found also in use among Latin Christians, as we learn from Tertullian. From this we are justified in concluding that at that time the thanksgiving had achieved special importance in Christian worship.

The word εὐχαριστήσας had already been employed in several passages of the Gospels, especially in the accounts of the Last Supper. It is interesting to observe that Matthew and Mark, in their account of the Maundy Thursday proceedings, use the term only before the words over the chalice; regarding the bread they use not εὐχαριστήσας but εὐλογήσας, a term that signifies a simple blessing. At the breaking of bread, the father of the family pronounced only a short benediction (εὐλογία): "Praised be Yahweh, our God, the King of the world, who brings the bread forth from the earth." Over the chalice, however, at the conclusion of the meal, he said the solemn thanksgiving prayer, the *eucharistia.* It is from this prayer of thanksgiving, as we have already seen, that the Christian Eucharistic prayer developed. Even in the Jewish table customs, this prayer of thanksgiving was introduced with a request uttered by the head of the household: "Let us give thanks." It is the same exhortation with which we today introduce our prayer of thanks: *Gratias agamus Domino Deo nostro.*

Naturally we would like to know what this prayer of thanksgiving and the Eucharistic celebration in general looked like in the second century. On this we possess some information from St. Justin, philosopher and later martyr, who wrote his *First Apology* about the year 150. Justin was born in Samaria (Palestine) but he was a Gentile; he had traveled extensively; finally he wrote his *Apologia* at Rome; he is therefore an excellent representative of the Church of the second century. Justin gives us a double description of Christian worship: first he describes a Baptism, giving in this connection a description of the celebration of the Mass which followed Baptism; after this he gives a special description of the Sunday's divine service. Let us read the first description:

> After we have baptized him who professes our belief and associates with us, we lead him into the assembly of those called the Brethren, and we there say prayers in common for ourselves, for the newly-baptized, and for all others all over the world. . . . After finishing the prayers, we greet each other with a kiss. Then bread and a cup of water and of mixed wine are brought to the one presiding over the brethren. He takes it, gives praise and glory to the Father of all in the name of the Son and of the Holy Ghost, and gives thanks at length for the gifts that we were worthy to receive from Him. When he has finished the prayers and thanksgiving, the whole crowd standing by cries out in agreement: "Amen." "Amen" is a Hebrew word and means, "So may it be." After the presiding official has said thanks and the people have joined in, the deacons, as they are styled by us, distribute as food for all those present, the bread and the wine-and-water mixed, over which the thanks had been offered, and also set some apart for those not present.[1]

In this first description a triple preparation precedes the celebration proper:

1. St. Justin, *First Apology,* c. 65.

(1) Common prayer by those calling themselves brethren. This is what was later called the "Prayer of the Faithful," with which the *oratio communis* was concluded. Only the faithful take part in it. For the neophyte it is, therefore, the first time that he is allowed to say this prayer with the brethren.

(2) The Kiss of Peace. The kiss of peace appears here in the first place as a conclusion, as a putting of one's seal on the prayer; it is called *signaculum orationis* by Tertullian.[2] After having prayed in common to God the Father of all, they affirmed, by means of the kiss of peace, that they all really wanted to be brothers and sisters of one family, because all are children of the Heavenly Father. This was obviously meant as a confirmation of the prayer, and in that sense a sealing. But because the kiss of peace preceded the celebration of Mass, it received still another meaning, one that gradually moves into the foreground; everyone is reminded of the Lord's statement (Matt. 5:34 ff.), that one has to be reconciled with one's brother, if one wishes to bring a gift to the altar. This kiss also was a custom which the faithful practised only amongst themselves. As we shall learn later on, the faithful were not allowed to exchange the kiss of peace with a catechumen; for, it was said, "their kiss is not as yet pure."

(3) The third and immediate preparation consists in this, that the gifts are brought to the "president" (προεστώς, lit. "one standing before"; as a rule the bishop is meant). It is the beginning of our offertory; but no special stress is placed on this rite. The faithful themselves do not bring the gifts to the altar. Nor is any offertory procession as yet in vogue. It is striking that not only bread and wine are brought, wine precisely called mixed wine (κρᾶμα, i.e., containing water), but that water is also mentioned separately: ποτήριον ὕδατος καὶ κράματος.[3] Apparently two separate chalices are meant, one containing wine mixed with water and the other containing water only. The puzzle is possibly solved if we consider what we have already said about the vestiges of the original rite of the meal: here we are dealing with the celebration of Mass after Baptism, and as we learned from the *Church Order* of Hippolytus, at the communion the neophyte should apparently be given, besides the Eucharistic chalice, and perhaps before it, the chalice with water, in token of his interior cleansing.[4] The further chalice of milk and honey, mentioned by Hippolytus, is not mentioned.

2. *De. or.*, 18 (CSEL, 20, 191).
3. "a chalice of water and of wine-mixed-with-water."
4. A. Ehrhard, *Die Kirche der Martyrer* (Munich, 1932), 334 f. But O. Casel disagrees: *Archiv für Liturgiewissenschaft*, 1 (1950), 283–285.

After this preparation there follows the prayer of thanksgiving, and immediately afterwards the communion. Before we consider these, however, let us first look at the second account:

> And on that day which is called after the sun, all who are in the towns and in the country gather together for a communal celebration. And then the memoirs of the Apostles or the writings of the Prophets are read, as long as time permits. After the reader has finished his task, the one presiding gives an address, urgently admonishing his hearers to practice these beautiful teachings in their lives. Then all stand up together and recite prayers. After the end of the prayers, as has already been remarked above, the bread and wine mixed with water are brought, and the president offers up prayers and thanksgiving, as much as in him lies. The people chime in with an Amen. Then takes place the distribution, to all attending, of the things over which the thanksgiving had been spoken, and the deacons bring a portion to the absent. Besides, those who are well-to-do give whatever they will. What is gathered is deposited with the one presiding, who therewith helps orphans and widows . . .[5]

In the main there is little difference in the two accounts; in both we find the Eucharistic prayer and then the communion. But in this second description the preparation is different, for this time there is no question of a Mass after Baptism but of the service on Sunday.

The service starts with lessons from Sacred Scripture, and both Old and New Testament are read: (*τὰ συγγράμματα τῶν προφητῶν* = the prophets; *τὰ ἀπομνημονεύματα τῶν ἀποστόλων* = the gospels). The reading is continued for "as long as time permits." Not merely single sections are read; the reading from the book in question is continuous. The system of the so-called *lectio continua* therefore prevails. It is not the "president" himself who is reading; a special lector is already in existence. The president, however, gives an explanatory and complementary speech, the homily. After this, there again follows a common prayer and the bringing of the gifts, consisting this time, as today, simply of bread on the one hand, and wine and water on the other.

What strikes us here most of all is that in the Sunday service there is already a Fore-Mass, a preparatory service, consisting of readings; whereas in the first case it was still lacking. We can probably guess the reason for this difference: the operation of the principle that the celebration of the Eucharist should not begin abruptly and suddenly. If a Baptism or some such function preceded, this could serve as preparation; if that was not the case, the service began

5. Justin, *op. cit.*, c. 67.

with readings from Sacred Scripture, followed by a sermon and the prayer.

It is well known that the Christian service of reading, sermon and prayer had its model in the service held each Sabbath morning in the synagogue. In the beginning, this service was probably held as an independent service; in fact, the Christians were obliged to do so since they did not or could not participate any longer in the Jewish service. In this passage from Justin, we see it for the first time joined with the celebration of Mass; since then such a coupling has gradually become a fixed rule.

But let us now turn our attention to what constitutes the real essence of the celebration in Justin's two descriptions of the Mass: The *Eucharistia.*

We do not learn much about its contents from St. Justin; we learn only that, at the end of this prayer, what up till then had been bread and wine has become now the body and blood of Christ, as Justin specifies more fully in Chapter 66. Moreover, he states that the transforming thanksgiving takes place through a prayer, the author of which is Christ (δι' εὐχῆς λόγου τοῦ παρ' αὐτοῦ).

The thanksgiving is pronounced by the president alone, in an untrammeled extempore style (ὅση δύναμις αὐτῷ = "as much as in him lies," or "according to his ability"). There are as yet no liturgical books and no fixed texts; there are merely some general principles to observe. The thanksgiving was a prayer to be directly addressed to God the Father "in the name of the Son and the Holy Spirit." Thus expression would be given to the truth that Christ is the Mediator through whom we go before God, and through whom we offer Him our thanks (the *per Christum* of our orations is thus indicated). Furthermore the truth is expressed that the Holy Spirit is the force which makes the real Christian prayer possible. Later, in the third century, a fixed formula was gradually devised to close the prayer or even to begin it—a formula of praise to God "through Christ in the Holy Spirit." Inklings of such a formula are already present here.

The subject of the prayer is only hinted at in the first account: "the gifts we were worthy to receive from Him"—gifts such as those just now granted also to the neophyte, namely, that we have been redeemed by Christ, cleansed from sin, and illuminated and graced with life eternal. It is the theme which has always constituted the main subject of the Christian's prayer of thanksgiving. There are still other prayers connected with the thanksgiving, about which, however, nothing further is said.

At the end of the prayer, as he points out in both descriptions, all answer: *Amen,* so be it. Justin is a layman. With a certain pride he emphasizes this right of the Christian congregation to declare its assent to the president's prayer of thanksgiving. The service is, therefore, truly a community service, corporate worship; there are no idle spectators or listeners; all are actively cooperating. This is especially shown by the fact that all receive Holy Communion and that it is brought by deacons even to those absent.

In the total picture of the Mass-liturgy of the second century, the principal point undoubtedly is that the prayer of thanksgiving, the celebration of the thanksgiving, stands in the foreground. This is not an accidental phenomenon which could perhaps be explained by saying that the prayer of thanksgiving at the end of the meal was the starting point for this development. The Christians of those days, having just emerged from the night of paganism, had a vivid urge and a strong desire to thank God. Gratitude towards God is the characteristic feature of their piety. Like a warm breath it permeates the writings which are preserved to us from those times. Clement of Alexandria explains: what man owes God is a lifelong thanksgiving; always and everywhere, not only on certain feast days and in holy places, but throughout one's whole life, "whether he be alone or with fellow believers, always does he [the perfect Christian—the Gnostic] honor God by giving Him thanks for having come to know the right path in life." [6] And he continues: "Rightly we do not offer God, who has need of nothing, who however has given men everything, an (external) gift; on the contrary, we glorify Him who dedicated Himself to us, by dedicating ourselves to Him." [7]

St. Justin explains: We must thank God "both for having founded the world, with all that is in it, for man's sake, and for having freed us from the wickedness in which we were born, and for having totally weakened the powers and principalities through Him who submitted Himself to the passion according to His will." [8] The gifts of nature, too, are included in the area of benefits for which we should give thanks: "We offer Him in spirit solemn prayers and songs of praise for our creation and for all the means of prosperity, for the variety of all things and for the changes of season."

In order that we may be enabled to give God due thanks, Christ gave us "the bread of the Eucharist." In Origen we read: "We are

6. PG, 9:457 C.
7. PG, 9:459 C.
8. Justin, *op. cit.,* 13.

not people with ungrateful hearts; it is true, we do not sacrifice . . . to such beings who, far from bestowing their benefits upon us, are our enemies; but to God who has bestowed upon us an abundance of benefits . . . we fear being ungrateful. The sign of this gratitude towards God is the bread called Eucharist." [9]

While the Christian writers of those early days propounded ideas such as these, at the same time they found themselves in conflict with an all-powerful paganism, a paganism they feared, a paganism they had to resist with might and main. They therefore describe their opposition to paganism as sharply as possible, and lose no opportunity to point out the differences between it and Christianity. Hence they stress in every way the spiritual character of Christian worship. We have already seen earlier how, for a long time, they avoided transferring the pagan terms for priest (ἱερεύς, *sacerdos*) to the Christian bishop and presbyter; Christians have something quite different. In like manner they stress other points of contrast. Minucius Felix, writing at the end of the second century, says:

> Do you think that we hide the object of our worship because we have no shrines and altars? What image am I to contrive of God, since logical reasoning tells you that man himself is an image of God? What temple am I to build for Him, since this whole world, fashioned by His hand, cannot hold Him? Am I to confine so vast and majestic a power to one little shrine, while I, a mere man, live in a larger place? Are our mind and heart not better places to be dedicated to Him? [10]

Note particularly the phrase, *Delubra et aras non habemus,* "we have no shrines and altars," that is, not as you pagans have. In the same vein, too, we find remarks in which sacrifices are rejected: "God has no need of blood-oblations and libations, nor of the smell of flowers and of incense, because He Himself is the perfect perfume, without want or blemish." [11] "Prayers and thanksgivings performed by worthy men," says Justin, "are the only perfect sacrifices pleasing to God." [12]

Small wonder, then, that about 1910 a fierce controversy broke out in Germany over the question whether the Church of the first two centuries acknowledged any real sacrifice at all. Franz Wieland, a good Catholic theologian, proposed the thesis that before Irenaeus there was no other sacrifice known to the Church except the one contained in the prayer of thanksgiving. God was praised, God was

9. Origen, *Contra Celsum,* VIII, 57 (PG, 11:1601 f.).
10. Minucius Felix, *Octavius,* c. 32; in *The Fathers of the Church,* 10 (New York, 1950), 389; transl. by Rudolph Arbesmann, O.S.A.
11. Athenagoras, *Legatio,* c. 13.
12. Justin, *Dialogue with Trypho,* 117.

worshipped only by prayers of thanksgiving, only with hymns and songs; the gifts which were lying upon the table and which they received at the communion were not considered as sacrifices. As proof for his contention, Wieland referred to expressions like those just adduced. But his opponent, P. Emil Dorsch, was able to show that the very authors cited as stressing the spirituality of the Christian service also saw in the Christian Eucharist the fulfillment of Malachy's prophecy of the clean oblation which is offered everywhere from the rising of the sun even to its setting.[13] Already in the *Didache* the Eucharist is clearly called a sacrifice (θυσία).[14] Clement of Rome speaks of the "offering of the gift," which surely does not refer merely to prayer in words.[15] It was not difficult to show, therefore, that the thanksgiving prayer recited over the gifts was at the same time an offering of the gifts, and that theologically, therefore, the Eucharist was considered during the first centuries, as now, a unique but real sacrifice.

And yet we have to confess that there exists a noticeable tension between the two concepts of thanksgiving and sacrifice. We are inclined to ask: Why did the Christians of the second century emphasize so one-sidedly the concept of thanksgiving in the mystery that Christ had bestowed on the Church? Thanksgiving, it would seem, is only a prayer secondary and accessory to the sacrifice, perhaps a cloak enveloping the mysterious sacrifice, but surely far removed from the thing itself. Moreover we know full well that thanksgiving is not the only end and purpose of Mass; the Mass is also adoration, petition, expiation. May we not then ask, why was the Mass at that time considered a thanksgiving, and why was the notion of sacrifice repressed?

This is a very practical question, of more than mere historical value, for even today the Mass is still shaped essentially as a thanksgiving. The main section of the Mass, what we may call "The Great Prayer," still opens with the significant invitation: *Gratias agamus* . . . ! Let us hold a thanksgiving before the Lord our God! And the ground plan of the subsequent prayer, preface and canon (as we will see more in detail later on), is still a prayer of thanksgiving, although into it many other and perhaps alien concepts have been inserted. Thanksgiving and sacrifice—how can this tension be resolved and this contradiction reconciled? It will repay us to continue on this point.

13. See the account of the controversy in G. Rauschen, *Eucharistie und Buszsacrament in den ersten sechs Jahrhunderten*, 2nd ed. (Freiburg, 1910), 71–95.
14. *Didache*, c. 14.
15. Clement of Rome, *Corinth.*, 36, 1.

Three considerations can be adduced to help us see that the two ideas of thanksgiving and sacrifice are not really as foreign to one another as they may appear at first sight.

(1) Though the liturgy of the Mass was formulated as a prayer of thanksgiving, this does not mean that it is, or should be, solely a prayer of thanksgiving. This prayer forms the beginning, because a sense of gratitude should be aroused and expressed. To all appearances, the thanksgiving prayer is in the forefront. But then the words develop into an activity; God is offered a gift which alone wholly expresses our gratitude. Yet it is not always necessary to speak of the gift or to do more than imply its relationship to the prayer. When we wish to honor some well-deserving person, we organize some festivity and present a gift in his honor, perhaps a scroll or a work of art, a picture, a golden ring or a medal. But in the festive address read out to him, there is not much mention of this present to be given in his honor; the speaker rather stresses the merits and accomplishments of the one to be honored.

Such was the procedure from the beginning with regard to the Eucharistic celebration. At the start we have a great prayer of thanksgiving, like the festive address, praising the grand works of God. After that the gift is presented. Thus the sacrifice evolves from the prayer of thanks. Of course in this way the giving of thanks was brought into bold relief, and this need not make us wonder. For it is entirely in keeping with the essentially supernatural character of the Christian religion and of the Christian economy of salvation. The fact that Christ came down from heaven and redeemed us is wholly a grace, a free gift of God's goodness. Our eyes aglow with wonder and awe before such munificence, what else can we do but give thanks? *Vere dignum et justum est . . . semper et ubique gratias agere*. A sense of gratitude must be the basic sentiment of every true Christian.

(2) Let us approach the subject from a different direction by considering the sacrifice, the Christian sacrifice. But we must try to view that sacrifice as it appeared to the Christians of the first centuries.

The Christian sacrifice is not like the pagan or even the Jewish sacrifice, where the outward gift, the material and physical action, the tangible effort was considered the main thing, where almost always blood had to flow, where (it was thought) the quantity and the value of a gift could influence the deity. The Christian sacrifice is different; it is spiritual. Although they knew it to be a real sacrifice (θυσία = *sacrificium*), those early Christians took great care to stress the difference between their oblation and any other; Christians did not want to be taken for pagans. The term θυσία, "sacrifice," is, therefore, employed at first with caution and reserve. If they use the term at all, they link to it an explanation that the sacrifice is spiritual (λογικὴ θυσία), that it is an *oblatio rationabilis*, a *sacrificium laudis*. And this is, of course, perfectly sound theology. In our Christian sacrifice the material components almost disappear, they mean so little. Our sacrifice is worth something because it is the expression of a mind wholly given to God. In our sacrifice, what matters most is the inner surrender, the adoration in spirit and in truth, which expands into a holy life and evokes a sense of gratitude. Thus it is first of all a sense of gratitude that must be expressed in the words that accompany our offering. The outward gift we offer is merely a shadow, as it were; the true offering is something entirely spiritual, heavenly and sublime, which cannot be measured by earthly standards. It is quite possible, therefore, that this is the reason why the outward gift received its name from the accompanying prayer, and could be called *eucharistia*. And for this reason, the celebration of the sacrifice was called *eucharistia* and the sacrament itself was given this name.

(3) There is yet a third consideration. The prayer of thanksgiving is the appropriate garb for the Christian sacrifice because our Lord's command has to be fulfilled, and that command was not just "Do this" but "Do this for a commemoration of me." As St. Paul writes: "As often as you eat this bread and drink the chalice of the Lord, you proclaim the death of the Lord." We must, in other words, consider the action enjoined upon us a memorial, a remembrance. Our sacrifice is at the same time also a commemorative celebration in which we are reminded not only of our Lord's passion and death but also of all He means to us and all He has done for us. But remembering and reminding are closely allied to being mindful and thankful; "to think" and "to thank" are cognate words derived from the same root. In thinking about benefits received, in calling them to mind, recollection spontaneously becomes a thanksgiving.

Therefore our Christian sacrifice is enclosed in a prayer of thanksgiving, in a prayer whose main subject is that salvation we have received through Christ. That prayer is but a thankful remembrance that recalls, with gratitude, how the Father sent His Son into the world, into a Virgin's womb, to accomplish our redemption, and how the Son, by the struggle of His passion and the triumph of His resurrection, made that redemption effective for us. Through considerations such as these, the first and second centuries were led to shape the Mass liturgy into a *eucharistia.* And such it is still at present—a Eucharistic celebration, beginning with the invitation, *Gratias agamus,* and the preface which heeds that invitation. Perhaps, as far as content goes, our Roman preface has lost a great deal, looking merely at the wording. This is particularly true of the Common Preface. But the ancient theme of thanksgiving for the work of redemption is still to be found, split up, it is true, but still present in the prefaces for feast days and festive seasons. If we put all these together we have a perfect *eucharistia* in the olden style: giving thanks that Mary bore the Son of God in the undiminished splendor of her virginity; that in His coming a new light shone forth upon us; that He wrought our salvation on the wood of the cross; that He conquered death by dying, and allowed His heart to be pierced to create for us a haven of refuge; that He won life for us by His triumphant resurrection, and granted us a share in His divinity by His ascent into heaven; that He has poured out upon us the spirit of adoption, He whose kingdom is eternal, a kingdom of holiness and grace, of justice and love and peace. We feel the poverty of our thanksgiving prayer especially in the Common Preface; nevertheless we must grant that even this formula does possess a certain grandeur, a certain nobility even in its very simplicity. For it presumes that the Christian already knows what he has to be thankful for, that he experiences in his own consciousness the divine benefits, both natural and supernatural. Only one thing is mentioned: we must thank God always and everywhere, *semper et ubique,* through Christ our Lord, *per Christum Dominum nostrum.* What more need be said? Christ has been sent to bridge the chasm that separates fallen man from God. In Him and with Him and through Him, therefore, the almighty Father, in the unity of the Holy Spirit, receives that honor and glory due from us poor banished children of Eve.

It would be a beautiful task for us—and for all Catholics!—again to learn from the liturgy of the Mass that fundamental attitude of mind which animated the Christians of those heroic ages long ago when the sense of incessant thankfulness towards God, the sentiment of undying gratitude, first evoked those words so full of meaning: *Gratias agamus Domino Deo nostro.*

Section II

THE THIRD CENTURY

CHAPTER SIX

The Eucharistic Liturgy of the Third Century

I. St. Hippolytus of Rome and His 'Apostolic Tradition'

WHEREAS in the first and second centuries we can distinguish only the shadowy outlines of the shape of Christian worship, once we come to the third century we can begin to see it clearly. For the first time we learn the actual wording of a Eucharistic prayer; for the first time we are given a full description of the daily devotions of the faithful and of the discipline of the sacraments, especially Baptism and Holy Orders. This we owe in the main to a document already known for a long time but not properly evaluated until about forty years ago, when its origin and importance were at last recognized. This document is what we have since then learned to call *The Apostolic Tradition* of St. Hippolytus of Rome.

Who was Hippolytus of Rome? Until late in the nineteenth century we knew little more about him than what could be disengaged from the legendary materials read in the breviary lessons for his feast on August 13. These present a fantastic jumble of several romances, so distorted that the only facts that can be retained from them are that Hippolytus was a presbyter and martyr of the Roman Church. Some few particulars are to be found in the Church history of Eusebius, who mentions him as a Christian writer, a disciple of St. Irenaeus. Few, however, of his writings were known until the nineteenth century. Then suddenly their number was increased, and with their discovery and publication not only was Hippolytus' reputation as a theologian restored but some of the circumstances of his life were at last explained.

Hippolytus was a presbyter of the Roman Church at the beginning of the third century. He wrote a number of works—all in Greek, of course, for that was still the language of the Roman clergy. These writings of his, in the main exegetical and apologetic, won him renown. However, because of his teaching regarding the Trinity, he became embroiled in a conflict with Pope Zephyrinus. The dispute grew more embittered when, after the death of Zephyrinus (217), not Hippolytus but Callistus, a former slave, was elected to succeed to the papacy. To the theological disagreement was now added a quarrel over matters of penitential discipline, with Hippolytus sponsoring a stricter point of view. Finally there ensued an open break; Hippolytus allowed himself to be chosen by his followers as an anti-pope. But when a new persecution of the Christians broke out in 235, Hippolytus, as one of the heads of the Church, was deported to the mines of Sardinia, along with Pope Pontianus. Both died soon afterwards. From the fact that Hippolytus was venerated in the Roman Church as a martyr—a fact attested to by the oldest sources—we may rightly conclude that before his death he returned to the unity of the Church.

In a crypt on the Via Tiburtina where he was buried, Hippolytus' friends erected a memorial to him in the form of a statue, which was discovered in 1551 and is at present preserved (with the head restored) in the Lateran Museum. The scholar is shown seated on a *cathedra;* on either side of the *cathedra* are engraved the famous Paschal tables he had drawn up and a list of the books he had written. It is an imposing list, but one that has given considerable annoyance to historians who have attempted to identify the writings. For these writings, which might have kept Hippolytus' memory alive, were soon forgotten in Rome. As we mentioned, they were written in Greek, and as early as the middle of the third century the Roman clergy began to speak and write in Latin. Because Hippolytus' writings were in Greek, perhaps, too, because his fame was clouded by the unpleasant memory of the schism he had occasioned, Rome forgot its talented scholar. In the East, however, the title of a "Bishop of Rome" which was associated with the works of Hippolytus, while it caused much perplexity to the learned of a later era, lent authority to his teaching and served to preserve his writings.

Many of the works listed on his statue have, therefore, been discovered; the *Philosophumena,* for instance, turned up at Mount Athos in 1842. Others, however, are still missing. Amongst the most intriguing was the title Ἀποστολικὴ παράδοσις, the *Apostolica Paradosis* or, as it is now generally called, *The Apostolic Tradition.*

Of all his major works, this surpasses the others in interest and lasting worth. For a long time it was known under the title of *The Egyptian Church Order,* and had to be disentangled from a whole series of canonical collections dealing with discipline and the liturgy, a certain part of which was attributed to the fourth century. The merit of isolating and identifying the work belongs chiefly to Dom R. H. Connolly, who showed that what had hitherto been called *The Egyptian Church Order* was in reality the *Apostolic Tradition* of St. Hippolytus.[1] He had been preceded in this work by another scholar, E. Schwartz, in 1910; both labored independently and without knowing of each other's findings until later on. Dom Connolly's work, published in 1916, was the most complete and had the most decisive effect. Any lingering doubts—and there were some reasons for hesitation—were dissipated by the thorough review of all the arguments for and against Hippolytus' authorship presented in the masterful work of H. Elfers, *Die Kirchenordnung Hippolyts von Rom.*[2]

The work thus restored is our chief authority for the picture we present of the liturgical life of the third century. In citing the treatise, however, we must endeavor to give the reader an exact portrayal of the facts regarding its restoration, for, as already indicated, the treatise does not exist in its original form and the recovery of the true text has not been without its problems, truly complicated problems. It will, therefore, be of interest to us to discuss Dom Connolly's thesis and to see how he arrived at his conclusion.

In the past few centuries, a number of oriental documents have come to light which deal with disciplinary problems and the regulation of worship and which, in part at least, purport to derive from apostolic sources. They are known under the generic title of Church Orders, and bear a striking resemblance to one another. The study of their mutual relationship and interdependence, in fact, exercised all the ingenuity of nineteenth century scholarship.[3]

Of these documents those that concern us here are the following:

(1) *The Egyptian Church Order,* so called because it first came

1. Dom R. H. Connolly, *The So-Called Egyptian Church Order,* in Texts and Studies, VIII, 4 (Cambridge, 1916).
2. publ. Paderborn, 1938.
3. See, e.g., Adrian Fortescue, *The Mass* (London, 1912), 57–66.

to the knowledge of the Western world in languages connected with Egypt. As early as 1677, the Dominican Wansleben had published a brief account of these canons, which were found in a collection of Ethiopian laws, and a fragment of this collection was printed by Ludolf in 1691. At present we possess several versions. The earliest and most faithful—apparently a very slavish rendering—is a Latin translation discovered in a palimpsest at Verona;[4] unfortunately this manuscript is mutilated and lacks a few sheets at the beginning. There are also four Eastern versions: in Coptic or Egyptian (Sahidic and Bohairic), Ethiopic and Arabic.[5]

(2) The *Canons of Hippolytus,* which exist in Arabic and Ethiopic versions.[6]

(3) The *Apostolic Constitutions,* a collection in eight books, probably drawn up by a Syrian writer, at the end of the fourth century, as mentioned above. Their text was not known to the Western world until 1546 when Capellus published a Latin version of a text found in Crete.[7] The eighth book, which alone concerns us here, contains the so-called "Clementine Liturgy."

(4) The *Epitome* ("The Constitutions of the Apostles through Hippolytus"), an abridged redaction of the material contained in this eighth book of the *Apostolic Constitutions,* but reproducing a different text for the ordination of bishops and lectors. It exists in Greek.[8]

(5) *The Testament of our Lord Jesus Christ* or *Testamentum Domini,* a Syriac apocryphal work already mentioned.[9]

Dom Connolly's thesis, to explain the mutual relationship of these several documents, may be summarized as follows. The *Apostolic Tradition* of Hippolytus of Rome was accepted in Egypt as an authoritative legal source and therefore incorporated into the Egyptian collections of canon law, being translated, in the course of time, into the various vernaculars. Later it was rewritten and adapted to new circumstances, but retained its author's name, in the *Canones Hippolyti.*

In Syria, too, the treatise was regarded as important, and about the year 400 the author of the *Apostolic Constitutions* made it the basis of the section of his work that dealt with the regulation of the

4. E. Hauler, *Didascalia apostolorum fragmenta Veronensia* (Leipzig, 1900).
5. An English version in Horner, *Statutes of the Apostles* (London, 1904).
6. Latin translation and commentary in Achelis, *Die ältesten Quellen der orientalischen Kirchenrechtes* (Leipzig, 1891).
7. Best edition in Funk, *Didascalia et Constitutiones Apostolorum* (Paderborn, 1905), Vol. I.
8. In Funk, *op. cit.,* Vol. II.
9. Publ. by T. E. Rahmani (Mainz 1899). Cf. above p. 7.

liturgy. Later another redaction was made under the title *Constitutiones per Hippolytum,* the so-called *Epitome.* Still later, in the fifth century, portions of Hippolytus' treatise were embodied in the *Testamentum Domini,* originally written in Greek but extant now only in Syriac.

In the West, however, the work of the Roman scholar was forgotten, although, about the year 400, a collection of Church laws containing the *Apostolic Tradition* was translated into Latin; of this translation only one manuscript is preserved.

The use of the name of Hippolytus in some of these derivative documents is cited by Dom Connolly in support of his thesis. This argument, however, was called into question a decade ago by a German Benedictine, H. Engberding.[10] Such ascriptions, he objects, can have no more value than the similar ascriptions to apostolic authorship implied in the headings of kindred documents, especially the *Apostolic Constitutions,* which appeals to the authority of Pope St. Clement. In Egypt, Engberding points out, Hippolytus was called a disciple of the apostles, *γνώριμος τῶν ἀποστόλων*; this is a legend found in various sources, beginning with the *Historia Lausiaca* about the year 420. This assertion is true and not at all something new; in fact I myself referred to it almost three decades ago, and at the same time pointed out the explanation. Far from being an objection to the authorship of Hippolytus, it is rather a confirmation of it.[11] Hippolytus was mistaken for a disciple and put in the company of those "acquainted with the apostles" precisely because a Church Order was in circulation with the title "Apostolic Tradition" and with Hippolytus' name as author. People drew from this the erroneous conclusion that the title intended to convey or imply an immediate derivation from the lips of the apostles. The existence of the legend regarding Hippolytus is, therefore, a testimony to the fact that a collection of Church laws was circulating under the name of the Apostolic Tradition of Hippolytus. A similar case is to be found in the Ethiopian liturgy: a Mass formulary, which derives from the Church Order we are discussing, is designated "The Anaphora of the Apostles"; and this title is easily explained if we suppose that the original heading read "of the Apostolic Tradition."

10. H. Engberding, "Das angebliche Dokument römischer Liturgie aus dem Beginn des 3. Jh.," *Miscellanea Mohlberg,* I (1948), 47–71.

11. J. Jungmann, "Beobachtungen zum Fortleben von Hippolyts Apostolischer Überlieferung," *Zeitschrift für kath. Theologie,* 53 (1929), 579–581. Cf. also B. Botte, "L'authenticité de la Tradition Apostolique de s. Hippolyte," *Recherches de théol. anc. et méd.,* 16 (1949), 177–185. H. Elfers, "Neue Untersuchungen über die Kirchenordnung Hippolyts von Rom," *Abhandlungen über Theologie und Kirche* (Düsseldorf 1952), 169–211.

In using the title "Apostolic Tradition," Hippolytus himself did not, of course, intend such a misinterpretation to be made. He lays no claim to discipleship. His title was meant to suggest that the author was presenting the ordinances and customs which the Roman Church had inherited from apostolic times. As we know from his biography, St. Hippolytus was a stickler for ecclesiastical precedent; his *Tradition* is, therefore, a summary of the rites and regulations of the Church as he knew them. His object in compiling it was "that those who have been rightly instructed may hold fast to that tradition which has continued until now, and fully understanding it from our exposition, may stand the more firmly therein." [12] A thorough conservative in matters of Church order, as these words suggest, he undoubtedly incorporated in his treatise the liturgical practices as he saw them in use in the Rome of his day. In certain details, perhaps, he may have modified or stressed the formulae in accordance with his personal preference; the style of the prayers, and even the theological views they reveal, are often distinctively his, and offer further proof of his authorship. But the work is not polemical, and we can be sure that he fully respected the main features of the prayers and ceremonies he describes. And since the book was written about 217 or perhaps even a few years earlier (as we shall see), we may confidently turn to it for information about Roman liturgical practice at the end of the second and the beginning of the third century.

However, if anyone is still sceptical about accepting this treatise as the work of Hippolytus of Rome, we might add that in any case it is a work of the third century and reflects, if not the liturgical life of Rome, then that of Egypt and Alexandria. We must bear in mind that one of the results of the study of the comparative history of liturgy has been to prove that throughout the era of our present investigation—the first five or six centuries—Rome and Alexandria had much in common. A lively interchange of thought and practice existed between the two cities and the two Christian communities they contained. As a matter of fact, during the lifetime of Hippolytus, his Alexandrian counterpart, Origen, paid a visit to Rome and was present one day at a homily preached by Hippolytus, who contrived to introduce into his talk an allusion to the illustrious visitor from Alexandria. The greatest of sceptics must, therefore, grant that in the document we now call the *Apostolic Tradition* we will find a picture of the Church's liturgical life as it existed in the centers of Christendom in the third century.

12. Gregory Dix, *The Apostolic Tradition of St. Hippolytus of Rome* (London, 1937), 2.

We have already indicated that the work was written about or before 217. Some have ventured the opinion that the date should be after 217, after the rupture with Pope Callistus; they see in the treatise a work written by the anti-pope for the government of his own community. But the work contains no trace of any polemic against Callistus. On the other hand, Richardson, an Anglican scholar, proposes the idea that the treatise was written during the pontificate of Pope Victor, about 197, when Hippolytus occupied an office of importance in the Church. But a young man is not usually so concerned about correct tradition and custom, and in 197 Hippolytus was probably only about twenty-five years old. Therefore I am inclined to follow Gregory Dix, who considers the year 215 as decidedly the most probable date of composition.

It is Dix's edition that we will be quoting in these chapters. As yet no definitive critical edition of the *Apostolic Tradition* has appeared. Since we no longer have the original Greek, the text must be restored—not an easy task. Canonical collections are, more than any other works, exposed to modifications; they do not bear the personal mark of one writer; they present legislation and forms which may have been altered in the course of years. The work we are examining must be studied all the more carefully because the text is now represented by two different groups of versions, one of which is incomplete and the other not very faithful. The question is one of sorting out conflicting texts from a number of translations and from several revisions embodied in other collections. The best edition at present, and the one we shall employ for the most part, is that prepared by the late Dom Gregory Dix, of the Anglican Abbey of Nashdom.[13]

II. Contents of the 'Apostolic Tradition' of Hippolytus

The *Apostolic Tradition* of St. Hippolytus is a collection—the earliest we possess—of laws or ordinances regulating the clergy and the conduct of liturgical functions, the order of rites and ceremonies to be observed by clergy and laity. In this collection we can distinguish three parts. The first is concerned with the clergy from both the canonical and the liturgical viewpoint. It begins with prescriptions regulating the consecration of a bishop, and these

13. See note 11. Another English translation is B. L. Easton, *The Apostolic Tradition of Hippolytus* (Cambridge, 1934). Very valuable also is the French edition by B. Botte, *Hippolyte de Rome, La Tradition Apostolique* (*Sources chrétiennes* 11; Paris 1946).

are followed by a section which is of particular interest to us because it presents a complete formulary for the Mass of the newly-consecrated bishop. Then follow the rules for the ordination of the presbyter and the deacon. And finally, suggestions are given concerning the lesser ecclesiastical states—confessors, widows, lectors, virgins, subdeacons and exorcists.

The second part deals with the reception of converts into the Church; it presents regulations for the catechumenate and for the administration of Baptism (and Confirmation). This text is all the more interesting because it includes the formula of a creed.

The third and last part gives various prescriptions for the regulation of Christian life—rules about fasting, about the *agape,* about times of prayer and devotion, about the reservation of the Blessed Sacrament in the home, and about the Sign of the Cross.

The materials contained in the second and third parts of the *Apostolic Tradition* will be dealt with in their place in other chapters of this book. The Eucharistic formulary also deserves special consideration, and will, therefore, be studied separately. We shall content ourselves here with a discussion of the other matters dealt with in the first part of the collection, namely, the various grades of the clergy and other ecclesiastical states, and the services of consecration and ordination.

Here we find mentioned not only the three major orders which were given to the church by divine institution: the episcopate, the presbyterate and the diaconate, but also the subdeacon, the lector and (at least by implication) the exorcist. Apparently relating to the exorcist, at the end of this section appears the sentence: "If any one among the laity appear to have received a gift of healing by a revelation, hands shall not be laid upon him, because the matter is manifest." [14] In the version of the *Apostolic Constitutions* the exorcist is expressly inserted. For the main task of the exorcist was to pronounce an exorcism or blessing, not only over those really possessed, but also in general over the sick; it was assumed that in all or most cases of sickness some demoniac influence was at least partly responsible. Medical knowledge in those days was very limited and the science of medicine only in its infancy. The Church did the only thing she could do: she had blessings and exorcisms pronounced over the sick, and sometimes, it seems, God vouchsafed in those days of great trials a real *gratia sanitatum*. But the *Apostolic Tradition* very cautiously remarks in this connection, that the reception of such a gift is to be tested by experience; it is

14. Dix, *op. cit.,* 22.

not the result of an ordination. However, if the gift had actually been granted, the ecclesiastical office was apparently given as well.

Of the *ordines minores* as we list them today, only the acolyte and the *ostiarius* or porter are missing in the *Apostolic Tradition.* But the group of ecclesiastical states mentioned also includes one that is rather surprising: the *confessor*. The confessors were those courageous Christians who had suffered for the faith in time of persecution but had not been obliged to sacrifice their lives. As is but natural, such people were greatly honored, and in the course of time, after the great crises of the third century, their power increased to the point that they arrogated to themselves the right to absolve by giving certificates of pardon (*libelli pacis*) to those who had lapsed but repented. Obviously things had not yet come to such a pass in the period when Hippolytus was writing his book, for here he clearly numbers them among the clergy.

> But if a confessor has been in chains in prison for the Name, hands are not laid on him for the diaconate or the presbyter's office. For he has the office of the presbyterate by his confession. But if he be appointed bishop, hands shall be laid on him.
>
> And if he be a confessor who was not brought before a public authority nor punished with chains nor condemned to any penalty but was only by chance derided for the Name, though he confessed, hands shall be laid on him for every order of which he is worthy.[15]

Those, therefore, who really had suffered for the faith could receive the rank or the honor of deacon or priest without ordination. This statement is, no doubt, puzzling, particularly in regard to the presbyter. But we must remember that in the first centuries, especially in a center like Rome, the presbyter was mainly an advisory assistant or counsellor of the bishop. Moreover, the statement must have been puzzling even in ancient times, for some of the translations changed the text and dropped the mention of the presbyterate, apparently because the authors were not in favor of granting such a high rank to the confessor.

In our present-day liturgy, there is still one passage where the confessors, in this ancient Christian sense, appear in the midst of the clergy: in the Solemn Prayers on Good Friday. In the third prayer they are mentioned after the four minor orders: *Oremus et pro omnibus episcopis, presbyteris, diaconibus, subdiaconibus, acolythis, exorcistis, lectoribus, ostiariis, confessoribus, virginibus, viduis. . . .* The word "confessor" here has been given many different explanations: for example, that it must mean the singers.

15. Dix, 18–19.

But Anton Baumstark is surely right in interpreting the term in the sense we have already indicated; he correctly concludes that these prayers must go back to the days of persecution.[16] These Good Friday prayers are, therefore, evidently the oldest prayers in our Roman missal.

The Good Friday prayer quoted above also includes two other groups among the ecclesiastical personnel: *virgines* and *viduae*. Hippolytus also mentions them with the clergy, but stresses the fact that they are not numbered among the clergy. In fact, the whole weight of the legislation here is on the negative side: what widows and virgins are not to be, or not to do, or not to have. The tone is not at all friendly, and seems to imply the fear of a danger that did actually arise towards the end of the century, the danger of such privileged groups forming a sort of aristocracy and disputing with the hierarchy the right to govern. St. Ignatius of Antioch had already admonished widows about their pride and had warned the unmarried not to plume themselves on their profession or to set themselves above their bishops. Hippolytus, therefore, had grounds for stressing the fact that the virgins and the widows were not to be counted among the clergy, and that in their "appointment"—as in the case also of lectors and subdeacons—there was no laying on of hands. Regarding virgins, the *Apostolic Tradition* points out further that virginity is a matter of personal resolve, not of some ecclesiastical ordination. And regarding widows, the treatise explains that they do not offer the sacrifice and do not have any liturgical function. However, they are given recognition in the *Church Order;* they are distinguished—this must be noted—from the ordinary laity, and given a special rank as ecclesiastical persons.

Perhaps the hostile tone of the *Apostolic Tradition* is not unwarranted. Nevertheless we must admit that ecclesiastical legislation—including this very treatise and the several documents derived from it—has, through the years, accorded virgins and widows special consideration. The beginnings of this development are already discernible in the New Testament. St. Paul speaks about a "list of widows" as, apparently, a fixed group, a sort of inchoate but recognized religious institution devoted to works of piety and charity (I Tim. 5:9 ff.). The Church undertook to provide for them, and they were entrusted—but with some hesitancy—even with tasks connected with the cure of souls. But the admission of widows to this class was hedged in with stringent conditions; the minimum age

16. A. Baumstark, *Missale Romanum. Seine Entwicklung, ihre wichtigsten Urkunden und Probleme* (Eindhoven-Nimwegen, 1929), 20–21.

required for acceptance was at first set at sixty, but later reduced to fifty and finally to forty. Virgins, too, were apparently admitted to some kind of dedicated life, and entrusted with such tasks as caring for orphans, providing hospitality for traveling missionaries, and visiting the sick. They were also engaged in certain services connected with the catechumenate and the Baptism of women.

In this way, the institution of the so-called deaconesses came about and, at least in the East, this office developed into something quite effective. Those who were admitted to this office received a special consecration. The first reference to the term—outside the disputed one in St. Paul's letter to the Romans—is in the letter of Pliny the Younger to Trajan (about the year 112), where he speaks about torturing two Christian female servants who are called *ministrae,* the Latin equivalent of "deaconesses." But it is in the third century *Didascalia* and in the *Apostolic Constitutions* that we find a more detailed description of the office and the functions of this class of Church workers. However the state of culture in the period of Christian antiquity was not favorable to the employment of women in the Church's ministry, and so the institution of deaconesses was never fully developed. In the Western Church, the office appears to have been gradually abandoned as early as the third century. It was to take the Church many years of accumulated experience before she finally found suitable ways in which to make use of the services of dedicated women in the work of caring for souls. Not until after the Renaissance, did the idea which the Church had adumbrated in the institution of the deaconesses at last attain realization on a grand scale in the women's congregations founded in the past few centuries.

With great detail, as the nature of the subject demands, the *Apostolic Tradition* treats of the higher ecclesiastical offices and the corresponding ordinations. For each of the major orders, a minute description is given of the ceremonial, and the prayers used in the rite are carefully noted. The first function described is the consecration of a bishop. The bishop is chosen by all the people. When he has been named and unanimously accepted, all assemble on a Sunday, together with the *presbyterium* and other bishops. All consenting, the bishops lay hands on him. The presbyters stand by in silence and, together with the assembly, they pray quietly, asking for the descent of the Spirit. Then one of the bishops, at the request of all, recites the prayer of consecration—a very extensive prayer begging the God and Father of our Lord Jesus Christ to grant His chosen servant the gifts necessary to feed the holy flock entrusted to him, to give due regard to the primacy of the priesthood and the requirements of a holy life, and to distribute God's favor by loosing all that is bound "according to the power Thou hast given to the apostles." After his consecration, as we shall see in the next chapter, the new bishop is greeted with the kiss of peace, and then celebrates the Eucharistic sacrifice.

The prayer said at the ordination of a deacon runs as follows:

> O God who hast created all things and hast ordered them by the Word, Father of our Lord Jesus Christ whom Thou didst send to minister Thy will and reveal unto us Thy desire; grant the Holy Spirit of grace and earnestness and diligence upon this Thy servant whom Thou hast chosen to minister to Thy church and to bring up in holiness to Thy holiness that which is offered to Thee by Thine ordained high priests to the glory of Thy Name; so that ministering blamelessly and in purity of heart he may, by Thy goodwill, be found worthy of this high and exalted office, praising Thee, Through Thy Child Jesus Christ. . . .[17]

The outward sign that accompanies the prayer of ordination is, in every instance, the laying on of hands. But the ceremony is carefully graded in accordance with the relative rank of the order administered. At the consecration of the bishop, as we have seen, several bishops were to be present and all of them were to participate in the ceremony of the laying on of hands, as is still the custom today. At the ordination of a presbyter, several presbyters should be present with the bishop, and they too should lay hands on the candidate—again a custom still followed today. But at a deacon's ordination, the regulation is that the bishop alone should lay on hands, and the reason for this is carefully noted: because he is ordained not for the priesthood, but for the service of the bishop.[18]

Here we must remark a very interesting coincidence. The *Pontificale Romanum* has preserved this custom and provides the reason for the practice, in the very wording found in Hippolytus. This is all the more striking because liturgical books in general do not present reasons for their ordinances. In the *Pontificale Romanum*, the reading of the rubric is:

> *Hic solus pontifex manum. . . . ponit super caput cuilibet ordinando et nullus alius,* quia non ad sacerdotium sed ad ministerium consecrantur.

In Hippolytus, according to the old Latin translation, the wording of the regulation is:

17. Dix, *op. cit.,* 17–18.
18. Dix, 15.

Solus episcopus imponat manus, propterea quia non in sacerdotio ordinatur, sed in ministerio episcopi.[19]

There are other passages in the liturgical books, especially in the Roman Pontifical, which similarly display a remarkable likeness to Hippolytus. How is this to be explained? It would be hard to believe that a tradition stemming directly from Hippolytus was preserved at Rome itself; this would be contrary to what we have already learned about the history of the *Apostolic Tradition.* How, then, did Hippolytus' ordinance get into the Roman liturgical books? I think that the course the tradition took can be traced with fair accuracy. Hippolytus' *Church Order,* as we have seen, found its way back from the Orient and was translated into Latin either in northern Italy or southern France. At the beginning of the sixth century, an order for ordination was written and inserted in the collection of canons known as the *Statuta Ecclesiae Antiquae,* compiled at Arles, where Caesarius was bishop; the basis for this Order was the text of Hippolytus in its Latin dress. From here it found its way, about 950, into the so-called Germano-Roman Pontifical composed at Mainz. This Pontifical served in turn as the model for the one prepared by John Burchard and Augustine Patrizi Piccolomini, papal masters of ceremonies, and published in 1485, in the pontificate of Innocent VIII.

So, we might say, after a lengthy journey, Hippolytus returned in spirit to where his body already lay, to Rome, to be honored with Callistus, his old foe, and Pontianus, his fellow sufferer, and Fabian, the first four Roman martyrs to be commemorated yearly in the Church of Rome. Here, in the ancient city, the eternal city, his memory is kept in reverence; as we read in the Roman Missal:

Die 13 Augusti
SS. Hippolyti et Cassiani
Martyrum

III. The 'Eucharistia' of Hippolytus of Rome

The section in the *Apostolic Tradition* of Hippolytus of Rome which awakens by far the greatest interest, and which also has been most written about, is the Eucharistic prayer which the author adduces in connection with the episcopal consecration. It is the oldest text of a Mass formulary to come down to us. What is really astonishing is that a text from such early times has come down to us

19. Dix, *loc. cit.*

at all. For we have heard Justin the martyr saying that the president offers up prayers and thanksgivings "in as far as he is able" (ὅση δύναμις αὐτῷ), that is, he makes up the text *extempore;* apparently no official texts were then extant.

In Hippolytus, this idea is expressed much more clearly; at the end of various rules about ordinations, to which are added set prayers for the bishop's consecration, for the priest's ordination and for the deacon's, we find the remark:

> And the bishop shall give thanks according to the aforesaid models.
>
> It is not altogether necessary for him to recite the very same words which we gave before as though studying to say them by heart in his thanksgiving to God; but let each one pray according to his own ability.
>
> If indeed he is able to pray suitably with a grand and elevated prayer, this is a good thing. But if on the other hand he should pray and recite a prayer according to a fixed form, no one shall prevent him. Only let his prayer be correct and right in doctrine.[20]

The expression here translated "according to a fixed form"—*lit.,* in measure, according to a measure, moderately—is differently interpreted.[21] But no matter! The basic idea is that texts are not generally fixed. If Hippolytus suggests fixed formulas, these are to be considered as samples, as models. The train of thought alone should be fixed; the words should be composed by the celebrant himself, just as in his sermons, where he also has to find the words for himself.

For this reason, the system of prayers presented by Hippolytus is of interest from another standpoint as well. Whereas elsewhere Hippolytus only puts down what to him appears to be apostolic tradition, in these prayers he has to express, at least partly, his own ideas. And, indeed, it has been established that in the Eucharistic prayer alone six passages are found expressing Hippolytus' favorite ideas, ideas that turn up again and again in his genuine writings. (This is, by the way, a valuable confirmation of the opinion that Hippolytus of Rome is the real author of our Church Order and that the sceptics are wrong.) One group of the oriental translations of this work omitted this text, either because they did not want to be limited in their freedom, or because they already possessed their own formularies. Only the Ethiopian tradition (as well as the Latin) contains the Eucharistic prayer. In the Ethiopian Church of Abyssinia, the Eucharistic prayer of Hippolytus' *Apostolic Tradi-*

20. Dix, 19.
21. The text is rather difficult. Cf. Connolly, *op. cit.,* 64–66.

tion has become the nucleus of a Mass formulary which is still said by the Abyssinian priests at the present time, and it bears the significant name: "Mass of the Apostles."

But let us now consider the text itself. After the consecration of the new bishop, he is greeted by those present with the kiss of peace, just as in Justin's account in reference to the newly baptised. The kiss here is a ceremony of acknowledgment and reception. Then he is acclaimed: ἄξιος. According to Dix,[22] the text would be: "saluting him, for he has been made worthy." This is wrongly translated; it should run: "saluting him, *that* he is worthy . . ." According to the older custom observed in ancient Greek and Roman ceremonial, when a high public office was conferred on someone, he was acclaimed with the words: he is worthy; ἄξιος! And indeed, it is still the custom, for example, in the Byzantine rite of the ordinations, that those present shout this old acclamation: ἄξιος!

Then the action of the Mass begins. It begins immediately with the offertory, as is the case in St. Justin's account of the Mass after Baptism. The Fore-Mass is therefore not as yet firmly connected with the sacrificial Mass: it can be omitted if another celebration, like an ordination, precedes.

In Hippolytus we do find, incidentally, another passage in which there is something which we could call a complete Fore-Mass, although it also bears a resemblance to other types of prayer service. According to Hippolytus, the presbyters and the deacons should appear every day, in the morning, at the bishop's residence and should then instruct those present in the church. Then they should say prayers and, after the prayers, each should go about his own business.[23] The faithful are correspondingly admonished in other passages to come every day to church in the morning when an instruction is given there (*καθήγησις*); for God speaks through the mouth of the teacher and thus strengthens the faithful. Hence on weekdays services of instruction took place which concluded with a prayer. Sacred Scripture forms the basis of the teaching or instruction: hence the service consisted of reading from Scripture, with explanation and prayer, the very outline which constitutes also the plan of the Fore-Mass. But here it appears separated from the Mass of sacrifice.

Hippolytus' description, then, begins with the offertory. The deacons bring the gifts. Then the bishop extends his hands over the

22. Dix, 6.
23. Dix, 60; cf. 61.

gifts and the presbyters present do the same, and with this gesture, the bishop begins the prayer.[24] It can be seen here how closely the presbyters partake in the bishop's Mass: they are concelebrating. And what about the faithful? There is no trace here of the faithful bringing gifts to the altar. In another passage, however, there is such a trace, where the order for the day of Baptism is given. There we read: "Moreover those who are to be baptized shall not bring any other vessel, save that which each will bring with him for the Eucharist. For it is right for everyone to bring this oblation then." Hence at least in the Mass of Baptism, everyone brings an oblation with him for Mass. Whether this was true of other Masses it is hard to say, for evidence is lacking.

The bishop now starts the prayer. Let us take the old Latin rendering, for we can thus the more readily sense the relationship to our present Latin Mass. The dialogue precedes:

> Dominum uobiscum; et omnes dicant: et cum spiritu tuo. Susum [*sic*] corda. Habemus ad dominum. Gratias agamus domino. Dignum et iustum est.[25]

These are almost the identical words we use today. The people are called upon to pray; and the point is stressed that the people should also give the responses. We see again that worship is a community exercise; all should actively cooperate in it.

Then follows the Eucharistic prayer itself; again we read the text of the old Latin translation:

> Gratias tibi referimus, Deus, per dilectum puerum tuum Iesum Christum quem in ultimis temporibus misisti nobis saluatorem et redemptorem et angelum uoluntatis tuae; qui est uerbum tuum inseparabilem per quem omnia fecisti et bene placitum tibi fuit; misisti de caelo in matricem uirginis quique in utero habitus incarnatus est et filius tibi ostensus est ex spiritu sancto et uirgine natus; qui uoluntatem tuam conplens et populum sanctum tibi adquirens extendit manus cum pateretur ut a passione liberaret eos qui in te crediderunt.
>
> Qui cumque traderetur uoluntariae passioni ut mortem soluat et uincula diaboli dirumpat et infernum calcet et iustos inluminet et terminum figat et resurrectionem manifestet, accipiens panem gratias tibi agens dixit: Accipite, manducate: hoc est corpus meum, quod pro uobis confringitur. Similiter et calicem dicens: Hic est sanguis meus qui pro uobis effunditur; quando hoc facitis, meam commemorationem facitis. Memores igitur mortis et resurrectionis eius offerimus tibi panem et calicem gratias tibi agentes quia nos dignos habuisti adstare coram te et tibi ministrare.

24. Dix, 6.
25. Dix, 7.

Et petimus ut mittas spiritum tuum sanctum in oblationem sanctae ecclesiae; in unum congregans des omnibus qui percipiunt sanctis in repletionem spiritus sancti ad confirmationem fidei in veritate, ut te laudemus et glorificemus per puerum tuum Iesum Christum per quem tibi gloria et honor patri et filio cum sancto spiritu in sancta ecclesia tua et nunc et in saecula saeculorum. Amen.[26]

Having read this prayer, we can now begin to understand more clearly why, in the second and third century, the Mass was called "Eucharistia." This is the only prayer in the Mass proper—what we would call the canon. In fact, it is the only prayer said at the service, for no Fore-Mass ordinarily precedes. Although immediately after the *eucharistia,* Hippolytus does remark that the faithful may bring foodstuffs for blessing, and for this purpose two samples of blessings are given, yet these blessings do not belong to the regular course of the Mass; they are merely extraordinary insertions. Sometimes, however, especially in later times, these blessings were inserted into the canon of the Mass, to form the last clause or phrase of the canon. There is still just such an insertion to be found in the Mass on Maundy Thursday, when the bishop blesses the oils.

Besides these prayers of blessing, the later Egyptian texts also present prayers for communion, but they almost certainly do not belong to the original contents of the Mass as proposed by Hippolytus; they are later Egyptian additions. In the Mass of the third century there is only this one prayer, and this one prayer is essentially a prayer of thanksgiving, an *eucharistia.*

But this prayer contains some further elements which evolve organically from the prayer of thanksgiving but go beyond a simple prayer of thanks, in the direction of sacrifice. The development is towards that form of the Mass which now is familiar to us. We see, first of all, the account of the institution, built right into the prayer of thanksgiving. It does not tally with the wording of any of the accounts of the New Testament; it still has a very simple form, without any ornamentations; it therefore represents a tradition all its own. It is, of course, extremely important that the oldest text of the Mass, as we know it, possess as its innermost core the words of the institution. In spite of this, Gregory Dix, in his book *The Shape of the Liturgy,* tried to prove that originally forms of the Eucharistic celebration must have existed without the words of

26. Dix, 7 f. Note the word *puer* at the beginning and end of the prayer corresponds to the Greek παῖς, a term which means "servant" as well as "child," and which comes from the Septuagint where it is applied to the Messias, the "servant of Yahweh." Thence it passed into certain texts of the New Testament, and into some of the early Fathers, the *Didache,* Barnabas, Athenagoras, Clement of Alexandria.

institution.[27] But his proofs are extremely weak; it has not been difficult to show that none of them is valid.[28]

We cannot enter into the details here, but Dix's main argument consists in this, that in the East-Syrian liturgy there exist some manuscripts in which the principal formulary of the Mass of the apostles Addai and Mari do not contain the words of institution. Dix tries to show that this must have been an especially old Mass formulary, in which an original tradition survived. But the philological examination already made has shown that this formulary belongs to a time in which the East-Syrian Church was already separated from the rest of the Christendom because of the Nestorian heresy, a time also in which the *epiclesis* had begun to be stressed in a high degree.

Another important point is that in Hippolytus, immediately after the words of institution comes the so-called *anamnesis* in a form quite similar to our own today, only a little simpler: *Memores igitur mortis et resurrectionis eius offerimus tibi* . . .

Notice, too, the statement that a sacrifice is *offered.* As we all know, the reformers of the sixteenth century opposed the idea that the Mass is a sacrifice, and, especially, that we men can give something to God, that we can offer something. And since the canon of the Mass, before the words of consecration and, more especially, after them, expresses this idea of sacrifice, they simply left the canon out (except for the biblical words), believing that they were thus restoring the genuine Christian tradition. (See, for example, the Anglican *Book of Common Prayer.*) We see, however, that the oldest tradition of the form of the Eucharistic celebration in existence already contains the *offerimus,* just as all later texts contain it; and we have no reason to suppose that it ever was missing in the Mass prayers of the primitive church. H. Lietzmann, the second successor of Harnack as professor of church history in Berlin, is of the same opinion. In a commentary devoted to this text he says: "What stands there, could . . . also have been spoken at the time of the Apostle Paul at Corinth or Ephesus." [29] The Mass, therefore, in spite of the original emphasis on thanksgiving, has been considered from the very beginning as a sacrifice which we offer to God.

27. Dix, *The Shape of the Liturgy,* esp. 240.

28. See M. Bévenot, S.J., "Some Flaws in the Shape of the Liturgy," *The Month,* 82 (1946), 50–57; J. D. Crichton, "The Shape of the Liturgy: A Review," *Magnificat,* 1946, 1–7; also my own review of the book: *Zeitschrift für kath. Theologie,* 70 (1948), 224–231.

29. H. Lietzmann, *Messe und Herrenmahl* (Bonn, 1926), 181.

After the offering there follows, in Hippolytus' Eucharistic prayer, what we usually call the *epiclesis:* the calling down of the Holy Spirit upon the sacrificial gifts. As we all know, the *epiclesis* is one of the main points of controversy between the Oriental and Latin churches. It is therefore very instructive to see how the oldest extant *epiclesis* is formulated.[30] It is a petition that God send the Holy Spirit upon His Church, so that all who receive of the gifts may be filled with the Holy Spirit.

Hence it is an *epiclesis* which does not ask for the transformation of the gift, but for a fruitful communion; its sense is the same as in the present canon of the Roman Mass in the words: *ut quotquot, ex hac altaris participatione sacrosanctum Filii tui Corpus et Sanguinem sumpserimus, omni benedictione coelesti et gratia repleamur.*

There is also a similarity between Hippolytus and our Roman mass in the final doxology. We say: *Per ipsum, et cum ipso, et in ipso, est tibi Deo Patri omnipotenti, in unitate Spiritus Sancti, omnis honor et gloria.* In Hippolytus it is simpler still: *per quem;* but here, just as at the end of other prayers, there is the idea that we offer God our prayers through Christ. The same idea was already expressed at the beginning of the prayer of thanksgiving, in the words *per dilectum puerum tuum.*

We say: *est tibi Deo Patri omnipotenti.* In Hippolytus, this address is expanded with theological correctness: *tibi . . . Patri et Filio cum Sancto Spiritu;* for if we want to express ourselves with theological precision, it is the whole Trinity which receives our adoration.

We say: *in unitate Spiritus Sancti.* In Hippolytus we find instead: *in s. Ecclesia.*[31] This is a more accurate expression of what is also meant by the words: *in unitate Spiritus Sancti.*

The main thought, however, is expressed in both cases with almost the same words, *tibi gloria et honor et nunc et in saecula saeculorum.*

Besides these similarities which we can notice between our Mass and Hippolytus', there are also considerable differences. What strikes us most is that there is in Hippolytus one simple prayer, in which the train of thought is never interrupted, whereas in the canon of our Mass various insertions are made.

30. cf. Lietzmann, *op. cit.*, 80–81. See the interesting discussion between J. W. Turner and Dom Connolly in *Journal of Theol. Studies,* XXV, pp. 139–150 and 331–364; also Dom Casel in *Jahrbuch für Liturgiewissenschaft,* IV (1924) 169–178.

31. This is a favorite formula of Hippolytus and is found not only in other liturgical prayers of his but also in his other writings—further evidence of his authorship of this treatise.

First of all, we have the insertion of the intercessions for the whole Church, for the living and for the dead. Of these intercessions, Hippolytus makes no mention at all. But we met them in the descriptions of the liturgy in Justin, although there they stand at the end of the Fore-Mass, before the gifts are brought in. Later on, since the fourth century, they were introduced into the canon of the Mass in most liturgies; so also in the Roman Mass.

Something more we find lacking: the *Sanctus.* This is all the more surprising because we find the *Sanctus* in all liturgies. As early as the beginning of the third century, that is, at the time in which our *Church Order* originated, we find indications that elsewhere the *Sanctus* was part of the Mass. Allusions to it are extant in Tertullian and in Origen. Probably Hippolytus left it out on purpose, perhaps because he wished to develop the unity and harmony of the prayer as a *Eucharistia* as purely as possible and without interruption; perhaps too, because the *Sanctus* belonged to the Old Testament and Hippolytus apparently wanted to leave aside everything of the Old Testament in his Eucharistic prayer, which is concerned with the *novum pascha novae legis.*

If now we turn from a consideration of details to the Eucharistic prayer as a whole, we have before us a prayer of thanksgiving, solemn and well proportioned. And if we consider the prayer of thanksgiving as such, what are its contents? It is a thanksgiving for our redemption through Christ. First the mystery of the person of Christ is described: He is the Word which cannot be separated from God: this is the profession of the divinity of Christ. And it is a profession of the divinity of Christ in a form personal to Hippolytus; for he had at one time been reproached with having, in his trinitarian doctrine, separated the Word (the Logos) from the Father. Here he says: He is the Word which cannot be separated from God. But the Word has become flesh in the womb of the Virgin; this is a profession of the humanity of Christ. However, this profession is not expressed merely as a sober statement of fact, but in words of profound gratitude for the divine mercy, which therein made its appearance: "Whom in the last times thou didst send to us (to be) a Savior and Redeemer and the Messenger of Thy counsel." [32]

But this work of the divine mercy has been completed in the passion of Christ. The passion itself is paraphrased in a few words: He was handed over to voluntary suffering; He extended His hands when suffering (viz., on the cross). All the greater, then, is the

32. Dix, *The Apostolic Tradition,* 7, 4.

emphasis with which the significance of the Passion is described: what was its purpose? "To prepare for Thee a holy people, . . . that he might abolish death . . ." [33] This is a magnificent picture of the work of redemption; we can feel the enthusiasm and the gratitude behind these words.

Notice, too, that the redemption is viewed as a battle: it is the battle against the devil, and against hell, and against Hades (which they were accustomed to personify). It was a war of liberation ending with a splendid victory in the Resurrection; the just of the Old Covenant, to whom Christ has brought the light, have been the first to benefit by the victory.

This way of considering the work of salvation is characteristic of Christian antiquity; they did not stop short at a sympathetic meditation on the pains which our Lord suffered in His Passion, as the later Middle Ages were wont to do; their vision went beyond what the Lord suffered to what He had gained through His Passion; and this view is facilitated by the image of battle and victory. They saw not only the grain of corn which falls to the earth, but also the fruit which it bears. The same method of consideration is found in the Apostles' Creed; here too the Passion of Christ is described in a few bold strokes: "suffered under Pontius Pilate, was crucified, died, and was buried." But then immediately the profession of the Resurrection is added, and here words are no longer economized; the line is continued till the final triumph and till the completion of the kingdom in the *parousia.*

This is the mode of thinking we already encountered in our consideration of the ancient ecclesiastical year. As we saw, Easter was, from the very beginning, celebrated every year as *the* feast of the Redemption. It was the solemn commemoration of the historical fact that Christ through His Passion had rid the world of sin and through His Resurrection opened a door for us into life everlasting; that He has redeemed us and gathered us under the sign of the Redemption to be a new people of God, to be His Church. True, our redemption is attributed in the first place to our Lord's suffering and death on the Cross, but it was in the Resurrection that His own transfigured body became the evidence of what that suffering and death had won for us. In early Christendom it was the victory that became focal, even to the extent of accumulating an added fifty days, the days of Pentecost, to the festival of the Resurrection.

And the same picture is repeated in the Christian week. Even at present it is Sunday, the day of the κύριος, that is celebrated with

33. Dix, *op. cit.*, 8.

special impressiveness. Perhaps we think too little about it; we forget that the Lord's day is a sort of weekly Easter. It is not at all a mere accident that Christian antiquity celebrated the Eucharist on Sunday and only on Sunday. For on the day of the Lord, the day when He rose victorious over death, what better or more suitable celebration could there be than the corporate and communal service in which the mystery of Redemption, the *memoria passionis* is observed.

Christians of old, as we said, liked to think of Christ's Passion as a battle—Christ coming to grips with the enemy. The Preface of the Cross, which is used during Passiontide, still employs the image of a combat: "he who conquered through a tree should on a tree himself be conquered: through Christ our Lord." Or as Hippolytus words it: "He extended His hands in His Passion, in order to deliver from suffering those who believed in Thee."

Truly, then, Hippolytus' Eucharistic prayer is not only the oldest extant text of such a prayer, a venerable monument of the past, but also a vivid and brilliant exposition of Eucharistic thought at the start of the third century, a record of the theological thinking of the pre-Constantinian Church.

CHAPTER SEVEN

Baptism and Preparation for Baptism

For the Christian religion in the Roman empire, the third century was an era of progress; Christianity grew strong. In 250, it is stated that the Roman community regularly supported 1500 poor; hence the faithful altogether must have numbered many tens of thousands. At the time of Diocletian's persecution, there were as many as forty basilicas in the city. In spite of the persecutions, by the time that Constantine appeared at least one fourth of the population in the Roman empire and also in the city must have been Christian.

How can we explain this growth? Ultimately, of course, it was the inner vitality of Christianity and the supernatural origin of the Church that produced such growth. But what means were at the Church's disposal to reveal and exercise that inner vitality? We might imagine some grand propaganda activity of the Church; we might picture a clergy devoting itself with great energy to missionary effort amongst the heathen. But if we look at the *Church Order* of Hippolytus we receive quite a different and surprising answer. The entire second part (which is about one third of the whole work) deals with the reception of new Christians; it is a consideration of the catechumenate and of Baptism. But there is not a word about propaganda, nor about missionary enterprise nor about relief for the new converts.

On the contrary, a long series of conditions is enumerated which must be fulfilled before a candidate is even admitted to instruction.

We get the impression that the Church built walls and barriers around herself, making it difficult for the heathen to enter. And yet Christianity made such progress as we have seen above.

Here is proof of the extraordinarily fine standing and reputation of the Christian communities of those days. From other sources, too, the same impression is obtained. Harnack, in his work on the mission and the spread of Christianity during the first three centuries, (1902) arrived at the conclusion: "We cannot doubt that the great mission of this religion was essentially accomplished through unprofessional missionaries." [1] In the first place, as we learn from many accounts, it was the example of the martyrs and of the confessors which had the greatest effect. But it is true also, as Harnack adds, that laymen were zealously alert to the possibilities of an apostolate: "It was characteristic of this religion, that every serious adherent served also towards its propagation." [2] Every real Christian, whether merchant, slave or man of letters, was a missionary through his example and through his ordinary everyday conduct. The Church could thus afford to be strict with regard to the conditions she made for those wishing to enter her fold. And this strictness and high standard only served to increase all the more the magnetic power of the Church.

Let us look at the more important conditions as Hippolytus sets them down. The candidate had to be introduced to the representatives of the Church (they are called teachers) by someone who was a Christian: "And let them be examined as to the reason why they have come forward to the faith. And those who bring them shall bear witness for them, whether they are able to hear. Let their life and manner of living be inquired into, whether he is a slave or free." [3]

First, therefore, it is ascertained whether the intention of the candidate is honest and what is his condition in life. Of slaves it is demanded that they give their masters no ground for complaints.[4] Concerning those who are married, an inquiry is to be made as to whether they fulfill the postulates of the Christian moral law.[5]

Next comes a long list of professions which are incompatible with being a Christian. We should expect as a matter of course that all professions would be excluded which were connected with ob-

1. A. Harnack, *Die Mission und Ausbreitung des Christentums in den ersten drei Jahrhunderten* (1902), 268.
2. *op. cit.*, 267 f.
3. Dix, *The Apostolic Tradition*, 23, v. 1–3.
4. Dix, *op. cit.*, v. 4 f.
5. Dix, v. 6 f.

vious unchastity or with idolatry: "If a man be a priest of idols, or a keeper of idols, either let him desist or let him be rejected." [6] But the list of forbidden professions goes far beyond this; in the culture of those days the theater could hardly be separated from immorality; again, the games in the circus were for the greater part a careless playing with human lives or (as in the case of gladiators) pure murder. Hence, all who were engaged in theaters, be it in the capacity of actors or of organizers, and all who cooperated in the circus or in the amphitheater were excluded. So also those going to these games as mere on-lookers.[7]

Only with great distrust might those be accepted for instruction who were in the pay of the pagan state. Among these were soldiers. Tertullian, also, dealt with soldiers in a special work (*De Corona Militis*), demanding their rejection on the grounds that they often have to execute unjust orders of punishment, that they have to guard pagan temples, but, above all, that they take the pagan military oath. We read also here in the *Church Order:* "A soldier of the government must be told not to execute men; if he should be ordered to do it he shall not do it. He must be told not to take the military oath. If he will not agree, let him be rejected." [8] Higher state officials are not accepted because they cannot avoid having to organize pagan sacrificial feasts nor escape taking part in them.[9] It has, indeed, also come to the attention of historians of the epoch of the martyrs that only few men martyrs could be proved to be from the higher ranks.

Artists and teachers, again, are only hesitatingly accepted; at that period, the making of idols was the main work of artists, while the teacher (the *grammaticus:* i.e. one who introduces into literature) had to explain the fables of the gods to his pupils. Their profession was, therefore, at least a difficult one as seen from the Christian viewpoint, and they were warned as to its dangers, though they were not absolutely refused.[10]

We see, therefore, that the Church maintained the stern standpoint of a decisive either-or. She did not want mere half-Christians; she preferred to remain small in numbers rather than to be unfaithful to her principles, or to endanger them.[11] Many who could not muster the required strength to make such a decision

6. Dix, v. 16.
7. Dix, 25 f., v. 12, 14, 15.
8. Dix, v. 17.
9. Dix, v. 18.
10. Dix, v. 11, 13.
11. These manifold interdictions show the extent to which paganism permeated public life, and what precautions the Church had to take to safeguard her children.

must have gone away again sad. On the other hand, however, this very insistence on her standards must have exercised a powerful attraction for the more noble-minded.

What was the catechumenate like for those who were admitted? The regulations about it are short and sufficiently clear.

The catechumenate lasted for three years.[12] We know, from other sources as well, that these three years were not meant primarily as a time of systematic doctrinal instruction; they were rather a period of moral trial, a sort of novitiate with religious and ascetical exercises, together with suitable instructions; to become a Christian in those days was comparable to entering some strict Order at the present time.

But these three years of the catechumenate also involved a regular course of instructions; its very name is derived from this: *κατηχούμενος* = one who receives instructions.

The catechumen enjoyed the right to take part in the readings and sermons of the community services; in the homilies of Origen, the catechumens are often addressed as part of the audience. But they received also special instructions, which consisted mainly in hearing a teacher (διδάσκαλος) read selected passages from Sacred Scripture. Those books were selected which contained suitable moral instructions; Origen mentions the books of Esther, Judith, Tobias, the books of Wisdom.[13] Almost the same books are mentioned later on by Athanasius, who adds also non-biblical works, namely the *Didache* and *The Shepherd* of Hermas.

This instruction was always concluded with prayers; moreover, on departing the teacher (who might be a layman) gave his pupils the blessing, that is, he imposed his hands upon them. Whereas nowadays we give the blessing with the Sign of the Cross, it was given then with the imposition of hands; the symbolism being that the one imparting the blessing is transfusing something of the sanctifying power within him to the one who is blessed.

When the three years of the catechumenate were over, the candidates for Baptism had first to be examined. But this was not an examination regarding the knowledge which they had acquired, but rather an examination of their conduct to ascertain whether it corresponded with Christian ideals: "And when they are chosen,

12. Dix, *op. cit.*, 28, v. 1. But the period of probation could be shortened by good conduct or prolonged by bad: "If a man be earnest and persevere well . . . because it is not the time that is judged but the conduct [let him be received];" Dix, 28, v. 2. Cf. Dom P. de Puniet, in the article *Catechuménat*, DACL, esp. 2583–2584.

13. In Num. hom. 27, 1.

who are set apart to receive Baptism, let their life be examined, whether they lived piously while catechumens, whether they honored the widows, whether they visited the sick, whether they have fulfilled every good work." [14]

Only after passing this examination could the candidate be admitted to the *proximate preparation* for Baptism.

This took place regularly during the time before Easter; since the number of the candidates for Baptism had increased, their instruction had to be given in common, and Baptism, too, was administered in common. It naturally followed that a definite date was fixed beforehand; and this was Easter, as we already learned from Tertullian. At the same time a beautifully symbolic idea was connected with this chosen day; in Baptism, the one to be baptized is buried with Christ and is allowed to rise again with Christ. Before Easter, therefore, the proximate preparation, the second degree of the catechumenate, began. (Lent as such did not exist as yet.)

This second degree or step in the preparation of the prospective convert was of a different character from the first. Now a more systematic instruction was given. Its main content was no longer the moral law, but dogmatic theology, the glad tidings of salvation, presented in a coherent form: "If those who bring them, bear witness to them, that they have done thus, let them hear the gospel." [15]

Hippolytus does not give any particulars, but from other sources (although these are of a later date, from the fourth century), we know that this final instruction was sometimes also scriptural: the history of salvation, the prophecies in the Old Testament and their fulfillment in Christ, His life and His Passion—all this was told them. Then followed, in any case, a systematic summary of the faith in a short formula: the Apostles' Creed. The text was explained in one or more catechetical instructions; then the candidates had to learn the formula by heart. The Apostles' Creed was, you might say, the oldest Roman catechism for the instruction of candidates for Baptism. Some time before the day of Baptism, the candidates were expected to recite the formula in front of the bishop.

But for all the emphasis on theory, practice was not neglected. During the last few weeks of preparation, the prospective convert was initiated into many ecclesiastical practices. As we learn more in detail from Tertullian, the candidates for Baptism were obliged to fast, to pray a great deal, even on their knees, and to keep the

14. Dix, *op. cit.*, 30 f.
15. Dix, 31, v. 2.

night-watches or vigils: *Orationes crebrae, ieiunia et geniculationes et pervigilia.*[16] Several times (even daily, according to Hippolytus) the exorcism was pronounced over them, the bishop himself performing this function during the last few days. Thus Satan's power, which still held sway over them, was gradually weakened, as it were, and broken. Finally, during Holy Week, they were to wash themselves in readiness for the baptismal ceremony, and to spend Friday and Saturday in a strict fast.[17]

The Sacrament of Baptism was administered during the night between Holy Saturday and Easter Sunday. That night they were to spend in vigil, listening to the Scriptures and the instructions.[18] But let us hear the regulations from Hippolytus himself:

> And at the hour when the cock crows they shall first pray over the water. When they come to the water let the water be pure and flowing.
>
> And they shall put off their clothes. And they shall baptize the little children first. And if they can answer for themselves, let them answer. But if they cannot, let their parents answer or someone from their family.
>
> And next they shall baptize the grown men; and last the women, who shall have loosed their hair and laid aside the gold ornaments.[19]

Let us notice, in passing, that Hippolytus describes the Baptism of children, even little children who cannot themselves respond to the questions put to them before Baptism. This is important, for it shows how wrong those writers are who still insist that infant Baptism was introduced into the Church only much later, perhaps after the fifth century. That is a mistake. From the very beginning, it was taken for granted that the children of Christian parents would be baptized in infancy. However, there were those who opposed infant Baptism; Tertullian was such a one. But Hippolytus' contemporary says categorically: "The Church received from the apostles the tradition of also baptizing children." [20] Parents were, however, permitted to delay the christening of their children, and during the fourth century in particular this permission appears to have been used very frequently. In fact those were the days of the so-called *clinici*—people who waited to receive the Sacrament on their *κλίνη*, their deathbed. This, many thought, entailed two advantages: their life could be spent with less restrictions, and then

16. De Bapt., 20.
17. Dix, *op. cit.*, 32, v. 5–8.
18. Dix, 32, v. 9.
19. Dix, 33, v. 1–5a.
20. Origen, In cap. VI., Ep. ad Rom.

before death they could be baptized and so (this was the second advantage) they would go to eternity in their baptismal innocence. The Church, of course, attacked this abuse vigorously, warning against the danger of a sudden death.

During the period under discussion, however, the Baptism of children from Christian families was common. We can see this very clearly from the following incident, which took place in North Africa about the year 250. A certain Bishop Fidus had voiced the opinion that parents should put off the Baptism of infants until the eighth day, because, according to the Old Law, the rite of circumcision took place on the eighth day. St. Cyprian, bishop of Carthage, proposed this question for discussion at a synod of sixty-six bishops then in session. The synod unanimously decided that no one should wait till the eighth day, but that the babies of Christian parents should be baptized immediately. From this it followed that children were not to undergo any formal preparation; the catechumenate was for grown-ups; the small children were simply brought for Baptism. Apparently this held true even if the Baptism was to take place during the night before Easter.

Let us now consider the procedure of Baptism more in detail. The first important act at Baptism was the renouncing of Satan: "And when the presbyter takes hold of each one of those who are to be baptized, let him bid him renounce, saying: I renounce thee, Satan, and all thy service and all thy works." [21]

The baptizing presbyter asked the questions and the baptized answered: *Renuntio*. Tertullian, also, frequently speaks of this renunciation, and from his words we can reconstruct the formula (it is about the same as the one in Hippolytus, and the same we still use today at Baptism): *"Renuntiasse nos diabolo et pompae eius et angelis eius ore nostro contestamur."* [22]

We have renounced Satan and his *pompa*. What is the meaning of *pompa diaboli?*

A *pompa* was, in the culture of antiquity, a festive procession, a triumphal procession, a marching around at some god's feast, at which all idols were carried along. The devil is, as it were, constantly conducting such a triumphal procession in the world; all who serve the devil and live in sin are running along in this procession. But in Baptism the candidate drops out of this procession, he leaves the devil's camp, and enters into the camp of Christ's army. This is made even plainer in the oriental ceremonial, where

21. Dix, *op. cit.*, 34, v. 9.
22. *De spect.*, 4.

the renunciation of Satan was called ἀπόταξις and this was followed by the σύνταξις to Christ. After the renunciation of Satan there followed the profession of faith, that is, the entry into the τάξις, the army of Christ.

The profession of faith, like the renunciation of Satan, was conducted in the form of questions and answers. In forswearing Satan, the answer was a simple and straightforward: *Renuntio;* here in the profession of faith it is a simple and straightforward: *Credo*. Let us continue with Hippolytus' description:

> Then after these things [the anointing with the "Oil of Exorcism"] let him give him over to the presbyter who stands at the water; and let them stand in the water naked. And let a deacon likewise go down with him into the water.
>
> And when he goes down to the water, let him who baptizes lay hand on him saying thus: Dost thou believe in God the Father Almighty? And he who is being baptized shall say: I believe. Let him forthwith baptize him once, having his hand laid upon his head.
>
> And after this let him say: Dost thou believe in Christ Jesus, the Son of God, Who was born of Holy Spirit and the Virgin Mary, Who was crucified in the days of Pontius Pilate, And died, And rose the third day living from the dead, And ascended into heaven, And sat down at the right hand of the Father, And will come to judge the living and the dead? And when he says: I believe, let him baptize him a second time.
>
> And again let him say: Dost thou believe in the Holy Spirit in the Holy Church, And the resurrection of the flesh? And he who is being baptized shall say: I believe. And so let him baptize him the third time.[23]

This liturgical formula gives us a description of the baptismal rite in all its details: Baptism is administered by immersion; this immersion is repeated three times, accompanied each time by an interrogation and reply: the neophyte professes his faith in each of the Persons of the Holy Trinity, the Father, the Son and the Holy Spirit. The description raises some interesting problems. And first there is the manner of Baptism, by immersion.

In the most explicit account of Baptism in the apostolic (or post-apostolic) age, given in the seventh chapter of the *Didache,* immersion is prescribed as a general rule, but allowance is made for Baptism by infusion if a suitable place is lacking.

> Regarding Baptism. Baptize as follows: after first explaining all these points, baptize in the name of the Father and of the Son and of the Holy Spirit, in running water. But if you have no running water, baptize in other water; and if you cannot in cold, then in warm. But if you have

23. Dix, *op. cit.,* 36, v. 11–18.

> neither, pour water on the head three times, in the name of the Father and of the Son and of the Holy Spirit. Before the Baptism, let the baptizer and the candidate fast, as well as any others who are able. Require the candidate to fast one or two days previously.[24]

This is the earliest mention we have of Baptism by infusion, although the circumstances detailed in the accounts of the Baptism of the Pentecost crowd and other Baptisms mentioned in the *Acts* allow us to infer such a procedure. But in the third century the construction of the baptismal *piscinae* had caused this mode of baptizing to fall into desuetude except in the case of the sick, and it might be noted that the reference to Baptism by infusion was suppressed when the text of the *Didache* passed into the *Apostolic Constitutions,* VII, 22. St. Cyprian had to defend the validity of baptism by infusion;[25] and Pope Cornelius, discussing the case of Novatian in his letter to Fabius of Antioch, observes that one so baptized could not be admitted into the ranks of the clergy.[26]

In both the *Didache* and the *Apostolic Tradition,* the baptismal ritual prescribes a triple immersion or a triple infusion. The triple immersion is frequently mentioned in documents of the third and fourth century. But a curiosity of the text of Hippolytus is that no baptismal formula is indicated other than the three interrogations and replies. Dom de Puniet, after noting other similar texts, remarks that it is difficult to avoid the impression that the interrogations regarding faith containing the express mention of the three divine Persons, took the place of the baptismal formula.[27] It is worthy of remark that two well-versed liturgical scholars of an earlier era, Dom du Frische (1693) and Dom Le Nourry (1724), held the same opinion.

The rite described by Hippolytus was further enriched, perhaps not as early as the third century, but surely by the fourth. In the *Canones Hippolyti,* an Egyptian adaptation of the *Apostolic Tradition,* the rite has the following form: The baptizand should first turn to the west (that is, the direction of darkness, because that is where the sun goes down) and should address the devil: "I renounce thee, Satan, and all thy following." After that he should turn towards the east (that is, the direction of the sunrise, the direction of Christ) and should cry out: "I believe and bow before Thee and all Thy servants, O Father, Son and Holy Spirit." And in another redaction, also Egyptian in origin, the contrast is stressed

24. *Didache,* c. 7.
25. Ep. 69, 12–16.
26. Eusebius, *Hist. Eccl.,* VI, 43, 17.
27. art. *Baptême,* in DACL, II, 342.

still more pointedly, for the positive profession runs: "I believe in Thee, Christ, my God, and I believe in Thy saving law, and all Thy lifegiving angels."[28] Satan and Christ are thus made to confront each other; the baptizand must separate himself from the *τάξις* of Satan and shift his allegiance to the *τάξις* of Christ.

To the foregoing was added yet another custom which was widespread in the fourth century and which Doelger assumes was already in vogue in the time of Hippolytus. After the baptizand had faced westward and pronounced his renunciation of Satan, he was instructed to expectorate forcibly before turning eastward towards Christ; in other words, he was to spit on Satan. This was simply a robust symbol of hostility, a token of the irreconcilable enmity which from then on must exist between himself and the powers of evil.

Several unctions were connected with the ritual of Baptism. By the third century they were essentially the same as those which are in use at present in the Roman rite. Before the actual Baptism, directly after the renunciation of Satan, the baptizand was anointed with an exorcised oil—the oil we nowadays call "the oil of catechumens." This unction was designed to help drive out the devil.

> And when the presbyter takes hold of each one of those who are to be baptized, let him bid him renounce, saying: I renounce thee, Satan, and all thy service and all thy works. And when he has said this let him anoint him with the Oil of Exorcism, saying: Let all evil spirits depart far from thee.[29]

Hippolytus gives no particulars regarding the form of this anointing, but perhaps we may infer from our present Roman custom and from references in other documents of the period that at least the breast and shoulders were anointed. In the baptizing of women this involved the delicate problem of modesty and, at least in the Orient, deaconesses were appointed to handle this part of the ceremony and to assist in the actual Baptism. Possibly the earliest reference to the deaconess and her ministry is found in the third or early fourth century *Didascalia Apostolorum,* which probably reflects the customs of Syria or Transjordania. It admonishes the bishop to appoint "a woman for the ministry of women," and speaks specifically of the problem of Baptism: "When women go down into the water, those who go down into the water ought to be anointed by a deaconess with the oil of anointing. . . . But where there is a woman and especially a deaconess, it is not fitting that women should be seen

28. Ethiopian Baptismal Order, in Denz. I, 123.
29. Dix, *op. cit.,* 34, v. 9–10.

by men; but with the imposition of hand, do thou anoint the head only. . . . But let a man pronounce over them the invocation of the divine Names in the water." [30]

After Baptism, the priest was to anoint the neophyte again, this time with another oil over which a prayer of thanksgiving had been pronounced (today we call it the "chrism"). This anointing was intended to represent the adherence of the newly baptized to Christ, for Christ means "the Anointed."

> And afterwards when he comes up he shall be anointed by the presbyters with the Oil of Thanksgiving, saying: I anoint thee with holy oil in the Name of Jesus Christ. And each one drying himself they shall now put on their clothes and after this let them be together in the church.[31]

This is obviously the same anointing which is still retained in the present-day Roman baptismal ritual. But there is still another anointing, this time by the bishop, who lays hands on the neophytes, pours oil on their heads, and signs their foreheads.

> And the bishop shall lay his hand upon them invoking and saying: O Lord God, Who didst count these worthy of deserving the forgiveness of sins by the laver of regeneration, make them worthy to be filled with Thy Holy Spirit and send upon them Thy grace, that they may serve Thee according to Thy will; to Thee the glory, to the Father and to the Son with the Holy Spirit in the holy Church, both now and ever and world without end. Amen.
>
> After this, pouring the consecrated oil and laying his hand on his head, he shall say: I anoint thee with the holy oil in God the Father Almighty and Christ Jesus and the Holy Spirit. And sealing him on the forehead, he shall give him the kiss and say: The Lord be with you. And he who has been sealed shall say: And with thy spirit. And so he shall do to each one severally.[32]

One of the Roman features of the baptismal ritual described by Hippolytus is this second unction, distinct from the unction given by the priest to the neophyte as he comes up from the *piscina*. This second unction is reserved to the bishop, and takes place after the imposition of hands. The first is a secondary rite of Baptism, in the other we recognize the Sacrament of Confirmation. This distinction, which would be looked for in vain in documents of Latin Africa, appears in the famous decretal letter of Pope Innocent I to Decentius, Bishop of Gubbio (March 19, 416). The text of Hippolytus gives us the first testimony of this two centuries earlier.

30. *Didascalia Apostolorum,* 16; ed. & tr., Dom R. H. Connolly (Oxford, 1929), 146 f.
31. Dix, *op. cit.*, 38, v. 19.
32. Dix, 39, v. 1–3.

After the neophytes receive the kiss of peace from the bishop, they are allowed to join the faithful at Mass. As new-born babes, they are permitted to run at once to the bosom of Holy Mother Church. They are permitted to enter the company of the faithful, to pray with them for the first time, to celebrate the Eucharist with them and to receive Holy Communion. (About the special practices at the Communion after Baptism we have already spoken.)

But the care of the Church for the neophytes did not end with the day of Baptism. Hippolytus observes that the bishop should supplement the instruction the new Christians had received by catechising them after their Baptism. As subject of this lesson, he indicates "the resurrection of the flesh and the rest according to the Scripture." [33] Later on we learn that these catechetical instructions were given for a whole week, during which those matters were discussed which were still subject to the *disciplina arcani;* these included especially the more detailed doctrine about the sacraments, the significance of the baptismal ceremonies, the mystery of the Eucharist and of the celebration of the Eucharist.

Baptism occupied a position of eminence in the life of the early Church. Even the very simplest of Christians knew the meaning of Baptism and its import. This is made plain in the various customs which are reported to us from the very period under consideration. Thus, for instance, the notion had already developed that no bath should be taken during the first week after Baptism—out of reverence for the baptismal bath. Later on Augustine mentions the custom then in vogue of not walking barefoot for one week, for the same reason.[34]

What the Christians of the first centuries thought of Baptism is reflected also in the numerous inscriptions and paintings in the catacombs. When we have a memorial card printed for one of our dear dead, we are glad when we can insert the words, "died fortified with the Last Sacraments." Ancient Christians, too, had a similar practice, but with this difference: they referred not to the Last Sacraments but to the first. In this period of frequent adult Baptisms, it was generally Baptism that was mentioned or indicated—Baptism and the salvation acquired through Baptism. The favorite themes of the paintings in the catacombs are, as all of us know, themes representing the effects of the Redemption. In many of these themes water plays an important role: Noe saved from the deluge, Moses striking water from the rock, Jonas thrown out of

33. Dix, 43.
34. Augustine, *Ep.* 55, 35; cf. Tertullian, *Cor. Mil.*, c. 3.

the sea onto the land of life eternal, chaste Susanna in her arbor bath, the Samaritan woman at the well. But there are also other themes connected with baptismal grace: the young men in the fiery furnace, Daniel in the lion's den—these are pictures of the Christian who has obtained salvation in Baptism and who therefore no longer fears death.

Through faith, the Christian has found Christ; and now, through the sacrament of Baptism, that faith in Christ has been sealed. For Baptism is the seal (*sigillum, signum*) which has been impressed upon the faith of the Christian, on the faith which he professed in his Baptism. Christians are a "people having a resplendent seal," as we read in the Epitaph of Abercius. The faithful departed are described as those *qui nos praecesserunt cum signo fidei*—who have gone before us sealed by Baptism with the sacramental seal of faith.

CHAPTER EIGHT

The Apostles' Creed

IN THE rite of Baptism as we observe it in the *Church Order* of Hippolytus, immediately before the administration of Baptism comes a profession of faith. Though it is couched in the form of a threefold question, as we have seen in the preceding chapter, it conforms fairly closely in its wording to the other ancient forms of the symbol, the Apostles' Creed, for example, which is the subject of this chapter.

During the last century, this short formula was the object of thorough investigation. Joseph de Ghellinck, S.J., recently published a noteworthy volume of 321 pages, about the history of the researches into the Creed: *Les recherches sur les origines du Symbole des Apôtres*. In this volume the list of the books and essays published on this subject comprises more than twenty pages.[1] Such a long bibliography not only gives us an idea of the astonishing amount of work devoted to this tiny formula, but also an insight into the many problems and the solutions suggested to them, which this formula involves.

The Middle Ages, in their unaffected simplicity, had a very naive explanation about the beginnings of the symbol. The symbol was called *Symbolum Apostolorum*, the Apostles' Creed; hence, so they concluded, the apostles had composed it, each one of the apostles at their last meeting contributing one of the twelve articles

1. J. de Ghellinck, *Les recherches sur les origines du Symbole des Apôtres* (2nd ed., Paris, 1949). Cf. also B. Altaner, *Patrologie* (Freiburg, 1950), 35–37. This present chapter on the Apostles' Creed is revised from my *Catechetics*, ed. *Lumen Vitae* (Brussels, 1956).

of the symbol.[2] In European churches dating back to the Middle Ages, therefore, we not seldom find portraits of the apostles under each of which is written the article of the creed ascribed to that particular apostle. This naive opinion was called into question several centuries ago, towards the end of the Middle Ages. In 1443, the noted humanist, Laurentius Valla, was listening at Naples to a Franciscan explaining to children the old legend of the origin of the symbol. He was annoyed, and challenged the Franciscan to a public disputation. The disputation did not take place because the King of Naples prevented it, but the incident caused a great sensation.

It took a long time, however, before a scientific examination of the question was undertaken. It was not till 1842 that any attempt was made to collect and collate the pertinent texts; in that year, A. Hahn first published his *Bibliothek der Symbole und Glaubensregeln.*

It is, however, only since about 1890 that research started in earnest, the occasion being the constant dwindling of the faith within the Protestant church in Germany. The Protestant church authorities demanded the contents of the symbol as the minimum of what each pastor who wished to serve in the church had to believe. Some pastors, however, declared that they were unable to accept even this minimum. A number of Protestant theologians, Adolf Harnack amongst them, sided with the recusants. The so-called "Controversy over the apostolic symbol" had begun. This controversy was the occasion for reopening the question of the origin of the formula with renewed vigor. The work of research was carried on, in the main, by Protestants, first in Germany and then in England.[3] Later on Catholics also entered the lists.[4] It would consume too much space even to outline the course of the debate. Our main concern here is with the results of these innumerable investigations. We purpose here to synopsize the most important of these.

The beginnings of the Apostles' Creed are found, of course, in the times of the apostles. But only at the commencement of the third

2. Cf. J. N. D. Kelly, *Early Christian Creeds* (London, 1952), 1–4.

3. Of the works that still have value today the most important are: F. Kattenbusch, *Das Apostolische Symbol,* 2 vols. (Leipzig, 1894/1900); H. Lietzmann, "*Symbolstudien,*" in *Zeitschrift f. d. neutest. Wissenschaft,* 1922–1927; A. Harnack, *Apostolisches Symbolum* (in Hauck's Realencykl., I, 741 ff.). In English there are H. B. Swete, *The Apostles' Creed* (London, 1894) and more recently O. Cullmann, *The Earliest Christian Confessions* (trans. J. Reid; London, 1949). See also J. Kelly (note 2).

4. S. Bäumer, *Das Apostolische Glaubensbekenntnis* (Mainz, 1893); C. Blume, *Das Apostolische Glaubensbekenntnis* (Freiburg, 1893); and of course recently J. de Ghellinck (note 1 above). The texts are collected in A. Hahn, *Bibliothek der Symbole,* 3rd ed. (Breslau, 1897); a selection in H. Lietzmann, *Symbole der alten Kirche* (Kleine Texte, 17/18; Bonn, 1935). A short orientation in Denzinger.

century was a fixed formula arrived at, such as we possess today. For two separate forms had developed, one trinitarian, the other christological, and only about the year 200 were these combined into one formula.

I. The Trinitarian Formula

As we see from the Acts, the main theme of the Apostles' preaching to the Jews was the announcement that Jesus is the Messias, the Christ. Among the pagans, however, it was necessary first to preach faith in the one God. Hence the missionary sermon to the pagans contained a twofold theme: God and Christ. God our Creator and last end, and Christ who leads us to God: these are the two basic concepts of the Christian *kerygma,* then and always. But a somewhat complete summary of the Christian doctrine includes still a third theme: the teaching of what Christianity brings to a sin-bound world: a new life and a new people of God; the Church, and everything contained in the Church by way of powers and institutions, the grace of the Holy Spirit, the Sacraments, life everlasting.

Depending on the way in which the latter theme was summarized, three or four or even five main points of Christian teaching were arrived at. In the so-called *Epistola Apostolorum* (about 150), the Christian doctrine is compared to the five loaves in the miracle of the multiplication of the loaves: as there were five loaves, so in the Christian doctrine there are five dogmas or lessons: namely we believe: "in the Father, the Ruler of the universe (παντοκράτωρ), and in Jesus Christ our Saviour, in the Holy Spirit the Paraclete, in the holy Church, and in the remission of sins." Sometimes only three main points were enumerated: God-Christ-resurrection, or sometimes God-Christ-the Church.

The favorite summary, however, was: God-Christ-Holy Spirit. Thus was obtained a concise expression of the belief in the three Divine Persons; this was especially natural and understandable when the formula was used in the profession of faith at Baptism, for Baptism was administered, according to the command of our Lord, in the name of the Father, and of the Son and of the Holy Spirit. For the rest, the profession of faith in the three divine Persons was included in the symbol in diverse ways, even at a later period. There are symbols, for instance, which place the profession of faith in the Trinity in the beginning: "I believe in God the Father and the Son and the Holy Spirit, and I believe in Jesus Christ our Lord who was born . . ." The Athanasian symbol for example, is still constructed in this way: first come, very extensively, the trinitarian dogmas, then follows the christological profession of faith.[5]

But already in the second century a different combination came to prevail: a connection of the trinitarian with the other dogmas in such a way that with the dogma of God was connected the mentioning of the Father, with the doctrine of Christ the mentioning of the Son as such, and with the dogma of the means of salvation the mentioning of the Holy Spirit. Or put it the other way around: to the mention of the Father, the doctrine of God the Creator was added, etc. In any case, God-Christ-the grace of the Holy Spirit, these are the great themes which we today still place as the headings over our theological treatises: *De Deo Uno et Trino; De Christo Redemptore;* and *De gratia et sacramentis.*

Thus there existed probably as early as about the year 100, tripartite baptismal symbols, consisting of three equally long articles in a wording quite similar to our present symbol, if we exclude from it the christological clauses. However, there were various redactions, and not one of them corresponds exactly to the wording we use today. Even the trinitarian formula of the oldest Roman *symbolum* runs differently (we replace the original Greek by the later Latin text):

Credo in Deum Patrem omnipotentem,
et in Jesum Christum, Filium eius unicum, Dominum nostrum
et in Spiritum Sanctum, Sanctam Ecclesiam, (remissionem peccatorum,) carnis resurrectionem.[6]

From this Roman Symbol, all the different forms of the *symbola* of the West have developed. A second and similar primitive symbol, also trinitarian, arose in the Orient: from it are derived the oriental forms of the symbol. An example, though rather enlarged, is familiar to us all: the Credo of the Mass: this was originally, in a somewhat shorter form, the baptismal symbol of Jerusalem.

II. The Christological Formula

Beside the basic formula comprising the trinitarian profession of faith, there existed also a formula, or more correctly, various formulae, containing the christological profession of faith (or as it

5. The *Te Deum* is similarly constructed: first praise of the Triune God—*Patrem immensae majestatis,* etc.; then the reference to Christ—*Tu rex gloriae, Christe.*

6. cf. Kelly, *op. cit.,* 121 f.

is called: the *kerygma* of Christ.) The beginnings of such a formula are already observable in St. Paul (I Cor. 15:3 ff).[7] Such a formula existed at Rome at a very early date. About the year 200, it was combined with the tripartite trinitarian profession of faith, and thus the older Roman symbol—called *R* by the scholars—was finished. In the Roman redaction this christological *kerygma* runs thus:

qui natus est de Spiritu sancto et Maria Virgine,
qui sub Pontio Pilato crucifixus est et sepultus,
  tertia die resurrexit a mortuis,
  ascendit in caelos,
  sedet ad dexteram Patris.
    unde venturus est iudicare vivos et mortuos.[8]

As against the present wording (called *T*, that is, *textus receptus*), only stylistic differences are worthy of note: the division of the *kerygma* into two parts by means of the twofold *qui*. This corresponds with the two main mysteries in the christological dogma: the Incarnation and the Passion: in other words, with the two principal feasts of the ecclesiastical year: Christmas and Easter. It is therefore not accidental that both these items in the present baptismal rite are stressed in the questions before Baptism: *Credis in Jesum Christum filium eius unicum natum et passum?* "Do you believe in Jesus Christ, His only Son, our Lord, who was born and suffered (for us)?" I.e., Christ's birth; Christ's passion and death. *Natum:* The miraculous birth through the Holy Spirit and the Virgin Mary sheds light on the mystery of the person of Christ. He is more than a man; He is at the same time the Son of God. *Passum:* The Passion is the work of Redemption for the sake of which He came. We must note that, in the symbol, the Passion is immediately followed by the glorification, described in hymnodic phrases.[9] This resembles the celebration of Easter, in which the glorification of the Lord is stressed rather than His bitter suffering—a celebration which continued for a period of fifty days. In Christian antiquity, Easter was celebrated before any celebration of Christmas came into being; later on, it was celebrated with greater solemnity than Christmas.

7. The ancient acrostic ΙΧΘΥΣ (= Jesus Christ, God's Son, Savior), or the fish symbol which replaced the word, is precisely such a confession of Christ.
8. Denz., n. 2; cf. Kelly, *op. cit.*, 102.
9. Even the phrase, "He descended into hell," inserted in the later text, is an expression of triumph. In Byzantine art Christ's descent into Limbo ("The Harrowing of Hell") usually replaces the picture of the Resurrection; cf. K. Kuenstle, *Ikonographie der christlichen Kunst,* I (Freiburg, 1928), 494–500.

Here also in the symbol, the Passion, together with the Resurrection, is more strongly emphasised and more extensively described than the Nativity. We might note that, in conformity with this same spirit, in the symbol a chronological definition is affixed not to the Nativity, as would have been done later on (for since the sixth century we reckon the years *post Christum natum*), but to the passion: *passus sub Pontio Pilato*. With this dating, Christ's work is fitted into the course of the world's history; for it is not a question of a myth, but of a positive and palpable fact: *passus sub Pontio Pilato*. Historical dates were usually reckoned according to rulers and their years of rule: *sub Tiberio Caesare: Consulibus Marco et Duilio:* here the date is fixed by the mention of the insignificant governor in Palestine—a sign that this form of dating the life of Christ had already come into use as a settled formula when Christianity was still confined to the narrow borders of the Holy Land.

The opinion has been expressed that the twofold *qui* of the old text has still another significance; the two subordinate sentences would be in conscious parallelism with the two attributes which had already been added to the name of Jesus Christ. The first clause: *qui . . . Virgine*, would thus be, so to speak, a commentary on the definition; *Filium eius unicum;* He is the Son of God, as is seen from the manner of His birth. And for this they referred to Lk. I, 35: *Spiritus sanctus superveniet in te. . . . Ideoque quod nascetur ex te sanctum vocabitur Filius Dei*. Here, too, the miraculous birth is taken as a proof of the divinity of Christ. Likewise the second subordinate clause: *qui sub P.P. crucifixus . . .* , seems to illustrate the second attribute of Christ, the title: *κύριος ἡμῶν—Dominum nostrum*. And here too a passage in Sacred Scripture (Phil. 2, 11) has the same train of thoughts: *Humiliavit semetipsum factus oboediens usque ad mortem. . . . Propter quod et Deus exaltavit illum . . . ut . . . omnis lingua confiteatur quia Dominus Jesus Christus in gloria est Dei Patris* (in the Greek text: "that Christ is the *κύριος*"). I might mention that de Ghellinck rejects this interpretation put forward by K. Holl, but I do not know whether rightly so.[10]

III. The Third Section of the Creed

Of particular interest is the third part of the symbol beginning with the profession of belief in the Holy Spirit and treating of the means of salvation. We could entitle it: The doctrine of grace in the Apostles' Creed. The expression is somewhat different here from

10. Discussion in Kelly, *op. cit.*, 123–126.

that found in our catechisms and in our treatises on grace, but it is, nevertheless, the doctrine of grace. The train of thought obtaining here can perhaps be paraphrased as follows:

First the Holy Spirit is mentioned as the principle of the new life brought by Christ. This living principle dwells in and works in the Church which is made holy through it. It takes hold of the individual through the remission of sins, and works its final effect in the resurrection of the flesh.

In the first place, mention is made of the Holy Spirit, who is the third person of the Divinity, but also at the same time the uncreated grace for mankind. When wishing to speak of grace, Christian antiquity was accustomed to mention the Holy Spirit who dwells in us and incites us to good. This terminology is less accurate than the one we are used to from theology. Yet the essence of grace is nevertheless well described, for it is thus made clear that there is question of an interior gift, and one that is supernatural. The very term makes it plain to everyone that something is meant to which we cannot make a claim; namely, God bestowing upon us His own Spirit, His own life.

The Holy Spirit has here on earth, in Holy Church, His first dwelling. The holiness of the Holy Spirit leaps upon her like a spark, as it were: *Credo in Spiritum Sanctum—sanctam Ecclesiam.* It must be intentional that two words *sanctum sanctam* follow immediately, the one after the other, in order to point out the source of the holiness of Holy Church. The other attributes of the Church, which we mention in the creed of the Mass, *una, catholica, apostolica,* are mentioned early (2nd or 3rd cent.), but it is the term *sancta* which is connected with the word *ecclesia* earliest of all, for the Church is essentially holy. This is already included in the very concept of the term *ecclesia:* she is the assembly of all those "called" by God, all those called to grace and sanctity.

In the later text of the symbol which we use today—which was in vogue in the Gallican Church and which, since about the tenth century, supplanted the older Roman text even in Rome (T = *textus receptus,* in contradistinction to R = *textus romanus*)—an explanatory phrase is added here: *sanctorum communionem.* The term *sancta Ecclesia* or *sancta Ecclesia catholica* had become a somewhat stereotyped expression which no longer conveyed a great deal of meaning. Here the old idea of holiness is rendered prominent again with a definite and new coloring: Holy Church is a community of men made holy by Baptism. Hence it is not our relations with the saints in heaven which is the object of this phrase;

primarily it is the Church on earth: she is a community of saints. Even in modern times many catechisms, e.g., the *Catechismus Romanus,* have given this interpretation. There is, however, another possible translation of this expression; *sanctorum* (*communio*) could be the genitive not of *sancti,* but of *sancta* (*sancta* = τὰ ἅγια, holy things); hence *sanctorum communio* would mean a community about holy things: faith, hope, the sacraments, the powers and privileges which are in the Church, above all the Eucharist, as a common possession of those belonging to the Catholic Church. St. Augustine explained the term *communio sanctorum* repeatedly in this sense. But when all is said, it comes to about the same thing: the Church is a holy community, holy through what is given her in grace, holy in those gifts she communicates to her children.

In any case, therefore, the life of grace is considered primarily under a communal and social aspect. Then there is also mention of the grace bestowed upon the individual. Those sacraments are specifically mentioned which initiate the Christian into the life of grace: Baptism and Penance—sacraments of the forgiving of sins. The *remissio peccatorum* refers in the first place to Baptism. This is clearly seen in the Creed of the Mass: *Confiteor unum baptisma in remissionem peccatorum.* The remaining sacraments like the Eucharist are implied. They are not mentioned individually. Nor was this necessary because, having once entered into the life of the Church through the door of Baptism, the Christian as a matter of course participates in the whole life of the Church.

By the phrase *carnis resurrectio,* there is meant above all the glorious resurrection of the just. Grace changes into glory and glory now takes hold of man's body, transforming it. The term: *et vitam aeternam,* added in the *textus receptus,* is, therefore, only an explanatory extension of the phrase, in which the eternity of that state of perfection is expressed.

We may certainly state that, according to the mind of the primitive Church, all these declarations about the means of salvation are merely an unfolding of the first declaration in which the Holy Spirit is mentioned. The Holy Spirit it is who fills the Church; He is, as we say, the soul of the Church. The Holy Spirit effects in Baptism the remission of sins: *ipse est remissio omnium peccatorum,* as a Pentecostal oration has it. The Holy Spirit works also in the resurrection, and brings it about that our earthly body becomes a "spiritual" body (I Cor. 15:44).

From another viewpoint, however, we can say that the Church is the climax, the principal concept, in this third part of the symbol.

The Holy Church is the comprehensive element wherein everything else is contained. Hence there were formulas of the symbol that read: I believe in the Holy Spirit (and in the remission of sins) and in the resurrection of the flesh in the Holy Church. Even the *Apostolic Tradition* of Hippolytus of Rome in the last baptismal question puts it thus: "Dost thou believe in the Holy Spirit in the Holy Church?" The whole process of salvation takes place within the Church.[11]

Deserving of our attention also is the parallelism to be discerned in our symbol between the lines sketched in the life of the Redeemer and the lines sketched in the lives of the redeemed. At the beginning of the description of Christ stands the Holy Spirit, and the Virgin Mary of whom Christ was born. In the description of the life of the Christian, there stands the Holy Spirit, and Holy Church, who too is virgin and mother, of whom Christians are born. On the one hand we have the descent to the Passion, to the grave and then the glorious Resurrection to eternal glory at the right hand of the Father; on the other, the being buried in Baptism, followed by the labors of a Christian's life, and then likewise the resurrection which finally embraces the body and brings it into the glory of life eternal.

From this study, we can clearly discover the natural divisions of the symbol. The division into twelve articles does not correspond to the original disposition of the formula: it is a later and artificial division, obscuring rather than illustrating the connection of the sentences. True, this division is already found in Rufinus (d. 410); but its origin is obvious: the symbol was always called apostolic, because it summarized the faith handed down by the apostles. Because there are twelve apostles, the formula was divided into twelve articles. From this fact originated the medieval legend. The Middle Ages, however, also employed other divisions. St. Thomas Aquinas, for example, divides the symbol into fourteen articles; seven of them, as he explains in his commentary, deal with the mystery of the Trinity, and seven with the humanity of Christ. The same construction is also to be found in some of the liturgical works of the Middle Ages, particularly in England.[12]

Finally we must comment on the surprising formulation of the phrase "I believe *in*" (*Credo* in *Deum*). The older Fathers of the Church did not attach any special significance to this particular usage. Even Rufinus, when discussing the differences between his

11. Cf. P. Nautin, *Je crois à l'Ésprit Saint dans la Sainte Église* (Unam sanctam, 17; Paris, 1947).
12. Maskell, *Monumenta ritualia Eccl. Anglic.*, I, 76 ff.

own credal formula, the one in use at Aquileia, and the one which he regarded as the Roman creed, takes notice of the grammatical dissimilarities but does not consider them important. However, since the time of St. Augustine this phrasing has been interpreted as a firm declaration of both an intellectual adherence to God and a loving effort to attain him.[13]

Naturally the Apostles' Creed enjoyed a great reputation in the ancient Church. The esteem in which it was held led to its being called a *σύμβολον* (= something put together, a sign of recognition). It was the passport with which a traveling Christian proved his identity before a strange Christian community. Therefore it had to be kept secret from the pagans. It was not allowed to be written down; it was to be inscribed only on the tablets of the heart. Catechumens, therefore, had to learn it by heart. And in order that they might not forget it, they were admonished to recite it daily, along with the Our Father, similarly held sacred. St. Augustine, for example, admonished the catechumens: "Say it daily. When you rise, when you go to bed, say your symbol, say it before the Lord. Call it to mind, and do not tire of repeating it." [14] And this admonition was actually carried out. The recitation of the *symbolum* and of the *Pater noster* formed the beginning of every Christian's morning prayer and the conclusion of his night prayer. And so it was all through the Middle Ages. Hence it is not to be wondered at that the same custom found its way into the order of prayer for monks and clerics. At the start of the day's office, at Matins and at Prime, it was customary to recite the Apostles' Creed and the Our Father (and since the late Middle Ages also the Hail Mary), and the same was done at the end of Compline before retiring.

This practice is no longer observed in the recitation of the Divine Office; but we still say the Apostles' Creed before our Baptism and after our Confirmation, and we still preface it to the recital of the rosary. And so even in the twentieth century we treasure this precious heirloom from the early Church, and to our lips today, as to the lips of the Christian of long ago, comes the strong and forthright word: *Credo,* "I believe."

13. Christine Mohrmann, *Credere in Deum: Mélanges J. de Ghellinck* (Museum Lessianum, sect. hist., 13; Gembloux, 1951), 277–285.

14. *Serm.* 58, 11 (*PL,* 38:399 f.) Cf. St. Ambrose, De virg., 3, 4 (*PL,* 16:225).

CHAPTER NINE

Daily Devotions of the Early Christians

IN THE present-day liturgical movement, primitive Christianity is often held up before our eyes as a model, an exemplar of liturgical observance. We are to believe that Christians of old, contrary to the tendency of modern individualism, knew no other, or scarcely any other, form of prayer than liturgical prayer: the common celebration of the Sunday, the common celebration of the Eucharist, the common liturgical prayer-hours and vigils for which clergy and people assembled regularly. A certain type of literature—dwindling now in volume—serves to embellish such a picture with vivid details. The members of the outlawed Christian communities are portrayed as creeping stealthily out of the city and stealing by devious paths to their underground refuge. There in the catacombs they are to be seen gathered round the patriarchal figure of the bishop as he offers the mystic sacrifice of the Divine Victim, the only light a flickering lamp, the only sound the hushed whispers of the assisting clergy and the responsive faithful.

Unfortunately this ideal picture is not correct. Today we know—and we should have known long since—that this is not all fact. It is a mistake to palm this off as reality. True, it is wrong to disregard the past. But it is equally wrong to be blindly attached to things of the past, just because they are ancient, especially when such an attachment distorts the facts, when it grows fond of unreality.

The idea that the life of the primitive Christians revolved exclusively around the liturgy is not correct. And it cannot be correct, simply because it would be unnatural and in contradiction to the rules laid down in the Gospels. How could the Christian life exclude private and personal prayer? Not only does the *Mediator Dei* of our late Holy Father point out explicitly that the Christian's life of prayer must comprise both the liturgical and the private, but our Lord Himself gave the example of such a duality. It was He who instituted the Eucharist; but it was also He who said: "When thou art praying, go into thy inner room and shut the door upon thyself, and so pray to thy Father in secret." [1] He Himself not only prayed with His apostles but also, and above all, He prayed alone, on the mountain and for whole nights.

But there is another and perhaps even more important reason for considering it a gross exaggeration to restrict the prayer of Christian antiquity to liturgical prayer alone. Such a restriction would have been most improbable because of the practical fact that communal devotions must have been largely hampered. To have assembled very often would have been dangerous, and in all likelihood that would have been reason enough to have confined such assemblies to Sundays.

We do not need, however, to make rough guesses in this matter, for we possess concrete and unequivocal accounts of the practice of private prayer among the Christians of the early centuries. And once again it is the *Apostolic Tradition* of Hippolytus of Rome that furnishes us with the most detailed and exhaustive data. Fortunately these data do not stand isolated; they are reinforced and confirmed by almost identical statements in other writings, both earlier and later—Clement of Alexandria, Tertullian, Cyprian, Basil and others of the Fathers. These references, separately and together, tend to prove that private prayer played a more important role in the life of the early Christians than we are ordinarily led to think.

The first notice regarding the daily devotions of the early Christians is to be found in the *Didache*. The text paraphrases our Lord's warning and injunction: "Do not pray as the hypocrites, but as the Lord directed in his Gospel"; then it adds the wording of the Our Father, with the doxological ending "for Thine is the power and glory forever," and ends with this rule: "Three times in the day pray thus." [2]

Three times in the day—there is a rule that crops up time and again in the following decades, usually in the form: The Christian prays at the third, the sixth and the ninth hour. As everyone immediately recognizes, here we have the first inkling of what have become our canonical hours of Terce, Sext and None. But here

1. Matt. 6:16.
2. *Didache*, c. 8, 2–3.

they are not canonical hours, not periods of public and common prayer, but times for private prayer. The observance of those hours from which the little hours of the Office have sprung was entirely the affair of the individual.

The choice of these particular times is founded on Jewish prototypes. Of the Prophet Daniel we read: "Three times a day he would open his chamber window towards Jerusalem eastwards, doing reverence on bended knee and praising his God." [3] Traces of this practice are to be found in the Acts of the Apostles, especially for None. It was at the ninth hour, "which is an hour of prayer"—*ad horam orationis nonam*—that Peter and John went up to the temple and cured the lame man; and it was in the afternoon, at the ninth hour, that Cornelius was at prayer when he had his vision.[4] The sixth hour, too, is referred to: "Peter went up to the house-top about noon, to pray there." [5] And perhaps a hint of Terce is to be discovered in the fact that it was at the third hour of Pentecost, as the apostles were gathered together, that the Holy Ghost came upon them with the sound of a strong wind blowing and in the shape of fiery tongues.[6]

These were the times which the early Christians also observed, and in fact the earliest writers, writers of the end of the second century, who give any account of this, expressly founded the practice on the example of the apostles who—they pointed out—observed the same hours as hours of prayer.

Tertullian dedicates a whole chapter of his book *De oratione* to this custom. In the twenty-fifth chapter he says:

> Concerning time, however, the keeping also of certain hours will not be useless from an external point of view—I mean of those common hours that mark the intervals of the day, the third, sixth and ninth, which in Scripture are to be found the most usual.

Then, after presenting in detail the examples already cited, he adds:

> Although these facts are stated simply without any commands about the practice, yet it would be a good thing to establish some prior standard which will both compel the remembrance of prayer, and as it were compulsorily at times drag one away from affairs to such a duty.[7]

3. Daniel 6:11.
4. Acts 3:1; 10:3, 30.
5. Acts 10:9.
6. Acts 2:15.
7. Tertullian, *De Oratione*, c. 25; in *Tertullian's Treatise Concerning Prayer, Concerning Baptism* (trans. Alexander Souter; New York, 1919), 41, 42.

This remark seems to indicate that the times mentioned are merely suggestions, but suggestions founded on good and solid custom. But there is a further remark about two other times for prayer; quite casually he adds: "Of course, quite apart from the regular prayers which without any reminder are due at the beginning of day and night." [8] Notice the word "regular": morning prayers and night prayers are simply taken for granted. *Exceptis legitimis orationibus . . . ingressu lucis et noctis.*

Tertullian also mentions another time of prayer—and he is not the only writer to call attention to it; it is a time that appears to us somewhat unusual and must have been rather troublesome to observe: prayer at midnight. But from the tone of his observations it is obvious that such prayer was required even of Christians who were not especially fervent. Tertullian considers the case of a woman wedded to a pagan man. Such a marriage puts her in an awkward situation, he avers, and such marriages ought therefore to be avoided if possible, precisely because in such a situation fulfilling the obligation of prayer becomes difficult. What, he asks, should the wife do when she gets up from her bed at midnight to pray? Should she thus "cast the pearls before swine"? for it is a slave of the devil who is at her side.[9]

Tertullian also advises the good Christian to pray before meals and before taking a bath. But this does not seem so surprising as that prayer should be stipulated for the middle of the night. We might remember, however, that the rhythm of life in the average household of antiquity differed no little from ours. Because of the paucity of lighting facilities in particular, it followed more closely the rhythm of nature. When it got dark it was time for bed. At certain times of the year, therefore, the sleeping period included almost twelve hours, and an interruption of sleep around midnight was not exactly an heroic act. In fact the idea of sanctifying the day and the night by periodic prayer was not a purely Christian notion; it is, in all probability, rather a tradition appropriated from Judaism. This probability is strengthened by a remark contained in the so-called "Manual of Discipline" which came to light through the discovery of some Hebrew manuscripts at Qumran near the Dead Sea in 1947, writings somewhat earlier than the time of Christ. The pious association whose rules we thus possess was wont to pray "at the start of the dominion of light, at the height of its course and when it once again returns to its established place, at the

8. *ibid.*, 42.
9. Tertullian. *Ad. uxor.*, II, 4 f.

start of the night-watch . . . , and at the climax of its [the night's] course, and when it again recedes before the rising light."

Tertullian has told us nothing about the contents of the prayers at these various hours. Apparently nothing was actually prescribed. But we do discover that it was an almost universal custom to meditate on the successive phases of our Savior's Passion up to the moment of His glorious Resurrection from the dead. Hippolytus of Rome, for example, presents us with a rather detailed description of the method of prayer followed by the Christians of old, beginning with the third hour:

> And if indeed thou art at home, pray at the third hour and praise God; but if thou art elsewhere and that time comes, pray in thy heart to God.[10]

Evidently there is question here of private prayer—prayer at home, or, if preoccupied with some business, prayer in the chamber of one's heart. Then the author goes on to point out the thoughts that should occupy the mind during these prayers. Because it is the third hour, think of Christ being nailed to the Cross and beginning His redeeming suffering. Hippolytus alludes to the loaves of proposition, the shewbread, to be offered at the third hour, and to the dumb lamb that was slain; for Christ is the living bread that came down from heaven for the life of the world, He is the Good Shepherd who gave His life for His sheep.[11]

Regarding the sixth hour, that is midday, the *Apostolic Tradition* has this to say:

> Pray also likewise at the sixth hour, for at that hour when Christ had been hanged upon the wood of the cross the daylight was divided and it became darkness. And so let them pray a prevailing prayer, likening themselves to the cry of Him who prayed and caused all creation to be made dark for the unbelieving Jews.[12]

At midday, then, the mind should consider the moment when Christ uttered His last words on the cross and with a loud voice yielded up His spirit, and darkness fell upon the earth.

Regarding None the author suggests:

> And at the ninth hour also let prayer be protracted and praise be sung that is like to the souls of the righteous glorifying God who lieth not, who remembered His saints and sent to them His Word to enlighten them. For in that hour Christ was pierced in His side and shed forth

10. Gregory Dix, *The Treatise on the Apostolic Tradition* (London, 1937), 62, v. 2.
11. Dix, *op. cit.*, 62, v. 3.
12. Dix, 62, v. 4.

> blood and water and brought the rest of the time of that day in light to evening. Whereby He made the dawn of another day at the beginning of His sleep, fulfilling the type of His resurrection.[13]

Praise God, he says, as did the souls of the just when about to be freed from Limbo. For now our salvation is accomplished—such is the significance of the blood and water which in turn symbolize the saving water of Baptism. Thus even though night is approaching, a bright day dawns for the world, heralding the glory of the Resurrection.

Throughout the day, therefore, the theme of the prayers is the redemptive passion of Christ. Its phases are distributed among the three hours more or less in accordance with their actual historical sequence. But they are so distributed that in the very last hour there is already a foreshadowing of the coming resurrection. This is a favorite device among the early Christians, one that we have met with repeatedly: to the combat is joined the victory.

As is obvious from the description, the prayer itself was not so much vocal prayer but rather mental prayer. However it was, no doubt, concluded with some form of vocal prayer, probably the Our Father, as is indicated in the *Didache* cited above.

The other usual hours of prayer, morning and evening, are mentioned only casually, and without indicating their form or contents; in a sense to do more would be superfluous, for their contents, as in the case of meal prayers, are determined by their very nature. But Hippolytus does treat more in detail the prayers said during the night, which he likewise inculcates. *Media nocte surgebam ad confitendum tibi,* sang the Psalmist (Psalm 118:62), and Hippolytus is as forthright in his regulation regarding prayer in the dead of night:

> And at midnight rise and wash thy hands with water and pray. And if thou hast a wife, pray ye both together.[14]

Already at None the process of nature—in the setting of the sun—was used to point out a process in the order of grace, but in a contrary sense; whereas in nature it is getting dark, we are reminded of the light, of the illumination that proceeds from the redemptive sufferings of Christ. Again when he describes the midnight prayer, Hippolytus first presents a picture of nature praising God in the stillness of the night.

> It is necessary for the following reason to pray at this hour, and truly those men of holy memory who handed on the Tradition to us taught

13. Dix, 63, v. 5.
14. Dix, 65, v. 8.

> us thus: because in this hour every creature hushes for a brief moment to praise the Lord; stars and plants and waters stand still in that instant; all the hosts of the angels ministering unto Him together with the souls of the righteous praise God.[15]

But then the transition is made from the midnight in nature to that midnight which our Lord spoke of in the parable of the Ten Virgins:

> . . . Behold a cry was made at midnight of them that said: Behold the Bridegroom has come. . . .

The *parousia*—again the favorite theme of primitive Christian thought appears; the *parousia,* for which everyone must always be ready.[16] And so the connection with Christ's Passion is resumed and continued: Christ is risen and will come again.

The same idea is afterwards adduced as a reason for another hour of prayer which is not generally mentioned, prayer at cock-crow; then, too, one should rise from bed and meditate on the resurrection of the dead on the last day.[17]

You may have noted a rather curious practice mentioned in connection with the midnight prayer (and it may be supposed, also in connection with the prayer in the early morning)—the washing of the hands. Obviously this is the same idea as that of the *Lavabo*—to wash the hands before undertaking something sacred. But then a second washing is mentioned, more curious even than the first. This is a symbolical action, and profoundly significant; Hippolytus instructs his readers to breathe into their hands and then sign themselves with the Sign of the Cross. For the moisture of the breath is said to come from the heart, where, since Baptism, the Holy Ghost has His dwelling.

> By catching thy breath in thine hands and signing thyself with the moisture of thy breath, thy body is purified even unto thy feet. For the gift of the Spirit and the sprinkling of the font, drawn from the heart of the believer, purifies him who has believed.[18]

From all these examples we see clearly that it was a healthful spiritual food that was suggested to the faithful for their daily devotions. Not just prayer formulas spoken by the lips; not merely prayers of petition outlining one's own personal needs and wants; but rather meditative prayer, thoughts of faith, fundamental concepts of the Christian religion. What is here proposed is an orderly and systematic remembrance of those things that make a Christian

15. Dix, 67, v. 12.
16. Dix, 67, v. 13; cf. Matt. 25:6.
17. Dix, 67, v. 14.
18. Dix, 66, v. 11.

a Christian, of those things that help him to lead a truly Christian life. As Hippolytus himself states in the closing paragraph:

> These things, therefore, all ye faithful, if ye perform them and remember them and instruct one another and encourage the catechumens to do them, you will not be able to be tempted or to perish, having Christ always before your minds.[19]

Whoever has the thought of Christ always in his mind, whoever keeps his heart warm with the memory of His Passion, will never be unfaithful to his dignity as a Christian, a follower of the Crucified.

This order of prayer and system of meditation is not peculiar to Hippolytus' *Church Order*. It reappears in the most diverse places, both East and West. If any changes occur, if any differences are to be noted, they are all in the direction of better order and a further enrichment of the contents. St. Athanasius (if he is the author), in the work *De Virginitate*, presents much the same plan. At the third hour, he advises, pray because at that time the wood of the cross was being assembled; at the sixth hour, because our Lord was raised upon the cross; at the ninth hour, because at that hour He gave up His spirit. He adds a thought, too, for night prayers; before going to bed, he says, recall to mind how our Lord descended to the realm of the dead. For the midnight prayer he suggests recalling to mind our Lord's Resurrection.[20] The order he proposes is more accurately accommodated to the chronological order of the Biblical account, and it is for this reason, no doubt, that he adds the night prayer to the series. Others again connect the morning prayer, said at rising, with our Lord's Resurrection from the dead. Thus the train of thought centering on Christ's redemptive work is made to continue round the clock.

This linking of the hours with the various phases of our Lord's Passion did not survive in the later development of the canonical Hours. But to some extent it did remain alive in the piety of the people all through the Middle Ages. This is particularly true of the numerous Books of Hours (*livres d'heures, libri d'ore*) or primers which represented popular abbreviations of the canonical Hours and contained such devotions as the well-known *Officium parvum B. M. V.* or similar types—*Officium parvum SS. Trinitatis* and *Officium parvum S. Crucis*. These booklets for the use of the faithful preserved the traces of the old themes not so much in the prayers themselves as in the miniatures inserted to illustrate the different

19. Dix, 68, v. 15.
20. *Enchiridion Ascet.*, 221.

Hours. Thus, for example, at Prime will be found a picture of our Lord being judged by Pontius Pilate; at Terce, our Lord being nailed to the cross; and so on. The illustration for Vespers is generally a picture of the body of our Lord being taken down from the cross and laid in the lap of His blessed mother—the Pietà; it is a curious fact that to this day such a picture is called in German a *Vesperbild*—a Vesper-picture.[21]

There were even attempts to focus the prayers of the day on other events of Christ's life, especially on His Incarnation and Nativity. Thus at the end of the Middle Ages, the custom arose of ringing the bells after evensong or Vespers in honor of the mystery of the Incarnation—the so-called *Ave*-bell or *Angelus*. This is linked with the notion, then current, that the Annunciation took place at twilight. When later the interrupted ringing of the bell took place three times a day, sometimes a special theme—one of the Christmas or Easter mysteries—was assigned to each. Thus even as late as 1605, a Synod of Prague explains the morning bell as a remembrance of our Lord's Resurrection, the noon bell a remembrance of His Passion and death, the evening bell a remembrance of His Incarnation. (As we all know, it is now the mystery of the Incarnation that is the theme for all three, except during paschaltide, when the Resurrection is recalled by the recital of the *Regina coeli.*) The order insisted on by the Prague synod, and already inculcated e.g. in the *Enchiridion* of the Jesuit Simon Verrepaeus (1580), is of course the inverse of the chronological, and so it is not surprising to find St. Robert Bellarmine (d. 1621) attempting a sort of reform or correction. In his famous Catechism, he gives the rule as follows: In the morning call to mind the memory of the Incarnation, at noon the memory of the Passion, and in the evening the memory of the Resurrection. And so almost to our own day there was kept alive a vestige of the order of prayer followed by the early Christians, the faithful of the second and third century.

As is clear from what we have already studied, the regime of prayer and devotion described by Tertullian and Hippolytus is remarkably akin to what we now know as the canonical Hours. But it cannot be sufficiently emphasized that for the most part these prayers were private and the observance of the hours entirely the affair of the individual. But, as we shall see, the liturgical Hours sprang from this private regime of prayer. This is plainly seen in regard to the three hours of the day, corresponding to Terce, Sext

21. J. Stadlhuber, "Das Laienstundengebet vom Leiden Christi in seinem mittelalterlichen Fortleben," *Zeitschrift für kath. Theologie* 72 (1950), 282–325.

and None. Even the prayer at midnight may be said to survive in the nocturns of Matins which are still recited—at least at times—in the dead of night by some of the strict orders (Carmelites, Capuchins). It was the fourth century that saw the conversion of these private "hours" into liturgical prayer, but even then the change did not occur as one might expect. The "hours" did not become the liturgical prayer of the community (they were never that, except in two instances, as we shall see) or of the clergy at large. It was monasticism which zealously snatched up the ancient tradition and continued to foster and refine it. Thus what had been private prayer became corporate prayer, but within the narrow precincts of the religious communities. And because the monks gradually became ecclesiastical corporations and had in every monastery ordained priests who could lead the prayers of the community as representatives of the Church, these hours of prayer developed into liturgical prayer. These are the canonical Hours which later became the official prayers of all the clergy.

From this general description, however, we must except two hours, the two we today call Lauds and Vespers, corresponding to morning prayer and evening prayer. Even at present they stand out from the others in their structure and in the greater solemnity with which they are often conducted. Their structural peculiarity and their comparative splendor is in part due to the fact that they alone, of all the canonical Hours, are associated with the corporate worship of the early Christian communities.

The first effect of the changed conditions brought about by the Constantinian edict of toleration was the increased share in the conduct of public worship which fell to the clergy. Another was the growth of that public worship. Once the Church was free, it was but natural that the faithful, at least in the cities and towns, should assemble oftener than for Sunday Mass alone. But only two periods were invested with the character of public corporate service, the morning hour, corresponding to the private morning prayer of the individual and to what we call *Laudes* (it was often called *matutinum,* "Matins"), and the evening hour, corresponding to night prayer and what we today call *Vesperae* (it was often called *lucernarium,* because it coincided with the lighting of the *lucerna,* the lamp).

But something resembling these public morning and evening services is found even before Constantine. Thus there is evidence of a common morning service in Rome as early as the beginning of the third century. In the *Apostolic Tradition* of Hippolytus of

Rome, we read the regulations concerning a regular instruction of the people. Deacons and presbyters, as we have already seen, were to appear before the bishop in the morning, and were to instruct the people and pray with them. The laity, in turn, were admonished to come to the church if and when such instructions were to take place:

> If there is a teacher there, let none of you be late in arriving at the assembly at the place where they give instruction. . . . And therefore let each one be careful to go to the assembly to the place where the Holy Spirit abounds.[22]

Such instruction obviously included a lesson from the Sacred Scriptures. A lesson and prayer were also constituents of the later canonical Hour.

The same source is our witness for common evening service at least on those days when an *agape* was held. The *agape* was an evening meal, a supper sponsored by some well-to-do member of the community for the benefit of the poor or the widows. A representative of the clergy always presided, either the bishop himself or a presbyter or deacon.[23] Hippolytus' *Church Order* includes detailed instructions regarding the conduct of such a meal. First, blessed bread was distributed (and the author stresses the point that it is only blessed bread, *eulogia,* and not the *eucharistia,* the Lord's body). At the meal itself, strict order had to be observed; no one was to speak unless invited to do so by the presiding clergyman. And finally they were to go home promptly.[24]

But before the meal began, there was an evening prayer-service. Since it was already dusk, the first ceremony was the blessing of the light. Then psalms were sung, usually the so-called Alleluia-Psalms, so that the assembly could respond to the cleric's recital of the psalm-verses with the Alleluia as a refrain. (It is remarkable indeed that even today at Sunday Vespers the Alleluia-Psalms, 110–113, are still in use; to suggest a connection here seems to be more than mere conjecture.) However such an evening celebration was a restricted one, since only certain groups were invited, and it was not a daily occurrence.

This evidence from Hippolytus of Rome clearly proves that Lauds and Vespers, at least in their initial stages, already existed in the third century. They were the liturgical Hours of the primitive Church.

Thus we acquire a rather full picture of the devotional life of

22. Dix, *op. cit.,* 62, v. 3.
23. Dix, 47, v. 10; 48, v. 11.
24. Dix, 45, vv. 1–2.

early Christendom, a life maintained not only by participation in the sacred mysteries but by prayer, liturgical and collective, as well as by prayer of a more intimate and domestic sort. No wonder that, in those years of intermittent but yet never halted persecution, the race of heroes did not die out. In public and in private, in common and alone the Christians of that age—as Christians always and everywhere—followed the counsel of the Master, "Watch and pray."

CHAPTER TEN

The Defense Against Gnosticism

IN THIS chapter, which closes our survey of the development of Christian worship during the second and third centuries, we must treat a peculiar phenomenon that appeared throughout the period, the menace of Gnosticism. What is most surprising about Gnosticism is not that it should have had its repercussions in the field of theology, but that its effects should have been felt also in the field of liturgy. I must confess that for a long time I myself was unaware of this liturgical reaction. Ancient writers nowhere make mention of it. But now, after due investigation, I am persuaded that only in the light of this conflict with the forces of Gnosticism can some liturgical developments be properly explained.

Albert Ehrhard, one of the last generation's foremost Catholic scholars in patrology, contended that during the first three centuries Christianity was threatened by three dangerous enemies: the pagan state, Montanism and Gnosticism.

The first enemy was the pagan state which tried, in ever renewed attacks, to repress Christianity by force and violence. From Nero to Diocletian, the persecutions continued, now gentle, now harsh, their persistence as well as their ferocity highlighting the apparent antinomy between Christendom and the pagan Empire. The seeming paradox in the development of Christianity is that it took place in spite of the opposition of the Roman government, and the paradox is made all the greater by the attitude of the Christians themselves, who offered absolutely no resistance to persecution. "The martyrs were bound, imprisoned, scourged, racked, burnt, rent, butchered—and they multiplied." [1] Their weapon was heroic constancy, and with this weapon Christianity emerged the victor.

The second enemy was Montanism. Montanism, which appeared somewhere in Phrygia towards the end of the second century, pretended to possess new revelations which would lead to a purer form of Christianity. Prophecy and not the hierarchy was to guide the Church. The Church was to be only a Church of saints, leading a strict life of fasting and penance and avoiding all contact with the world. At first it was only a movement of religious enthusiasm and attracted especially the more fervent Christians (Tertullian, for example, became a Montanist). But it was a dangerous doctrine, for on the one hand it would have led to the dissolution of the Church's constitution, and on the other, it would have brought about such an isolation of Christendom from secular culture that the Church would have been kept forever in a sort of ghetto. Hence the convocation of synods—the first which history records—to condemn the heresy and draw up measures of defense. Hence Rome's firm anathema, pronounced by Pope Zephyrinus about the year 200.

But by far the most dangerous enemy was the third, Gnosticism. This was a religio-philosophical sect or group of sects whose origin antedated Christianity. Through its genealogies and subtle speculations, it strove to give a perfect explanation of the problem of evil in the world and to teach a way of salvation. And since Christianity was also a religion of salvation, Gnosticism pretended a certain kinship and attempted to establish contacts with it.

Even before the preaching of Christianity, Gnosticism was already widespread in Syria, Palestine and Egypt. In the first centuries of our era, it invaded the whole Greco-Roman world, coming into collision with the Hellenic and Jewish religions before attacking Christianity. Its origins must be sought in the religious syncretism which, from the time of Alexander's conquests and still more after the Roman subjugation, had mingled and fused the many Oriental cults. The name *gnosis* indicates the object aimed at: the knowledge, or rather the vision, of God. It is a divine revelation which almost always claims to be based upon some ancient and secret message transmitted by a chain of initiates. Thus the hermetic books present themselves as revelations made to Hermes or Asclepius. Similarly the Christian Gnostics place their revelations under the patronage of an apostle or Mary Magdalene (who is supposed to have received them from the risen Christ before His ascension).

1. St. Augustine, *The City of God,* XXII, 6. Augustine adds: *Non erat eis pro salute pugnare nisi salutem pro Salvatore contemnere.*

Gnosticism claimed to be a doctrine of salvation as well as a revelation; it taught the soul how to free itself from the material world in which it is imprisoned, and to ascend once more to the spiritual and luminous world from which it had fallen. This liberation is brought about by the communication of a heavenly revelation, often accompanied by magical formulas and rites; moreover, participation in the *gnosis* is not accorded to all indiscriminately, but reserved for initiates—and this was one of its most powerful attractions.

The religious doctrine thus transmitted was marked by a dualism that taught that matter was to be despised and hated. The Supreme Deity is removed as far as possible from all contact with matter. The creation of the material world is ascribed either to an inferior god or demiurge or else to angels or *archontes*. Between this god and the visible world there are more or less numerous intermediaries; it is by these that the divine action is extended and abased as far as the material world, and it is through them that the soul is able to elevate itself step by step up to the Supreme Deity.

Perhaps the most perilous aspect of Gnosticism was its elasticity, its apparent ability to adapt itself to all religions. It seemed to provide a framework for the syncretism of all religions and philosophies. This elasticity or adaptability is manifested in the episode of Simon Magus narrated in the Acts of the Apostles.[2] Here was an attempt at a rapprochement—the first of many such attempts during the first Christian centuries. But, as in the case of Simon Magus, all these contacts with Christianity were made not with a view to accepting Christianity and submitting to Christian revelation, but for the purpose of assimilating Christian notions and reshaping them. Out of such syncretistic mixtures, arose a third quantum, namely the various Christo-gnostic systems of the early Christian era.

Through Christian writers of the second, third and fourth centuries, we get to know quite a number of such Gnostic systems: oriental systems of a wild and chaotic character, and Hellenistic ones of a more spiritual and philosophical kind, like those of Valentine, Ptolemy and Heracleon; some which were gross and hardly influenced by Christianity, and others which had a wholly Christian appearance, like that of Marcion. The more spiritual these systems and the nearer they approached Christianity, the more dangerous they were. For to the men of those times, especially the more educated men of the Hellenistic world of culture, these

2. Acts 8:9–13.

systems presented themselves as a higher Christianity, as a spiritual teaching in which all the good points of Christianity, but without its rigors, were combined with the best knowledge of Greek wisdom, into a system more spiritual and refined than Christianity.

The battle against the *gnosis* was begun even in the writings of the New Testament, and continued unflagging all through the first three centuries of Christianity. Thus St. Paul warns Timothy against the travesties of true teaching which led others away from the faith, the empty words of a false knowledge that is knowledge only in name (ψευδώνυμος γνῶσις).[3] Even in the apostolic writings, we can gather a vivid picture of the kind of Gnosticism which then threatened Christianity. Among its features was a dualism which showed itself by contempt for the flesh. This led to a denial of the Resurrection (I Cor. 15:12), or to its being understood in a figurative sense (II Tim. 5:18). From this principle divergent moral influences were drawn: sometimes in a libertine sense—everything is allowed, because all that is fleshly is to be despised (I Cor. 6 and 10; Apoc. 2:14; II Pet. 2:10; Jude 8); sometimes, on the contrary, in the sense of a rigid asceticism—forbidding contacts deemed impure, and even marriage (Col. 2:16–21; I Tim. 4:3). Then there was the "philosophizing"—the odd theogonies and cosmogonies, the personified abstractions conceived as the principles of all life, all being; "There were some," says the Apostle of the Gentiles, "who needed to be warned against teaching strange doctrines, against occupying their minds with legends and interminable pedigrees or genealogies." [4] He warns against accepting ambitious speculations and elaborate myths: "Take care not to let anyone cheat you with his philosophizings, with empty phantasies drawn from human tradition, from worldly principles; they were never Christ's teaching. . . . You must not allow anyone to cheat you by insisting on a false humility which addresses its worship to angels. Such a man takes his stand upon false visions; his is the ill-founded confidence that comes of human speculation." [5] St. Peter, too, admonishes the faithful to be wary of "cunningly devised fables" (II Pet. 1:16).

But the worst dangers from Gnosticism were its perversions of the doctrine of the Incarnation of the Son of God. These resulted in putting Christ below the angels or even denying Him altogether (I John 2:29; II Pet. 2:1; Jude 4). Many who did not go so far

3. I Tim. 6:20.
4. I Tim. 1:4 ff.; cf. Titus 3:9.
5. Col. 2:8, 18.

as this radical denial rejected the reality of the Incarnation: Jesus Christ had not come in the flesh. The docetic Christology taught by a heretic like Cerinthus was a great danger for the Christians of Asia Minor; hence the vehemence of St. John's expression: "Every spirit which acknowledges that Jesus Christ is come in the flesh, is of God: and every spirit which would disunite Jesus, is not of God. And this is Antichrist, whose coming you have been told to expect" (I John 4:3).

From the very beginning, then, the storm raged around the mystery of the Incarnation. And it remained the crux of the problem in every controversy with the Gnostic forces. The Hellenistic *gnosis* was bent on "dissolving Jesus," as St. John put it; for it was concerned with endless genealogies and emanations from divine beings, and with eons gradually departing from the original divinity. All this, however, takes place beyond this terrestrial sphere, in a realm of spirit, or in a former stage of this world's existence. But that the Son of God has become man, that the Word was made flesh and dwelt amongst us, that God assumed our very nature and became, in our own time, on this very earth of ours, a man of flesh and blood—of this the Hellenistic *gnosis* does not want to hear. "In the fifteenth year of Tiberius Caesar, in the time of Pontius Pilate, Jesus descended from heaven at Capharnaum, a town of Galilee, and taught there in the synagogue"—such is the commencement of Marcion's Gospel. The good God, the Supreme God, who owed nothing to the miserable human race, willed however to save it by sending His Son, who is distinct from Him only in name. Passing through the heaven of the Demiurge, the evil god, Jesus appeared here below. He could not take a material body, for matter is essentially evil. Hence there was no Nativity in Marcion's Gospel, no childhood, no Baptism, but only a sudden appearance in the synagogue at Capharnaum. The Son of God who came into the world could at the most wear an apparent body, could only appear to have eaten and drunk with men, and could have suffered in appearance only. That He actually condescended to lower Himself to earthly matter, this, according to the Gnostics, would not have been worthy of Him.

With the apostolic Fathers, therefore, it is a question of defending the real human nature of the Lord. With marked realism, Ignatius of Antioch stresses again and again precisely the earthly and human side of the christological mystery: "Be deaf," he says, "when anyone speaks to you apart from Jesus Christ, who was of the race of David, the son of Mary, who was truly born and ate and drank, who was truly persecuted under Pontius Pilate and was really crucified, and died in the sight of those in heaven and on earth and under the earth. Moreover He was truly raised from the dead." [6]

Around the same time, as we have seen, the *kerygma* of Christ which we have preserved in the Apostles' Creed was being formed. Here, too, we find a strikingly energetic emphasis on the earthly events surrounding the work of salvation: Born of Mary the Virgin, suffered, crucified, and buried. This is apparently expressed with such vigor in order to exclude all Gnostic or Docetist interpretations. Hence the time is mentioned, for all that happened, happened really and truly in our human history: under the governor Pontius Pilate; and the Resurrection followed: on the third day after His death. In an earlier chapter, we saw how the Church at the beginning kept stressing her spiritual character. Now we see how the Church starts to proclaim not only the spiritual and supernatural contents of her Gospel, but also precisely the material and earthly elements in it—in order that the Gospel may not be misunderstood in a Gnostic sense, and thus despoiled of its power.

This battle against the *gnosis* continued throughout the whole of the second century and lasted until far into the third century. In the doctrine of the Gnostics, the contempt for matter became more and more pronounced—not only a contempt for the human nature in Christ but for the entire material creation. According to Gnostic teaching, matter is the seat and the very origin of evil, created by an evil spirit, the Demiurge, who sometimes is identified with the God of the Old Testament. The human body also belongs to the domain of evil; only in the soul is there a divine spark. Through the *gnosis,* this divine spark is strengthened and only in this way can salvation be obtained.

There you have a rough outline of the basic principles of Hellenistic Gnosticism. To defend itself and its doctrines, therefore, the Church had to defend the material creation. We then notice how, towards the end of the second century, this defense against the *gnosis* shows effects also in the sphere of the liturgy. We have already seen how the Church from the very beginning stressed the spiritual, as against the coarse and materialistic, concepts of religion and culture rampant in Judaism and paganism: no restriction to a certain locality, no temples and altars, no outward show with music and pomp, but a pure worship, rising up from the hearts of the faithful, a holy *eucharistia.* But now the Fathers felt compelled to

6. *Ad Trall.,* 9, 1 f.

defend the exterior and material phenomena of the Christian religion.

In worship, too, attention began to be focused on the material side which was now gradually brought into the foreground. This change we are able to notice particularly well in St. Irenaeus, bishop of Lyons, who about the year 185 wrote his great work *Adversus haereses* which is devoted especially to combating the various Gnostic systems of which he had first-hand knowledge.

In Irenaeus, passages are to be found which follow the same line of thought already manifest in the earlier apologists. For Irenaeus, no less than for his predecessors, it was the inner intention, the offering of the heart, that was decisive in God's sight. "God," he says, "does not require sacrifice, but the conscience of the offerer." [7] And he quotes Psalm 50: *sacrificium Deo spiritus contribulatus* —a perfume pleasing to God is the heart that praises His name. At the same time, because he is taking a strong position against the exaggerated spiritualism of the Gnostics, he appears to be compelled to defend the value of the material element of the sacrifice. In fact without minimizing the spiritual side, it is the material aspect that the Bishop of Lyons emphasizes time and again.

Sublime and celestial though the Christian Eucharist is, yet it takes its origin in material things; it begins with the material gifts of bread and wine. Irenaeus says: "It behooves us to make an oblation to God, and in all things to be found grateful to God our Maker, in a pure mind, and in faith without hypocrisy, in well-grounded hope, in fervent love, offering the first-fruits of His own created things. The Church alone offers this pure oblation to the creator, offering to Him, with giving of thanks, from His creation." [8] Thus it is from earthly creatures that the heavenly sacrifice is prepared.

Irenaeus shows also how such an order is entirely in keeping with the fundamental principles of Christianity, and is even demanded by them. The world is not something created by an evil spirit, by some malignant eon, but it has been created by the Father of our Lord Jesus Christ, that is, through the Word. Therefore when Christ came into this world, He was coming into His own possession; and when He instituted the Eucharist, He took bread and wine from His own creation.[9] Christ came into the world, that He might

7. *Adversus haer.*, IV, 18, 3.
8. *op. cit.*, IV, 18, 4.
9. *op. cit.*, IV, 33, 2; V, 2, 2.

lead back to God the creation which had fallen away from God; and everything divine and human, heavenly and earthly, He summarized in His person. Irenaeus calls this the ἀνακεφαλαίωσις = "recapitulation."

Thus "does the Eucharist consist of two elements, one an earthly one, the other a heavenly one." For the Lord taught His disciples "to offer God the first fruits of creation—not as if He Himself had need of them, but in order that they be not ungrateful and unfruitful; when, therefore, He took the oblation of bread, He gave thanks and said: 'This is my body,' and likewise the chalice, which is a product of this earthly creation, He declared as His blood, and made it the oblation of the New Covenant; and thus does the Church . . . offer Him to God, Him who is nourishing us; these are the first fruits of His gifts in the New Covenant." [10]

Thus is revealed a marked change in the concept of the Eucharist in consequence of the need of defense against the teachings of the *gnosis*. Nothing is changed with regard to the basic dogma, but a new aspect is stressed and emphasized for practical devotion—for practical devotion as well as also for practical worship. It cannot be accidental that precisely since this time, namely, just since the end of the second century, the first traces appear of the practice of bringing offerings to the altar. Thus we read in Tertullian that offerings are made by the laity, for he ironically addresses someone wishing to defend a second marriage: "You will therefore (after both your wives have died) offer for both (*offeres pro duabus*) and you will recommend them both to God through the priest?" [11] Thus Tertullian supposes that a layman can do something in the nature of an oblation. This expression, that the faithful offer individually, that apparently they themselves contribute something towards the sacrifice, is not met with before. In Hippolytus, too, we find a definite trace of an offering by the laity: every *baptizandus* was to bring along an oblation for the Mass of Baptism.

A few decades later, in Cyprian (about the middle of the third century), this practice is perfectly clear. Cyprian points out that the faithful regularly (hence apparently every Sunday) bring an oblation along to church, for he is rebuking the rich lady who comes to church without any oblation (*sine sacrificio*) and therefore communicates of what the poor have offered.[12] So we must presume that an offertory procession has already been introduced,

10. *op. cit.*, IV, 17, 5.
11. *De exh. cast.*, c. 11.
12. *De opere et eleem.*, c. 15.

namely that offertory procession of the faithful which subsequently was to be found in all countries, and which flourished in the Occident for over a thousand years.

Whereas formerly mention was hardly ever made of the material gifts of bread and wine, but only of the thanksgiving which was pronounced over them, now it is precisely this material side which is stressed. Bread and wine are not only brought to the altar (as in Justin) but they are *offered*—offered to God. The sacrifice, therefore, is already begun with the Offertory. And in order to add still more weight to this action, the gifts are offered by the entire community in a solemn act, in a well ordered procession, which since the fifth century is further accompanied also by a special song: the *offertorium*. In this way, a significant symbolism previously only latent is explicitly brought out. The gifts over which the thanksgiving is pronounced are gifts of this earth, gifts that include something of our own labor and our toil, gifts that help to preserve our life. Our goods and possessions, our toil and sweat, our entire life is included therein. And through these gifts, our entire lives and the whole of this earthly creation is taken up into the holy sacrifice which Christ our High Priest is offering together with us; the whole of creation is thus returned to God.

This changed the picture of the Mass quite considerably, for now the gift, the oblation, the sacrifice, stood out much more strongly than had been the case hitherto, when only prayers of thanksgiving were given any emphasis. Now the stress is on the oblation, even the material oblation. In our Canon, in more than one place, are still to be found phrases that safeguard the material aspect of the sacrifice. Take for example the phrase before the final doxology: *per quem haec omnia semper bona creas;* this means: what Thou dost create (from which we have taken our offerings) is good. At the mentioning of the sacrifice of Melchisedech which consisted of bread and wine, a significant qualification is added: *Sanctum sacrificium, immaculatam hostiam*. The gifts of bread and wine offered by Melchisedech were holy and pure gifts. And in the solemn prayer of offering after the consecration we read: *offerimus praeclarae majestati tuae de tuis donis ac datis:* it is a gift of Thine we offer, both as to its immaterial and its material part. It is, therefore, not accidental that about the same time also there was a change in the name for the celebration. During the first and second century, the favorite name for the Christian celebration was *Eucharistia*. But now the term *oblatio* or *sacrificium* is preferred. Cyprian as a rule uses *sacrificium, sacrificium Dei, novum sacrificium*. This word, indeed, became so common, especially within the area of the Gallican liturgy, that the sacred host itself was called *sacrificium*. In Ambrose and Augustine, the common designation is *oblatio, offere*. Aetheria, in that invaluable account of her pilgrimage, *Peregrinatio ad loca sancta* (about 400), when speaking of worship, regularly uses the term *oblatio*.

This change also exerted its influence on the conception and furnishing of the church building. The church building was in the beginning called "the house of the Church," *domus ecclesiae*, or simply *ecclesia;* the accent was on the community, which gathered here around the bishop or his representative to hear the word of God and to pray. In the apse of the church, the bishop had his *cathedra;* from here he gave the homily; from here he recited with a loud voice the prayer in the name of the community. The *cathedra* was, so to speak, the point of gravitation in the church; from here the community was governed. The *cathedra* was, therefore, also the symbol of the bishop's authority; we speak today of the *cathedra Petri* and the church where the *cathedra* of the bishop stands is still called the cathedral.

The description of pontifical ceremonies contained in the *Ordines Romani* of the early Middle Ages vividly recalls this focal position of the papal throne. Here the pope's *cathedra* is still found in the center of the apse, with places for the bishops at the right and for the presbyters at the left. Even today its influence is to be perceived in the arrangement of the readings at what we now call the "epistle side" and the "gospel side" of the altar. Medieval commentators were hard pressed to explain why the Gospel is read at the left side of the altar (as viewed from the nave of the church). Of course they found profound reasons for such an arrangement: the Epistle signifies the preaching of the apostles to the Chosen People, to the Jews (symbolized by the right side of the altar), but the Jews did not accept the Word of God; thus it came about, that the Word of God was taken away from them and was transferred to the pagans, who are signified by the left side. Or it was said that this arrangement denotes that Christ did not come to call the just, but sinners. The real reason, however, was no longer known to the commentators. The Gospel should, of course, be given the place of honor; but the place of honor was considered from the point of view of the bishop's *cathedra;* the Gospel had to be read at the bishop's right-hand side, which, seen from the nave of the church, was the left side.

The *cathedra* was, therefore, the center of the church, while the altar was not stressed to the same extent. We ought not to be astonished at this. The celebration of the Eucharist certainly was then, as now, the climax of the Christian worship; this follows from all that we have already said. But the *altar* is not an essential element in Christian worship, as we shall soon see; while the *celebrant* (bishop or priest) is. Furthermore, the celebration of the Eucharist took place only once a week, in one short hour of the Sunday. And during this hour, it was the lessons, with the appertaining prayers and the bishop's homily, which surely took the most time, lasting much longer than the celebration of the Eucharist itself. This holds true even now in the case of a *missa solemnis;* the Fore-Mass, with its orations, readings and singing, last longer than the sacrificial Mass even if no sermon is given. And if it is the pontifical High Mass of a bishop, there is the added fact that the whole procedure centers on the bishop's throne; it is not until after the Creed that the bishop proceeds to the altar.

Such was the case also in the Church of antiquity, but with this difference, that the altar was generally not prepared until the Fore-Mass, with its lessons and orations, was finished. For the most ancient altars, in accordance with their very purpose, were simply tables—tables upon which the gifts of bread and wine could be placed. More was not required. Christianity did not need altars in the sense in which the Old Testament and the pagan cults of old needed them. In the ancient pagan cults (and even in the cult of the Old Testament), the altar was the sanctuary and sacred place, belonging to the deity; by placing the oblations on the altar, they were transferred to him, becoming the deity's property and sacred. The Christian oblation, however, being the body and blood of Christ, does not require such a previous sanctification; the Christian oblation is already holy and is already God's property, because it is the Savior's immolated body and immolated blood.

Hence in the ancient Church there was for a long time no thought of attributing to the altar any special importance and of furnishing it after the fashion of pre-Christian cults. It was merely a technical necessity, a place for the bread and chalice, nothing more. Minucius Felix, therefore, could with truth protest: *Aras non habemus*—we have no altars; [13] for what the Christians had were simply tables. This conception of the Christian altar was clearly manifested in the material out of which the oldest Christian altars were made. Although for the service they were adorned with precious cloths, they were only simple wooden tables. Wood was still the ordinary ma-

13. *Octavius,* c. 32, 1.

terial during the whole of the fourth century and even later. From North Africa we have accounts of how the Donatists invaded the churches of the Catholics and broke their altars to pieces, using them as firewood. In other places where wood was scarcer, the Donatists were content to scrape off tne surface of the wood of the altar, and then they employed it again for their worship. The archeological explorations which have been undertaken during the last decades, particularly in North Africa, have confirmed this information. The ruins of many churches of the fifth to the seventh century have been unearthed; but in most cases, although the place where the altar stood has been located (the place was marked by special stone slabs or by a stone frame), no trace of the altar itself has been found.

Since the fourth century, however, there existed also altars of more solid materials. The *Liber pontificalis* recounts how Constantine donated to the basilicas of St. Peter and of St. Paul each an altar of silver, studded with gold and jewels, weighing three hundred and fifty pounds. It was also probably about the same time, if not earlier still, that altars of stone began to be erected and built firmly into the structure of the basilica. Again it is from Christian North Africa that such examples are forthcoming.

It is evident—and it has already been remarked by liturgists—that this development of the altar is somehow related to the religious and intellectual developments of the conception of the Mass.

In the beginning, the spiritual element in the Christian worship was stressed as against the pagan cults. Although occasionally mention was made of the fact that the Church likewise possesses a sacrifice, a corrective note was immediately added: It is a spiritual sacrifice, λογικὴ θυσία, *rationabile sacrificium*. But in the Church's campaign against the *gnosis*, she was forced more and more to stress the outward, the material and the objective in Christian worship. No more do you hear that the Church's sacrifice is a spiritual sacrifice, but rather that it is a real sacrifice. And so, naturally, the table upon which this sacrifice is celebrated gains in importance. From a table of wood it becomes a table of stone. And the whole many-sided development of the altar sets in—a development which gradually reshaped the simple primitive altar of antiquity into the elaborate structure of a later age, surrounded it with railings or other enclosures, raised it upon steps and platforms. Over it baldachines and canopies were to be built, and behind it the rear screen that became the dossal and reredos. The glorious history of the Christian altar had begun.

Section III

THE AGE OF CONSTANTINE

CHAPTER ELEVEN

The Impact of Paganism on Christian Worship

We now begin a new period in our study of the liturgy of the early Church. We are entering the fourth century and with it the dawn of a new era. Hitherto we followed the development of the liturgy as it evolved from its own intrinsic principles. Now it is our task to learn how the Church, and her system of worship, reacted to the influences of pagan antiquity.

I. Christian Worship and Secular Culture

It was a decisive hour in the history of the primitive Christian Church when, in February 313, Emperor Constantine issued at Milan the so-called Edict of Toleration, granting to Christians full freedom of religion and worship, and ordering the restitution of the Church's property and her places of worship.[1]

As a result of the "Constantinian Peace," there began a great mass-movement of people from all classes towards Christianity. Among these new converts were not only people of a deeply religious nature, but also the timid and the weak who wished to join because it was now an advantage to be a Christian. True, many resisted the "new" religion, not only among the lower section of the peasant proletariat—*pagani*—but even many of the aristocracy.

1. It is not necessary here to enter into the question whether there was an "Edict of Milan" in Feb. 313. The term is used for convenience.

But the emperor himself was in the forefront of the promotion of Christianity and Christian worship. He and his family erected great buildings for worship in the Holy Land—at Jerusalem and Bethlehem—as well as in Constantinople and especially in Rome. It was then that the Lateran basilica, the old church of St. Peter, and Santa Croce were constructed. These buildings were, for the greater part, colossal and magnificent structures (like St. Peter's and the Lateran), churches worthy of an emperor.

But the erection of such public buildings highlighted the fact that now the Church, whether she wanted it or not, would be entering into a closer relationship with secular culture, with the culture of pagan antiquity. Certainly it was the bishop and the Church authorities who gave the directives for the building of churches, but it was the lay architect's concept of his art and the wealthy benefactor's love of pomp that were to have the greatest effect in the actual building. It is easy to imagine how often, under such circumstances, crises arose not only in connection with the building of great basilicas, but in many other fields as well. For the Church was certainly aware of the hazards inherent in the influence of antiquity upon the Church and her institutions, and the perils arising from its secular and pagan culture. She faced the danger of materialism and of secularism, the danger of losing as much in spiritual values as was gained in material splendor.

With regard to church building, a middle course was soon found. The old Christian basilica was really a Christian building. The name itself is derived from profane culture. The word *basilica* originally meant "royal building," palace. But it was further extended to other types of structure; it could even include a marketing hall. The ruins of many such civic buildings can still be seen today at Rome in the vicinity of the *Forum Romanum,* for instance, the *Basilica Julia,* the *Basilica Constantini.* Long before the Christian epoch, various pagan sects and associations had adapted the basilica type of building to worship. Christianity thus continued an existing tradition, accommodating it to the requirements of its liturgy. Thus it came about that the larger churches were also called basilicas, even though they differed from the civic structures that bore the name. Gradually these buildings took on definite forms, akin to the secular types, and yet having distinctly Christian characteristics. Here we will speak only about the general features of these buildings.

The history of art tells us that the ancient Christian basilicas, when compared with the churches of later times, display a greater simplicity and austerity. For the exterior, little ornamentation was used. There was no magnificent façade, no tower; plain, smooth walls only. The door was an invitation to enter, but there was first a porch or portico separating the basilica from the outer world. The real beauty of the ancient basilica is revealed in the interior. It is a beauty pure and austere. There are huge colonnades and the great, resplendent mosaics in the apse. But everything fanciful and purely ornamental is lacking. Lacking, too, are the representations copied from nature, from the organic and inorganic kingdoms, to be employed so profusely later on in the Gothic and in the Baroque styles. Heinrich Lützeler says therefore of the basilica: "It exists without the world; it exists against the world, drawing men forcibly inside." [2]

Quite a similar problem also arose with regard to instrumental music and singing. How far should such music and singing be admitted into the framework of Christian worship? [3]

According to the concepts of antiquity, music was a part of each sacrifice even when only incense or a libation were offered. Flutes, various stringed instruments, noisy kettle-drums, trumpets, and little bells, the so-called *sistrum*, were employed. The music was meant to ward off the demons and to invite the coming of the gods. It must be granted that the philosophers, especially those of Plato's school, voiced their rejection of things so worldly, demanding a *λογικὴ θυσία*; but they went unheeded.

An absolute rejection of such noisy music as a whole was achieved only by Christianity. The Church excluded in those days all musical instruments from her worship; plain homophonic singing only was allowed, unaccompanied by any musical instruments. The human voice and the human heart alone were to sing God's praises; the use of the one voice only was to symbolize the unity which was to obtain in the Church. Here there was question only of the so-called dialogue or responsorial form of singing, that is: one singer chanting and then the congregation answering with a short versicle. We have already seen an example in the order of the *agape* in the *Apostolic Tradition* of Hippolytus of Rome, when he described the singing of the psalms: one of the clergy sang the psalms; the people answered with an *Alleluia*. Moreover the rule was that the melody should be a very simple one.

Not all bishops however were equally strict. Of Athanasius, St. Augustine tells us that he ordered the leading singer to deliver his

2. H. Luetzeler, *Geschichte der christlichen Kunst des Abendlandes* (Bonn, 1932).

3. On this problem consult J. Quasten, *Musik und Gesang in den Kulten der heidnischen Antike und der christlichen Frühzeit* (Muenster, 1930).

song with so little inflection of the voice that it constituted a recitation rather than singing; *Ut pronuntianti vicinior esset quam canenti.*[4] St. Ambrose was less strict. He practiced singing psalms with his Milanese congregation and even composed hymns himself. St. Augustine narrates in his Confessions how deeply the singing in the church at Milan had moved him:

> I was deeply stirred by the voices of Thy Church sweetly swelling in the singing of Thy hymns and canticles! Those voices flowed into my ears, and truth was distilled into my heart, and a feeling of piety welled up from it. The tears poured forth, and I was happy with them.[5]

Thus finally for the singing, too, a compromise was effected, similar to the one regarding the architecture of the Church.

Although the Church thus preserved in her worship an attitude of great reserve towards pagan pomp and riches, yet she took over from the surrounding world many elements which were of an indifferent nature and belonged simply to general culture. This process had already set in long before the beginning of the period we are now considering. Among such elements, we shall consider two more in detail: the language and the style of prayers.

It was more or less a matter of course that in the divine services the language employed should be the language prevailing in the locality concerned, especially if it was a language of culture with a literature. The oldest documents of the Christian liturgy are in the Greek language. The divine services, therefore, first took on Greek colorings. Even in the Latin West, the divine services were conducted for a long time in Greek. This does not mean that the Church held her services in Greek amongst a Latin speaking population; it means that in the western part of the Roman empire up to the third century the majority of the Christians were Greeks. In Rome, in Lugdunum, and elsewhere, Christianity was chiefly propagated in the Greek colonies. Only gradually did the Latin element grow in strength; this was first the case in North Africa where Tertullian wrote in Latin. Since the middle of the third century this became true also in Rome. This is the language that now determines the style and the make-up of the prayers.

But first a few words about the Greek elements. The oldest Christian prayers preserved to us show certain peculiarities found also in pre-Christian prayers. They favored solemn addresses in which a long series of the Deity's attributes are strung together, especially of those consisting of negations of things proper to this

4. *PL*, 32:800.
5. *Confessions*, IX, 14.

world; unexplainable one, incomprehensible one, the infinite, ineffable one. This manner of expression we find also in the Greek prayers of the Christian liturgy (Serapion, *Anaphora*).

But at the same time, too, many ideas from the philosophy of the prevailing Hellenistic culture were adopted, for words and ideas can never be kept distinctly apart. It is commonly taken that St. John already adopted from contemporary philosophy the concept of the "Logos" in the prologue of his gospel. Similar phenomena we find also in the liturgy. The philosophers of the Stoa did their best to describe the Deity's revelations in nature and to praise Him for the wonders displayed through the whole of creation. Though their concept of the divinity as a rule was pantheistic, yet what they said could as well be predicated of our personal God.

Thus the Hellenistically educated Jew Philo gives a prescription as to how God is to be praised: "If thou wilt praise God for the coming into being of the world, so say thy thanks for the whole as well as for its parts . . . for the sky, the sun and the moon, the planets and the fixed stars, the earth, the animals, and plants thereon, then for the sea and the rivers, . . . further for the air and its changes; then for winter and summer, spring and autumn, the yearly returning and fruit-bringing seasons, constituting conditions of the air changed to the welfare of what there is beneath the moon; and if thou sayest thy thanks for man, then do not merely give thanks for the whole mankind, but also for its species and its most important parts: for man and woman, for Greek and barbarian, for the inhabitants of the continent, and for those of the islands. . . ." [6]

This expression of praise for the wonders of nature we find again in Christian prayers. Justin reports that the Christians praised God and addressed hymns to Him for creation and all the means of well-being, for the constitution of the species, for the changes in the seasons. And the so-called Clementine liturgy of the fourth century, in its prayer of thanksgiving (we would perhaps call it a "preface"), contains a long description of nature, in order to praise God for it (*Apost. Const.* VIII, 12, 9–16).

In regard to the Latin liturgy, too, we can make similar observations. Here also, together with the language, much has been adopted from the Roman treasury of thought. In passing over to the Latin liturgy, the Romans were not satisfied merely to translate older

6. Casel, *Gedächtnis des Herrn in der altchristlichen Liturgie* (Freiburg, 1918), 22.

Greek prayers; the genius of the Latin language and the Roman's particular intellectual character were allowed to make their own contribution. The great English liturgist, Edmund Bishop, wrote a famous article on the genius of the Roman rite, bringing out some of these features.[7] Shortness and conciseness, clarity and austerity are significant characteristics of the Roman orations. In addition there is what might be styled "a juridical way of thinking." A typical example is to be found in the canon of the Mass, in the prayer: *Quam oblationem:* the condition of the sacrificial gift we are asking of God is described with five expressions, in order to exclude any possible doubt: *Quam oblationem tu Deus, in omnibus, quaesumus,* benedictam, adscriptam, ratam, rationabilem, acceptabilemque *facere digneris: ut nobis Corpus, et Sanguis fiat dilectissimi Filii tui Domini nostri Jesu Christi.*

A familiar stylistic form of liturgical prayer which seems to be based on pre-Christian Roman custom is the litany, or at least one kind of litany, that which consists of a series of invocations, like those at the end of the Litany of the Saints, to which the response is given: *Libera nos Domine, Te rogamus audi nos.* For example, we are told of the emperor Licinius, who was still a pagan, that he taught his soldiers to cry before the battle:

> Summe Deus, te rogamus; Sancte Deus, te rogamus. . . .
> Summe sancte Deus, preces nostras exaudi.
> Brachia nostra ad te tendimus.
> Exaudi sancte, summe Deus! [8]

Furthermore the use of pre-Christian forms can be ascertained not only from the language of written words, but also from the language of the oldest ecclesiastical art. In the Christian paintings of the catacombs, there appear to a large extent the same motifs as in the paintings of ancient pagan art. And here, too, the same rejoicing in nature becomes manifest which we discovered in the prayers. We find doves and peacocks, sheep and lambs with their shepherds, vines and wine-pressers, fishermen with their nets and fishing rods, representations of the four seasons—all quite like those found in pagan paintings on non-Christian tombs. Sometimes, indeed, we even find Amor and Psyche and Orpheus depicted, but usually they stand in the midst of unmistakable Christian signs and symbols, letting us know that the artist associated with these traditional forms of ancient pagan art other ideas than did the pagans.

7. E. Bishop, *Liturgica historica* (Oxford, 1918).
8. Lactantius, *De mortibus pers.,* 46, 6 (CSEL, 27, 226).

The Christian knew the significance of shepherd and flock; he knew who was the vine; and even under the figure of Orpheus he recognized Christ.[9]

Furthermore, it is not surprising that some current forms of etiquette were introduced into the Christian liturgy. Among these we must mention especially the kiss. As a form of greeting, the kiss had in ancient culture a much greater significance than it has today. When someone was initiated into a fraternity or a society, it was the kiss which formed the sign of such an initiation. The Christians did likewise; the initiation into the Christian community took place through Baptism; immediately afterwards when the neophyte was confirmed by the bishop, he gave him a kiss. After that he was allowed to pass down to the faithful in the church, and by them too he was greeted with a kiss. The bishop's kissing of the newly confirmed still survives, it seems, in the rubrics of the *Pontificale Romanum*. There we read: *Deinde leviter eum in maxilla caedit, dicens: Pax tecum*. F. J. Doelger, at least, is of the opinion that the original kiss became first a hand kiss and then later on (perhaps under Germanic influence) was changed into a slight tap on the cheek.[10] Another custom related to this is the priest's kissing of the altar when he has ascended the steps after the prayers at the foot of the altar, as well as the kissing of the altar at the end of the Mass before the last blessing, just before leaving the altar. This custom is also derived from the culture of antiquity. It was a general custom to pay reverence to the temple by kissing the threshold or the doorpost. An idol, too, was reverenced by kissing it or by blowing a kiss to it, as Italians are still accustomed to "kiss" a statue by putting their hand to their mouth and then extending it in the direction of the object. In the apologia of Minucius Felix, we are told of a conversation between a Christian named Octavius and the pagan Caecilius; while going through the town they passed a statue of Serapis; the pagan upon seeing it raised his hand to his mouth and blew a kiss from his lips, "as is the superstitious custom of the vulgar." This is the starting point of the conversation narrated in the *Octavius*. The altar, too, the pagans used to greet with a kiss. And because the table at which meals were taken was considered something holy, it was kissed before meals. (This, by the way, is still a custom among the Capuchins in Austria.)

9. St. Beissel, *Bilder aus der Geschichte der christlichen Kunst und Liturgie in Italien* (Freiburg, 1899), 194. Hertling-Kirschbaum, *The Roman Catacombs and their Martyrs* (trans. Costelloe; Milwaukee, 1956), 161–179.

10. F. J. Doelger in *Antike u. Christentum*, 1 (1929), 186–196.

A kiss of this sort was, therefore, simply a sign of the veneration of holy objects, a form of greeting, and so it is not to be wondered at that Christians adopted it in their worship. The theory that our kissing of the altar at the beginning of the Mass dates back to Christian antiquity and ultimately to antique culture is confirmed by the fact that it exists not only in the Roman but also in the Oriental liturgies. In the Byzantine, the Syrian and Armenian liturgies, the altar is kissed in the beginning of the divine services. In the Middle Ages (since the twelfth century) the custom grew of kissing the altar each time one turned away from it; this is a practice of the Roman liturgy and of it only. But in the first instance at least, the kiss is really a form of greeting and nothing more. That this is the real meaning of the ceremony is clearly seen also from the fact that the same kissing of the altar is still prescribed also on other occasions when the priest ascends the altar: before the Gospel at the blessing of the palms on Palm Sunday, and on Good Friday before the solemn prayers.

The *Ite missa est* at the end of the Mass is also a custom derived from ancient Roman custom. It is not a specifically religious formula, but one which could be employed just as well at the end of a profane assembly. For the words literally mean nothing else but "Go, this is the dismissal" (*Missa* = *missio* = dismissal).

This explanation is entirely in keeping with the origin of the formula. About the year 500, the Burgundian King Gundobald, in a letter to Bishop Avitus of Vienne, asked for information about several questions. Amongst them was also the question about the meaning of the *Ite missa est*. The bishop explained to him that it was a general custom, in use in the imperial palace and in the public courts as well as in the church, simply to declare or announce the dismissal of the people after an audience or after a session of the courts or after divine service: *missa fieri pronuntiatur*. Hence Avitus still knew of forms of dismissal of a similar nature in secular usage.

The formulas were of different sorts. Not only *Ite missa est*, but several other formulas too are mentioned as having been customary with the Romans, e.g. *Ilicet* (ire licet); *Discedite Quirites*. Doelger, who wrote a long article about the formula, arrived at the conclusion that our formula, *Ite missa est*, must have been in use in any case about 400, but that it could have been in existence already in Tertullian's time, about the year 200.[11]

The court of the Roman emperor was another source from which

11. F. J. Doelger in *Antike u. Christentum*, 6 (1940), 81–132.

various customs of ancient Roman culture flowed into the Christian liturgy. But here very clear-cut distinctions had to be made before the practices were adopted.

Before Constantine's time, besides sun-worship, the cult of the emperor was one of the principal forms of idolatry and the Christians had to reject it absolutely. They possessed a very fine sense for distinguishing anything containing even a trace of divine worship paid to a created thing. The Christians refused to drop even a single grain of incense on the burning coal in front of the emperor's statue; they refused to garland the emperor's image with flowers; they refused, too, the Greek *προσκύνησις* or prostration in front of the emperor's picture; they refused to give the emperor the title *κύριος*. When Polycarp of Smyrna had been arrested, well-meaning friends said to him: What harm is there in saying, *κύριος καῖσαρ*—Caesar is Kyrios? But Polycarp refused to say it on the grounds that only One was our *κύριος*, and so he died a martyr. Early Christian literature is replete with expressions emphasizing Christian opposition to paying any divine honors to the emperors, and especially to the use of the title *κύριος*. They made a point of noting Christ's unique right to the title. Ordinarily in dating a letter or document, some date in the ruler's or governor's reign was given. But the Christians seldom did that without indicating their *κύριος*; thus, for example, the report on Polycarp's martyrdom says: "This took place under the proconsul Status Quadratus, but under the everlasting kingship of Jesus Christ." Or in St. Cyprian's martyrdom: "The blessed Cyprian suffered under the Emperors Valerianus and Gallienus, but under the kingship of Our Lord Jesus Christ, to whom there is due honor and glory in all eternity." Even centuries later the dating of important events was done in a similar manner.

Things changed rapidly, however, after Constantine's conversion and after the emperor had waived his claims to divine honors. Various external forms remained: they belong to the ceremonial of the court, but they no longer bore any religious significance. The emperor continued to be called *Dominus* or *κύριος*, he was called *divus*, and mention could even be made of the emperor's "genius"—all things which formerly simply were not done. The *προσκύνησις*, the prostration, continued to be performed in his honor. But all these were now considered matters of court ceremonial, empty of all religious meaning.

But now a new process began. Emperor Constantine had already felt moved to manifest his faith by paying honors to the bishops of the church and especially to the pope. The bishops were granted special privileges; in the *audientia episcopalis* they could sit in judgment just like secular judges. They were granted the right to special honors such as were due the highest officials of the Roman empire and even to the emperor himself. Among these, it seems, was the ceremony of *προσκύνησις*. The *Caeremoniale episcoporum* (I, 18, 2), as you know, still commands that whenever the clerics pass the episcopal throne during pontifical High Mass they have to genuflect before the bishop. In Germanic countries today these rubrics are no longer generally observed but they are still observed elsewhere.

Still another custom in the rite of the episcopal pontifical High Mass is also derived from the ceremonial of the imperial court. If a bishop is celebrating pontifical High Mass, there assist him not only deacon and subdeacon and a *presbyter assistans,* but also two *canonici in habitu diaconi* besides. The two *canonici* have no other duty but to stand next to the bishop, assisting him perhaps a little at the vesting, and to accompany him. In the *Caeremoniale episcoporum* where we find this rubric, the words are added: (*deducunt eum*) *si opus est, eius brachia sustentantes.* This *sustentare* was originally the essential point; it had nothing strictly to do with aiding a helpless bishop, *si opus sit!* It was a ceremonial of honor.[12] In the papal liturgy of the seventh century, two deacons always accompanied the pope, *sustentantes eum.* In the Middle Ages, this was a papal prerogative and a prerogative of the emperor. And this rubric, too, goes back to the ceremonial of the imperial court. This custom can even be traced back to much earlier times. In IV Kings (5:18) Naaman the Syrian, after having been cured asked the prophet whether he could continue "sustaining" his king as he had done hitherto:

> Yet one fault pray the Lord to pardon in me thy servant. My master will still be going up to offer worship in the temple of Remmon, leaning on my arm for support. At such times, if I do reverence, as my master does reverence, in Remmon's temple, the Lord grant me pardon.

This narrative shows again the nature of the ceremony—a court ceremony, obviously of eastern origin, adopted by the imperial court from the princely courts of the East. How essentially this little ceremony was considered in the first centuries of Christianity to be due to a king or a prince, we may learn by the recital of the Resurrection of our Lord as given in an apocryphal writing of the second century, the so-called Gospel of Peter (n. 35–40): Two

12. Cf. L. Vaganay, *L'évangile de Pierre* (Paris, 1930), 292–300.

tall figures enter the tomb of our Lord; soon afterwards three figures emerge from the tomb, the two sustaining the one in the middle whose figure reaches to the sky (that is: two angels are sustaining our Lord, symbolized in this way as a heavenly King).

This ceremony from the court of the emperors has passed over, not only to the court of the pope and to the papal and hence to the episcopal liturgy, but even into the ordinary solemn Mass. At every solemn Mass, when the celebrant incenses the altar, the levites have to accompany him, and to hold or touch the border of the chasuble (for the solemn Mass was derived in the Middle Ages from the pontifical Mass, and so it retains many of the latter's ceremonies).

Only remnants of the *sustentatio* therefore remain. But there is still another custom derived from the ceremonial of the Roman imperial court which has become a general rule in our liturgy and continues so. I refer to the use of lights and incense. On this topic, we have a stout volume by the English scholar Atchley: *A History of the Use of Incense in Divine Worship* (London, 1909).

The Roman consuls had the right to have lights carried before them when appearing in public—a torch or a thick candle, together with a basin or pan containing a fire to relight the torch in case it should perhaps go out. Because aromatic spices were put into the fire, the censer evolved from this fire-pan. The Roman emperors kept this custom in their court ceremonial. In fact the ceremony continued in use during the Middle Ages in the imperial court at Byzantium as well as at the courts of the kings and emperors in the West. Of Richard the Lion-hearted we are told that, when he was conducted to his coronation at Canterbury, all the nobles of the country gathered and entered the cathedral before him, but immediately in front of the king walked four barons carrying four lighted tapers before the king. In Austria, where the traditions of the Roman empire made their influence felt longest, this custom also remained longest. An old countess some years ago told me that when a member of the imperial family, an archduke, came on a visit to the house of a nobleman, it was still a custom before the last World War, even in the 1930's, for the master of the house to wait for him at the entrance with a servant standing next to him with two lighted candles.

This privilege must, therefore, have been adopted by the papal court during the fourth century. In the Roman *Ordines* describing the ceremonies of the papal services of the Stations we clearly see that the torch bearers—*ceroferarii*—have as their chief function the task of walking in front of the pope. Also when the deacon goes to the ambo with the Gospel book, two torch bearers—*ceroferarii*—walk before him as a retinue for the holy book which contains the word of God and in which Christ is somehow present.

This custom still obtains, as we know, at each *Missa Sollemnis*. At least two torch bearers precede the priest when going from the sacristy to the altar and the same *ceroferarii* walk in front of the deacon when he goes to read the Gospel. And in both cases the censer is carried also.

Originally the candlesticks were simply placed somewhere next to the altar during Mass. Since the eleventh century, the practice began of putting them upon the altar. And so lights and candles began gradually to be considered as a sign of reverence offered to the Blessed Sacrament, and even to be employed whenever we go before God in public divine services.

The incense, too, gradually was given a deeper and richer significance, as was already indicated in the Old Testament: *Ascendat oratio mea sicut incensum in conspectu tuo*. Thus a segment of the ceremonial of the court of the Roman emperors has become a religious ceremony of our liturgy.

II. Christian Worship and Pagan Religious Customs

Christian culture and pagan culture cannot be considered so completely antagonistic to one another as to make any compromises impossible, compromises in the field of literature, compromises in the field of the other arts. In fact, the first *entente* between the Church and the state constituted the starting point of a new era for the Christian arts—literature, music, painting and architecture. The Church is in the world even if she is not of it. It is no wonder, then, that echoes of the Roman world should be discovered in the literature of Christianity, or that the painting and sculpture and building of the Christians should bear traces of the cultural environment, pagan though it was. Nor is it surprising that the Christian liturgy should display some marks of its secular surroundings.

But what explanation do we give when we find in the forms of Christian worship resemblances to the forms of pagan religious rites?

Up to now we have been discussing various profane and secular customs of pagan culture which were somehow adopted into the liturgical life of the Church. Even the ceremonies involved in the ancient worship of the emperor as a deity found their way into the Church's worship only in their secularized form. This process of assimilation, striking though it may be, is not wholly unexpected. The early Christians were, after all, men and women of the Greek and Roman culture and, although they became Christians, they yet retained the material and ideal formalities of their own cultural life. *Gratia non destruit naturam, sed eam elevat.* The new Christian order was not called upon to demolish the wholesome cultural values—civic, social, and artistic—of the past, but to transform them to the honor and glory of God.

Now, however, we must deal with the fact that forms of the *religious* culture of the ancient world were also adopted into the worship of the Church. This is really surprising, for we know how strictly the Church insisted on avoiding any admixture with pagan religions, and how the heroic fight of the martyrs found its very climax, in the majority of cases, precisely in the fact that they refused an act of worship to a pagan idol or other sacred object. The transformations and adaptations which we are now to discuss were certainly taken from the religious sphere; but either these were made at a time when paganism no longer held sway and the danger of a pagan interpretation was either eliminated or minimized; or else they involved border-line cases, matters touching only on the external organization of worship, or formalities capable of different interpretation and of becoming vehicles of Christian ideas.

Amongst these, we mention first of all the orientation during prayer and in the position of the church and of graves. To turn toward the east while praying was a fixed custom not only among the Greeks and Romans, but also among most civilized people of the ancient world, as well as among various primitive races. The east, where the sun rises, appeared to men as the place whence proceed life, power, and happiness. Thus the rising sun became a symbol of divinity; from this it was, of course, only a short step to deify the sun itself, and that was often enough the case. But the orientation itself remained independent of these false notions and could thus be adopted into Christian practice.[13]

One might have expected that Christianity would retain the customs of the Jews in regard to the bodily attitude during prayer, as it did in many other matters related to prayer in which it continued the practices of the synagogue, as in the use of psalms, responsorial singing, and the like. The Jews turned towards Jerusalem when praying. Of Daniel it was said (6:10): "Now when Daniel knew this, that is to say, that the law was made, he went

13. The best treatise on orientation is F. J. Doelger, *Sol Salutis. Gebet und Gesang im Christlichen Altertum* (2nd ed., Muenster 1925).

into the house: and opening the windows in his upper chamber towards Jerusalem, he knelt down three times a day and adored and gave thanks before his God, as he had been accustomed to do before."

The Mishna, too, commanded the Jews all over the world to follow this practice; only with great reluctance were any exceptions permitted if this command was impossible to fulfill:—"Whoever is riding on a donkey descends for his prayer, and if he is not able to alight, so let him turn his face, and if he is unable to turn his face, so let him turn his heart to the house of the All Holy." But as early as the first century, the Christians, it seems, turned towards the east when praying. For we have the information from the founder of a Judaeo-Christian sect by the name of Elchasai; he demanded of his adherents that they turn towards Jerusalem while praying, forbidding them expressly to pray in the direction of the east; obviously this latter was then the practice among the Christians.

Why did the Christians turn to the east while praying? In paleo-Christian literature various reasons were adduced. The Lord had ascended into heaven to the east of Jerusalem, from the mount of Olives; and in confirmation they pointed out that the Old Testament had already predicted it with the words of Psalm 67, *Psallite Deo qui ascendit super coelum coeli ad Orientem*. As He ascended to heaven in the direction of the east so they believed He was to come again from out of the east. Another reason for thinking that He ascended into heaven towards the east was a cosmographical one. As we are accustomed to think of heaven as only above ourselves, so they imagined the dwellings of the blessed somewhere in the eastern sky, where the sun rises. The paradise in Genesis, too, was situated in the east: God planted the garden of Eden towards the rising of the sun (Gen. 2, 8). The angel of the Lord in the Apocalypse (7, 2) comes *ab ortu solis,* from the direction of the rising sun. The Ecclesia, too, the personification of the Church in the visions of *Pastor Hermae* (Vis. 1, 4, 3), comes down to the earth from the east.

Hence Christ's second coming was expected from the direction of the east. Here we must keep in mind how vivid was the desire for Christ's second coming in the early days of the Church. *Veni, Domine Jesu,* concludes the last chapter of the Apocalypse. And the invocation *Maranatha,* which has the same meaning, belongs to the oldest Christian liturgy. Thus we understand the importance which this turning to the east during prayers had for the early Christians. It is a turning towards the glorified Christ, who had conquered sin and death and who, as the head of the Church, is living in heaven. It was likewise the expression of the hope and the desire that He come again to redeem His own, *qui venturus est judicare vivos et mortuos.*

This thought was further strengthened when Christ Himself began to be called the Sun. The Lord had called Himself the light of the world. This was the starting-point for applying to Him also other passages that speak of light and sun: He is the *Oriens ex alto* (Lk. 1, 78s) of which the *Canticus Zachariae* speaks. He is the *Sol Justitiae* of the prophet Malachy (4, 2). He is the sun which sees everything and illumines everything and which with its light brings justice and prosperity. All the attributes of praise which the ancient world had bestowed upon the sun were referred to Christ. He is, in a word, the *Sol salutis,* the sun bringing health and happiness.

This line of thinking was given a further impetus when, towards the end of the third century, the sun-cult began to expand in the Roman empire. Emperor Aurelian purposely imported it to Rome from the Orient, and declared the *Sol invictus* as the god of the empire. Now Christians began all the more to emphasize the important fact: Christ is our sun. "Who is so invincible as our Lord who conquered death?" queries an old Christmas sermon.[14]

With new converts it could easily happen that, however seriously they took their rejection of the pagan cults, and however earnest they were in their faith in Christ, many forms and practices would continue to survive, which were capable of a pagan interpretation. It is well known that for some years excavations of the foundations under St. Peter's at Rome have been under way. Underneath the southern wing of the basilica, a whole city of tombs was discovered with streets between the tomb-structures. Several years ago I had the opportunity to view these excavations for myself. Most of the tombs are pagan ones of the second and third century; but among them individual Christian tombs are also to be found. On the walls of one such Christian monument of the third century can be seen the familiar picture of Jonas who is being thrown into the sea. But in a mosaic on the ceiling of the same memorial, Sol, the sun-god, is represented driving the sun-chariot, with his hands on the reins of the horses and the light spreading out before him; but without doubt it was Christ who was meant, for among the Christians the sun had become an image of Christ. The same locality, the basilica of St. Peter, is also the scene of a later custom obviously related with the sun-cult. Pope Leo the Great

14. Doelger, *Sol Salutis,* 291.

(about 450) in a sermon deplores the fact that some Roman Christians still greet the morning sun; after having climbed the steps leading up to the church of St. Peter's, they turn around and bow before the rising sun; he knew well enough that they did not have in mind worshipping the sun itself, but all the same there was cause for scandal in Christians acting thus.

In the light of such information, we can understand why it was a matter of course for Christians to turn to the east during prayers. They turned to the east during private prayers at home, or wherever they might be. We even know of some instances as early as the second century where in some Christian houses the room where the prayers were to take place was specially marked with a cross painted on the east wall.[15] More strictly still was the orientation observed during prayers in church. The clergy, especially the priest at the altar, and all the people prayed standing up and with their eyes turned east.

It is in connection with this idea that the church itself was orientated. And as a rule, this is still done wherever possible, at least in German countries. This was customary as early as the second century. Tertullian informs us about it: *Nostrae columbae etiam domus simplex, in editis semper et apertis et ad lucem.*[16] *Nostra columba* is the holy Church; her house is built *ad lucem:* in the direction of the rising sun. Here we meet again a tradition of the religious cult of antiquity. For the temples of the Greeks and Romans were also as a rule built in such a way that they faced east; in such a way namely, that the rays of the rising sun fell upon the idol when the doors of the temple were opened. The façade of the temple was, therefore, in the direction of the east. The oldest Christian churches, too, at least in Rome, were thus built with the façade towards the east. This we can still see in the case of some of the most famous Roman churches, e.g. St. Peter's or the basilica of the Lateran. This had the disadvantage that the congregation, wishing to look east during prayers, had to turn together with the priest towards the door of the church. For the priest this meant no inconvenience, for he faced east and at the same time looked towards the people; but for the people it was less convenient, because they were obliged to turn away from the priest and from the altar. In such churches, therefore, the altar was placed *versus populum,* "facing the people."

Apropos of the insistence nowadays on the position of the altar as

15. E. Peterson, *Eph. liturg.* 49 (1945) 52–68.
16. *Adv. Val.,* c. 3.

a factor in bringing about a closer union between celebrant and congregation, it may be well to make clear that the historical precedent for the orientation of the altar is often highly exaggerated. The different Oriental rites have never countenanced the practice of celebrating the liturgy in this position. This is worthy of note, because these rites have generally preserved the primitive, traditional practices of the Church most faithfully and because they have retained to this day a very active and close participation of the faithful. The principal reason for the existence of such a custom in the position of the altar can be traced, as we have already pointed out, to the general rule of orientation in prayer. With the apse of the church turned toward the west—as commonly occurred in Rome—the priest was compelled to turn his back to the apse and toward the people. And it may be remarked in passing that the people also had their backs to the priest while he thus stood in prayer. So it may well be that the disposition of the altar in the Roman basilicas is linked with this orientation in prayer, for in these churches the priest is able to face the altar while at the same time facing eastward. But for the people the necessity of turning away from the altar was a distinct inconvenience. However, it seems they made nothing of this disadvantage, for the faithful had to turn round only during prayers. In the Egyptian liturgies, there is preserved the command, in Greek, by which the faithful are told to turn to the east at least during the main prayer of the liturgy, before the Sanctus of the Mass: εἰς ἀνατολὰς βλέπετε!

But it was probably this inconvenience which finally led to a change in planning the church building. As early as the fourth century, some churches were built with the apse towards the east, in accordance with what became the general custom later on. Now the priest is standing at the altar, generally built of stone, as the leader of his people; the people look up to him and at the altar at the same time, and together with the priest they face towards the east. Now the whole congregation is like a huge procession, being led by the priest and moving east towards the sun, towards Christ the Lord.

The same idea of orientation was also carried out in the lay-out of the cemeteries. In most of the old cemeteries in the villages of my country, in Tyrol and Austria, the graves are laid out in such a way that all the dead lie facing towards the east, to the rising sun. This is sometimes very striking. It can happen, for example, that a broad avenue is cut through the cemetery, e.g. the road to the church (for most cemeteries are still adjacent to churches), but, even in this case, the graves, the crosses and the gravestones do not face the road, neither do they face the church, but if necessary they face away from the road and away from the church: towards the east. The dead therefore are like a large army looking out for Him who has risen and awaiting His call, when He will summon them also to the resurrection. This certainly is a symbolism full of meaning. Over the entrance of one of the larger cemeteries in Tyrol this symbolism is expressed in the single word: *Resurrecturis.*

How this symbolism made its influence felt also with regard to the ecclesiastical year, especially with regard to Christmas time, we shall see later. But first we shall speak about some other customs which go back to the religious culture of the ancients and which at least for some time continued to survive in the Christian liturgy. There are three times in every man's life that, in every religion, are celebrated with religious ceremony and surrounded by religious usages, namely: birth, marriage, and burial.

In Christianity, ever since the earliest times, the birth of a child is followed by the ceremony of re-birth: Baptism. In connection with Baptism, a custom dating from the pre-Christian era was observed for a long time, namely, the giving of milk and honey to the child. With the pagans this was a sign that the child had been received into the family; at the same time they wanted to ward off the demons. The Christians continued to observe this practice: In the *Apostolic Tradition* of Hippolytus, as we mentioned above, it is ordered that after Baptism the newly-baptized should be led into the church, there to take part for the first time in the celebration of the Eucharist and to receive communion under both species. But before receiving the Precious Blood from the chalice they were to receive a drink of water and after that a drink of milk and honey. What was meant by this usage in the Christian liturgy was, in the first place, to preserve on this solemn occasion the ancient custom of a meal in connection with the holy Eucharist. But the nature of the meal was determined by the pagan tradition of the Roman people, a tradition to which a new Christian meaning was given. The symbolism would appear to be that the newly-baptized were conducted into a land flowing with milk and honey. The custom vanished, but vestiges of it are seemingly to be found long afterwards. Even in the tenth-century *Pontificale* of Egbert of York a blessing is prescribed for the Easter Mass—a blessing of milk and honey after the canon of the Mass.

With marriages, also, a custom has been preserved, at least in the oriental Church, originating from the religious culture of antiquity.

At marriages and at other occasions as well, the wreath played an important part: bride and bridegroom wore a wreath of natural flowers, the στέφανος νυμφικός. This wreath seems to have had for its purpose the warding off of harmful spirits, but at the same time it signified a religious consecration.[17] It was for this reason that at first the Christians rejected the marriage-wreath as a pagan custom; Tertullian especially objected to it. Yet the custom continued. Chrysostom testifies to it, giving it a new significance: the wreaths are victory-wreaths; they are worn by the bride and groom as a sign that they have never been overcome by lust and are thus now proceeding to their wedding. The putting on of wreaths was finally taken into the marriage ceremony of the Byzantine liturgy, the church ceremony even taking its name from it, being called στεφὰνωσις, the crowning with a wreath. The priest puts the wreaths over both the bride and groom; then the first of the witnesses exchanges the wreaths three times by placing the wreath of the bride on the head of the groom and vice versa. Thus the wreath becomes the symbol of the oneness of bride and groom; but principally it is to signify, as with Chrysostom, victory. Today the wreaths are no longer made of natural flowers, but of precious metal and of artificial flowers; they now look like a diadem or a crown. The wedding wreaths are kept in high honor by both marriage-partners; whoever dies first is decorated with the wedding wreath for the burial.

In the West, too, the putting on of wreaths was a ceremony customary at church weddings. Pope Nicholas I (in the ninth century) testifies to it for his time. Then it gradually disappeared. But at least the popular custom remained that the bride should wear a myrtle wreath as a symbol of purity.

With regard to burial, also, many customs are preserved which go back to pre-Christian times. We already spoke of the orientation of the graves, for this too is a pre-Christian custom with various peoples. The pagan burial included a sacrifice for the dead. In Christianity, also, even as early as the second century, we find indications that the Eucharist was celebrated after the funeral. Gradually the Mass for the dead became a part of every Christian funeral. But the Christians of the fourth and fifth centuries had still another custom which was judged differently by different Fathers of the Church: the so-called *refrigerium* for the dead. The *refrigerium* was a meal held on various occasions by the grave of

17. K. Baus, *Der Kranz in Antike und Christentum* (Theophaneia, 2; Bonn, 1940), esp. 96 ff.

the deceased at which the deceased himself was deemed present, a place being set for him and a portion of the meal put aside. At Rome we can see pagan burial places with little holes in the floor and a pipe leading down to the corpse; through this pipe some drink was poured down to him.

This custom of the death-meal was also kept by Christians, although not in order to feed the deceased himself, but merely to keep alive his memory. So far it was an indifferent practice which Christians could observe. In some places, however, abuses crept in; the *refrigeria* became occasions for excessive drinking parties and thus they were finally prohibited. Thus it is clear that the Church had to forbid the custom, not because it was pagan, but because it led to intolerable abuses. Both Augustine and Ambrose were concerned with this burial practice, but it is interesting to note the difference in their attitude and their mode of attack. At Milan, Ambrose forbade the *refrigeria* absolutely. Augustine did not abolish the custom absolutely, but he did transform it. He was willing to allow gifts to be brought to the tombs of the dead, provided that they were moderate; and he demanded that the gifts of the banquet be destined for the poor. It was with this alms that St. Augustine connected the idea of solace (*refrigerium*) for the dead. This was a very prudent way of proceeding, a way which was followed by many leaders of the Church afterwards.[18] This substitution of ideas is a procedure of the utmost importance both for the history of religion and for the history of culture. We shall see it at work in another field of relationship between ancient religious culture and Christianity.

III. Traces of Paganism in the Christian Calendar

The task undertaken by the Catholic Church, to transform the ancient pagan world into a Christian one, was indeed a formidable one. Dom Gregory Dix gives us a description of that world in a picture at once splendid and horrifying.

> The pagan Roman empire was like some great crucible, into which were poured all the streams of culture welling up out of the dimness of pre-history; from Egypt and Mesopotamia, even in lesser degree from Persia and in thin trickles from the alien worlds of India and China; in Anatolia from the long-dead Hittite empire and old Phrygia;

18. Th. Klauser, *Die Cathedra im Totenkult der heidnischen und christlichen Antike* (Liturgiegeschicht. Forschungen, 9; Muenster, 1927). J. Quasten, "Vetus superstitio et nova religio. The problem of *refrigerium* in the ancient Church of North Africa," *Harvard Theological Review*, 33 (1940), 253–266.

> as well as from Minoan Crete and Achaean Greece and Ionia, and from semitic Tyre and Carthage. All these, with the raw cultures of the North and West, were formed by the dying flame of Hellas and the hardness of Rome into the unified mediterranean world of the first and second centuries—the *Civitas Romana.* Into that had flowed all the forces of antiquity.[19]

This was the world that had to be refashioned. Not destroyed, but reshaped; not demolished, but converted, moulded into something Christian, transformed into the *Civitas Dei.* The Church did not bow to the forces of paganism; this was impossible. But she did assimilate what she could of the pagan culture by which she was surrounded. Social forms, civic ceremonials, national usages, artistic practices—all these could be (and were) adopted or at least adapted to Christian life and worship. The whole pagan world had to enter the kingdom of God in order to be sanctified. No sphere of life was exempted from Christian "Baptism."

Nowhere are there more striking examples of the impact of the pagan world on Christian worship than in the calendar. The influence of the religious culture of antiquity is apparent, for instance, in the choice of days on which divine services were held in memory of the dead. In the Roman missal, at the end of the *Missa in die obitus,* we still find the rubric: *In die tertio, septimo et trigesimo depositionis defunctorum dicitur missa ut supra;* the same special Requiem Mass can be said not only on the day of burial but likewise on the third, seventh and thirtieth day after death. This rubric is not just a relic; it is still of practical importance, at least in part. The "month's mind" is a living tradition in many countries, and even Protestants in some localities have a memorial service a month after death.

But why on these particular days? What is the significance of this particular usage, and where does it come from? In the Roman liturgy it is the third, the seventh and the thirtieth day that are singled out; the same days are observed in Christian Egypt. Among the Syrians, it is the third, the ninth and the thirtieth day, and in the Greek church, the third, the ninth and the fortieth day that are observed. All these dates for the commemoration of the dead go back to pre-Christian traditions, particularly to traditions of the ancient Orient.[20]

The ancient Greeks used to commemorate especially the third

19. Dix, *The Shape of the Liturgy,* 385.

20. Cf. E. Freistedt, *Altchristliche Gedächtnistage und ihr Beziehung zum Jenseitsglauben und Totenkultus der Antike* (Muenster, 1939).

and the ninth days after a death; the same was the practice of the ancient Persians (Parsees). According to an old Syrian custom, when someone died a three-days' fast was kept for the deceased; on the evening of the third day the banquet for the dead was held. Similar customs are already recorded in Homer's *Iliad*.[21] Achilles mourned the death of his friend Patroclos for three days. He took no bath and partook of no food. The corpse was not cremated till the fourth day.[22] From other sources we learn that on the third day sacrifices for the dead were offered in connection with the funeral, the so-called *τρίτα*.

In all of Asia Minor and also in ancient Israel, the mourning for the dead lasted as a rule seven days. The funeral rites for Jacob lasted seven days; the mourning for Judith after her death lasted seven days.[23] Among the ancient Persians and Greeks, as already mentioned, a period of mourning for *nine* days was observed. The *ἔνατα*, that is the sacrifice on the ninth day, was observed by the Greeks along with the *τρίτα*, the sacrifice on the third day. In the myth of Niobe, it is related that Niobe mourned nine days and nights for her lost children; only after that did she partake of food again. And so with the thirtieth and fortieth day. They are testified to be the closing days for mourning at several localities of the ancient world. Among the Israelites it is said that the mourning for Moses and for Aaron lasted thirty days (Num. 20, 29; Deut. 34, 8). Plutarch tells us of the town of Argos in Greece where the custom was that the relatives offered for their dead first sacrifices to Apollo, and then thirty days later to Hermes, adding an interesting explanation: "for they believed that as the earth received the corpses, so did Hermes receive the souls." [24]

It now becomes apparent why the particular days mentioned were selected for honoring the dead. The reason is found in the opinions of the ancient peoples about the manner in which the process of the soul's separation from the body takes place. When somebody dies, the soul does not immediately depart from the body; it lingers on for a while in the vicinity of the body. Generally it was assumed that this took three days, but some people believed that this delay lasted for seven days.[25] This opinion is probably connected with the fact that the decay of the corpse becomes apparent

21. *Iliad,* 16, 855 ff.
22. Freistedt, *op. cit.,* 77 ff.
23. Genesis 50:10; Judith 16:29.
24. Freistedt, *op. cit.,* 167.
25. Freistedt, *op. cit.,* 60.

only after some time. Not till after seven days, according to popular belief, or after three days, must the soul take definite leave of the body.

But the view was also widely held that the soul remained on earth till the body was definitely decayed. (This seems to be the reason why the ancient Egyptians, in order to delay this decay as long as possible, preserved the corpses of their kings and princes so carefully.) The decay of the body and the final departure of the soul from the world appears to have been put as a rule on the thirtieth or fortieth day.

This eschatological theory is connected, at least among the Greeks, with their view about the origin of the individual. For they were of the opinion that here too the third, ninth, and fortieth day had special significance. Only on the fortieth day did the embryo take the form of a child and only then was it joined by the soul. After death the process was more or less reversed.

These popular concepts continued to live on, as is easy to understand, even after the people had become Christians. A Greek writer of the early Middle Ages summarizes these views as follows: "After death the soul stays on earth for three days; on the fourth day the angels lead her up; on the ninth day a battle for the soul breaks out between the spirits in the air and the angels; on the fortieth day after death the soul is led before the judgment seat of God and receives from God the final decision." [26]

We can well understand that the Fathers of the Church challenged these notions vigorously. St. Chrysostom opposed them in a sermon dealing with the parable of Dives. He points out with emphasis that "from other passages and also from this parable it is clear that the souls, when departing from the body, do not stay here any longer, but are immediately led away." But in vain. Popular practices and beliefs have long lives, and so a compromise had to be found by keeping these commemorative days, but giving them a Christian meaning: The third day is the day of the resurrection of Christ after His death; and the fortieth day is the day of His ascension into heaven; thus the dead may be helped on the third and fortieth day, in order that they might follow the same path that Christ had trod.

As we have seen, the seventh and thirtieth day are mentioned in the Old Testament and thus sanctioned. The seventh day, moreover, at least in a later reckoning, signifies a commemoration of the Sunday and thus again of Christ's resurrection. The third,

26. Freistedt, *op. cit.*, 180.

seventh and thirtieth day thus became in the Roman liturgy fixed days for commemorating the dead. In the Orient, however, where partly different traditions existed and where people did not like taking the example of the prescriptions of the Old Testament on account of their enmity toward the Jews, the third, ninth, and fortieth day continued to be observed.

Service for the dead, however, is something that concerns only a small circle, namely, the relatives and friends of the deceased. Being therefore a semi-private matter, we can well understand that here popular opinions exerted a stronger influence. But was this true also when not some private circle but the whole community was gathered together on feast days? Did pre-Christian and pagan traditions also exercise any influence here, at least with regard to the choice of certain days? The answer is, yes.

The *litania major* on April 25 is a clear example of it. It is evident that this *litania major* has nothing to do with the feast of St. Mark celebrated on the same day. The very color of the vestments shows this; the feast is celebrated with red, the *litania major,* however, in a purple cope. This *litania major* is a remnant of a pre-Christian custom of ancient Rome. Every year on April 25, a procession through the fields was held in Rome in honor of the goddess Robigo (*robigo* = rust, wheat rust), seeking to obtain the favor that the wheat be kept free from rust. Christians could ask the same favor of the true God, and so the procession simply continued to be held. It generally proceeded a fairly long way; hence it was and is called *litania major*. The Christians kept to the same road which the pagan procession had taken; but whereas the former procession had gone on to the grove of Robigo, the Christian procession turned and proceeded on to St. Peter's on the Vatican, where the *statio* is still kept to this day.

A procession in purple vestments is also held on February 2. This procession seems to correspond with the subject of the feast; candles are carried in the hands and the words of Simeon are sung: *Lumen ad revelationem gentium*. Striking, however, is the purple color used during the procession. In former days its penitential character was stressed much more than today: the procession began with the antiphon: *Exsurge Christe adjuva nos* and the pertinent Psalm 43; the litany was sung exactly as in the case of the *litania major* and the *litania minor*. The presbyter and his assistants walked barefoot, *discalceati*. The explanation here also is that the procession of Candlemas had originally nothing to do with the feast of the day. In all probability, it is a continuation of an old Roman procession, an *amburbium* or *amburbale* (in which they walked around the city = *ambi* + *urbs*).[27]

During the month of February, another day is also celebrated the source of which is a custom of pre-Christian Rome: the feast of the *cathedra Petri* on February 22. We find a witness to this feast in the so-called Roman *Chronograph of 354* under the title: *Natale Petri de cathedra.* This is a curious work, half calendar, half note-book; its author is probably Furius Dionysius Philocalus who so artistically executed the inscriptions of Pope Damasus. Scholars now agree in considering this feast a survival of the pagan festival of the *charistia* or *cara cognatio.* During the month of February the ancients celebrated the feast of the *Parentalia,* which was the great feast for the dead, lasting eight days. In conjunction with this feast of eight days, a family feast was also held, during which all relations gathered to honor the dead, sitting down to a meal in common which served to strengthen concord and love. Hence its name *charistia* or *cara cognatio.* This meal was at the same time a funeral banquet, with an empty chair meant for the dead. The only question is, how did the Christian feast originate from it? The older opinion, last put forward by J. P. Kirsch, is this: The Church wished to react against the pagan practices connected with this death-feast, and to substitute for it some Christian feast. For this purpose, a feast in honor of St. Peter seemed very suitable in the fourth century, because feasts in honor of the Prince of the Apostles were very popular. Furthermore, at that time the anniversary of each bishop's consecration and entry into his episcopal office was celebrated with a special divine service, so they also wanted to devote such a feast to the first bishop of Rome, to St. Peter: *Natale Petri de cathedra.*

But in 1927, Theodor Klauser put forward a new theory which is, perhaps, more probable.[28] He suggested that this feast was introduced not in opposition to an already existing festivity, but in celebration, on the part of the Church, of a death-feast in honor of the Apostle Peter (or originally probably for Peter and Paul), in conjunction with the customary banquet for the dead at which a chair—*cathedra*—was placed for the dead. Hence its name. This occurred perhaps as early as the third century. Later on, in the fourth century, the name of this feast of *cathedra* was given a different interpretation, and thus there originated from it a feast of the episcopal office of St. Peter, the feast that we celebrate today. In fact, we celebrate this feast twice: on the 22nd of February (that is

27. Cf. D. de Bruyne, in *Revue Béned.*, 34 (1922), 14–26.
28. Th. Klauser, *Die Cathedra im Totenkult* (see note 18 above).

the old Roman tradition) and on the 18th of January (which is the Gallican tradition); it was not till 1558 that both feasts began to be celebrated in the Roman Church in such a way that the one is referred to the Cathedra Romana and the other to the Cathedra Antiochena.

The most famous example, however, of a feast the date of which was taken over from a pagan feast is *Christmas*. In the time of Hellenism, it was customary to celebrate birthday feasts: the birthdays of princes and especially of the Roman emperors, but certainly also of other famous personalities. So it was quite natural the Christians should solemnly celebrate the birthday of their Lord, their *κύριος* and king. And since the actual birthday was unknown, another symbolically important day was chosen: in Rome it was the 25th of December.

Duchesne, it is true, held a different theory. He maintained that the 25th of December was reached by an independent calculation on the part of Christians. Christ must have died on the same day or near the day of the vernal equinox, on the 25th of March, the same day, too, on which the creation of the world had begun. But since in Christ any imperfection was excluded, His life-span must have represented a full number without any fractions; therefore His life must have begun on the 25th of March; hence they would have calculated that the conception of Christ took place on the 25th of March and consequently His birth on the 25th of December. A fourth century work, *De solstitiis et aequinoctiis,* puts these ideas in the following form: Since Christ is the true sun, it was befitting that the start of His life should coincide with the high point of the sun-year. Christ must, therefore, have been conceived on March 25 and born on December 25. As a scriptural clue to this sort of reasoning, the unknown author attempts to prove that the announcement of John's birth took place on the Great Day of Atonement (which he fixes on September 24) so that his birth then occurred at the summer solstice. But it is quite reasonable to ask whether this reckoning does not actually presuppose the Christmas feast of December 25. At any rate, this explanation is generally considered obsolete, though not abandoned by all scholars.

On the contrary, it has become progressively clear that the real reason for the choice of the 25th of December was the pagan feast of the *dies natalis Solis Invicti* which was celebrated in those days with great splendor.[29] The birthday of the unconquerable sun: the

29. Thus H. Frank, O.S.B., "Frühgeschichte und Ursprung des römischen Weihnachtsfestes," *Archiv f. Liturgiewissenschaft,* 2 (1952), 1–24. But in the same volume, pp. 25–43, H. Engberding, O.S.B., defends the other opinion.

sun has seemingly lost its power during the time when the days are shortest, only to be new-born (as it were) and to grow again and become strong. In an old Greek calendar of the year 239 B.C. originating in Canopos, we read regarding this day: Ἡλίου γενέθλια. Αὔξει φῶς.[30] Hence the Orient was the home of this feast, where (of old) sun cult and Mithras worship were indigenous. Emperor Aurelian introduced it in Rome after his victory over Palmyra in 274. He wanted to introduce one uniform religion for the empire with the *Sol invictus* as the principal god. He erected a huge temple of the Sun on the Campus Martius, appointed a special college of priests and made the 25th of December a national holiday. This was the last great pagan cult that opposed Christianity and still wielded tremendous power even in the fourth century. Hence we can understand that the Christians clung all the more closely to Him who was their Light and their Sun, and that they now began to celebrate this day as the *Dies natalis Christi*. For, as we have already seen, they called Christ *Sol salutis, sol justitiae, oriens ex alto;* and they even described Him as their *Sol Invictus. Hic sol novus noster*, as St. Ambrose some time later puts it. The author of *De Solstitiis* cited above speaks of the *Natalis Invicti* and asks: "Who is as unconquered as our Lord, who overcame and conquered death?" The feast of Christ's birth, therefore, fittingly provided the Christian antithesis of the pagan feast of the sun.

The first indication that the 25th of December was celebrated in Rome as Christ's birthday is found in the so-called *Chronograph of 354* already mentioned. This Chronograph contains a list of the Christian feasts which were then celebrated. Here we find mentioned: *VIII Kal. Jan. natus Christus in Betleem Judaeae.* That is our Christmas, the 25th of December. Probably this information goes back to an older writing of the year 336, and, therefore, Christmas would already have been celebrated during the last years under Constantine. It is quite possible that the emperor himself demanded this feast and that it was at that time that the old pagan national holiday received its Christian character, although the pagan feast still survived, for St. Augustine still speaks of the crying and shouting of the pagans on this day. On the other hand, however, it seems that the Christian Christmas feast existed even before Constantine. For it appears that this feast was also celebrated by the Donatists; in which case they would have possessed it before their separation from the Church, hence before 312.

In this way our Christmas came into existence, the feast on which

30. A. Baumstark, *Comparative Liturgy* (Westminster: Newman, 1958), 152.

we celebrate the mystery of the Incarnation, the coming into the world of the Logos. The great emphasis on the light in the darkness, *Lux fulgebit hodie, lux nova,* the use of the psalm-verse about the sun, *tamquam sponsus . . .* , can be looked upon as remains of that opposition to sun-worship out of which the feast originated. In the course of the century, the feast rapidly spread in all directions, also to the Orient. And this took place in spite of the fact that the Orient had meanwhile evolved its own feast for the celebration of the Incarnation, a feast which, as a closer study has shown, also evolved from an originally pagan feast, namely *Epiphany.*

Regarding this feast of Epiphany, a Belgian Benedictine scholar, B. Botte, has suggested some very important and surprising conclusions.[31] From time immemorial, the feast of the winter equinox was celebrated in the Orient, especially in Egypt and elsewhere, on a day which in the course of centuries, on account of the inaccurate calculation of the leap years, was gradually shifted until finally it coincided with the sixth of January of the Julian calendar. On this day, or rather during this night, processions were held in the temples amidst the cries: "the virgin has brought forth; the light is increasing." Or according to another version: the virgin has brought forth the Αἰών. This feast, too, must originally have been a feast of the sun-god who was highly venerated in Egypt (Osiris). At this time of the year, the sun becomes weak and small but it is newly born and will grow again: *αὔξει φῶς.* In the Hellenistic period, the sun-god became a more spiritual figure: the Αἰών. It can therefore be no mere accident that, about the middle of the fourth century, in the Orient the Christian feast of the *ἐπιφάνεια* is celebrated on the same day, namely on January 6. *Ἐπιφάνεια* was then in Greek theology the designation for the incarnation of the Logos: the Son of God appearing in the world as man. In our preface of Epiphany, too, we read: *unigenitus tuus in substantia nostrae mortalitatis apparuit* (*apparuit* = *ἐπεφάνη, ἐπιφάνεια*). Hence Epiphany meant the coming of the Son of God into the world, and this included of course the idea of the coming of a divine being. But chiefly it signified that with Christ the true light has arisen, the light of the world was born, in a far fuller sense than that announced in the old pagan worship with its cry: *αὔξει φῶς.*

In pre-Christian popular belief, a second tradition was connected with this day, or more accurately with the fifth of January, namely

31. B. Botte, *Les origines de la Noël et de l'Epiphanie* (Louvain, 1932). Concerning some items, different views are proposed by Christine Mohrmann in her lecture, "*Epiphany*" (Nijmegen-Utrecht, 1953).

that on this day certain springs yielded wine instead of water; various towns claimed to have such springs. Obviously it was this popular belief which the Church tried to overcome by connecting with the same day the commemoration of the miracle of Cana: she wished thereby to say: Here in reality is the miraculous water become wine.

Besides this, the Church confronted the popular belief with still another idea, the idea of Baptism. The waters of Baptism really do possess miraculous powers; they have the power to enlighten man; indeed, Baptism was called φωτισμός (enlightenment). In this way at the same time the connection with the idea of light was made and thus also a certain unity in the significance of the feast was established: the illumination of the world by the Son of God.

The basic concept of Epiphany is, then, the coming of Christ into this world; the mystery of the Incarnation. The other two subjects, namely, Baptism and the miracle of Cana are only secondary. (The opinion formerly proposed, that in the beginning Epiphany was a feast of Baptism, cannot be held any longer. True, there is an account of some in the adherents of a Gnostic sect in the third century celebrating the Baptism of Christ on the tenth of January, but it seems that there is no connection between this feast and Epiphany.)

This feast of Epiphany was adopted in the West at a very early date, just as Christmas started to spread also in the Orient during the fourth century. It is interesting to see how in the Roman liturgy the unity of the meaning of the feast was established in a very different fashion. In the antiphon to the *Benedictus* of the Epiphany feast, the thought of marriage is fundamental:

> Hodie caelesti Sponso juncta est Ecclesia, quoniam in Jordane lavit Christus ejus crimina; currunt cum muneribus Magi ad regales nuptias, et ex aqua facto vino laetantur convivae.

By allowing Himself to be baptized, Christ cleanses not Himself but the Church, His spouse; therefore the Magi come from the east with their wedding presents; and therefore also the marriage joy and the miracle of the wine at Cana.[32] It is not known, where and when this association of ideas was created. Baumstark thinks that here, too, the suggestion for it came from a pre-Christian, pagan feast. With the ancient Greeks and also in Hellenism there existed

32. The triple manifestation of the mystery of the wedding of Christ and the Church is brilliantly studied in P. T. Camelet, O.P., "La triple épiphanie de la gloire du Fils de Dieu," *Vie spirituelle*, 92 (1955), 5–15. On the origin of the antiphon cf. H. Frank, O.S.B., "Hodie coelesti sponso," *Vom christlichen Mysterium* (Düsseldorf, 1951), 192–226.

the idea of a ἱερὸς γάμος. It is possible that the Church seized this idea and confronted it with the Christian reality. But this is at best only a more or less vague conjecture. The fundamental idea of Epiphany is the Incarnation just as this is the basic thought of Christmas: it is the feast in honor of the God-man. But after both feasts had come into being, it became necessary to differentiate them to some extent. The differentiation was made in such a way that on Christmas the fact of the birth of Christ is considered mainly from the standpoint of His weakness and the poverty of His human nature, while on Epiphany it is viewed from the standpoint of the divine majesty shining through the human nature of Christ and illuminating the world. Jesus' Baptism in the Jordan and the miracle at Cana also fit nicely into this concept of the feast's mystery: "Jesus made known the glory that was His" (John 2:11).

Thus Christianity absorbed and made its own what could be salvaged from pagan antiquity, not destroying it but converting it, "Christianizing" what could be turned to good.

CHAPTER TWELVE

Pagan and Christian Mysteries

IN THE previous chapter, we have seen a demonstration of the multiple influences of the ancient pagan culture on the Christian liturgy. But we have seen that these influences touched only the fringes of the liturgy, in matters of linguistic form, of outward ceremonial, in the selection of certain calendar days for festivities. Moreover, the effect of these influences took mainly the form of a counteraction, a substitution for, and not an actual adoption of, pagan forms. But when we come to the study of the pagan mysteries, we are faced with a serious problem. For we must pose the question—a question already answered by many in the affirmative—whether the influence of pagan antiquity was even more profound, whether it did not in reality enter into the very core of Christian worship. The similarities apparently found between the Eucharist and the pagan mysteries present a problem which we cannot evade if we are to understand fully the Christian tradition of liturgy. Are these merely analogies, or are they the result of an interplay of the pagan upon the Christian mystery?

I think we can safely answer that the pagan mysteries did not, directly or indirectly, affect Christian worship in its inception. Those evolutionary theories of religious history—proposed by scholars like Lietzmann and Loisy—which try to explain Christianity entirely in terms of a more or less happy syncretism of paganism and Judaism, with the mysteries playing a special role (because they were the origin of the sacramental system) are today abandoned or at least greatly restricted in scope, for it has become increasingly clear how little occasion there was, when the sacraments were first proposed, for any real contact with the pagan mysteries, and also how essentially different the concept of the sacraments is from that of the mysteries.

Nevertheless the analogies which these scholars have pointed out cannot be set aside without discussion. It is our purpose in this chapter to study the pagan mysteries in the light of the hypothesis proposed during the past thirty or forty years by Catholic scholars, especially by the school of Maria-Laach and its chief representative, the late Dom Odo Casel, O.S.B. (+ 1948). Dom Casel and his school did not reject the materials proposed and explained by the historians of comparative religion; their contribution to the question was to propound a new interpretation of these materials.

The main point of Dom Casel's theory is this: The mysteries provided a sort of providential preparation for the sacramental idea presented by Christianity. While it is true that the sacraments were instituted by Christ and determined in all essentials by Him, yet paganism was already prepared to some extent to accept them because in the mysteries paganism already possessed something that was of the same *typus* (or the same εἶδος) as the sacramental system. Thus the pagan mysteries did not influence the origins of the sacramental idea, but they provided a framework for Christianity to fill with divine grace, a pattern which showed how grace brought with it, through earthly means, precisely those benefits which human nature had been seeking to obtain for itself. And, later, when Christianity entered into the sphere of Hellenistic culture, it made use of the technical terms of the mystery religions in order to introduce the sacraments, and especially the Eucharist, to the heathen world.

This theory is one of the most important Catholic contributions to the study of comparative religion and the history of primitive Christianity, and deserves our earnest study. Let us therefore look into the matter more closely.

What were the mysteries? Among the ancient Greeks, and afterwards among the Romans as well, the mysteries were secret rites held in honor of a deity, chiefly an underworld divinity who was believed to take charge of souls after death. These rites were not public but secret; they were performed only by a small group of initiates. Every participant was received into the circle of members by a special initiation rite; thus he became a μύστης. This initiation or introduction into the mystery included a preliminary purification (καθαρμός) and the crowning or garlanding of the mystic, who was thus, as it were, marked out as a privileged person. But the climax of the initiatory rite consisted in the communication of the mystic knowledge (τελετῆς παράδοσις) and the ἐποπτεία, or revelation of the holy things, the exhibition of an object which had been brought into contact with the deity. We know that this central revelation was not something spoken, or not merely spoken, but something done (δρώμενον), that is to say, a ritual enactment of the death and return to life of the god, this enactment being carried out in such fashion as to make the initiate in some way a partaker of the life of the god. One who reached this level amongst the membership was called an ἐπόπτης, "one who had seen the mystery."

The rites of initiation have to be distinguished from the recurring celebration of the cult. This celebration consisted in the more or less dramatic representation of scenes from the mythology of the deity in question, for instance in the Eleusinian mysteries, the abduction of Proserpina: the loss, the search and the recovery. All the initiated were present and played some role. Those who represented and relived incidents from the deity's fate hoped thereby to participate in some way in the god's life and so to find salvation after death.

These mysteries already existed during the classical age of ancient Greece; even then they were probably already very old. In all likelihood, the beginnings are to be sought in the agrarian rites of the ancient nature religions. Traces of them have been found especially amongst primitive peoples: in the fertility rites, in the consecration of their youths and their puberty ceremonies, where, likewise, only the initiated were allowed to take part. Andrew Lang, therefore, called the initiations amongst primitive peoples "rude sketches of the mysteries of Greece." [1] The origin of these cults is thus expounded by scholars: It was observed how each year nature dies and revives again. So nature was personified and made into a cult-hero. This cult-hero was given human form and his fate compared to that of man. Man, too, must die; but man has the undying desire to live again and to share in the immortality of the gods. Hence the alliance of those who wanted to worship the hero and unite themselves with him.

Our knowledge of the mystery religions is necessarily unsatisfactory, owing especially to the paucity of available evidence which consists mainly in scattered references, verses of poetry, fragments of hymns and prayers, inscriptions, cult emblems and a few ruins. In addition, much of the evidence is late in date. However, from this elusive evidence certain facts can be extracted with some

1. Quoted by K. Prümm in *Zeitschrift für kath. Theologie*, 57 (1933), 271.

assurance. They were "salvation" religions, as we already indicated, but the precise nature of the "salvation" which they promised to their adherents is hard to determine; in some way it was to be a deliverance from the uncertainties of social life, from the upheavals of political life, from the burden of grief and sorrow and the oppressive tyranny of fate climaxed in death. But the mystery religions did not insist so much on doctrines as on a way of life. The chief emphasis appears to have been on external ceremonials designed to aid in the achieving of "salvation." Not only were there dramatic performances and the presentation of mythological scenes, but there were lustrations, consignings, anointings, impositions of hands and the like. At the celebration of the mysteries those cult-forms were especially valued which could induce ecstasy and wild enthusiasm; noisy music and frenzied dancing seem to have been part of the celebration. Not only were there cleansing baths but also sacred meals. Often these celebrations were held during the night, by the light of torches. The dramatic solemnities or performances which accompanied these celebrations were given the name ὄργια; the same word is also contained in the word λειτουργία, from ἔργον. But the pejorative meaning which the word "orgies" received, likewise in the English language, indicates the excesses and revelries which took place during them. The Bacchanalian consecration rites were so excessive that the Roman senate forbade them in the year 186 B.C. But these mysterious rites exercised a great attraction on the people of those times. Especially during the era of the Roman emperors, they kept spreading more and more; they were, as somebody has remarked, the last outcry of the pagan religions. But just for this reason they constituted a serious obstacle to the Christian religion, and the Fathers of the Church, therefore, energetically combatted these mysteries. In their war of defence they even used phrases like "Come to us—here are the true mysteries." Hence, they seemed to acknowledge some kind of kinship between the Christian and pagan mysteries. Their attitude appears to be similar to their reaction in regard to the sun-cult where they kept saying: We have the true sun. Of special importance here is a passage of Clement of Alexandria:

> Come, O madman, not leaning on the thyrsus, not crowned with ivy; throw away the mitre, throw away the fawn-skin; come to thy senses. I will show thee the Word and the mysteries of the Word, expounding them after thine own fashion. This [that is, Christianity] is the mountain beloved of God, not the subject of tragedies like Cithaeron but consecrated to dramas of the truth,—a mount of sobriety shaded with

> forests of purity; and there revel on it not the Maenades . . . but the daughters of God, the fair lambs, who celebrate the holy rites of the Word, raising a sober choral dance. The righteous are the chorus; the music is a hymn of the King of the universe. The maidens strike the lyre, the angels praise, the prophets speak. . . . Come thou also, O aged man, leaving Thebes, and casting away from thee both divination and Bacchic frenzy, allow thyself to be led to the truth. I give thee the staff [of the cross] on which to lean. Haste, Tiresias; believe and thou wilt see. Christ, by whom the eyes of the blind recover sight, will shed on thee a light brighter than the sun; night will flee from thee, fire will fear, death will be gone; thou, old man, who saw not Thebes, shalt see the heavens. O truly sacred mysteries! O stainless light! . . .[2]

Clement of Alexandria seems to have had in mind the Bacchanalian mysteries, also called Dionysian mysteries (Bacchus = Dionysos). The subject of these mysteries was the myth of the death of Dionysos. Dionysos, son of Zeus, is attacked by Titans while playing at his nursery games; he transforms himself into a bull, but even so he is pursued by the Titans and torn to pieces. But Athene saves his heart and brings it to Zeus: Zeus devours it and generates a new son, the new Dionysos, in whom the one torn to pieces by the Titans lives again. Thus a two-fold action is celebrated: the killing of Dionysos by the Titans, and his coming to life again. These celebrations, it seems, were preferably held at night and in the hills; it was believed that Dionysos himself appeared there. Since this was a feast of the wine-god Bacchus-Dionysos, wine played a great part in the celebration; through an abundance of wine and resounding music a wild enthusiasm was engendered. A holy frenzy was characteristic of the Bacchanalia. By becoming "beside himself" (ἔκ-στασις), in an ecstacy, the participant sought to free himself as it were, from his own life. However, that the participant in such a frenzy also sought to have a part in the death and revival of the god is denied by some scholars.[3]

Similar in kind, but less wild were the mysteries of Eleusis, which were held in the fall every year at Eleusis near Athens. The subject of these mysteries was the myth of Proserpine who had been abducted by Pluto and taken to the underworld; her mother Demeter searches for her and finally finds her. The yearly solemnity took place on the seashore near Eleusis. At one point of the celebration, the people were allowed to participate, even those who were not initiated. In a huge procession they left Athens; the abduction of

2. *Protrepticus,* XII, 119 f.
3. K. Prümm, *Der christliche Glaube und die altheidnische Welt,* I (Leipzig, 1935), 308.

Proserpine was dramatically represented; the Mystae ran along the coast with torches searching for Proserpine. Amidst all sorts of artificial illuminations, with dancing and singing, the goddess was finally found, and all joined in the rejoicing.

Other mysteries were those of Cybele, of Isis, and of Mithras.[4]

I have already alluded to the fact that the mystery cults gradually gained a wide popularity. For in the mysteries people were touched personally. The official state-cults were merely outward show; besides, they merely considered the earthly welfare of the state. But the mysteries were meant to bring salvation—σωτηρία—to each individual. Hence they won the praise and eulogy even of grave men like Sophocles and Plato. Cicero says of them: These mysteries have taught the people who took part in them to live with joy and die with a greater hope.

The mystery cults were a manifestation of vivid desire for salvation. In the later years of the epoch of the emperors, some people had themselves initiated not only into a mystery cult, but into as many as possible, in order thus to make sure of their salvation. In the year 376 a Roman donated a marble altar to the Magna Mater Cybele. The inscription upon it enumerates the mysteries into which he had been initiated: *Pater patrum Dei Solis invicti Mithrae, hierofanta Hecatarum, dei Liberi archibucolus, taurobolio criobolioque in aeternum renatus.*[5] These expressions indicate at least four different mysteries. Therefore Rahner says of them: [6] "The ancient mysteries are an altar bearing the inscription: 'To the Unknown God.' " At any rate we can thus begin to understand the fascination the mystery cults held for those interested in the history of Christianity during the first centuries.

And now we come to the question: How much did the ancient mystery cults actually influence Christianity and Christian liturgy? or at least, how closely are they related to each other?

To answer these questions fully we have to distinguish three different periods: (1) the apostolic age; (2) the era of the early Fathers of the Church; and (3) the period of the decline of pagan-

4. B. Heigl, *Antike Mysterienreligionen und Urchristentum* (Muenster, 1932); S. Angus, *The Mystery Religions and Christianity* (New York, 1925); Karl Prümm, *Der christliche Glaube und die altheidnische Welt*, 2 vols (Leipzig, 1935). An up-to-date survey of the discussion regarding the relation of the mystery religions and Christianity in Hugo Rahner, "The Christian Mystery and the Pagan Mysteries," in *The Mysteries: Papers from the Eranos Yearbooks*, ed. Joseph Campbell (New York, 1955), 337–401.

5. *Corpus Inscriptionum Latinarum*, VI, 510. Other records of such mystery initiations in Gustav Anrich, *Das antike Mysterienwesen in seinem Einfluss auf das Christentum* (Goettingen, 1894), 55.

6. *Op. cit.*, 346.

ism after the fourth century. Now first, the apostolic age, roughly the first century. It has been pointed out that the word μυστήριον occurs in St. Paul very often; the Christian religion itself is called a μυστήριον, a mystery. We must note, however, that here, as well as in the older Fathers down to Irenaeus, the word does not have any connotation of cult. Here it is regularly used in the singular, whereas in the mystery cults the plural is employed. It is used to designate God's counsel to save the world; at first this counsel remained hidden and inscrutable; then it was revealed and realized in Christ. Hence it is called a μυστήριον.[7] In this first century, the mystery cults were not as widespread as later on.

It was during the second period that Christian writers busied themselves in attacking the pagan mysteries which meanwhile had spread far and wide and become a menace to Christianity. Christians took up the cudgel; the most important of these writers were Clement of Alexandria and the two apologists, St. Justin and Tertullian. They accused the pagan mysteries of adopting and imitating Christian concepts and institutions, like baptism, rebirth, catharsis, sacred repast. Clearly, then, these Fathers recognized similarities between Christian and pagan mysteries, but they claim the priority of Christianity and they address the pagans: "Come to us! here are the true mysteries!" The passage from Clement of Alexandria which we cited above is characteristic of the attitude of the Christians of the second and third centuries.

After this there follows a third period, the era of the decadence of paganism and also of the mysteries, beginning in the fourth century. Paganism is no longer a peril; it is not necessary to attack it any more. So now Christian writers are not afraid to borrow expressions from the language of the mysteries; to a certain extent it even becomes the fashion to speak in the terminology of the mysteries. The baptised are the initiated: μεμυημένοι, *initiati;* the teacher is the μυσταγωγός and his teaching the μυσταγωγία. *Norunt initiati,* ἴσασιν μεμυημένοι: with this formula the preachers indicate that they are not allowed to reveal certain words and formulas. The writings of Pseudo-Dionysius Areopagita, written about 500, are already replete with expressions from the mysteries: ἱερουργία, ἱερολογία, τελετή, etc. The same must be said also of the Byzantine literature now emerging, which differs precisely in this from the literature of the foregoing age. However, although the language of the mystery cults was borrowed by Christian writers, there can be

7. This sense of μυστήριον and its association with liturgy are well explained by L. Bouyer, *Liturgical Piety* (Notre Dame, 1955), 70–242.

no question of borrowing the cults themselves. It was a matter only of externals.

It is not until this third period—hence about the fourth century—that there can be any question of an influx into the liturgy of customs and institutions connected with the ancient mysteries, a carry-over of mystery forms into Christian worship. However, the sole example which can be adduced with some certainty, in addition to the expressions just mentioned, is the *disciplina arcani,* which cannot be proved to have existed before the third century, and which reaches its climax in the fourth and still endures to a certain extent in the fifth century.[8] Objects of the *disciplina arcani,* which, therefore, had to be kept secret, were not so much certain doctrines, but certain practices and formulae—chiefly Baptism and the celebration of the Eucharist and what is connected with it: the words spoken during these rites, especially the words of the consecration, the *symbolum,* the *Pater noster.* All these things and words had to be kept secret from all non-baptized, the heathen and the catechumens. Hence, if these came to the services, they had to leave the church after the lessons, before the real celebration. Sacred formulae were not allowed to be spoken in their presence. Possibly it is from this that the custom is derived (which we observe even today) that except in Baptism and the Mass where none but the baptized are supposed to be present, only the introductory and closing words of the Pater noster and of the *symbolum* are said aloud: *Pater noster. . . . Carnis resurrectionem.*

Not all the authors, however, are unanimous about the origin of the *disciplina arcani.* Various factors, too, may have worked together: the necessity of preserving the sanctity of the Christian mysteries, the catechumenate, caution in the face of persecutors. But in all probability the main factor leading to the formation of the *disciplina arcani* was the contact with the mystery cults; not as if this institution had been borrowed directly from them; but in the culture of those days the *disciplina arcani* was a safeguard for sacred things already customary in the mystery cults and there was, therefore, no reason why the Church should not herself make use of a similar safeguard.

But what is of special interest for us in regard to the mysteries is not the question whether perhaps a certain rite, a certain liturgical institution, can be explained as derived from the ancient mystery cults, but the question whether or not the concept of

8. O. Perler, "Arkandisziplin," in *Reallexikon f. Antike u. Christentum,* I, 667–676.

mysterium is necessary for a correct understanding of the Christian liturgy. What Odo Casel asserted again and again is this: The mysteries of the ancient world were a preparatory school, a preparation for Christianity somewhat as the Old Testament was a preparation for Christianity, for what the pagans sought for and desired in the mysteries, precisely that and much more has been brought to mankind by Christianity, precisely that and much more is contained in the Christian liturgy.

What did they seek? They dramatically represented the life and suffering of a deity in order themselves to take part in the immortal life of the gods and thus to obtain salvation. It is precisely this that has been brought to men by Christianity. The Son of God came into the world, lived amongst us, suffered and died and is risen again; we Christians seek to obtain salvation by taking part in His passion and resurrection—through the sacraments, through Baptism and the Eucharist, through the liturgy. Therefore, Casel holds, we can understand the liturgy only if we interpret it by an analogy with the antique mysteries, if we take it as cult-mystery. Casel does not deny the essential difference between the ancient mysteries and the Christian liturgy. The former is only myth, the latter historical reality, for Christ, who suffered and died under Pontius Pilate, gives us its basis. In the former, a process in nature is personified, namely, the yearly return of life in spring; nobody believed that the deity had any desire to do anything for mankind's welfare. But the latter is the work of divine grace for the salvation of mankind. In the mysteries everything remains in the plane of nature and the senses; moral demands are scarcely made. But in the Christian liturgy a new life is supposed and demanded, a new moral life, a supernatural life.

However, Casel emphasizes that the *typus mysterium* contains precisely what constitutes the essence, rightly understood, of the Christian liturgy: the redemptive act, the fact of salvation in the passion and resurrection of Christ; the representation of this fact of salvation in a ritual, particularly in the sacraments; and thirdly, the communication of salvation or grace to all those participating in the rite. Hence Casel presents the following brief definition of the liturgy: "Liturgy is the cult-mystery of Christ and the Church." [9] The meaning of this little phrase is this: The liturgy is that mystery whose object is the saving act performed by Christ and now made present in the worship of the Church. Since about 1925 this definition and what it entailed became the issue in a great controversy. We cannot enter here into the details—the battle is not yet won—

9. *Jahrbuch f. Liturgiewissenschaft*, 8 (1928), 212.

but we need to discuss certain points that are perhaps clearer than the rest.

First of all, the concept of liturgy as the cult-mystery of Christ and the Church in the sense explained above cannot be applied to the whole liturgy, but at most to the sacramental rites. For example, it is not applicable to the celebration of the ecclesiastical year. You cannot, for instance, say at Christmas, when *Hodie Christus natus est* is sung: the birth of Christ is made present or becomes present. Similarly at Easter the resurrection of Christ is not, in any true sense, realized anew. Moreover, the application of this concept to the Church year is apparently rejected in the encyclical *Mediator Dei:*

> The liturgical year, devotedly fostered and accompanied by the Church, is not a cold and lifeless representation of the events of the past, or a simple and bare record of a former age. It is rather Christ Himself who is ever living in His Church. Here He continues that journey of immense mercy which He lovingly began in His mortal life, going about doing good, with the design of bringing men to know His mysteries and in a way live by them. These mysteries are ever present and active not in a vague and uncertain way as some modern writers hold, but in the way that Catholic doctrine teaches us. According to the Doctors of the Church, they are shining examples of Christian perfection, as well as sources of divine grace, due to the merit and prayers of Christ. . . .

The central point in Casel's theory is that in the cult action—hence certainly in the sacraments and in the Mass—it is Christ's saving act itself that becomes present and not merely the effect and fruit of this saving act. Accordingly we must say that Christ's passion and death and resurrection are made present, and not merely the grace that these acts won for us. Casel admits that this is a rather difficult concept, for how can a past happening become present again? He confesses that this is a mystery, and like all the mysteries of faith, a concept which our limited intellect cannot grasp. But he tries to prove that this mystery is to be found in ecclesiastical tradition; he gathers a large number of passages from the Fathers and other early and medieval authors which seem to substantiate his theory.[10] His critics, however, have contended—and generally established—that though individual ecclesiastical writers use expressions that can be interpreted in the sense that Casel maintains, there can be no question of a common tradition. This point in Casel's theory, therefore, central though it be, must be dropped.

10. O. Casel, "Das Mysteriengedächtnis der Messliturgie im Lichte der Tradition," *Jahrbuch f. Liturgiewissenschaft,* 6 (1926), 113–204.

Gottlieb Söhngen, accordingly, presents a modification of Casel's theory by explaining its meaning in terms of sacramental reality.[11] According to Söhngen the saving act of Christ, the Redemption, becomes present in so far as an image of the Redemption is created in those participating in the sacraments or in the Mass. The Church's external ritual is a figure and memorial of Christ's saving act, and since that ritual is an effective sign, it contains the reality which it signifies. A person baptized is buried with Christ and permitted to rise with Him. One who takes part in the Mass and communicates is offered up with Christ and is thus sanctified, etc. According to many theologians who view Söhngen's theory favorably, this theory is a really progressive development in theological thought. If the theory means anything, it means that the image of the Redemption, the symbol produced in the participant, is not the redemptive act itself but its effect, namely, grace; but here grace is viewed as an effect not only in the line of efficient causality but also in the line of exemplary causality. The teaching of the mystery has been under constant attack, but if it endures it will probably do so in this modified form.

Now we must ask, what are the practical results of all these considerations? Why is there such a live interest in the concept of the *mysterium?* This theme has, indeed, great practical importance. The theory of the *Mysteriengegenwart*—the "presence of the mystery"—is a reaction to that excessively abstract and intellectualistic conception of the liturgy in favor up to a few decades ago, which was obviously not advantageous to liturgical life. Of course we always knew that in thc liturgy, in the ecclesiastical year, and especially in the Mass, there is celebrated a commemoration of the life, passion, death and resurrection of Christ—*memoria passionis et resurrectionis*. But did we not consider this simply as a subjective recollection of what had happened nearly two thousand years ago? It was chiefly this emphasis that Casel and his colleagues wanted to combat. In the liturgy, they asserted, a commemoration is taking place not only in our subjective thoughts, but also really and objectively. By enacting the liturgy, by consecrating bread and wine, a commemoration takes place even if nobody is thinking about it. The Christian liturgy is not like a profane commemorative celebration in honor of some famous person in which perhaps a long speech is made about him but the person himself is absent and

11. *Symbol und Wirklichkeit ım Kultmysterium* (2nd ed., Bonn, 1940). Cf. also G. Söhngen, *Der Wesensaufbau des Mysteriums* (Bonn, 1938). On the whole of the controversy cf. Th. Filthaut, *Die Kontroverse über die Mysterienlehre* (Warendorf, 1948).

nothing of him can be made present. In the Christian religion it is different; the Redemption is not something which is simply past; the reality is still present, especially in the liturgy of the Church. For the Church itself is present—the *plebs sancta,* the people assembled, which is the very fruit of the Redemption. And Christ is there, for He is the head of the Church; did not He Himself say: "Behold I am with you all the days that are coming, until the consummation of the world"? He is not someone who lived once upon a time but now is no more; He it is *qui vivit et regnat per omnia saecula saeculorum.* Indeed it is Christ who is active in the sacraments: *ipse est qui baptizat, ipse est qui consecrat.* He is the High Priest. And at the same time He is the sacrifice; He is present in the sacrament *vere, realiter et substantialiter.*

But this presence in the sacrament is only part of the multiple presence of the redemptive reality given us in the Church and in the liturgy. The liturgy is, therefore, much richer in content, more pregnant with power than we may have thought. True, to consider all this, and thus to make our concept of the liturgy more vital, it is not absolutely necessary to hold Casel's theory of the *mysterium.* But it can certainly be said that this concept of the *mysterium* and the study of the mysteries of the ancient world have been a means to help us gain a better understanding of this aspect of the liturgy and to prompt theologians and historians to look more closely into this element of liturgical devotion and Christian life.

CHAPTER THIRTEEN

The Role of the Liturgy in the Transformation of Pagan Society

THE world of the fourth century was a world that was gradually being transformed from a pagan into a Christian one. The Church was the one living creative force in the spiritual life of the age, and so, although Christianity was the religion of a minority, its influence spread far and wide. For some two hundred years a constant change was going on in the world of the Mediterranean basin, a development that slowly converted pagan society into a society dominated by the Christian spirit, the spirit of Christ and of the Church He founded. It may be well to delve into the question of the part played by the liturgy in bringing about this vast transformation. Other factors, of course, were at work, but it is our task to study the role of the liturgy in changing a pagan society into a Christian one.

In the last two chapters, we tried to describe how the traditions and beliefs of the pagan masses who flocked into the Church, especially since the fourth century, made their influence felt in the liturgical life of the Church. They exerted a very powerful influence indeed. They impressed upon the liturgy the stamp of the Hellenistic Greek and Roman cultures. Nor should this be surprising. Because the Church is in the world, though not of it, it must be somehow affected by its milieu. The life of the Church is determined, to some extent at least, by the people living within the Church.

The life of the Church can be regarded as a continuation of the Incarnation: new men, new nations, new cultures are constantly being taken up by the Church and built into the Mystical Body of Christ. These, in turn, determine to a certain extent the particular forms which the Church's life assumes. The process exemplifies the famous principle: Grace supposes nature; grace does not destroy but perfects nature. Or, to paraphrase the axiom: Liturgy supposes culture, which it does not destroy but rather perfects. Not a little of the cultural wealth of the Greco-Roman world has been embodied in the Christian liturgy. The fact is generally admitted; and the extent of this embodiment is becoming increasingly clear through recent liturgical research.

But the question can also be stated the other way around: What influence did the Christian liturgy exert on the masses of the Greco-Roman peoples who came into the Church? Did it contribute anything to the Christian formation of these peoples? Was it merely a matter of fulfilling an obligation when those Christians, whether from newly converted families or from the Christian populace in general, regularly frequented the divine services of the Church; or did the liturgy really exercise a formative influence upon them: was it effective, in other words, from the pastoral point of view?

The answer is unequivocal. The formative power of the liturgy was both profound and vast. We are speaking about the fourth and fifth centuries, the era of the great Fathers, and the period in which a tremendous process of transformation within the ancient nations was taking place: the transformation of society from paganism to Christianity.

Christianity in this epoch progressively extended its triumph; and it did so, as in the earlier centuries, primarily through the inner attractiveness of its content and message and the enthusiasm of many of its adherents. Society, political life, the lives of the people, family life, the position of woman, the appreciation of man's dignity, whether slave, child, or infant yet unborn—all this was transformed in a slow but sure process of fermentation: out of a pagan society a Christian society was born. And from the womb of the Christian communities new groups emerge: the multitude of monks and virgins endeavoring to live the Christian ideals in their full splendor, thereby preparing the way for the Christian culture of the Middle Ages.

To appreciate what happened, we must keep in mind above all that what we now understand by the term *cura animarum,* "the care of souls," was then very little developed, and that institutions were lacking which today are taken as a matter of course and considered essential even in mission countries. There existed, it is true, an extensive organization of charity, supervised by the deacons. But there were no Christian schools, either for the elementary level, which was mostly a matter of private enterprise, or for higher education. On the contrary, in the public, or more correctly in the semi-public schools, the pagan element still predominated for a long time. The Church gave no systematic catechetical instruction to the children; their religious training was left entirely to the parents. The Church made no special provision for the care of youth; they were left to fend for themselves. There were no Christian societies or confraternities or institutions comparable to organized Catholic action. All this was lacking. In addition, the penitential discipline was for centuries in a critical state. And Rome was an old, dying nation.

And yet there existed a flourishing Christian life, for there existed a living liturgy. The liturgy, then, somehow substituted for other institutions which, according to our way of thinking, should have been objectively necessary. From the effects which the liturgy achieved through these, so to say, compensative functions, we can conclude the force which lay hidden in it.

In what way could the liturgy obtain such results? The liturgy was something of the people. It had been created in forms of expression taken from the people's own living culture. In buildings, clothing, gestures, song and language, it possessed elementary forms familiar to all. It was, however, not of the people to such an extent that, for example in the Latin West, it was formed of local elements only; the essentials, what was of divine institution, had come from outside, from the Orient, and together with them a great number of forms which the primitive Church, i.e., the apostles, had taken over from the worship of the synagogue: e.g., the manner of beginning and concluding prayers, the use of the psalms, the divisions of time into the third, sixth and ninth hour even in domestic prayer, and many other elements. But what had thus come as a mysterious gift from above and from the East was now clothed and furnished with forms of expression from their own cultural world. The language was the national language. Up to the middle of the third century, the worship of the Roman Church had been in the Greek tongue, obviously for the reason that Christianity was at first limited largely to Greek colonies. After that, apparently at the time when the Latin element had obtained preponderance, the transition to the Latin language took place also in the divine services, in any case in the papal divine services.

That the liturgical language was understood by all participants was naturally a great advantage, not only immediately, for intelligent cooperation in worship, but also in other ways. The liturgy was thus enabled to exercise its function as teacher. In the worship of the ancient Church, there was much reading of Holy Scripture, of the Old Testament and the New, much more than today. The "lesson" occupied a prominent role in the Mass of the Sunday; it had its place also in Vespers and in the prayer-hour of the morning. And it was ordinarily a *lectio continua:* it was an unbroken reading of whole books. Hence the complete commentaries on them by various Fathers, i.e., the sermons with which they accompanied these readings of the Scriptures.

Thus it was that the people gained a very extensive knowledge of Holy Scripture, so extensive that the Fathers could constantly make allusions in their sermons to various passages in the Bible and especially to the figures and types of the Old Testament.

The result was that a large treasury of figures and types in which Christ and His work were represented became familiar to the ordinary Christian. The Fathers in their homilies interpreted the Old Testament not chiefly according to its literal, but much rather according to its typical, figurative sense, according to the principle: "The New Testament is latent in the Old, the Old becomes patent in the New." They saw in Adam and Abel, in Noe, in Isaac and Joseph, in Moses and David, figures adumbrating the Savior. Eve, the ark of Noe, the temple in Jerusalem and the holy City were figures of the Church. And in the passage through the Red Sea, in the bath of Susanna, in the deluge, and in many other figures, they saw Baptism prefigured. The result of this way of thinking is already evident in the paintings of the catacombs, which in ever new repetitions represent these themes and thereby constantly represent only the one theme: Christ and His work. But the basis for it all was the knowledge of Scripture, which had become the common property of the Christians through the homilies in the liturgy.

The psalms, too, in an especial manner, became familiar to the faithful through public worship. After each lesson there followed, as a rule, a psalm sung in common. In the dialogue or responsorial mode of singing customary at the time, the chanter first sang the refrain which the congregation repeated after him; then he began the psalm, after each verse of which the refrain was repeated by the faithful. The refrain-verse itself was determined by the celebrant, i.e., the bishop or priest.

We read, for instance, that when St. Athanasius was besieged by the emperor's soldiers in the church of Theonas at Alexandria, he ordered the deacon to start the singing of Psalm 135 and to have the people after each verse repeat the refrain: "For His mercy endureth forever" (as is already provided for in the text of this psalm). St. John Chrysostom, at Easter, ordered the people to sing as a refrain: "This is the day which the Lord hath made. . . ." With Psalm 41 he connected the refrain: "As the hart panteth after the fountains of water. . . ." Such verses, with which the people had become thoroughly familiar through singing, he was then wont to make the subject of edifying explanations in his sermons. St. Augustine, too, seems to have done the same. We can imagine how deeply such words of the psalms, and the thoughts associated with them by the homilies, became imprinted into the minds and hearts of the faithful. St. Augustine often refers with pride and joy to this congregational singing. Thus he says: "We have sung the psalm. We encouraged one another: we cried with one voice, with one heart, *Venite Exsultemus*."

The psalms themselves, too, at least those heard again and again, of necessity became to some extent familiar to the people. We must not, however, think that the faithful in general knew all the psalms, or even a great part of them, by heart; this was the privilege of the monks, who, of course, had an ambition to know the complete psalter. Among the people, the knowledge of the psalms must have been quite modest. St. John Chrysostom says in a sermon: "Most of you know dirty songs, but who of you is able to say even one psalm?" Yet in another place, he also supposes that all knew by heart at least the morning Psalm 62 ("O God, my God, to Thee do I watch at break of day") and the evening Psalm 140 (". . . The lifting up of my hands as an evening sacrifice . . ."). St. Caesarius of Arles wishes that all learn by heart Psalm 50 (*Miserere*) or Psalm 90 (*Qui habitat*). At Naples, the candidates for Baptism were ordered to memorize, besides the short Psalm 116, also Psalm 22 (*Dominus regit me*), and to recite it in thanksgiving for Baptism, Confirmation and the Eucharist. It was a state of affairs similar to that existing today in congregations that sing hymns: a certain number of strophes are familiar to all, and, if the hymns have good content, a treasury of religious ideas is thus inculcated.

During the following centuries, a certain number of individual psalm verses must have been common property. This is particularly true of the so-called *capitella de psalmis*—a series of psalm verses which formed the basis of the oldest experiments in the way of a prayerbook. Just as nowadays every cleric knows the response to *Adiutorium nostrum in nomine Domini* or *Dirigatur Domine oratio mea,* so in those days every Christian, cleric or lay, must have known the common responses. Thus a form of communal prayer, full of variety and of substantial content, was quite possible—a not unimportant precedent for our own problem of popular prayer.

But the liturgy does not exercise its educational influence by teaching alone; more important, it actually introduces the participants into the midst of prayer. It makes them sharers. That is, at least, the ideal. What, we may ask, was the practice of the early Church in this regard? The answer is: the people took their own part in the liturgy alongside the clergy. Prayer, including the celebration at the altar, was purposely performed in such a way that the people were taken up into it. This was the practice from the beginning, and it was the living practice at the time of the great Fathers of the Church. Not only was the prayer spoken in the plural, but it had also to be explicitly co-executed by the people. We know from St. Justin how important this was considered; proudly he tells of the people's *Amen* after the great prayer of the Eucharist. And St. Jerome boasts that in the Roman basilicas the *Amen* resounds like heavenly thunder.[1] But even this confirmation of the prayer by the *Amen* of the congregation was not enough. An express invitation to join in preceded the prayer: *Oremus; Gratias agamus.* Yet more. Before the invitation the priest turned toward the faithful and conveyed to them a formal greeting, one which they in turn had to answer, thereby again expressing their union with the celebrant. Such was the care the earlier centuries manifested that the faithful might take an active, a living part in the liturgical prayers.

These brief responsorial prayers of the faithful derive, as we know, from the Jewish antecedents of the Christian liturgy. Like so many of our traditions, they are a reflection of the Judaic background of our Christian heritage. But at the same time they also correspond well with the conceptions and customs of other ancient peoples. Among both Greeks and Romans the people were accustomed to voice their assent or dissent in public assemblies by means of acclamations. If satisfied with a proposed candidate, they shouted: ἄξιος, *dignus est.* When he accepted the office, they cried out: εἰς πολλὰ ἔτη, *Ad multos annos!* Such acclamations as these were carried over into the service of the Church. The Church wanted to hear the voice of the people, wanted them to voice their consent, not, of course, as if the prayers and the sacrificial action would otherwise lack validity, but because only through and with

1. *In Gal. Comment.*, 1. 2 (*PL*, 26:355).

the consent of the people does prayer become in the fullest sense a prayer of the whole people, of the *plebs sancta,* of the Church. Only when the people take part actively does prayer truly become the people's prayer.

The participation of the people was also manifested in other ways. It was expressed, for instance, in their bodily posture. This corresponded to the celebrant's. Like him they stood facing the East, with him they raised their hands in the attitude of the *orante.* On certain occasions (which were very frequent) the deacon cried out, *Flectamus genua,* and all knelt down for silent prayer until the command, *Levate,* was heard. Later, in the sixth century, St. Caesarius of Arles was to complain in a sermon that this regulation was no longer being observed by many: "When the deacon calls out *Flectamus genua,* I often see the majority remain standing like pillars." And so he urged them to again observe the old rule.

The fact that the faithful could thus intelligently follow the prayer of the Church with the consciousness that it was their own prayer which the priest was reciting at the altar, constituted for them a very effective school of prayer and religious life. The very method of praying was itself a training in praying. The individual could not isolate himself from the community in his own personal concerns, withdrawing into a paltry particularism; he was drawn perforce into the prayer life of the Church Universal. The lifting of mind and heart to God was learned in adoration, thanksgiving and in the holy Sacrifice. They were reminded that it was Christ who leads us up to God, that it is through Him that our prayer reaches God: *per Christum Dominum nostrum.* They acquired an esteem for the Church, the assembly of the children of God, which could celebrate such a service of worship. And all this they learned not in theory but in practice, by activity. It was an application of the principle of "learning by doing" which we today value so highly in the conduct of our schools.

But besides the "doing" of prayer, there was another especially intensive "doing," in fact a twofold "doing," through which participation in the holy Sacrifice became still more intimate: the bringing of bread and wine by the people, and the communion of all those present. Both of these activities were a regular part of the order of Mass. Communion for everyone was so much a part of the Mass that it was very difficult to make an exception. The ease with which the faithful went to Communion in those days may not always have been to the good, for not all would be in the right frame of mind for a proper reception of the sacrament. Yet it was presupposed that every Christian, being a child of God by Baptism, is entitled to the food proper to the children of God, the daily bread which is the body of Christ.

However, the fervor for Holy Communion started to decline, in some countries as early as the fourth century. Among the Greeks especially the change was quite rapid, chiefly as a result of the reaction against Arianism. In the West, on the contrary, and particularly at Rome during the time we are considering—the fourth and fifth centuries—it was still taken for granted that all the faithful communicated whenever they assisted at the Eucharist, and especially on Sundays.

But in those days the faithful not only received the gift *from* the altar; they also brought a gift *to* the altar. We refer to the so-called offertory procession. Once this "procession" became a part of the order of service, it was obligatory for all to take part. In the Orient, the faithful had to bring their gift before Mass to the so-called *diaconicon;* this was a kind of sacristy near the altar. Here the clergy received the gifts and selected those that would be used for the sacrifice. Then, after the lessons, those gifts which were set apart for the altar were carried in and placed on the altar. In Gaul, too, a similar plan obtained. The deacon carried the bread for the sacrifice and the wine in the *turris,* a dome-shaped vessel. On feast days this became a solemn procession accompanied by singing.

In North Africa and Rome the procedure was somewhat different. Here the offering of the gifts was much more closely linked with the liturgy. The faithful made their presentation of the gifts during the Mass, at the offertory. Two different methods were followed; either the faithful themselves approached the altar and handed over their loaf of bread and their little bottle of wine to the priest and his assistants, or the clergy descended to the nave of the church and collected the offerings there. When the first method was used, it must have presented an impressive sight when the entire congregation joined in the offertory procession on Sundays and feast days. Unfortunately, we do not possess much information about it and are unable to describe the details very accurately. But there is a curious bit of information regarding a gift of the Emperor Constantine that is pertinent here; he donated to the Lateran basilica *altaria septem ex argento purissimo,*[2] "seven altars of the purest silver." Now we know that at that time every church, even the largest basilica, had but one altar. Why then the "seven altars" for the Lateran basilica? The answer can only be that these seven were

2. *Liber Pontificalis* (Duchesne, I, 172).

not altars for the celebration of the Eucharist, but altar-tables on which the faithful could place their offerings. The use of these subsidiary "altars" also explains the use of the plural in some *secreta* (offering prayers), e.g., *Tua, Domine, muneribus altaria cumulamus;* whereas in the post-communion prayer there is never mention of altars in the plural but only of the one altar, the *mensa coelestis.*

Naturally the gifts offered by the faithful were chiefly bread and wine. But from various churches we gain the information that other foodstuffs and other articles were also offered, especially those that might be of use for the divine service, like oil, wax, candles, church implements; and a part of these gifts was used for charity. But soon it was felt to be less fitting that all sorts of things, however necessary and important for the upkeep of the clergy and the support of the poor, be brought into the church. Already in the fourth century regulations were issued that in future bread and wine and other things necessary for worship be brought to the altar as heretofore, but that all other gifts be handed in elsewhere. It was understood that through the gifts of bread and wine, all the other things which the faithful wanted to give were symbolically represented and conjointly offered up.

Throughout many centuries, the ancient Church continued visibly and palpably to draw the faithful into the Sacrifice of Christ by means of the offertory procession. There can be no doubt that it contributed a great deal towards making the faithful understand the Mass, and that thus they realized more clearly that the holy Sacrifice was their Sacrifice which they should offer together with Christ. Holy Mass itself was the catechetical instruction and schooling for the most important doctrines of the Christial faith. The faithful must have been keenly alive to the fact that their entire lives belonged to God and that they all were one in the Sacrifice of Christ.

The latter point, viz., the unity of the faithful among themselves, was also strongly promoted by the mutual, active cooperation in the divine service. All prayed together, all sang together, all together cried out the responses, all offered at the same time, all or nearly all received the holy Sacrament. This community feeling was still more strengthened by the *disciplina arcani,* the so-called "discipline of the secret." All unbaptized and those unworthy were excluded. But even without the *disciplina arcani,* the sense of community would have made itself so strongly felt that any stranger would have immediately felt out of place. In a gathering where one merely has to stand and listen, every one can casually come and go. But where everything is moving in a definite order, an outsider feels immediately that he does not belong: he will therefore withdraw of his own accord. And inversely: one who belongs to the community knows that he must take part in the whole service. He will be there on time, and he will not be tempted to leave before the gathering is dismissed. Being on time, like being attentive, is part of a Christian's way of life. This idea is even given a liturgical stress; a Syrian source, the *Testamentum Domini,* a fifth century document, directs the deacons to shut the doors when the celebration starts, and on no account to open them to late-comers, but to insert a special prayer for them in the common intercessory prayers, that God may grant them more love and fervor.

But the question still forces itself upon us: Did the faithful really frequent the divine service Sunday after Sunday, so that the liturgical worship could in fact influence them in the manner just outlined? Was there a real Sunday obligation? An obligation in the form of a written ecclesiastical law did not, of course, exist for a long time. But it was considered a matter of course that every Christian would, if at all possible, assist at the divine service. The martyrs of Abitina during the persecution of Diocletian declared: *Sine Dominico (esse) non possumus*—"Without the Sunday Mass we cannot live." In earlier times also, we find references which seem to establish that on Sunday all were normally present: e.g., about the year 200, the Syrian *Didascalia* admonishes the faithful: That on Sundays they should come to the words of salvation and to the divine repast, and not shorten the body of Christ of its members.[3]

A formal law, together with the threat of punishment, is found for the first time in can. 21 of the synod of Elvira (this synod was held in about 305, in any case before Constantine s edict): "If someone is resident in the town and does not come to church for three Sundays, he shall be excluded for some time," i.e., he is excommunicated and has to do penance. It may be that this law was not everywhere equally strictly interpreted. In a recent study,[4] for instance, it is declared probable that as late as 390, in a town like Milan only one divine service took place, that, namely, which the bishop conducted. If this be correct, then it would obviously have been impossible for a great part of the faithful to go to Mass, for reasons of space, because no church at Milan could have con-

3. II, 59, 2 ff.
4. V. Monachino, *La cura pastorale a Milano, Cartagine e Roma nel secolo IV* (Rome, 1947), 54 ff.

tained them all. In any case, it was not so in other cities. Rome was well provided for during the same period: about the year 300 there already existed more than forty churches; twenty-five of them were, according to somewhat later information, titular churches which had regular Sunday services; among the remainder there were several basilicas of martyrs of which most probably the same can be affirmed. Thus we may safely assume that, in any case under the conditions existing in Rome, the Christians actually lived under the constant influence of the education which came from the liturgy.

Besides these regularly recurring divine services, which refreshed the soul like a steady yet intensive rain, there were also extraordinary occasions which served from time to time for a religious renovation. In Rome four times a year there were the Ember weeks, with their extraordinary divine services on Wednesday and Friday and the full vigil during the night from Saturday to Sunday. And every year there was the great spiritual renewal of Lent, with its increased fasts and the daily services of the stations. The Roman Lent, as it evolved since the fourth century and reached its full growth in the sixth, might be compared to a modern, successful mission, profoundly influencing the whole population and preparing it for Easter.

Easter itself, of course, was simply *the* feast: the feast of Christian hope and joy, the feast on which every Christian of necessity, as it were, became again fully conscious of what he had possessed ever since his rising with Christ in Baptism.

If we thus view the life of worship as it affected the Christians of the fourth and fifth centuries, we shall understand in some measure what kind of formative influence it could exert. In those days, we have seen, important institutions were lacking which we now consider essential to a proper *cura animarum* and which we could never dispense with. But there was a living liturgy. The liturgy was both Christian school and Christian instruction; the liturgy enriched the parents interiorly to such an extent that they were enabled to instruct their children; the liturgy made the Christians coalesce into one community. It was through the liturgy, i.e., through the word of God which it contains and through the strength of its sacraments, that pagan society became a Christian society.

CHAPTER FOURTEEN

The Veneration of the Martyrs

WE HAVE already seen how, in the fourth century, the liturgy received strong impulses toward further development from its now closer contact with the culture of antiquity. Traditions customary among the people which did not stand in opposition to the Christian faith were built by the Church into her own worship. By thus incorporating so many popular elements, the divine service really became "lit-urgy," the people's service.

But there is still another element that exercised a powerful influence in the development of the liturgy, an element that likewise resulted from contact with antiquity, not however a peaceful and amicable contact, but a conflict with the pagan state. I refer to the veneration of the martyrs.

Martyrdom has been a part of Christianity's program from the very beginning. On the day of His ascension into heaven, our Lord announced to His apostles their future task in life: "You are to be my witnesses (*ἐσεσθέ μου μάρτυρες*) in Jerusalem and throughout Judaea, in Samaria, yes, and to the ends of the earth" (Acts 1:8). The apostles were simply to give witness to what they had heard and seen. And those who, through their witness, received the faith were to carry on this witnessing. They were to uphold it, not allowing themselves to be shaken by anything in the world, not even if they were dragged into the presence of kings and governors (Luke 21:12). For that would be an opportunity for giving witness, and if their word were no longer sufficient testimony, they should be ready to sacrifice their very lives. The witness who sacrifices his life for Christ's sake is the "martyr" in the strict sense of the word.

Naturally the martyrs were, from the very beginning, held in high esteem; they were the real heroes of the faith. Also highly regarded were those who had been imprisoned and tortured for the sake of the faith but had escaped death. They, too, were at first called martyrs (even Tertullian and Cyprian still so employ the term), for they had given witness. But soon another name was coined for them: ὁμολογητής in Greek, *confessor* in Latin; in reality the word signified the same thing: one who has confessed his faith is one who has given witness to it. Like the martyrs, the *confessores* were given special honor. Often they were received into the ranks of the clergy. A confessor was given the honorary privileges of a deacon. There was even question whether he should not receive the rights of a presbyter. We recall what was said in the *Apostolic Tradition* of Hippolytus:

> But if a confessor has been in chains in prison for the Name, hands are not laid on him for the diaconate or the presbyter's office. For he has the office of the presbyterate by his confession.[1]

Another way in which the confessors were venerated was by giving them the right to present to every Christian who had to do penance for a grave fault, especially for apostasy, a *libellus pacis,* that is, a recommendation to the bishop that the penitent should be received back into the Church. The sufferings of the confessor should, so to say, be credited to the penitent.

So it is not astonishing that *a fortiori* the martyrs who had died for their faith were revered and honored. This veneration was shown first of all by gathering their bodily remains, often at great risk (because burial was frequently forbidden), and in spite of all prohibitions and dangers giving them decent burial. The blood of the martyrs was often soaked up in cloths and kept as a relic. But above all their memory was held in reverence and on the anniversary of their death a special service was held in their honor.

I. The Yearly Commemoration of the Martyrs

Originally this annual commemoration of the martyr was like that held for any dead person. For the cult of the martyrs may be said to have had its origin in the cult of the dead and so at first had no other liturgical form than that employed for the dead in general. Even in Cyprian's time, no formal distinction was made between prayers for the dead and the invocation of their intercession with God. From

1. Dix, *The Apostolic Tradition,* 18 f.

the very beginning, however, the funeral cult of the martyrs was distinguished not only by the greater part which the community played in it, but also by its more permanent character. Since it was a concern of the whole ecclesiastical community, it did not cease with the death of the martyrs' immediate relatives and friends. Moreover the annual commemoration did not have the character of mourning, but of a feast of joy.

The first information we have of a martyr's commemoration comes from Asia Minor. Bishop Polycarp was burned to death at the stake on February 23, in the year 155 or 156. The community of Smyrna thereupon sent a letter to the neighboring Christian communities to tell them of the event—the so-called *Martyrium Polycarpi,* which is still extant. The eighteenth chapter of this work tells how the Christians gathered the remaining bones, bringing them to a safe place like precious pearls and burying them. Then it adds: "There the Lord will permit us to meet together in gladness and joy and to celebrate the birthday of his martyrdom (τὴν τῆς μαρτυρίας ἡμέραν γενέθλιον) both in memory of those who fought the fight and for the training and preparation of those who will fight." [2]

In the West, the earliest accounts we have regarding the veneration of the martyrs come from North Africa about the year 180. This year marks the martyrdom of the Scilitan martyrs. A little later, in 202, there took place the martyrdom of Sts. Perpetua and Felicitas, whose beautiful memoirs have come down to us.

In Rome, traces of a yearly celebration of the memory of the martyrs are not found till the third century. The martyr popes Callistus, Pontianus and Fabian, and the presbyter Hippolytus are chronologically the first for whom a yearly celebration was held. This brings us, therefore, to the period between 220 and 250. At first only promient personalities, chiefly the bishops of the city who were martyred, were so honored. Later, after 250, martyrs who were not bishops were also accorded liturgical veneration. Among the earliest of these is the deacon Lawrence. Of the same period were the virgin martyrs, Agnes, Cecilia and many others.[3] And once the practice of honoring contemporary martyrs with a festive celebration was firmly established, it was but a simple step to create such a festive celebration also for great martyrs of the past. Since the third century, the feast of the Princes of the Apostles, Peter and Paul, has been celebrated on June 29.

2. See "Polykarpos," in *Real-Encyclopädie der klassischen Altertumswiss.,* 21, 2 (1932), 1680.

3. Kirsch, *Scuola catt.,* 55 (1927), 161–174.

The great era of the cult of the martyrs began with the edict of Milan in 313, when the period of persecution came to a close. The terrible battle had ended with the victory of the Church, and it was the martyrs above all who had won this victory by the heroic sacrifice of their lives. It was because of the martyrs that the state was finally forced to concede that it was impossible to conquer Christianity by fire and sword.

The development of the cult of martyrs in the fourth century was manifested in several ways, especially in the transformation of their graves. Even during the period of persecution small monuments, called *cellae* or *memoriae* (*Martyrum*), had been built over the graves of famous martyrs. Such monuments were already common among the pagans. There was little space in the subterranean corridors or passages for any fitting monument, so the larger monuments were built above them, in the open air. These *cellae* or *memoriae* were tiny open chapels. Here before such a *cella*, it was possible to assemble in the open field to conduct a memorial service; in fact, even a Sunday service could take place on the pretense of holding service for the dead, since there were no set forms for such a service.

After 313, the modest monuments erected over the graves of the martyrs were quickly transformed into magnificent basilicas. At Rome, Constantine himself erected the basilicas of St. Peter on the Vatican, St. Paul on the Ostian Way, and Ss. Pietro and Marcellino. Other martyr basilicas in Rome, all of the fourth and fifth centuries, are the following: S. Cornelio, S. Lorenzo, Sant' Agnese, S. Silvestro, S. Valentiano, S. Sebastiano, S. Pancrazio, S. Stefano, Ss. Nereo and Achileo.[4] All these basilicas, being crypt churches, were built along the periphery of the city, for at Rome, as elsewhere, it was around the periphery of the city that the cemeteries lay, and there consequently were also the graves of the martyrs. Among the Romans especially, it was a principle, protected by law, that graves were not to be disturbed, that corpses were not to be exhumed without special permission nor transferred to another place. Consequently the graves of the martyrs remained around the outskirts of the city and even today the great martyr-basilicas are found scattered along the edge of the boundaries of ancient Rome. It was the same elsewhere. At Antioch, St. John Chrysostom compares the sanctuaries of the martyrs to a ring of fortresses surrounding the city: "By the grace of God our city is fortified by the precious remains of the saints."

The multiplication of grave-monuments meant also a multiplica-

4. V. Monachino, *La cura pastorale*, 3–4 ff.

tion of divine services. The *Chronograph* of 354 contains, under the title *Depositio Martyrum,* a short festal calendar for the Roman churches in the middle of the fourth century; twenty-four feast days are cited. Of these only two, Christmas and *Petri Cathedra,* are not feasts of martyrs. The other twenty-two are martyr feasts. Naturally there are also the Sundays, including the two great feasts of the year, Easter and Pentecost. Of course these martyr feasts—to which a large number would soon be added—were not holydays of obligation for all. Each feast was simply celebrated at the grave of the martyr, at one of the crypt-churches. But in all probability we can assert of Rome what is recounted about other places, namely that the crowds that thronged to the martyr's grave were like a swarm of bees, for the whole city and its environs poured out to celebrate the feast day of a renowned martyr and so the basilicas were generally too small.[5]

The celebration itself consisted essentially in holy Mass; this is already indicated by Tertullian: *Oblationes pro defunctis annua die facimus.*[6] But at least for the feasts of martyrs, the Mass was introduced by a vigil. As at Easter, the greater part of the city assembled at the grave of the martyr for common prayer. Holy Scripture was read, and also the *Passio* of the martyr, in small sections. Each section was followed by a prayer, or by a song and a prayer, as on Holy Saturday or in the Fore-Mass on Ember Saturdays (as is still indicated in the Missal). Jerome makes mention of these vigils, and justifies them. Arguing with Vigilantius, he points out that such vigils *in basilicis Martyrum* take place quite often.[7] However he acknowledges that there are certain dangers connected with such vigils; in a letter to Laeta, in which he gives the Roman matron advice regarding the upbringing of her little girl, he warns that at the night vigils the daughter should stick close to her mother's side: *ne transverso quidem ungue a matre discedat.*[8]

Both the custom of holding these vigils and the perils connected with the practice must have been recognized very early. At the Council of Elvira in Spain which was held about 305, a special regulation was promulgated: Women were not to hold vigils in the cemeteries (namely, at the martyrs' graves); and the reason for the prohibition is appended: because often under the cover of prayer secret outrages are committed.[9] It would seem, therefore, that even private vigils were conducted at the martyrs' graves, per-

5. *DACL* 10:2434 f.
6. *De cor.*, c. 3.
7. *Contra Vig.*, c. 9.
8. Ep. 107, 9.
9. C. 35; Mansi, 2, 11.

haps on a pilgrimage. In the Breviary for January 28, we read of the parents of St. Agnes: Agnes appeared to her parents *ad eius sepulcrum assidue vigilantibus*. Even if this is not a historical record, it is at least a testimony to a custom that had survived from the period under consideration.

But the high-point of the vigil, at least of the public vigil held on the anniversary, was the celebration of Mass at the grave of the martyr. Here we recognize the genuine ecclesiastical conception of the veneration of the martyrs. For in the Roman sacramentàries and in the other liturgical books, a great number of Mass formularies are preserved which were appointed for the feasts of the respective martyrs at their basilicas. At the beginning, to be sure, the Mass on the feasts of martyrs was not celebrated very differently than on other occasions. The prayers, even the prayer of thanksgiving, had the usual content. The Oriental Church retained this practice even later; only the lessons and hymns were specially selected, for each individual instance. But in the Western churches, especially at Rome, the commemoration of the martyr influenced the prayers of the priest at the altar, even the chief prayer, the preface. The proper and original theme of the preface is to thank God for the benefits of redemption and for the graces He has granted us in Christ. Many of the Roman martyr-prefaces remain faithful to this theme; they praise God for permitting us to celebrate, time after time, the triumphs of the martyrs, "for these have confessed that name in which alone salvation is determined for us, and so that we may be enabled to confess it, Thou teachest our weak faith by their witness and strengthenest it by their intercession." [10] Or God is given thanks because He has brought it about that the enemy of humankind should be overthrown not only by Christ but also by the holy martyrs, "so that in the members also that victory might be repeated which was first won in the Head." [11] This last reflection is a favorite one in the ecclesiastical cult of the martyrs, namely, the parallel between the triumph of the martyrs and the victory of Christ.

In this notion, we have the foremost and the most profound justification for the cult of the martyrs. At the same time, we have an explanation of the fact that for a long time only martyrs were given any special honor. Other saints were not admitted into the festal calendar of the Church until later, and then only hesitatingly and diffidently. In doing so they were admitted as *confessores;*

10. Muratori, I, 304 f.
11. Muratori, I, 311 f.

they were given, as it were, the honorary title of martyr, because by their edifying lives they had accomplished no less than the *confessores* who had wasted away in prison for the faith.

St. Martin of Tours (+ 397) was the first non-martyr the anniversary of whose death was accorded a liturgical celebration in the West. But a text in the Roman Breviary echoes the hesitation which was shown in according Martin the honors of sainthood. The antiphon for the *Magnificat* at Vespers sounds like an apology: . . . *O sanctissima anima, quam* etsi gladius persecutoris non abstulit, *palmam martyrii non amisit!* In short, a saint had, in some sense, to be a martyr!

As a matter of fact there is a close parallel between the victory of Christ and the victory of the martyrs. Our Lord went to His death because He wished to bear witness to His mission and to His heavenly Father. Therefore St. Paul encourages his disciple Timothy to remain steadfast before God and "before Christ Jesus who bore witness to that great claim when He stood before Pontius Pilate" (I Tim. 6:12). Christ sealed His own witness by His own blood; with His own blood He gave testimony that He had come as the Messias for the salvation of the world. And, similarly, the martyrs sealed their testimony, their witness to Christ, by the shedding of their blood. And just as Christ rose from the dead and proved Himself the victor, so the martyrs too, sharers in His battle of suffering, will triumph with Him in His Resurrection. These were the thoughts that gave strength to the martyrs in their sufferings. Bishop Polycarp, standing at the stake, prayed: "O almighty Lord God . . . I bless Thee for having been pleased in Thy goodness to bring me to this hour, that I may receive a portion amongst the number of Thy martyrs, and *partake of the chalice of Thy Christ*. . . . Wherefore for all things I praise, bless and glorify Thee. . . ."

In the Roman liturgy, the mention of the wondrous suffering of the martyrs in the Prayer of Thanksgiving was not considered sufficient. The next step was to make mention of the martyrs in the canon itself. This did not happen at once, but in the course of the fifth and sixth centuries. The names of martyrs were inserted into the *Communicantes* and the *Nobis quoque,* thus giving expression to the desire to offer the sacrifice in union not only with the whole Church on earth but with the Church triumphant in heaven. The foremost representatives of that celestial Church were the apostles and martyrs, and hence their names were grouped around the consecration, before and after, in either instance in a series of sacred numbers. Before the consecration, there are twelve apostles and twelve martyrs, with the holy Mother of God at the head of the list. And after the consecration, there are seven men martyrs and seven women, and at their head he whom our Lord Himself named the greatest of those born of woman, John the Baptist.

When a martyr's feast was celebrated, all the variable prayers made reference to him. Even at present, we are accustomed to hear some allusion to the saint in the oration of the day as well as in the *secreta* and the Post-Communion. Mention is made of the feast we are commemorating, or we beg that we may in eternity enjoy the sight of the saint whose memory we are celebrating now in time. This manner of prayer was first devised for the celebration of the martyrs on the occasion of their anniversary.

II. Popular Features of the Cult of Martyrs

From what we have already said it can be seen that the veneration of the martyrs was already quite popular in the fourth century. The faithful of the era had an almost limitless faith and confidence in the intercessory power of those fearless heroes, the martyrs who gave their lives for their belief in Christ and the truths of the Catholic faith. This can be easily demonstrated by an examination of the *graffiti* which were scratched on the walls near the martyrs' graves. In the cemetery of Priscilla there is the petition: *Salba Me Domne Crescentione Meam Lucs* . . . (Lord Crescentio, heal my eyes for me!). Under the Basilica of St. Sebastian in Rome, excavations have revealed a wall almost wholly covered with *graffiti* invoking the intercession of the apostles Peter and Paul, inscriptions in both Greek and Latin, like: "Paul and Peter, pray for Victor," "Paul, Peter, pray for Eratus," "Peter and Paul, protect your servants." All of us have seen pictures of the Roman catacombs, their walls and ceilings decorated with venerable paintings from the early years of the Church, and here and there a verse or prayer scratched on the wall by some unknown hand to beg the prayers of the holy martyrs buried there.[12]

Another indication of the popularity of the cult of the martyrs was the wish, so often manifested, to be buried near the graves of the martyrs. Take those same pictures of the catacombs; sometimes a wall covered with beautiful paintings is partially destroyed in order to make room for a new grave near the grave of the

12. *DACL* 10:2450. C. O. Marucchi, *Le catacombe romane* (Rome, 1934), 261–265.

martyr. The idea seemed to be that if, in death, one lay near the martyr, one would be close to the martyr also on the great day of the resurrection from the dead. This popular belief, verging almost on superstition, had to be combatted. The Church had to point out with emphasis that it was not physical nearness to a martyr's remains that assured salvation, but imitation of his life and virtues.[13]

But the enthusiasm for the veneration of the martyrs which captured the popular fancy led to a problem of even greater proportions, a problem in ecclesiastical life that bordered on a crisis. This was the strange custom of the *refrigerium*, a kind of funeral banquet celebrated in honor of the dead. As we already learned in an earlier chapter, it was an ancient practice of long standing to prepare a meal at the grave on certain occasions, especially on the anniversary of the death, setting a special empty place as though the dead person were participating. This custom continued to be followed by Christians, especially at the martyrs' graves on the anniversary of their triumph. Naturally no one thought that the martyr had need any longer of earthly food, but it was considered a practical way to express companionship and communion with the dead, with the martyrs. Among the inscriptions scratched on the wall under the Basilica of St. Sebastian mentioned above are messages like the following: "I, Tonius Coelius, have held a *refrigerium* for Peter and Paul" or "On the fourteenth day before the Kalends of April [March 19], I, Parthenius, held a *refrigerium* in God. All of us in God."

The *refrigerium,* therefore, represented a cult act, an act venerating the martyrs.[14] But it was a practice that could easily lead to abuses, as was proved by events. Popular devotions, unless controlled, often tend in this direction, and this was no exception. It seemed that the greater the honor intended by the *refrigerium,* the greater and the more multiplied were the abuses. The meals were held not only in the open, near the grave of the dead, but in the very basilicas of the martyrs, like a divine service, and even in these sacred surroundings often turned into carouses and drinking-bouts. This was the case, for example, in the Basilica of St. Cyprian in Carthage at the time when Augustine was bishop of Hippo. It was not much better even in his own diocese, especially on the feast of St. Leontius, the martyr-bishop of Hippo. Combined action was imperative, and, in a letter to the Bishop of Carthage, Augustine asked for a thorough reform in this matter. He was successful. At a

13. *DACL* 10:2455 ff.
14. *DACL* 14, 2:2179–90.

Synod held in Hippo in 393, these banquets in the basilicas were forbidden.

St. Ambrose had attempted something similar in Milan even earlier. But carrying out his reform was not easy, because of the popular nature of the custom. It was especially difficult for Ambrose because he was attempting a sweeping reform, cutting out the *refrigerium* at the graves of the dead even in the cemeteries. St. Monica was stopped one day as she brought her basket filled with food and wine to the cemetery in Milan, preparing to visit the oratories of the saints there.[15] St. Augustine himself did not follow the example of his friend of Milan by forbidding the *refrigeria* entirely; he recommended that the faithful take the food and drink they had brought to the cemeteries and distribute it to the poor.

III. The Veneration of Relics

There is yet another example of popular enthusiasm—and excess—in the veneration of the martyrs, namely, the cult of relics. The *Martyrium Polycarpi* already cited is not only a clear record of the reverence shown by the faithful for the remains of the martyrs even in the post-apostolic age, but it is, as Dom Dix remarks,[16] a precise statement of the reasons why such touching reverence is shown. The account tells how, after the venerable bishop was dispatched by a dagger,

> the jealous and envious Evil One, the adversary of the family of the righteous, having seen the greatness of his witness and his blameless life from the beginning . . . managed that not even his poor body should be taken away by us, although many desired to do this and to touch his holy flesh. So the devil put forward Nicetes . . . to plead with the magistrate not to give up the body, "lest," so it was said, "they should abandon the Crucified and begin to worship this man" . . . not knowing that it will be impossible for us either to forsake the Christ who suffered for the salvation of the whole world of the redeemed, suffered for sinners though He was faultless, or to worship any other. For Him, being the Son of God, we adore, but the martyrs as disciples and imitators of the Lord we cherish as they deserve for their matchless affection towards their own King and Master. May it be our lot also to be found partakers and fellow-disciples with them. . . . And so we afterwards took up his bones, which are of greater value than precious stones or gold of the highest price, and laid them in a suitable place.[17]

15. St. Augustine, *Confessions,* VI, 2.
16. Dix, *The Shape of the Liturgy,* 344.
17. *Martyrium Polycarpi,* 17–19.

But the relics of the martyrs were cherished not only as keepsakes and mementos of the dear dead, but as a protection, a *munimentum*. On the occasion of the struggle of Perpetua, Felicitas and their companions in the arena of the amphitheatre of Carthage in 203, we find the martyr Saturus dipping the ring of the soldier Pudens in his own blood and handing it back to him as a *pignus* and a *memoria sanguinis,* because he had been very good to the Christians.[18]

Once the persecutions had come to an end and the faithful were able to celebrate at will the glorious past which remained so vivid in their memories, the martyrs (as we have already said) were given the most prominent place in these enthusiastic celebrations. And the relics played a large role. *Sanctus ubique beatorum martyrum sanguis exceptus est, et veneranda ossa cotidie testimonio sunt,* wrote St. Hilary in 361.[19] It would be superfluous to present all the facts which confirm this statement. Anyone who has the leisure to consult the texts of this period will find a great number of statements indicating the ardor with which the faithful gathered together the glorious remains of heroic fighters, *quae raptim sibi quisque vindicabat,* as the poet Prudentius says.[20] But the enthusiasm thus manifested carried the seeds of possible excess and abuse. What especially prepared the way for the indiscretions and deceits of later times was the custom, introduced very early in the East, of dividing the bodies of the martyrs into fragments, each one of which was thought to have the same virtue as the whole body itself.

It does not seem that this *cultus* of relics gave rise immediately to the strange abuses which sprang up later. But the popularity of this form of piety could not fail to encourage frauds resorted to for the sake of gain. In his treatise, *De opere monachorum,* St. Augustine criticizes certain mendicant wanderers who *membra martyrum, si tamen martyrum, vendunt.*[21] This traffic, which had become a profitable one, must have been extensive, for the civil government had to deal with it and bring it under some measure of control. A law of Theodosius forbids the transference of the bodies of the martyrs, or the cutting up of them into pieces, or the sale of these. On the other hand, it authorizes the erection of a *martyrium* over the tomb of dead persons regarded as saints.[22]

But even this permission to build a large monument over the

18. *Martyrium Perp. et Fel.,* 21, 3.
19. *Contra Constantium,* 9
20. *Peristephanon,* 6, 132.
21. St. Augustine, *De opere monachorum,* 28.
22. *Cod. Theod.,* IX, 17, 7 (dated Feb. 26, 386).

tombs of the martyrs led to difficulties. The cult of the martyrs betrays its connection with the cult of the dead by the fact that it was at first exclusively associated with the grave. Antiquity hardly knew what might be called an abstract worship of the saints. As we have already noted, the graves of the martyrs were the scene of assemblies and the destination of pilgrimages. The shrines built over the tombs became veritable basilicas. This created the rather odd situation that in the larger cities there were really two kinds of churches: within the city, the churches intended for community worship—what we would call parish churches—and on the outskirts of the city, the cemeterial basilicas of the martyrs. Sunday service was conducted not only in the city churches but often also in these basilicas of the martyrs, and the greater the enthusiasm for the cult of the martyrs, the larger the crowds that streamed to the cemeterial basilicas, to the neglect of the community churches.

There is extant an Egyptian document, the *Canones Basilii,* which presents us with a detailed picture of the situation, and the tension and strain it produced. The *Canones Basilii* takes a strong position against this excessive preference for the shrines of the martyrs:

> When uncultured people venture to deny the Catholic Church and its law at the very graves of the martyrs, and no longer desire to remain under its power, the Catholic Church cuts them off as heretics. Just as the sun does not need the lamplight, so the Catholic Church [the community church] does not need the corpses of martyrs. . . . The name of Christ is enough for the honor of the Church. . . .[23]

We do not know whether there was such a sharp crisis in other localities as well, but undoubtedly such differences and divisions must have been noticeable everywhere. And finally a solution to the difficulty was found.

This solution consisted in transferring the bodies of the martyrs, or at least parts of their relics, to the city churches. In Rome, and in the West in general, the authorities were somewhat reluctant to adopt such a practice. The West, accustomed to the strong sanctions of the Roman law against anyone who should disturb the bodies of the dead, contented itself with sending pieces of material (*brandea, palliola, sanctuaria*) which had been in contact with the tomb of the saint. A unique document from the period of Gregory the Great (590–604) shows how long this notion persisted. The *Papyrus of Monza* tells how Theodolinda, queen of the Lombards,

23. *Canones Basilii,* 33. (Riedel, *Die Kirchenrechtsquellen des Patriarchats Alexandrien* [Leipzig, 1900], 250.)

sent a priest named John to Rome to obtain relics of the Roman martyrs, but he got no first-class relic because the pope was opposed to opening the tombs and dividing the bodies of the saints; John had to be content with oil from the lamps which burned before the tombs. Gregory's attitude regarding relics may be gleaned from a letter which he addressed to the Empress Constantia. He refused her entreaty to have the head or some other part of St. Paul on the grounds that it was contrary to Roman custom to touch the bodies of the saints and unworthy of the respect due to them. He promised, instead, to send filings from the chains worn by the apostle during his imprisonment.[24]

In the East, civil regulations were not so strict and the translation of bodies and the division of relics took place at an early date without any direct opposition from the law. Constantinople, being but newly founded, naturally had no graves of martyrs. So the bishops of the city, starting with Chrysostom, were indefatigable in their efforts to obtain the bodies of martyrs from elsewhere and to bring them into the city. The Emperor Justinian turned to Pope Hormisdas and begged him for relics of the Princes of the Apostles and of St. Lawrence. His legates were refused with a sharp reference to ancient custom and the strict Roman law against disturbing the graves of the dead.[25]

Finally, however, Rome had to capitulate. After the fifth century, the outlying sections of Rome were subjected to continuous pillage due to the Lombard invasions and their attendant evils. People no longer dared to venture out to the graves of the martyrs, and so, in the course of the eighth and ninth centuries especially, the popes decided to transfer the remains of many of the martyrs to places of safety within the city. And it was not long before the bodies of the martyrs began to be dismembered, with churches far and near vying for relics, so that soon every church had its own relics and every altar was fitted with a *sepulcrum* wherein the relics of the saints might be laid. Thus the community churches merged with the churches of the martyrs and became martyr-shrines in their own right.

The veneration of martyrs and their relics thus affected the building of churches. According to the canon law now in force, every altar must have a sepulcher containing the relics of saints and closed up with stone. And so wherever divine service is held the Church militant on earth is united to the Church triumphant and with its foremost representatives, the martyrs.

24. *Ep.* 4, 30.
25. *DACL* 10:2436.

CHAPTER FIFTEEN

Christological Disputes and Their Influence on the Liturgy

THE fourth century is marked in Church history not only by the victory of the Church and the influx of the pagan masses, which now more or less quickly turned towards Christianity, but also by the disputes which raged within the Church in regard to the christological dogmas, disputes which were set loose by the rise of Arianism. These disputes attained special intensity and fierceness in the eastern part of the Roman empire. They led to divisions within the communities and to the expulsion of many bishops. They even entered the very sanctuaries of the churches, where they led not merely to the setting up of formulas, of professions of the faith, one against the other, but in many churches they influenced the prayers themselves and caused polemical changes to be made in them in this or that sense. We must remember, of course, that these disputes concerned a matter of vital importance to the Church's life, the very person of Christ our Lord.

By taking up and extending the train of thought of Origen and of Lucian of Samosata, Arius had arrived at the position that the Son is less than the Father. Although possessing divine dignity He is not from all eternity. He is a creature of the Father, made in time, hence subordinate to the Father. The doctrine caused tremendous reverberations. On the one hand, many hailed it, since it seemed that thereby the obscure mystery of the divine persons in the one divinity could be brought into harmony with the postulates of human reason. And at the same time, it was flatly contradicted and opposed by many, because it was manifest that it denied the traditional doctrine. At the Council of Nicaea, in 325, this doctrine was condemned. But it was not subdued; the whole century was still filled with this dispute and even in the following centuries the argument was carried on in one form or another. It is, of course, quite obvious that the decision about the Arian doctrine was of importance in the question of how prayer, and especially liturgical prayer, was to be organized. May the Son be honored and adored just like the Father? What position was Christ to occupy in the prayer? This question became all the more acute because the liturgical traditions of previous centuries contained formulas that seemed to favor the Arian point of view.

Liturgical prayer was addressed to God at first without relating it to any particular speculations; religion is worship of God and prayer is the raising of the soul to God. Further, in thinking of the mystery of the Most Blessed Trinity, God was called Father; in prayer He was addressed as the Father of our Lord Jesus Christ. This was quite correct; we can even say that if in prayer we address God as the prime fountain of all beings, then the Person who is thereby addressed is always the Father.[1] But even during the first centuries the point was insisted on that in liturgical prayer not merely was the name of God or of the Father to be mentioned, but in it the fundamental fact of the Christian order of salvation was to be expressed. Why do we appear before God with confidence? We appear before God with confidence only because Christ our Lord is with us and is leading us to the throne of God. Hence in liturgical prayer mention must be made also of Christ through whom we have "access" to the Father (Eph. 2:18).

Thus already in St. Paul, at least in two passages where he speaks of prayer or is himself praying, we find the phrase inserted: *per Christum*. "First I give thanks to my God, through Jesus Christ, for all of you" (Rom. 1:8). "To God who alone is wise, be glory through Jesus Christ for ever and ever" (Rom. 16:27). The same meaning must probably be attached to his saying that the faithful pronounce the *Amen* "through Him" (II Cor. 1:20); this manifestly means: the faithful, with the *Amen,* voice their consent to the prayer which has been offered to God through Christ. And it is not only St. Paul who uses this formula; it is also found in St. Peter (I Pet. 2:5) when he is exhorting the faithful to offer spiritual

1. Karl Rahner, "Gott als erste Trinitarische Person im Neuen Testament," *Zeitschrift für kath. Theologie,* 66 (1942), 71–88.

offerings, which are agreeable to God through Jesus Christ; or (in the same Epistle, 4:11) when he wishes God to be glorified by the faithful through Jesus Christ. The idea was, therefore, common in the primitive Church even from the beginning.

What exactly is meant when the Christian congregation offers prayer "through Christ"? This formula makes clear not only that Christ has redeemed us by the historical fact of His passion and death, but that He continues to be our Mediator with the Father. After His sojourn here on earth, He did not divest Himself of His human nature, but as man entered into the Father's glory. He is still one of us, the firstborn of new mankind, the head of Holy Church. And so He is with the Father "always living to make intercession for us" (Hebr. 7:25). When we pray, therefore, we do not pray alone, but our prayer reverberates as it were in His holy soul, and thus through Him, fortified, sanctified and ennobled through Him, fortified, sanctified and ennobled through His prayer, it reaches the Heavenly Father.

This mode of prayer is found in all the remnants of the liturgy preserved to us from the era of the primitive Church. We are not now referring to such turns of thought as are found in the *Didache,* wherein thanks is rendered to God "for the life and knowledge which Thou hast revealed to us through Jesus Thy Son"; for here there is question not of the ascent of our prayers through Christ but of the descent of God's gifts through Him. Similar expressions are found in our present day prayers. But even the prayers of the *Didache* end with a doxology, a note of praise by which the prayer is sent heavenward through Christ to God: "For Thine is the glory and the power through Jesus Christ forever."

In the account of Polycarp's martyrdom which the Smyrna community sent to the other churches, we find quoted the beautiful prayer which the holy bishop recited as he stood tied to the stake. After thanking Almighty God for the grace of martyrdom, he concludes in a loud triumphant voice, as though he were concluding a solemn liturgical prayer: [2] "For this and for all benefits, I praise Thee, I bless Thee, I glorify Thee through the eternal and heavenly High Priest, Jesus Christ, Thy beloved Son, through whom be to Thee glory, now and for all the ages to come. Amen." Thus we see that already in the first and second century, especially in the doxology with which prayers were concluded, the thought was expressed that our prayer and our glorification ascends to God through Christ.

2. *Martyrium Polycarpi,* 9. As to the authentic text of the doxology cf. J. A. Jungmann, *Die Stellung Christi im liturgischen Gebet* (Münster 1925), 127 f.

As the liturgy of the primitive Church continued to develop, so this type of prayer and especially the doxology developed also. The wording already included a mention of the goal of our prayer (God) and of the mediator of our prayer (Christ); now expression must be given also to the earthly sphere from which our prayer arises. This earthly sphere from which our prayer ascends is the community of the redeemed, holy Church. In Hippolytus of Rome, therefore, we find the doxology at the end of his prayers in this form: "That we may praise and glorify Thee through Thy child Jesus Christ [thus far this is also the form of glorification previously customary] through whom glory and honor is unto Thee, the Father and the Son with the Holy Spirit [this seems to be a more personal addition of Hippolytus; but now the continuation] in Thy holy Church (*in sancta ecclesia tua*), now and in eternity." Wherever in the *Apostolic Tradition* of Hippolytus, the solemn form of the final doxology recurs, there is always this addition, "In Thy holy Church." This formula, by the way, is found once also in St. Paul, with the same wording, in Eph. 3:21: "To whom be glory in the Church and in Christ Jesus." However, in later texts the same idea is more generally presented in another form. For what is the reason that the Church is able to glorify God worthily? It is the Holy Spirit dwelling in her; the Holy Spirit helps her to pray. Our Lord Himself said that the Father is seeking such adorers as adore Him in the "spirit" and in truth. So the Holy Spirit is included in the prayer formula and especially in the doxology, and this is formulated in the following words: "We praise Thee through Christ in the Holy Spirit."

This wording we find, for example, in Origen. Origen wrote a special book about prayer, referring not only to liturgical but above all to private prayer. He recommends that we conclude the prayer by "praising the Father of the universe through Jesus Christ in the Holy Spirit." The prayers contained in the eighth book of the *Apostolic Constitutions* are regularly constructed in this manner. This mode of praying was apparently well received also because of its expression of the mystery of the Most Blessed Trinity: We praise the Father through Christ in the Holy Spirit. The expression was made even more proportionate by putting the "Son" instead of Christ: We praise the Father through the Son in the Holy Spirit. The "Son" used in this connection was intended to signify, as it is evident, the Son in so far as He has become man; but it was possible also to obscure the humanity of Christ by emphasizing the divine Sonship.

As already mentioned, we possess in the *Euchologion* of Serapion a collection of Egyptian liturgical prayers from the middle of the fourth century. In this *Euchologion* the doxology already has this form, but it is frequently developed by stressing the divine nature in Christ. The author seems to delight in such phrases as: "Thy only begotten Jesus Christ, through whom there is glory and honor to Thee in the Holy Spirit in eternity." Or sometimes the name "Jesus Christ" is left out and the prayer simply says: "Thy only Begotten One"; thus in the prayer of the breaking of the bread: ". . . make us wise, God of mercy, through the participation in the body and blood; for through Thy only Begotten One there is to Thee glory and honor in the Holy Spirit now and in all eternity" (n. 14).

Now here was a possible starting point for Arianism. Arianism held, as mentioned, the doctrine that the Son is inferior to the Father, that, therefore, He is "subordinate" to the Father; Arianism is, therefore, also called Subordinationism. The Fathers like Athanasius, Basil, and other champions of the Catholic doctrine are, therefore, forced to defend the real and complete divinity of the Son, His unity in essence with the Father: *consubstantialis Patri,* as the council of Nicæa defined it and as we today still say in the Creed. A string of passages from Sacred Scriptures could be brought forward in evidence, together with the Church's tradition, to support this doctrine. The Arians, however, cited other passages, where the lowliness of the God-man is referred to; and they could point to the liturgical prayer, to the doxologies, everywhere customary in that time in the Catholic Church, which read: *Gloria Patri* per *Filium in Spiritu Sancto*. The Catholics themselves, so they said, grant that the Son is less than the Father, because they address their prayer to the Father *through* the Son, hence they consider Him as in some sort of intermediary stage below the Father.

It was not difficult to answer this. Without doubt there are numerous passages in the Bible in which it can be seen that the God-man stands below the Father. But this is precisely because He is the God-man; as man He is a created being, as man He subordinates himself to the Father's will, as man He prays just as He suffers and dies as man. And this is the meaning also of the *per Christum* or the *per Filium* of the liturgy: as man He is our Savior and High Priest, as man also He is now our Mediator with the Father.

We can, however, understand that these differentiations could not prevent a certain uneasiness from arising amongst the Christian people. People were troubled and uncertain. The Catholic party, therefore, began dropping the old doxology, not because it had been erroneous, but because it could be misunderstood and, as a matter of fact, was misunderstood. Therefore as a rule they no longer prayed (if we may reduce the various formulas into one scheme): *Gloria Patri* per *Filium* in *Spiritu Sancto,* but *Gloria Patri* et *Filio* et *Spiritui Sancto.*

The dispute was particularly fierce in the Greek area. Here the formula, as a rule, was so worded that at the end of a prayer the name of Christ was mentioned with the following phrase appended: δι' οὗ σοι ἡ δόξα ἐν ἁγίῳ πνεύματι. This was now replaced by μεθ' οὗ ἡ δόξα σὺν ἁγίῳ πνεύματι. Thus even the mention of the Holy Spirit was given a different wording, for soon after the Nicæan Council the dispute over the person of the Logos was quite logically carried over also to the person of the Holy Spirit. For the wording "In the Holy Spirit" was also misinterpreted in such a way that the Holy Spirit was taken as some impersonal force: hence that He was not a divine person.

This doctrine, too, was condemned by several synods and finally by the Second Ecumenical Council of Constantinople in 390. And in this sense, we still say in the Creed of the Mass the words: *Et in Spiritum Sanctum Dominum* (He too is Kyrios) . . . *qui cum Patre et Filio simul adoratur et conglorificatur* (He too is to receive all adoration and glory together with the Father and the Son). This simul-adoration was also expressed in the doxology with the formula: *Gloria Patri* et *Filio* et *Spiritui Sancto* or correspondingly in the Greek: μετὰ τοῦ Υἱοῦ, σὺν Ἁγίῳ Πνεύματι.

In Caesaria, during the episcopate of St. Basil, the Arians were bent on causing trouble, and here too they appealed to the doxologies. Then one day Basil started using beside the old doxology "through the Son in the Holy Spirit" (διὰ—ἐν) also the new one: "(to the Father be honor) with the Son together with the Holy Spirit" (μετὰ—σὺν). A storm was the consequence. The adversaries accused the bishop of using texts which were not merely foreign and novel, but which contradicted one another. Then, in the year 375, Basil wrote the work *De Spiritu Sancto* in which he thoroughly expounds the meaning of both the old and the new formula. In the older formula, prominence is given the voluntary abasement by which the Son descended down to us, becoming our Savior and Shepherd; therefore we can pray *through* Him. And in it, too, the Holy Spirit is pictured, so to say, as the place where we can adore God; therefore we can pray *in* Him. The new formula, on the other hand, expresses rather the adoration we owe equally to the Father and to the Son and to the Holy Spirit; and it harmonizes with the words with which we are baptized, "in the name of the Father and of the Son and of the Holy Spirit."

But the cause of orthodoxy was by no means won. Other bishops were hazy themselves as to how they should decide, or they themselves were inclined towards the heresy, or they did not have the courage to oppose it outright. In Antioch, the great capital of Syria, the conflict of opinions raged most fiercely. Bishop Leontius did not want to incur the displeasure of any party, so when he had to celebrate the liturgy in his cathedral, he was at a loss which doxology he should use at the end of the prayer. He had recourse to the expedient of pronouncing the words in question so softly and indistinctly, that even those standing next to him, could only catch the last words "from eternity to eternity." That such a dodge was no solution of the problem, Bishop Leontius himself was well aware; it is reported of him, in this connection, that he pointed to his white hair saying: "after this snow has melted away, there will still remain a lot of mud." This was about 350.

But by the end of the century, the dispute in the Orient had been settled with regard both to the dogmatic and the liturgical aspects of the question. The emperors at Byzantium no longer protected Arianism as had the Emperors Constantius and Valens, and so the Arian bishops were obliged to retire. After that, Arianism no longer mattered in the Orient. It was only in the West that it survived through the Teutonic tribes which had embraced a Christianity tinged with the Arian heresy.

With regard to the liturgy, the result in the Orient was the transition to the new anti-heretical and anti-Arian doxology. This was either employed in the form in which it had been evolved in the dispute against the heretics: Glory be to the Father with Christ together with the Holy Spirit (this form became dominant especially in the region of Antioch), or a form was used in which both the old and the new were combined: Our Lord Jesus Christ, through whom and with whom be to Thee glory together with the Holy Spirit (this form prevailed in Alexandria, hence in Egypt). Yet a third form arose in the Orient. It became dominant around Byzantium; although it probably came from Syria. This form is modelled after the words of Baptism in accord with our Lord's command in Matth. 28:19. In it the three divine persons are simply mentioned one next to the other. Thus at the end of many prayers in the Byzantine liturgy we find: "For Thou art a good and benevolent God, and to Thee we send up the glorification, to the Father and to the

Son and to the Holy Spirit, now and always and in all eternity." This same solution was connected with the psalmody, and the Western Church borrowed the formula as we use it at present: *Gloria Patri et Filio et Spiritui Sancto.*

From what we have said, it can easily be seen how deeply the Church's life was shaken by her dispute with Arianism, especially in the Orient. It even appears that not only were some words of the prayers altered, but also that the whole religious mentality of the people was deeply affected by this change, at least in the Oriental Church. For stress was now placed not on what unites us to God (Christ as one of us in His human nature, Christ as our brother), but on what separates us from God (God's infinite majesty). The doxology is not the only point in the liturgy where the effect of the dispute with Arianism became apparent. It was merely an issue where the reaction had been greatest. But the reaction is visible also in the calendar of feasts, only it is here much more calm and moderate. However, the war of defence against heresy in this case was not so much the cause, but much rather the occasion and additional incentive, to a further development.

This is particularly the case with regard to the two new feasts of Christ which arose during the fourth century both in the Orient and in the Occident: in the former the feast of Epiphany, in the latter Christmas. Of both feasts we have already spoken at some length. We cannot establish with certainty whether either or both were in existence before the beginning of the christological dispute. In any case, it was the zeal to defend Christ's divinity and greatness which helped towards the speedy dissemination of both feasts, so that the Oriental feast was even adopted in the Occident and vice versa, although both actually had the same theme. In both instances, the theme was the Lord's coming into the world, the Incarnation. But just as a ruler's coming is the occasion for welcoming him and for praising his greatness, so these feasts presented the occasion for praising the greatness of Him who came to us under the cloak of human nature. Especially in the feast of Epiphany can we notice this tendency, for the Introit of the Mass starts with the words: *Ecce advenit dominator Dominus.* It is to be noted that, in the Roman liturgy, the entire feast of Epiphany still keeps something of its primitive Eastern significance, so that it seems as though the principal mystery it has in view is actually the first manifestation of the Word made flesh.

But in the Orient the enrichment of the festive calendar did not stop there. While celebrating the birthday of a great son, it is almost a matter of course to honor also the mother. The worship of Christ, the Son of God become man, implies and compels a veneration of her who was the instrument of His Incarnation. A particular impulse toward such a move was supplied in the fifth century by the struggle against the Nestorian heresy which followed a course similar to that taken by Arianism a century earlier. Nestorius, who became Patriarch of Constantinople in 428, faced with the problem of explaining the union of the divine nature with the human in Christ, reduced that union to one of the moral order. He asserted that the Second Person of the Trinity, the Logos, and Jesus were two distinct persons, two individuals united in the moral person called Christ. His heterodoxy was unmasked when one of his priests openly preached against calling Mary "Mother of God" (θεοτόκος). The Catholic rejoinder was an increased devotion to Mary. The whole of the East arose to atone for the indignity to the Mother of God. St. Epiphanius had already warned against treating the Mother of God as a goddess and his admonition continued to restrain the faithful from giving to Mary the adoration that belongs to God alone. But this warning was not meant to restrain the faithful from celebrating with increasing solemnity the glories of her who was Mother of God and Mother of men. Churches were built in her honor, just as previously churches had been built over the tombs of the martyrs to honor the memory of these heroes of the Faith. It was in a basilica of the Mother of God that St. Cyril of Alexandria preached before the Fathers assembled for the Council of Ephesus what some regard as the greatest Marian sermon in the whole of antiquity.

It was in connection with the building of such churches to honor the Mother of God that two of the earliest Marian feasts took their origin. A church was built at Gethsemane, on the road between Jerusalem and Bethlehem, where pious belief placed the grave of Mary. This church was consecrated on the fifteenth of August, and from this festival of dedication, it seems, was evolved what later became the feast of the *Dormitio,* the Assumption of the Blessed Virgin. This feast was celebrated already before the year 500; it was extended to the whole Eastern Empire by the Emperor Maurice (+ 602).

Something similar occurred in the case of another Marian feast. A church was built in honor of Mary in Jerusalem, near the *Probatica piscina.* The feast of its dedication was held on September 8. This became the feast of the Nativity of Our Lady.

Two other feasts of oriental origin are linked with the Christmas cycle: the Annunciation (nine months before Christmas) and the

Purification (forty days after). Both of these feasts are basically feasts of the Lord. February 2 is still styled by the Greeks *Hypapante* (Ὑπαπαντή), that is, *occursus Domini,* the manifestation of the Word in human flesh to the aged Simeon. Its origin is probably to be sought in Jerusalem; here it was being celebrated about the year 400 when Aetheria pilgrimaged to the Holy Land. March 25 was also called *Annuntiatio Domini* or *Conceptio Christi.*[3]

These are the four great feasts of our Lady that originated in the Orient in the period between the fourth and sixth centuries, outgrowths, as we have seen, of the great christological conflicts against Arius and Nestorius. It was not until much later, after the time of Gregory the Great, that they were brought to the West, when countless priests and monks fled the pressure of the Islamic invasions and settled in Italy and Gaul.

We have to mention still another liturgical fact more or less connected with the reaction against Arianism, namely, the decrease in the reception of Holy Communion. It is a fact that during the fourth century there was a sharp drop in the reception of communion, especially in the East. St. Ambrose, while attacking those in his own church who communicated only once or twice a year, makes a pointed reference to this sad state of things: *quemadmodum Graeci in Oriente facere consuerunt.*[4] About the same time, Chrysostom gives vent to a similar complaint that few venture to approach the altar: [5] "In vain do we stand before the altar; there is no one to partake." But it is Chrysostom himself who makes us aware of a trend in oriental piety that might in some way account for this decline. Even before him, St. Basil the Great and other Greek Fathers had been using a language calculated to inspire awe and fear in the recipient. The pertinent chapter in Basil's *Shorter Rule* is captioned "With what fear . . . we ought to receive the Body and Blood of Christ." [6] Chrysostom speaks about "the terrible sacrifice," about the "shuddering hour" when the mysteries are accomplished, and about the "terrible and awful table." Those who approach the table of the Lord may do so only with fear and trembling.[7] Is it any wonder that the ordinary faithful, conscious of the pressures of their daily occupations, conscious too of their unworthiness before the divine majesty, lost courage?

This manner of expression is obviously related to the situation in

3. Baumstark, *Comparative Liturgy* (Westminster: Newman, 1958), 189 f.
4. *De sacr.,* V, 4, 25.
5. *In Eph. hom.,* 3, 4 (PG, 62, 29).
6. Basil, *Reg. brev. tract.* 172 (PG, 31, 1195).
7. Cf. Jungmann, *The Mass of the Roman Rite,* I, 39 and footnotes. See some further remarks on the question in the German edition of the same work, *Missarum sollemnia,* 4th ed. (Vienna 1958), II, 578.

the field of Christology. In the struggle with Arianism and Nestorianism, a struggle waged over the essential divinity of Christ, the eyes of church leaders were focused upon the point in danger, the divinity of Christ. They laid less and less stress on the human aspects of Christ's personality, on His relationship to us as friend and brother. For it was His divinity that had to be defended, and so the emphasis was on the rights that He exercises, His might as the judge of the living and the dead. Singular proof that there is a direct link between the opposition to Arianism and the peculiarly awesome attitude toward the Eucharist is furnished by the Monophysite groups. The Monophysites were the antithesis of the Arians; they completely denied the human nature in Christ and maintained only one nature, the divine. Now it is precisely the Monophysites who in their liturgy give the greatest expression to those sentiments of fear and awe towards the sacrament. The Thanksgiving should be begun in fear, in fear should one bow before the Lord, and for communion the rubric reads: Draw near in fear and partake in holiness!

So we must conclude that the struggle with heresy, though ultimately victorious, yet led in many points to losses. The conflict left its mark not only on the liturgy, especially in the East, but also on the peculiar character of oriental piety. This was probably unavoidable. But it is, and will always be, the task of the Church to do everything it can to restore equilibrium after the period of battle is over.

Section IV

DEVELOPMENTS SINCE THE FOURTH CENTURY

CHAPTER SIXTEEN

Ecclesiastical and Linguistic Provinces

THE existence of a busy traffic between the Christian communities from east to west, from south to north, and in all directions was a significant characteristic of the first centuries of Christianity. Christians availed themselves of the fine roads and the sea routes of the Roman empire; the Greek language was understood in all parts of the empire. St. Paul is an early example; he made numerous journeys far and wide. In the second century, we see the lines of communication within the Church running from Pontus to Italy, from Asia Minor to Gaul, from Phrygia to Africa. Thus it came about that also in matters liturgical a far-reaching harmony existed between the most distant churches.

About 154, Bishop Polycarp came to Rome from Smyrna to visit Pope Anicetus. The Pope invited the bishop to hold the divine service in the church in his stead. He was not afraid that the different character of his guest, the divergent rite, would create a disturbance. At the beginning of the third century, we see how Hippolytus wrote down his *Church Order* in Rome, presenting in it texts for the celebration of worship. One or two centuries later, we find these texts in use in Egypt and in Syria and, as has already been remarked, the Mass-formulary is today still in use in Abyssinia. We are thus able to establish that with regard to the liturgy there existed in the Church of the first centuries an extensive concord throughout the lands of Christendom.

We must not, however, imagine that for all particulars exact rubrics were then observed; much rather we must assume a fairly large measure of freedom allowed to each *liturgus* in word and rite. But in the main there was uniformity, and as we learn from the Easter controversy it was deemed intolerable if any one church differed in important matters from the rest. This was true, at least in general, not only with regard to the liturgy but also with regard to the whole range of ecclesiastical discipline.

But about the fourth century the situation changed; in the East and in the West various liturgies come into existence. And to some extent we can also understand this development. The communities had grown larger, the services were held with greater splendor, and thus they had to be organized with greater precision. The extemporary creation of the texts by the *liturgus* was possible and natural as long as the community was only an intimate circle of brothers and sisters. Larger communities demanded more organization. The wording of the prayers had to be fixed and permanent. This need was felt all the more deeply since the purity of the faith was jeopardized by the new heresy of Arianism and by the syncretistic Gnostic systems, which offered their own prayer formulas in numerous more or less popular devotional books, particularly in the apocryphal histories of the apostles.

Keeping this situation in mind, we can understand the canon agreed upon in the year 393 at a synod in Hippo in the presence of St. Augustine, and repeated at the synod of Carthage in 397: "In prayer one should not put the Father in the place of the Son, nor put the Son in the place of the Father; when standing at the altar one should always address the prayer to God the Father." There is question, therefore, of errors regarding the Trinitarian doctrine which had crept into the liturgical prayers; reference is probably to the apocryphal histories of the apostles from Gnostic circles which were then still very widespread. "And if a bishop is copying prayers for use in the liturgy, he should examine them beforehand with brother experts." [1] The individual bishop is, therefore, still allowed to select the liturgical texts, but the selection was to be controlled. This control is not further described; but it soon assumed definite forms.

Within the church organization, certain bishoprics began to stand out more and more as centers of authority in matters of church discipline and also in the liturgical sphere. This is the development of the metropolitan groups or patriarchal "dioceses." The beginnings of this development are traceable already in the times of the apostles. Antioch is, after Jerusalem, the first example of a

1. Mansi, III, 884; cf. 895, 922.

Christian community from which a large number of other communities was founded; these, therefore, have towards it the relationship of daughters to mother. Other metropolitan centers of a similar nature in the second century were Alexandria and Carthage, not to speak of Rome. They are, therefore, chiefly the great cities in the Roman empire which also became ecclesiastical metropolises. The opinion has been expressed that the Church from the very beginning purposely adapted her organization to the political organization of the Roman empire; this cannot be proved. But the fact remains that the ecclesiastical government was closely patterned on the civil. The great capitals were the natural centers. Here larger Christian communities could be formed, which could also raise the means for far-flung missionary activity. They were also the centers towards which the new foundations on their part gravitated. Here, around the bishop of the metropolis, the bishops of the daughter communities gathered for synods; in any case the bishop concerned presided, even though the synod took place outside his episcopal city. But the surrounding area was often larger than the corresponding political area or differently defined. Thus, for example, Mauretania did not belong to the African province, but the bishop of Mauretania came to Carthage for the provincial councils. Edessa in Syria, too, considered itself as belonging to the ecclesiastical unit of Antioch, although actually situated outside the Roman empire, in the kingdom of the Parthians.

As we see from the examples of Hippo and Carthage, liturgical questions were treated at these provincial councils. Whatever the explanation, the fact is that since the fourth century the differentiation of the liturgy was mainly along the lines of the patriarchal divisions. The great metropolitan or patriarchal churches became the centers of a particular liturgical rite. In these patriarchal sees an order of worship was fixed, and this order sooner or later became obligatory within the entire sphere of influence of the see in question.

But before we proceed to survey the individual liturgies which were thus formed both in the Orient and in the Occident, we must mention still another differentiating factor which, of course, had been operative before and alongside the influence of the metropolitan organization, namely, the language. In the world into which the apostles carried the glad tidings there were many peoples and many languages. Amongst those who were witnesses of the miracle of Pentecost, a number of languages are enumerated: "We Parthians and Medes, and Elamites . . . and Cretans, and Arabians, we have heard them speak in our own tongues the wonderful works of God." (Acts 2:9 f.). And amongst the elect assembled for the singing of the hymn of glorification to God and the Lamb, St. John sees "a great multitude, which no one could number, of all nations and tribes, and peoples and tongues" (Apoc. 7:9).

However, only three languages were of any importance for the development of the liturgy in Christian antiquity. They are the three great cultural and literary languages of antiquity, and the three languages in which the inscription on the cross over our Savior's head had been written: *hebraice, graece, et latine*—the Syro-Aramaic, the Greek, and the Latin languages.

It is to be taken for granted that the first community in Jerusalem held its divine services in the Aramaic or Syro-Aramaic language—in the language of the country—the language which our Lord Himself spoke, in which He prayed with the apostles and in which He taught them the Our Father: the language in which prayers were recited in the synagogue and the scriptures explained. The same holds good not only with regard to the Judaeo-Christian communities in Palestine, but also with regard to the whole missionary territory to the north and to the east, in so far as it was not Hellenised as were the bigger towns situated along the sea coast or its vicinity. Edessa became the center of a national Aramaic or Syrian Christianity. However, only very little information is extant about the origins of this community. About the year 190, there is an account of a synod of eighteen bishops of Osrhoëne, defining their attitude in the Easter controversy. In the year 201, there is mention of a church in Edessa which had been destroyed by a flood—it is the oldest account about a Christian cult-building. And only a little later the church of Dura-Europos came into existence, the ruins of which have been excavated during the last decades. As a literary memorial of this period of the third century, the Syrian *Didascalia* is preserved to us, telling us also something about liturgical matters. But it is not possible to speak of any period of real prosperity in the Syrian Church until the fourth century when Aphraat the Wise and St. Ephrem appeared on the scene. Aphraat, the "Persian Sage" (*fl.* 340), has left us a series of twenty-three *Demonstrations* in the form of questions-and-answers, which are of the highest value, abounding as they do in precious information regarding dogmatic and moral theology as well as liturgy and church history. St. Ephrem (d. 373), venerated as a *doctor ecclesiae,* has been called "The Harp of the Holy Spirit" because of his beautiful and inspiring hymns. Many of these were adopted for liturgical use, and so they may be said to have contributed to the shaping of the Syrian liturgy.

The Syrian liturgy, using the Syriac language, has survived to the present day. Today it is called the East Syrian liturgy, in contradistinction to the West Syrian, which was formed at Antioch in the Greek language. It is sometimes also called the Persian, because the Syrian Christians belonged to the Persian empire; during the sixteenth century, when some of those who used the rite returned to Catholic unity, it was given the name "Chaldean."

This liturgy must at first have had an entirely independent development. But later it was strongly affected by the Greek liturgies and thus underwent great changes; accordingly the greater part of the Syrian liturgy consists of translations from the Greek. In this mixed form, the East Syrian liturgy continues still as a living liturgy among the tiny handful of Nestorians and Chaldeans who live in Iraq—sorry remnants of a glorious past—and also, to some extent, among the "St. Thomas Christians" of Malabar on the southwest coast of India.

On the other hand, the Syrian liturgy for its part exerted a strong influence on the Greek and even to some extent on the Latin liturgies, chiefly with regard to singing in church: through a new mode of psalm-singing and through the composition of hymns. Whereas up to that time, as we have seen, ordinarily a solo singer chanted the psalm to which the people then responded, in the Syrian church the custom developed of having the psalms chanted by two choirs alternately, changing after each verse as we do even today. This is what is known as the antiphonal mode of singing. The innovation met with instant success, and gradually spread to various churches of the East and West.[2]

Another practice that appears to be Syrian in origin is the adding of the *Gloria Patri* after the psalms. This was probably intended as a verse with which the people could join in the singing of the psalm, because in general they did not know the psalms by heart.

We may note that the *Gloria Patri et Filio et Spiritui Sancto* which we add as a doxology to each psalm, corresponds exactly with the common doxology of the prayers in the East Syrian liturgy. In the Syrian liturgy, it is customary to end each prayer with a glorification of the Father, the Son and the Holy Spirit; and this form of the doxology (in prayer as well as in psalmody) was adopted into the Byzantine liturgy as a profession of the pure Trini-

2. Cf. *Vita Ambrosii*, 13. A very clear confirmation in Augustine, *Confessions*, IX, 7.

tarian faith. Thus the Syrian way of psalmodizing considerably influenced other liturgies.

This is also the case, and perhaps to an even greater extent, with regard to the composition of hymns. Not a few hymns of the Syrian liturgy, some by St. Ephrem, have later been translated and used in the Greek liturgies; and similarly they appear to have served as patterns for new compositions originating in the Greek language. The great melodist of the Greek liturgy, Romanos, has even been called by a modern scholar the very successor of the old Syrian tradition of the composition of hymns.[3] Even in our Latin liturgy, we meet with one case at least, it seems, of a hymn whose origin is Syrian: the *Popule meus* of Good Friday. If the strophes of the second half of this hymn are retranslated into the Syrian language, the result is that the initials of the strophes, as Baumstark showed, yield the letters of the Syrian alphabet in their regular order: for the Syrians, like the Hebrews, often composed their poetry alphabetically.[4]

The second liturgical language of Christian antiquity, one that subsequently obtained by far the greatest importance, is the Greek. As soon as the apostles stepped beyond the narrow confines of Palestine, they came within the sphere of Greek culture. The Greek language was the *lingua franca* as well as the literary language in the whole of the eastern half of the Roman empire and also of the various nations of the interior; it was understood even in the West. Therefore the written memorials of Christianity in the first centuries, beginning with the New Testament and the writings of the apologists, are in the Greek language. Greek, therefore, was the language also of the liturgy of this first epoch, and almost all the sources that inform us about the liturgical life of this period, till the fourth century, are composed in Greek.

The third liturgical language of Christian antiquity is the Latin language. But the Latin language appears in Christian literature (as far as original works are concerned) only towards the end of the second century, the writings of Tertullian being the oldest important examples. However, translations from the Greek go back to an earlier date. Latin Christianity first obtained greater importance in North Africa. And without doubt it was also here that the Latin language was first used in the liturgy.

At Rome—as we have seen—the Greek language was still

3. Baumstark, *Comparative Liturgy,* 104.
4. Baumstark, "Der Orient und die Gesänge der Adoratio crucis," *Jahrbuch für Liturgiewissenschaft,* 2 (1922), 1–17.

prevalent in the Christian community for two centuries. The first sources of the Christian liturgy of Rome are in Greek. It was not till about 250 that Latin came to the fore in Rome. And ever since Latin has been not only the language of church government, but for the entire West also the language of worship, the ecclesiastical language as such. Thus, the history of the Latin liturgies begins; there arose in the Latin language, besides the African and the Roman liturgy also an old Spanish, a Celtic, a Gallican and a Milanese liturgy. Later on we shall consider these more in detail.

Yet besides these three great liturgical languages—Syrian, Greek, and Latin—there existed in Christian antiquity also some lesser peoples among which the beginnings of a national liturgy can be established. There are, first of all, the Armenians who perhaps received Christianity from the apostles. At any rate even before the Constantinian peace, Christianity had been made the national religion of Armenia by King Tiridates (Trdat) III. There still exists a special Armenian liturgy in the Armenian language. But in the form which it has today and which, on the whole, is presented in the written documents since the tenth century, it is no longer an entirely independent liturgy; the greater part of its texts are derived from neighboring liturgies—from the Byzantine liturgy on the one hand, and from the Syrian liturgy on the other; in fact the Catholic Armenians have a liturgy hybridized by Latin customs. An Armenian liturgy fixed in writing was possible only since the origin of the Armenian script; this was invented between the fourth and fifth century. But unfortunately from this early stage of Armenian liturgy no documents have been preserved; most of what is extant dates from the Middle Ages.

One great group of nations, the old Germanic nations, is still of special interest for us. They, too, received Christianity only after the fourth century. We know with certainty that the Goths had their own church at Constantinople at the time of St. Chrysostom, where they praised God and heard the lessons and the sermons in their own Gothic mother tongue. Of the Vandals in North Africa we are told how they shouted out the *Kyrie Eleison* (*Frôja armês*) in their own language. Nevertheless we do not have any proof that there ever existed a complete Germanic liturgy in which the celebrant also used the vernacular. We do know for certain at any rate that the creation of a national Germanic liturgy was never considered when, after Chlodwig's baptism (496), the Germanic tribes within the sphere of western culture were converted to Christianity, to the Catholic religion.

Why was this? Why was a national liturgy in German unthinkable? We have seen that Christianity regularly used the vernacular, the language of the people in question, even in worship. It is therefore an error to say (as we sometimes hear said) that the Church prefers or preferred for worship a foreign, and if possible, a dead language. Why then no special Germanic liturgy for the Germanic peoples? We can suggest two reasons:

(1) The first reason is: The Christian liturgy needs a somewhat cultured language, a language in which one can write, and also express spiritual matters, a language with a literature; this was the case with regard to the Syro-Aramaic, the Greek and the Latin languages, but not with regard to the Germanic languages, at least in western Europe. Now the problem could have been solved, as was done by Mesrop for the Armenian language, by Ulfilas for the Gothic language, and later on by Cyril and Methodius for the Slav language: a literary language could have been created by translating the Bible into one of the existing dialects; but this was not done in the Occident. And so we come to the second reason.

(2) Since the fifth century, Germanic peoples had been penetrating into countries with Latin culture. Thus the Franks, the Burgundians and the Visigoths had overrun Gaul and Spain. Here they formed only a thin stratum within the population, and recognizing the superior culture of the Roman population they tried to adapt themselves to it. The governing groups quickly took to the Latin language, which must have appeared to them as the nobler and more practical language. In any case they soon understood Latin to some extent. So there was no pressing need for a Germanic language of worship. Latin remained the liturgical language because for several centuries it was the only written and literary language.

Now we have to return once more to that sphere in which the principle of church provinces or rather of patriarchates had been even more effective than the difference of language in producing a further division of liturgies. I refer to the countries where Greek was the liturgical language. Whereas, in the West, the leading centers, with the exception of Rome, gained but a small measure of importance, in the Greek Orient these centers were of decisive moment. We have seen already how two of these centers gradually took a leading position since they were also political centers: Antioch for Western Syria and Alexandria for Egypt.

At the council of Constantinople in 381, an effort was made to extend this organization. The canons outlined a plan to superimpose on the ecclesiastical system a wider division modelled on the political division of the empire which Diocletian had instituted. They set up new provinces fixing Caesarea as the center for Pontus, Ephesus for Western Asia Minor, and Constantinople for Thrace (i.e. the Greek Balkans). Indeed, Caesarea had already shown itself previously, during the time when St. Basil the Great was bishop there, to be a liturgical center. For here originated that Mass formulary which is known in the Orient as the Liturgy of St. Basil and which continues in use in Syria, in Egypt, and especially in the whole sphere of the Byzantine liturgy. Basil had given it the shape still employed today. For the rest, however, neither Caesarea nor Ephesus were able to maintain themselves as centers of a special liturgical province; both were outdone by Byzantium-Constantinople which, as the imperial city, continuously expanded its sphere of influence in regard to all ecclesiastical questions.

However, there was still another center that had always had a considerable importance, namely Jerusalem, which flourished again after Constantine and which was also awarded patriarchal rights by the council of Chalcedon (451). We are in possession of more detailed information about it through the *Peregrinatio Aetheriae,* written about the year 400. Pilgrims from all over the world returning home again from the Holy Land served as agents to diffuse a knowledge of the liturgy of the Holy City. The divine services in Jerusalem became the pattern for more distant churches. Thus, for example, the procession on Palm Sunday derives from the custom of Jerusalem. Similarly also the *adoratio crucis* on Good Friday. But Jerusalem, too, could not long maintain its position as a center of a special liturgical area; it was absorbed by Antioch, the great metropolis on the Orontes.

Thus there remained in the Greek Orient after the fifth century, three powerful centers of liturgical life: Antioch, Alexandria and Byzantium. From these three patriarchates, three different liturgical orders were formed on the basis of the common ancient tradition: the West-Syrian liturgy, the Egyptian liturgy and the Byzantine liturgy.

But division did not end with this triple partition. In the year 451, the heresy of Eutyches, Monophysitism, was condemned by the council of Chalcedon. The Monophysites were those antagonists of Arianism who, through their excessive zeal, fell into the opposite extreme: they not only maintained that Christ has a divine nature, but, going further, they acknowledged only one nature in Christ; what was human in Him was, according to them, absorbed by the divinity, just as a drop of water in a cup of wine is absorbed and dissolved. Quite logically, therefore, they did not practice the ancient custom of adding a little water to the wine, because—that at least was the explication given by later Armenian writers—that symbolizes the human nature as existing in Christ together with His divine nature. The Monophysites were condemned by the council of 451 already mentioned. Monophysitism had its headquarters in Egypt and here, as well as in Syria, the national instincts and the dislike of the regimen exercised by Byzantium coalesced with the theological question. Attempts to reach an understanding continued more than a century. But then the rupture became final, and it started to exert its influence also on liturgical life, especially by introducing a vernacular liturgy into the countries concerned. In the Syrian hinterland of Antioch and in the Egyptian hinterland of Alexandria, the liturgy began to be celebrated in the national language: Syrian in the former, and Coptic and Ethiopian in the latter.

Thus we have from that time on, a double Antiochene or West Syrian liturgy. On the one hand, there is the West Syrian liturgy in the Greek language, used by the Greek population principally along the coast. This Greek population adhered to the orthodoxy of the emperor; they were, therefore, mockingly dubbed Melkites (*Melech* = king) by the (Monophysite) national Syrians. The Melkites subsequently came more and more under the influence of the imperial city and thus finally lost their own West Syrian liturgy in the Greek language and adopted the Byzantine. Therefore the West Syrian liturgy in the Syrian language survives today almost exclusively among the national Syrians: they are for the most part Jacobites although there are also some Catholics. It also survives, but with many adaptations, among the Maronites in Lebanon who, by the way, have never been Monophysites.

Since this period, too, we have a two-fold Alexandrian or Egyptian liturgy. On the one hand there is the Alexandrian liturgy in the Greek language, used by the Greek population in the capital and on the coast. They, too, were called Melkites; their liturgy was also absorbed by the Byzantine liturgy and the Church itself was swept into the great Photian Schism. On the other hand, the same liturgy, but in the Coptic language and with an independent development, was used by the majority of the native population, the Copts, where it continues to survive. And besides there is also the Ethiopian liturgy used in the Abyssinian Mountains. The Ethiopian liturgy appears to be to a great extent an independent tradition and derived only in part from the Alexandrian liturgy.

This is a view of the more important divisions of the Oriental liturgies as they developed in the period to which we are confined, namely up to 600.

CHAPTER SEVENTEEN

The Oriental Liturgies

IN THE last chapter, we considered in outline the origin of the various Oriental liturgies and at the same time obtained a perspective of the geographical division and the relative strength of each liturgy. Now we shall consider their interior organization, their theological character, and some of the more important peculiarities of their liturgical forms. In general, we shall note only those characteristics which are more or less common to all the Oriental liturgies and in which they differ from our Roman liturgy. Only now and again shall we mention the peculiarities of some individual liturgies, and also include some later developments, because here there can be question only of a general survey.[1]

I. General Features

When considering the place liturgy occupies in the lives of Oriental Christians, we must first of all state that the liturgy is of much greater importance in their lives than it is in the lives of western peoples. For it is significant that if we wish to speak about Oriental Christianity, we speak as a rule simply about the Oriental Rites, meaning thereby the individual ecclesiastical communities as signified by their rites. The rite constitutes by far the most important expression of their ecclesiastical life. For in the rite the entire religious and ecclesiastical culture of these peoples, and even their national culture itself, is summed up.

1. Details can be found in Donald Attwater, *Eastern Catholic Worship* (New York, 1945), and in A. Raes, S.J., *Introductio in Liturgiam Orientalem* (Rome, 1947).

But this has its disadvantages and drawbacks. For one thing, it brings out the fact that other aspects of the Church's life and activity were cultivated only little or not at all, namely, theology, the sermon, catechesis, and Christian charity as an organized activity of the Church. Among the Jacobites of Syria, for example, sermons and catechetical instructions are not in use at all any more. Someone wishing to become a priest—and this is also the case in some Balkan countries—does not necessarily undergo any higher education; he merely has to learn the liturgical functions. A few weeks' stay in some monastery or with some parish priest suffices for this, and he can then be ordained, provided no other obstacle stands in the way. The Catholic communities, however, are of course much more exacting; and also among the separated communities there are today theological seminaries, but only a small fraction of the clergy is affected by them.

In general, we can say that even where ecclesiastical life is present, as a rule it has remained stationary at the stage it had reached at the end of Christian antiquity. This explains the archaic character of the Oriental liturgies. Nevertheless the Oriental liturgies, too, underwent one great crisis, strongly affecting them with regard to the manner of prayer; this was the crisis brought on by Arianism. We have already spoken about it, and some other matters concerning it we shall take up later. With regard to this point, our Roman liturgy remained much more conservative than all the Oriental liturgies. The Roman liturgy alone preserved during the time of the christological disputes and even to the present the ancient manner of praying *per Christum Dominum nostrum* in its pure form as used in the primitive Church. This is a matter of great importance. In other structural points, however, especially in the general structure of the Mass, the Oriental rites have kept many primitive characteristics which have disappeared from the Roman rite.

It might be well to mention at once one point in which the Oriental liturgies remained especially conservative, namely in the treatment of the language question. The Roman liturgy, too, remained conservative with regard to the language; it held on to the Latin language. The Orient, however, to a large extent maintained the principle by which antiquity had solved the language question: by keeping, as far as possible, the language of the people whom the liturgy is intended to serve.[2]

2. Cf. C. Korolevsky, *Living Languages in Catholic Worship* (Westminster, 1957).

However, this principle was not acted upon uniformly everywhere. For example, the East Syrians, who were most active missionaries, extended Christianity into Persia, but here, although Iranian was the vernacular, the liturgy on the whole remained in Syrian.[3] On the other hand when the Nestorian missionaries penetrated farther East, into China, we hear of a translation of the liturgical texts into the language of the country. The well-known Syro-Chinese memorial stone of Si-ngan-fu, dated 781, seems to speak of translating the liturgical books into Chinese. But when Christianity was propagated in India—in the territory of the Malabar coast where we find the so-called St. Thomas Christians—Syrian was generally retained as the liturgical language.

On the other hand, we have seen already, how within the Greek sphere, in the patriarchates both of Alexandria and of Antioch, towards the end of Christian antiquity the language of the people gradually gained the upper hand in the liturgy: in Syria the Syriac and the Coptic in Egypt. The Greek language had lost its importance in public life, and thus it was finally given up also in the liturgy. These people experienced, during the course of the Middle Ages, still another change of language: after the invasion of the Arabs who inundated the entire western Orient, the Arabic language gradually displaced the former vernaculars, both the Syrian and the Coptic. So the liturgy underwent another change, partly at least, for those portions of the liturgy destined in a special manner for the people. These were the lessons and the litanies which from time immemorial the deacon had said with the people. Now Arabic was introduced instead, and it has remained up to the present day.

These liturgies, therefore, did not insist on the whole rite being kept equally in one language; a language mixture was the result. The Coptic liturgy is particularly instructive in this respect; for here we have today a mixture of three languages; at various places there still remain in the Coptic liturgy the remnants of the original Greek liturgical language. For at the time when the first change of language, the transition from Greek to Coptic, was carried out, the introductory and concluding prayer formulas, in which the people in some way took part, continued to be spoken in Greek and to be answered by the people in Greek; for the people had already been used to it for centuries. The priest greets the people in Greek: Ὁ *κύριος μετὰ πάντων*, and the people answer in Greek. The priest still begins even the preface in Greek, and after the rest of the preface has been said in Coptic, priest and people say the *Sanctus*

3. A. Baumstark, *Vom geschichtlichen Werden der Liturgie* (Freiburg, 1923), 99.

together, again in Greek. All the rest the priest says in Coptic, except the lessons and the litanies, which are in Arabic. This order obtains not only among the separated Copts, but also among the Uniates, the Catholic Copts.[4]

What we have just considered is particularly important in the event that the Holy See might one day permit any extensive use of the vernacular in our Latin liturgy, e.g. for the lessons in the paschal vigil. For some people object to such a proposal on the grounds that it is not natural and contradicts the liturgical laws of style to use two different languages during one divine service. But who will dare to say that what we find in the Coptic liturgy, where three languages are used, is unnatural? In any case, we already use three languages in our Mass, for the *Kyrie* is Greek and the *Amen* and some other words are Hebrew.

Of all the liturgies, the Byzantine went furthest in its accommodation of the rite to the language of the country. The Byzantine is today by far the most important Oriental liturgy, for it comprises not only all the peoples of the Balkans, but also the whole of Russia. In the native country of this Byzantine liturgy, where Greek is still the language of the people, the Byzantine liturgy remained, of course, in Greek; it is so to the present day. But with the evangelizing of the Slavs, the liturgy began to be translated into the Slavic language (this has been the case since the ninth century). Old Slavonic (Staroslav) is today, as everyone knows, the liturgical language of the Russians, the Ukrainians, the Serbs, and the Bulgarians. It is not the language of the people of today, but is a language still understood on the whole by all Slavic peoples. Similarly the Greeks today speak modern Greek, although they use ancient Greek in the liturgy.

The principle of the sacred language was therefore operative here to some degree as it was in the Latin West. If a text has been used in worship for centuries, such a text has become sacred, and it is not likely to be changed as long as it is not necessary. This is a law which we can observe in all cults, even in pre-Christian ones. Thus it sometimes came to pass that a dead language was used in the cult. But it was not a dead language when it was first employed—this is a very important point. It was not introduced as a liturgical language *because* it was a dead language.

But it was not only in the case of the Slavic peoples that the Byzantine liturgy held to the principle of accepting the vernacular. Among the Melkites, the population in the region of Antioch which

4. F. E. Brightman, *Liturgies Eastern and Western*, I (Oxford, 1896), 164 ff.; 176. Cf. Attwater, *Eastern Catholic Worship*, 74 ff.

originally spoke Greek but later adopted Arabic as a vernacular, the liturgy has become Arabic. Among the Georgians in the Caucasus, the Byzantine liturgy has become Georgian. In the seventeenth century, the Rumanians adopted modern Rumanian as their liturgical language. The Byzantine liturgy is also celebrated not only in various Baltic languages, but also in Hungarian (Magyar), Finnish, Chinese and Japanese. Some of the orthodox immigrants into the United States even use English as their liturgical language. And even though some of these groups have returned to Catholic unity, they have retained their own liturgy and their own liturgical language: Rumanian, Hungarian, Arabic, Estonian.[5] The same also obtains, as is well known, with regard to the other Oriental liturgies: there are, therefore, within the Catholic Church also the Syrian, the Coptic, the Armenian, and the Georgian liturgical languages.

Another point of interest—particularly in view of the return of some of these oriental bodies to Catholic unity—is the *theological character of these liturgies*. As is well known, part of the Oriental church units separated themselves from us not only by schism, but also by heresy; the Syrians for the most part, as well as the Copts and the Ethiopians, became Monophysites. And in the theology of the adherents of the Byzantine rite, in Greek and Russian Orthodoxy, there are today some points of doctrine about which dogmatic differences arose. In spite of this, however, they all continued conservative in their liturgy, so much so that on their return to the Catholic Church, nothing or nearly nothing has had to be changed. The heresies in question hardly find any direct expression in the liturgy. The Armenians at the union merely gave up the practice of using at the Mass only wine without the admixture of water; for it was meant as a direct profession of the Monophysite heresy. But this was an exception. For the rest, almost the only change consisted in this, that some names were dropped from the diptychs—the names of those who led the people into, or kept them in, the heresy or the schism. All the rest can remain as before; at least such is the present policy of Rome. Thus is shown the magnanimity of the Roman Church, wishing to be the mother of all peoples, not wishing to touch the traditional national forms of the liturgy of these peoples.

But it was quite different during the Middle Ages and even at the beginning of the modern period. In those days, ecclesiastical officials and especially missionaries lacked this broad view and the necessary historical appreciation. They could not rid themselves of the notion

5. Raes, *Introductio,* 207 n. Cf. also C. Korolevsky, *op. cit.,* 41 f., 51 ff., etc.

that the Orientals could become Catholics only if they adopted from the Latin Church as much as possible of her liturgical practices. And those peoples themselves had the same idea. The Maronites borrowed the chasuble in its western form, although this is neither better nor more beautiful than the Oriental chasuble. The Armenians introduced Psalm 42 at the beginning and the Gospel of St. John at the end of the Mass. The Ukrainians, too, introduced many Latin customs. In many instances it was the Orientals themselves who did the adopting; they patterned themselves on the missionaries sent to them. Today it is Rome that tries to protect the Oriental liturgies within the Catholic Church, especially against the Latinizing tendencies emanating frequently from overzealous converts from these rites.

But now, let us proceed to take up some particulars of the Oriental liturgies, especially those in which they differ from our Roman liturgy.

(1) There is first of all the *use* the Orientals make of Holy Mass: they use it much more sparingly. Daily private Mass by the priest alone is almost unknown outside the Uniate groups. As a rule Mass takes place only if people have gathered for Mass. Hence each church has only one altar, and if more priests are assembled, they celebrate together; this is the custom of *concelebration*. Concelebration does not necessarily mean that all the priests present equally perform the whole liturgy of the Mass including the words of consecration, or that they say all the prayers together, as is the custom in the Latin rite. In the Orient, concelebration is in general not so understood. The model of concelebration is simply the solemn Mass of the bishop surrounded by his clergy. There each cleric has his function; some tasks of the celebrant are distributed to concelebrating priests: certain orations, the incensations taking place at various times; and then especially all receive Holy Communion. It is only since the end of the 16th century that Uniate communities began to link the oriental type of concelebration with the western idea of co-consecration and with the practice of pronouncing the words of consecration all together; and eventually in the 17th century this idea and practice spread outside the Uniate communities to the Russians.[6]

(2) One further important peculiarity of the Oriental rites is the use of the *deacon*. At every Mass said for the people, not only a

6. P. de Puniet, "Concélebration liturgique," *DACL*, 3, 2470–2488; J. A. Hanssens, "De concelebratione ecclesiastica," *Periodica de re morali, canonica, liturgica*, 16 (1927)–21 (1932); A. Raes, "La concélebration eucharistique dans les rites orientaux," *La Maison-Dieu* 35 (1953), 24–47.

server but a deacon assists. And the principal task of this deacon is to establish contact between the priest at the altar and the assembled congregation. The Oriental liturgies, therefore, do not ignore the people, as we do at least in the older praxis and as some liturgists, so-called, still seem to advocate. Neither are they content to have the celebrant address the congregation several times and thus give them occasion for replying; they also have the deacon acting, as it were, as leader of the prayers, to assist the people in following the celebration; thus the people are more intensively included in the procedure, especially since these prayers as well as the lessons, as we have seen, are in a language understood by the people. Hence an active participation of the people is included in the plan of the liturgy from the very start. This arrangement we find in the Orient as early as the fourth century. This active participation, however, is not such that the people immediately take part in the prayers of the priest and in the exact train of thought of the liturgy; but the people remain, as it were, with the deacon one step lower; they say prayers of petition; together with the deacon they recite litanies—or as they are called in the Greek liturgies: *Ektenes*—each time the priest starts some important prayer. The deacon announces the object of the petitions: Let us pray for the peace of the church; let us pray for the bishop; let us pray for suitable weather; and the congregation reply to each of these petitions with the invocation: Lord have mercy (*κύριε ἐλέησον*) or with some similar prayerful exclamation. Such litanies are said in the Byzantine liturgy at the beginning, after the Gospel, after the Great Entry, before the *Pater Noster,* after the communion. In the other Oriental liturgies, they are a little less frequent. The spread of the dialogue Mass, with its lector or leader reciting certain texts in the vernacular, is at last bringing to Latin Catholics an arrangement which the Orient has always possessed.

(3) One further fundamental difference between the Roman and the Oriental liturgies consists in the manner in which the *offertory* at Mass is treated. The Oriental liturgy has no offertory properly so called, within the Mass. Although an offertory-procession of the faithful had been customary in some places, it either disappeared long ago or it takes place before the Mass. In the place of our offertory, Oriental liturgies have the Great Entry. The sacrificial gift is prepared before the beginning of the liturgy proper, on a special table and with a more or less complex rite. This rite is very complicated in the Byzantine liturgy; accompanied by certain prayers and words taken from Sacred Scripture, especially from

Isaias' prophecy of the passion, certain pieces are cut off from the bread by means of the sacred lance and arranged in order on the sacred discos: one larger piece, called the lamb (ἀμνός) and several smaller pieces. The chalice is also made ready. After the Gospel, the offering is transferred in a solemn procession from this table to the altar; candles and torches are carried in front; the deacon follows, carrying the sacred discos, holding it high above his head, and then the priest with the chalice; they enter the nave of the church by the northern door of the Iconostasis put up between the sanctuary and the people, returning again by the central door to the sanctuary in order to deposit the oblation upon the altar. In the meantime the so-called Cherubikon is sung: ". . . let us now lay aside all worldly cares, that we may receive the King of the universe, who comes escorted by unseen armies of angels. Alleluia." This Cherubikon was already being sung in the sixth century. And the procession itself is described about the beginning of the fifth century by Theodore of Mopsuestia, who explains its allegorical significance. This is the Great Entry, in contradistinction to the little entry which takes place earlier, when the lessons are to begin and the Gospel book is similarly transferred in procession to the altar.

In regard to the gift itself, there is, of course, the great difference between Latin Christianity and the Orient, that the Eastern liturgies use fermented bread. This practice, it seems, was prevalent throughout Christendom in the early ages of the Church, both East and West. The faithful could, therefore, bring their ordinary white bread to church for use at the altar. It was not until medieval times that the West adopted the use of unleavened bread, led to this not only by considerations of symbolism but because the biblical accounts, too, indicate unleavened bread (ἄζυμα). At the Last Supper, "on the first day of the Azymes," unleavened bread was obviously employed. In olden times, nobody doubted the validity either of the one or the other matter. But in the twelfth century, the Greeks started to reject the use of ἄζυμα as heretical. The ἄζυμα, they jibed, are really ἄψυχα; if the leaven is missing, the soul is missing; to use unleavened bread is to deny the soul of Christ, etc. Later on, however, this controversy lost its intensity.

II. The "Anaphora"

And now we come to the most important part of our discussion, the description of the sacrificial portion of the Oriental Mass. What precisely does the core of the Mass look like—that part, namely, which corresponds to the primitive *eucharistia* of the ancient Christians?

In general, it can be said that the structure of the ancient Eucharistia has been kept very faithfully. (We speak in the main only of what is common to all the liturgies and of what belongs to the fixed stock of all the liturgies.) Everywhere the ancient introductory dialogue is preserved: *Sursum corda, Gratias agamus*—mostly with some elaborations. Then the prayer of thanksgiving starts, followed by the *Sanctus*. The prayer of thanksgiving is generally continued (in the Syrian and Byzantine liturgies) by enlarging on the work of Christ. Also after the words of institution, the train of thought is identical with that in the primitive examples: expression is given to the offering of the sacrifice and a prayer made for a fruitful communion. In this respect there is, therefore, no substantial difference from our liturgy, even though the outward picture differs somewhat, because, for example, the preface is spoken quietly and the words of consecration are said aloud (thus in the Byzantine liturgy). Also we find in all Oriental liturgies, just as in our own, that somewhere within this prayer are inserted the intercessions (a Memento for the living and the dead).

One difference, however, is very important, and it also became the subject of theological controversy. This is the *Epiclesis*. We shall only consider the liturgical side of this question.

In each Mass, according to Christ's institution, there are two points where the divine omnipotence is conjoined to the action of the priest, thus causing a supernatural effect: the consecration and the communion. Hence it is very natural that in the priest's prayer some acknowledgment should be made of the fact that here God Himself has to act. And its natural form is a petition, a petition addressed to God, that He effect the consecration, that He sanctify our souls in communion. This petition we may call *epiclesis,* an invocation of God by which that effect is solicited. If the petition concerns the consecration we call it a consecration-*epiclesis,* if the communion, a communion-*epiclesis*.

A communion-*epiclesis* is found at the end of the *eucharistia* of Hippolytus of Rome: may God grant to all who partake that they be filled with the Holy Spirit. With regard to the wording, the *epiclesis* can be formulated in many ways: simply that God may bring about the effect; or that He send His Holy Spirit over the gifts or into the souls of the recipients. During the fourth century, it became customary in the wide regions of the Orient to insert an *epiclesis* in the Mass in the latter form. Hence with regard to the *epiclesis* we can now distinguish three great liturgical regions: the Roman, the Egyptian and the Syro-Byzantine.

In the Roman liturgy, since most ancient times, we have the very simple first form, both before the consecration and before the communion. In the *Quam oblationem* we pray that God may make our oblation *adscriptam, benedictam,* etc., and change it into the body and blood of our Lord. In the *Supplices* after the consecration we pray that God may fill all recipients with every blessing: *omni benedictione caelesti et gratia.*

In the Egyptian liturgies, there exists also since ancient times a very pronounced *epiclesis* before the consecration immediately after the words of the Sanctus: heaven and earth are full of Thy glory. The prayer continues: Fulfill also this oblation through the descent of Thy Holy Spirit. And after that the words of consecration follow immediately. In Egypt, there seems to have been originally no communion-*epiclesis,* at least not in the form of an invocation of the Holy Spirit.

The homeland of the solemn and elaborate *epiclesis* after the words of consecration in the form of an invocation of the Holy Spirit is the Syrian (or the Syro-Byzantine) liturgical region. Here it must have become customary towards the end of the fourth century (not earlier) to insert such a prayer in the place of a more ancient formula. In this older form, the prayer must have been much like the prayer in the Roman rite, namely a petition that God may accept the oblation and grant us a fruitful communion.[7] Out of this was evolved a new form of petition, that God may make of the offering Christ's body and blood through the coming down of the Holy Spirit, and so grant us a fruitful communion. The point to note here is that the petition has been developed into a consecration-*epiclesis,* or rather into a consecration-plus-communion-*epiclesis,* and yet has been allowed to retain its place after the words of consecration. The reason for this phenomenon may be that no suitable place was found before the words of institution, because an *epiclesis* would here have interrupted the christological part of the prayer of thanksgiving. So the consecration-*epiclesis* was simply connected with the communion-*epiclesis*. From what has been said, it is clear that here there is no question of a tradition dating back to Christian antiquity. At the same time there is nothing to show that the new type of *epiclesis,* so placed, implied any theological opinion regarding the moment of consecration. Christian antiquity

7. Cf. Jungmann, *Mass of the Roman Rite,* II, 190 ff., 233 f. and notes.

as a rule gave but little thought to such problems as the exact moment of the consecration. Precisely for this reason it was possible to insert the *epiclesis* where it is actually found.

How the words of institution were interpreted during the early days of the Oriental liturgies can be seen from the ceremonies with which of old they were accompanied. Just as in our own liturgy, the words of institution are not simply spoken as an historical account of things which happened long ago. Instead the priest takes the bread into his hands (or, more accurately: he lays it on his hands; thus already in the fourth century) as Christ had done. He imitates Christ's actions: the looking up to heaven, the blessing. Among the West-Syrians and the Copts, even the breaking of the bread is re-enacted here. And when the priest says the words: take and eat (or: drink of it), in the Byzantine Mass, the deacon points to the bread and to the chalice in the priest's hands, as if he would say: it is *this* bread and *this* cup in the hands of the priest to which the words he is now saying refer. And after the words have been said the people cry "Amen," which cannot mean anything else but a profession that *hic et nunc* the sacrament has been performed as Christ the Lord had performed it.[8]

That our interpretation of these ceremonial actions is justified we can learn from the later history of the controversy. For later on, when the Orient began to place all the consecratory power in the *epiclesis,* there was a tendency to moderate the ceremonies accompanying the consecration and to abolish the acclamations. But these older ceremonies and acclamations really demonstrate the secondary position of the *epiclesis* and, therefore, the Uniate churches have all retained the *epiclesis* (interpreted in its ancient Catholic sense).

The Oriental liturgies have also retained some old traditions in the communion part of the Mass. The fraction has generally remained an important rite accompanied by special prayers. Then a special blessing is pronounced over the faithful wishing to receive Holy Communion. The priest then holds up the Lord's body saying: *sancta sanctis* (τὰ ἅγια τοῖς ἁγίοις); thus he invites the faithful to receive. Communion is given under both species.

There you have in bold outline the invariable pattern which has been basic to all Oriental liturgies since the fourth century and which has been preserved everywhere up to the present day.

But now we must discuss the question of how this scheme is supplemented from occasion to occasion. In other words, we must

8. Jungmann, *Mass of the Roman Rite,* II, 204 f.

now study the use the Oriental liturgies make of variable texts. In so doing we shall at the same time have occasion to consider more closely some peculiarities of individual liturgies of the Orient.

We are used to associating with the thought of Oriental liturgies the idea of uniformity, unchangeableness and monotony. Whereas our Mass changes day after day, the Orient constantly repeats the same invariable formulary. We are wont to describe this as a typical expression of the paralysis that grips Oriental Christianity. What is the truth in this matter? Not very much. In fact the Oriental liturgies are, in some ways, far richer in variety than ours, and even in that part of the Mass where we have an almost unvaried "canon." As variable texts, the lessons, the songs and the prayers come into consideration. Let us consider them one after the other.

(1) The lessons:

The readings from Sacred Scripture change in the Oriental liturgies in about the same way as with us. On feast days they are adapted to the feast. In the Byzantine liturgy, they consist, as with us, of two lessons, an epistle and a gospel. In other liturgies, the lessons are generally more numerous—three, four or more. The West-Syrian Mass has—or at least had in former times—as many as six lessons: three from the Old Testament and three from the New. We have already seen that in most of these liturgies the lessons were read in a language understood by the people, and in the Orient this is all the more important, because the sermon and catechesis are neglected.

(2) The songs:

In this respect great differences exist between the various Oriental liturgies. The Coptic liturgy is not rich in songs; as a rule there is no choir, so that only the people sing, and always the same songs. The Byzantine liturgy, on the contrary, having been the liturgy of the imperial court and having evolved a rich ceremonial in other points, is also rich in songs. In the ordinary liturgy, the presence of the choir is presupposed. Some of the songs of the Byzantine liturgy are invariable and recur again and again: the *Cherubikon,* the *Sanctus;* also the *Trisagion,* which we sing on Good Friday (Ἅγιος ὁ θεός) and which is usually sung in the beginning of the Mass; likewise another hymn of praise to Christ: the *Monogenes.* Besides these, however, there are several hymns scattered through the service which vary with the ecclesiastical year.

(a) At the very beginning, before the lessons, three antiphons are sung; this is really an abbreviated *hora* serving as preparation for the liturgy; just as among us Terce is sometimes sung as an introduction to a Pontifical High Mass. This song consists of three psalms or parts of psalms changing according to the festive season and interspersed with antiphonal verses which also change.

(b) Before the two lessons, the epistle and the gospel, there is again an antiphonal song corresponding to our Gradual and Alleluia.

(c) In the çanon also, the Oriental liturgies have a kind of *Communicantes* wherein our Lady is mentioned in the first place. This mention of the Blessed Virgin is connected in the Byzantine Mass with a special song by the choir; the priest loudly says the words (we render them in Latin): *Imprimis sançtissimae, immaculatae, benedictae, gloriosae Dominae nostrae Dei genitricis semper Virginis Mariae;* here the choir begins a Marian hymn, which changes according to the festive seasons. It is called the *Megalynarion* because in it the word Μεγαλύνει ("Magnificat") plays a part.

(d) Also at the Communion at least one varying hymn is sung, the *Koinonikon.*

(e) And at the end there follows a concluding song, also variable, the *Apolytikion.*

In the songs, therefore, there is quite a large variety, much greater than in our Roman liturgy.

(3) We come now to the *prayers* of the priest, the formularies he employs in saying Mass. In our study of the incidence of variety in these formularies, we must clearly distinguish the Oriental rites not only from the Roman but also among themselves. For here there exist great differences.

Let us first turn to the *Byzantine* liturgy. Here the prayers vary very little; there are only two formularies comparable to our *Ordo Missae.* The *Proskomide* and some other parts in the beginning of the Mass are not subject to any change and so both formularies are practically identical in the pre-anaphoral part. After that, the prayers in the two formularies differ, establishing contact again only in a few points—for example, in the *Sanctus,* or at the *Pater noster.* One formulary is called the Liturgy of St. John Chrysostom; it is the ordinary formulary used throughout the year. The other one is called the Liturgy of St. Basil; it is used only a few times in the year, chiefly on the Sundays of Lent; it is the longer and more solemn of the two. Of St. Basil's liturgy we have already spoken, and we ascertained that it indeed goes back to St. Basil, that it even existed before him, because he merely rewrote it. Its origins, therefore, reach back at least to the beginning of the fourth century.

The liturgy of St. Chrysostom, on the contrary, very probably has nothing to do with St. Chrysostom; it is of a later date and it has been given this name only in his honor. In these names, Liturgy of St. Basil and Liturgy of St. John Chrysostom, the world "liturgy" is taken in a different sense from the one we are used to: liturgy here means Mass, Mass-formulary; the Greeks and the Slavic peoples, hence the followers of the Byzantine rite, use the word "liturgy" almost invariably in this sense of "the Mass."

The other Oriental liturgies are all richer in Mass formularies than the Byzantine; they all possess a veritable stock of them. In making this statement, we must distinguish between the Fore-Mass and the Mass proper. In the Fore-Mass, the sacerdotal prayers remain much the same in all the Oriental liturgies; only the lessons and the songs vary. In the Mass proper, the sacrificial Mass, however, the prayers of the priest are subject to change. This part of the Mass has also a special name; it is called *anaphora, oblatio*. Hence the various formularies which the priest can use are called by this name. But these anaphoras do not differ among themselves by giving expression perhaps to a certain festive mystery; they are simply parallel creations formulating the identical theme but in a slightly different way. We might compare them to the various Sunday orations of our Roman liturgy which, although they vary in their wording, yet always formulate the identical idea in a different way.

One thing, however, is remarkable with regard to these Oriental anaphoras: each is conceived as a whole. True, there are a few individual prayers at the beginning of this part of the Mass, like a prayer at the uncovering of the chalice, a prayer at the kiss of peace (which in the Orient always takes place at the beginning of the sacrificial Mass). But then comes the ancient *eucharistia*, introduced by the exhortation: *Gratias agamus* (Εὐχαριστήσωμεν τῷ κυρίῳ) and continuing uninterrupted to the *Amen* before the *Pater noster*. After the *Pater noster* there is again a smaller series of individual prayers surrounding the communion, and then the Mass comes to a close. In this way, the theme of every Mass celebration stands out in the principal part of the Mass, in the anaphora, much more strongly than is the case with us: the glorification of God, and above all the thanksgiving for the work of Redemption. Especially after the *Sanctus* up to the words of institution, the redemptive work is described in ever new phrases in most of the formularies (especially of the Syrian liturgy).

Let us now briefly consider each one of these liturgies. The *East-Syrians,* separated from the Catholic church since 431 as Nestorians

—the Uniate branch are called Chaldeans—have only three anaphoras. The one considered to be the oldest is the anaphora "of the apostles Addai and Mari." It probably does not go back to these legendary apostles of Syria, but seems to have come into existence only much later. This anaphora is famous—or notorious—because of an altogether singular peculiarity it exhibits: in the oldest manuscripts that contain it the words of institution are lacking.

The liturgy of the *West-Syrians,* the liturgy from the Greek patriarchate of Antioch, possesses a rich store of anaphoras, not all of them ancient. The basic formulary is the so-called anaphora of St. James, named after the Apostle James, the first bishop of Jerusalem; this formulary originated in Jerusalem and was already in existence in the fourth century; for St. Jerome, living as a hermit in Bethlehem, once quotes a passage from it, and it is also quoted in the Mystagogical Catecheses ascribed to St. Cyril of Jerusalem. In the course of time, new anaphoras were composed according to the pattern of the anaphora of St. James, at first in the Greek language. Since about the seventh century, these anaphoras have been translated into the Syriac language and other anaphoras like them were then composed in the Syriac language.

The Syrians had become Monophysites, but before long the Monophysite heresy had been practically abandoned, and all that remained of it was only the schism from the main body of Christendom. In any case, during the following centuries the Jacobites developed a flourishing ecclesiastical life, cultivating even a little theology, especially exegesis. Chiefly, however, it was the liturgy which they developed by the composition of liturgical poetry and new anaphoras. This finds expression in the history of Syrian literature. Whereas among us the spiritual leaders of the advanced Middle Ages wrote commentaries on the Sentences and theological *Summae,* Syrian history of literature boasts concerning each important West-Syrian bishop that he composed some anaphora formulary. Altogether more than seventy anaphoras of the West-Syrian liturgy are known, though not all of them are still in use; some of them have been published in Latin by Renaudot. The papal Institutum Orientale began in 1939 to work on a Syro-Latin critical edition of all these anaphoras, *Anaphorae Syriacae,* but because of lack of funds the undertaking could be continued but slowly.

Finally, let us take a look at the *Egyptian* liturgies proceeding from the patriarchate of Alexandria. The fundamental formulary is here the so-called "anaphora of St. Mark"; this is very ancient, though, of course, its relationship to St. Mark is highly improbable.

The extant manuscripts, it is true, do not date before the twelfth century, but in the year 1928 a fragment on papyrus was found dating back to the fourth century. Branches of the Alexandrian liturgy are the Coptic and the Ethiopian liturgies.

The *Copts* still use the anaphora of St. Mark. In addition they use two other anaphoras; one of them is an ancient form of the anaphora of St. Basil which we already know; the other, the anaphora of St. Gregory, is quite singular in that its prayers are addressed to Christ from beginning to end. Although there is nothing contrary in this to any Catholic dogma—hence the Uniate Copts also use this formulary—it is quite striking in a Mass formulary because in the Mass we are offering up Christ's Body and Blood to God, the heavenly Father. For this reason we find that the liturgical prayers of the ancient Church, at least in as far as the sacrifice of the Mass is concerned, are generally addressed to God the Father. Various explanations have been suggested for this exception. It was sometimes taken as a sign of great antiquity, but quite wrongly so. Another explanation is much more probable: the anaphora of St. Gregory originates from the sixth century when Monophysitism flourished; the Monophysites, to be logical, were bound to arrive at some such formulation, in which Christ's divinity alone is taken into consideration, and the distinction between Christ and God (which is stressed in prayers addressed to God "through Christ") was obscured. Hence addressing the Mass to Christ was quite natural.

The *Ethiopian* liturgy of the Christians in Abyssinia is also derived to a certain extent from the Alexandrian liturgy, and the Ethiopians, too, had been dragged into the Monophysite heresy. Here a greater number of anaphoras are in existence than among the Copts: seventeen formularies are mentioned, although not all of them are used. Amongst them is the anaphora of St. Gregory just mentioned. But the Ethiopian liturgy has gone a step further; there is an anaphora, the anaphora of our Lady, in which all the prayers from beginning to end are addressed to the Blessed Virgin. The explanation is, of course, the same: the more exclusively Christ's divinity is considered, the more one is inclined to elevate Mary, not only by honoring her as the Mother of God, which she really is, but by attributing to her a kind of mediatorship which in fact belongs to Christ. For the same reason, therefore, the Abyssinian church developed an extraordinarily large number of Marian feasts and an exceedingly rich Marian poetry. Of course both the forms of the festive celebrations and the individual Marian poems may well be altogether orthodox; even the anaphora of our Lady contains nothing heretical, and is, therefore used also by the Uniates. As a matter of fact we might liken it to the custom of some Latins of reciting the Rosary during Mass, only here it is the priest who is doing so—and a beautiful Rosary it certainly is. But neither the one nor the other is an ideal form of worship.

Nevertheless the Ethiopian liturgy, apart from such results of a secondary evolution, has preserved some very precious things from the ancient Christian treasures; I mentioned already earlier that the *eucharistia* written by Hippolytus of Rome about 215 is still in use in Abyssinia, although now somewhat amplified; it is the Mass formulary which they ordinarily use under the name of "Anaphora of the Apostles."

CHAPTER EIGHTEEN

The Latin Liturgies

THE same diversity of liturgical forms which we found in the Orient we also find in ancient Western Christendom. In the fifth and sixth century, the West, too, was still far from that unity and strict uniformity of the liturgy, from that centralized regulation of all questions of worship on the part of Rome, which we are used to today. Rome, it is true, was conscious of the fact that she had been entrusted with the guidance of the Church—and not only of the Church of the West. The attitude of the Popes in questions of faith and also in many questions of discipline makes this abundantly clear. But, generally, Rome did not exercise her rights in questions of worship in those days or for many centuries to come.

Thus also in the Occident we have various liturgical domains which, save for certain fundamentals, are held together only by the unity of the Latin language. Latin remained the only liturgical language in the West, just as, in the Orient, Greek had been for a long time. Yet in the West the liturgical provinces were not so clearly formed by leading metropolises. Except for Rome, there was in the West no metropolis which could have undertaken the leadership for a large territory in so definite a manner as was the case, let us say, with Antioch and Alexandria.

In the West there were two large areas, each of which possessed its own liturgical order: Rome and North Africa on the one hand, and the rest of Europe on the other. We can, therefore, call one the Romano-African liturgy, and group all the remaining liturgies under the title of liturgies of the Gallic type or the Gallic liturgies, because Gaul seems somehow to have taken a leading part. First we shall speak of the Gallic liturgies.

The Gallic liturgies covered the entire large territory from the Iberian peninsula, over Gaul, up to the Danube countries. The British Isles and Upper Italy also belonged to this domain; for the latter was called Gallia Cisalpina. Within this large territory there was not one liturgy, but rather one common liturgical system. Everywhere more or less the same feasts were celebrated and the same liturgical order was basic for the celebration of the Mass. But the prayer texts varied from country to country. The one point all had in common was the principle of no fixed canon in regard to the priest's prayers; no prayers were to recur constantly, Mass after Mass, without change (as is the case in our Roman liturgy), with the exception of course of the words of consecration, the *Pater noster* and a few other formulas. Each feast, each votive Mass had its own Mass formulary from the beginning to the end; and these Mass formularies were not one single solemn prayer, a rounded-out anaphora, as in the liturgy of the Orient; each Mass formulary was divided into a lengthy series of individual prayers. For example, after the gospel came the reading of the names of the *offerentes,* followed by a prayer *Post nomina;* then came the kiss of peace and a prayer *Post pacem*. Then came the preface, which was here called *immolatio* or *contestatio;* then the *Sanctus,* followed by a prayer *Post Sanctus;* then the words of consecration beginning with the *Pridie quam pateretur* and after that a prayer *Post pridie* (elsewhere called *Post secreta*).

A certain restlessness is apparent in such a system. And this restlessness is shown also by the fact that many prayers and forms had already departed rather far from the ancient traditions, and that various liberties had been taken in remodeling the structure. For example, the preface, which ought to represent the old prayer of thanksgiving, has in many cases become a prayer of petition. The prayer after the consecration *Post pridie,* which ought to contain the anamnesis and an offering to God, has often hardly any trace of these. Rarely is there an *epiclesis,* a calling down of the Holy Spirit, according to the oriental pattern. The style of the prayers, too, is strikingly different from the Roman liturgy: much more involved, long-winded and sentimental; much more akin to the prayer-style of the Greek liturgy than to the Roman. In general, on many points the influence of the Orient can be felt. In this connection we may note that these liturgies had no offertory in the manner of the Roman offertory. The faithful, it is true, were allowed to offer their gifts for the sacrifice and it was even urged occasionally, e.g., in a synod of Mâcon (585). But these gifts were to be handed over in the sacristy before the Mass. From these offerings, all that was needed was selected and, after the Gospel, was carried in procession to the altar for the sacrifice. Also with regard to the use of incense and of outward solemnity, these liturgies kept more to the oriental pattern.

Within this Gallic type, we distinguish as a rule four different liturgies, each of which had its own liturgical texts and liturgical books. The four usually enumerated are the Old Spanish, the Gallican, the Celtic, and the Milanese. These certainly were not the only more or less independent forms. On the borderlines, for example in the Danube countries, there may have been still different shapes and forms, but of these we do not have any detailed knowledge. Let us study the above four in more detail.

(1) The old *Spanish* liturgy, which later, after the invasion of the Arabs, was also called the *Mozarabic* liturgy.[1] This liturgy had nothing to do with the Arabs; but because, after 711, the inhabitants of southern Spain came under the rule of the Arabs, they were henceforth called *Mozarabes* (i.e., the Arabianised ones), and because this old Spanish liturgy was still used by the people in these places till the eleventh and twelfth centuries (in contrast to the people in the new kingdoms in the north of the peninsula, who had adopted the Roman liturgy), their liturgy was called the Mozarabic liturgy. The Mozarabic liturgy, which we are treating now, was already fully developed in the sixth century. Its further development, the creation of new texts, had not as yet ceased by the year 600, but by that time the prayer-type was already fully evolved. And what is especially remarkable in this prayer-type is that it shows to a high degree the influence of the battle against Arianism.

About 411, Spain was invaded by the Visigoths. The invaders, who had embraced an Arian Christianity in the days of Ulfilas (d. 383), not only held fast to their Arianism, but from time to time they also actively propagated their heresy and persecuted the Catholic faith. We are all familiar with the persecutions of the Catholics under King Euric and later on under King Leovigild, who even had his own son Hermenegild, a convert to Catholicism, killed. The Visigothic tribe was not converted to Catholicism until the time of King Riccared in the year 589. Occasionally a fierce

1. Cf. H. Jenner, "Mozarabic Rite," in *Catholic Encyclopedia*, X, 611–623. See also Dom G. Prado, *Historia del Rito Mozarabe* (San Domingo de Silos, 1928); Archdale A. King, *Liturgies of the Primatial Sees* (Milwaukee, 1957), 457–631.

controversy must have been carried on between the Arians and the Catholics in Spain. And it must have extended again and again, as in other countries, to liturgical customs and institutions.[2] We see this clearly from the various examples of the same controversy coming to us from neighboring Africa where Catholics also opposed Arians, that is, the Arian Vandals. Even from Spain itself, we possess, for example, an account of how the Arians demanded from a Catholic going over to them a profession of faith by way of the doxology: *Gloria Patri per Filium in Spiritu Sancto*. This doxology was in itself in no way heretical; it could easily be given a Catholic interpretation, and it simply corresponded to the type of prayer in use in the whole Church during the third and fourth centuries. But the Arians meant it to be an expression of their belief that the Son (not only Christ, the God-man) is inferior to the Father and a creature. On this score, the Catholics hesitated to use this mode of prayer which could be misunderstood and misconstrued; they even began to avoid completely the ancient *per Christum* in liturgical prayer. This was much the same process that had occurred in Oriental liturgies.

Only in the most ancient prayers of the Spanish liturgy do we still find the idea of the mediatorship of Christ; in the more recent ones we do not find it any longer. Instead we find forms of prayer in which the consubstantiality of the divine persons is more pronounced. In the Mass, the liturgical prayer is indifferently addressed to God the Father or to God the Son. Often the prayer is even formulated in such a way that in the beginning it is addressed to God the Father and in the continuation to the Son; or at the end the Most Holy Trinity is addressed. The glorification of the Most Blessed Trinity occupies a large space in the prayers of the old Spanish liturgy. We remember the Trinitarian professions of faith, defined during the various synods of Toledo, with their clever expositions of the relationship between the three divine persons. The formulas of prayer, too, were created to parallel those formulas of faith. They are of special importance to us because not a few of these prayer texts later on found their way into the Roman liturgy, mostly via Ireland, England, and the Carolingian empire. Our preface *de ss. Trinitate,* which most probably originated in Spain, is an example. Our Mass prayers *Suscipe s. Trinitas* and *Placeat tibi s. Trinitas,* if not originally from Spain, surely came from the same atmosphere.

2. Cf. J. A. Jungmann, "Die Abwehr des germanischen Arianismus und der Umbruch der religiösen Kultur im frühen Mittelalter," *Zeitschrift für kath. Theologie* 69 (1947), 36–99.

(2) The second liturgy of the Gallic type is the one we call the *Gallican,* in the strict sense.[3] This is the liturgy as it was practised in the territory of ancient Gaul, in the kingdom of the Franks. This, too, during the time of which we are treating, was still in process of development. A series of documents of this liturgy has been preserved to us, but most of them date from the seventh century. Yet there are others which belong to the sixth or perhaps to the fifth century. A Gallican lectionary has been published, which has been called the oldest book of the Latin liturgy.[4] It displays the same peculiarity which can be found also in later lectionaries of the Gallican liturgy, that lessons were frequently compiled not from one section of Sacred Scripture, but from different books, or at least from different chapters. For instance, the gospel for the Mass on the anniversary of the consecration of a church is composed of thirteen passages taken from all four evangelists. In this case, we speak of a *cento,* i.e., a text patched or sewed together from various pieces. Here, too, we glimpse that great freedom and lack of control which we are led to expect in the liturgies of the Gallic type.

The same is the case in another document also belonging to the sixth century, namely, the Masses published by F. J. Mone.[5] They are Mass-prayers for the priest which are, in general, of much the same type as the Mass-prayers in the later sources of the Gallican liturgy. But amongst them there is a Mass formulary in which all the prayers are composed in hexameters. Poetry, it is true, had been employed in the liturgy in some form or other even in other liturgies, and at an early date, but only by way of variety in the songs of the choir and in the hymns of the hour prayers. This is something different. It is a singular case, to be found only here in the Gallican liturgy. It would appear to be in marked contrast to the seriousness of prayer to put the very prayers of the priest in verse. But this phenomenon, too, harmonizes with the restless character which we ascertained as the mark of the liturgies of the Gallic type. And it appears also to be linked with the character of the Celtic people; for the Romanized Celts, the descendants of the ancient Gauls, constituted the main part of the Christian population of Gaul even after the invasion of the Franks.

The Gallican liturgy, moreover, also shows, though not so strongly as the old Spanish liturgy, the influence of the battle against Arianism. For even in the country of St. Hilary, the Arians were for

3. H. Leclercq, "Gallicane (Liturgie)," *DACL,* 6, 473–493.
4. A. Dold, *Das älteste Liturgiebuch d. lateinischen Kirche* (Beuron, 1936).
5. *Lateinische und griechische Messen aus d. 2.–6. Jh.* (Frankfurt, 1850); Migne, *PL,* 138, 863–882.

a very long time dangerous adversaries. The Franks had embraced Catholic Christianity, but the Burgundians remained Arians for a long time, and in the south of the country it was the Arian Visigoths who were the rulers till 507. Thus the Gallican liturgy is also marked by an anti-Arian attitude, as was the case with the old Spanish liturgy. This is shown, for example, in the predilection for orations addressed to Christ. This is all the more important for us because later on, during the period of the Carolingians, the Roman liturgy was also affected and transformed by this influence. In fact, a number of orations were simply taken up into the Roman liturgy. An example of this is the second oration at Prime, with its genuine Gallican conclusion, *Salvator mundi. . . .* Under the influence of traditions from the Gallican liturgy, was likewise developed that popular devotion which was standard during the whole of the Middle Ages and beyond, with a predilection for the mysteries of Christ's childhood and Passion and an inclination to address prayers indifferently to Christ and to God.

(3) The third liturgy of the Gallic type is the *Celtic,* i.e., the liturgy of the Celtic peoples on the British Isles, especially the Irish and the Scotch.[6] It was, of course, in Latin, because the Celtic language did not become a written language until a much later time. We have but little knowledge of this liturgy, and what we know is only from documents of the close of the seventh century (in which, by the way, the Celtic language is used in part for the rubrics). It has been said, and rightly so, that the Celtic liturgy can hardly be considered as an independent liturgy. For it consisted for the greater part of foreign elements: of texts taken from the old Spanish, or the Gallican, sometimes also from the Roman and even the Oriental liturgies.

(4) The fourth liturgy of the Gallic type is the liturgy of *Milan.*[7] This is the only Gallic liturgy which still survives, not only in a church or two or in a single diocese, but actually in a whole ecclesiastical province. The Mozarabic liturgy also exists, but only in a single chapel in Toledo. The Milanese liturgy, however, although basically what it was fifteen centuries ago, is today very strongly permeated with elements from the Roman liturgy. In the Mass from the *Sanctus* on, the Roman canon is used with only minor changes. This permeation had begun early in Christian antiquity. On the other hand, however, it still contains many features and typical formulas of the Gallic liturgy. Among these, for instance, is the

6. L. Gaugaud, "Celtique (Liturgie)," *DACL,* 2, 2969–3032.
7. P. Lejay, "Ambrosienne (Liturgie)," *DACL,* 1, 1373–1442; Cf. King, *op. cit.,* 286–456.

litany which is said on the Sundays in Lent before the oration, in which the response recurs: *Precamur te . . . Domine miserere.* Also a great store of old prefaces, which were edited by Paredi some years back, shows the type of the Gallic preface. Even the Roman forms, it may be noted, display to some extent a more ancient shape than they have in the present Roman Mass.

These four liturgies all belong to one common type. Now there arises the question: how was it possible for a type of liturgy to be formed common to such an extensive territory? Where is there a center, a metropolis from which the law for such a liturgy, common in its fundamentals to all these countries, could proceed? Lugdunum (Lyons) or Massilia (Marseilles) never enjoyed such great importance, not even in Gaul. Toledo gained importance but only in Spain. Hence it was pointed out that only Rome could have been that center from which at a very early date this liturgical type had radiated. So the hypothesis was developed that later, after this liturgy had already spread throughout the whole West, Rome had abandoned its own original liturgy and adopted her present Roman liturgy. This hypothesis, put forward by Fr. Cabrol, is not tenable; even Cabrol himself has abandoned it in this extreme form.[8] For there is absolutely no trace of any such development at Rome. And besides, the Gallic type from the very beginning shows features which cannot be imagined as coming from Rome, because they contradict Roman simplicity and clarity.

Another solution to the problem which is, however, also only a hypothesis, is by far more probable; it is the one developed by L. Duchesne.[9] He is of the opinion that Milan was the center from which the Gallic type of liturgy proceeded. Duchesne points out that, in the fourth century, Milan was the residence of the emperors, and that at that time its influence in Church matters extended as far as Spain. Several bishops of Milan in the fourth century came from the Orient, amongst them the predecessor of St. Ambrose, Auxentius, who was a native of Cappadocia. This would help to explain the oriental influences noticeable to these liturgies.

* * * * *

The Gallic type of liturgy in the West is in marked contrast to the Romano-African type. As this term implies, this group contains two liturgies: the liturgy of North Africa and the liturgy of Rome. Of the liturgy of North Africa, no complete documents, no liturgical

8. F. Cabrol, *La Messe en Occident* (Paris, 1932), esp. 37, 106 ff.
9. L. Duchesne, *Christian Worship* (5th ed., London, 1927), 90–95. The theory of Duchesne has been contradicted by E. Griffe, "Aux origines de la liturgie gallicane": *Bulletin de littérature ecclésiastique,* 52 (1951), 17–43.

books, are preserved to us. But in the writings of Tertullian, Cyprian and Augustine and in some other writings, numerous details are mentioned from which we can put together a fairly complete picture of this liturgy.[10] North Africa had its own liturgical texts and they, too, would not have been uniform for the whole of the province, ,as we can see from the canon of Hippo which was mentioned earlier: Each bishop can provide himself with the liturgical texts but he should examine them *cum instructioribus fratribus.*

An examination of the various texts and occasional samples gives us an idea of the shape of the Mass liturgy and the structure of the Church year. This shows that the African liturgy was closely allied to the Roman. The offertory at which the faithful presented their gifts was, as in Rome, after the lessons. The orations concluded with an ending-formula similar to that in the Roman liturgy: *per Dominum nostrum*. Yet there are also considerable differences. In the Roman liturgy, for example, the faithful received the blessings after the Communion (in the *oratio super populum*), but in the African liturgy, as in the Gallic liturgies, such a blessing was given before the Communion, first to the faithful and then to the penitents, presumably so that they could then depart, like other non-communicants.[11]

* * * * *

And now we come to the last and most important of the Latin liturgies: the *Roman liturgy*. As a matter of fact we already dealt with this Roman liturgy in detail when we spoke of the liturgy of the third century, but it was the Roman liturgy in the Greek language. Now we must consider the Roman liturgy in the Latin language during the time up to Gregory the Great, and it is this liturgy that we shall treat in all the following chapters. Here we shall, therefore, sketch out a few outlines of the general history of the Roman liturgy up to Gregory the Great.

This history begins for the greater part in obscurity. Whereas with regard to the period of the Roman liturgy in the Greek language we are very well informed through Justin and Hippolytus, for the period following direct information is almost completely lacking. Of the liturgical books going back to the time before Gregory, really only two can be taken into account: the so-called

10. E. Dekkers, *Tertullianus en de geschiedenis der liturgie* (Brussels, 1947); W. Roetzer, *Des hl. Augustinus Schriften als liturgie-geschichtliche Quelle* (Munich, 1930).
11. Jungmann, *Mass of the Roman Rite*, II, 294–295.

Sacramentarium Leonianum and the *Sacramentarium Gelasianum.* First a remark on the term "sacramentary."

By sacramentary or *liber sacramentorum,* we understand the book which the priest and the bishop used at the celebration of the Mass and for the administration of the most important sacraments. It therefore contains especially the prayers of the Mass, both the invariable prayers or the *canon Missae,* and those that varied with the ecclesiastical year; these latter, of course, make up the main contents of the sacramentary. The sacramentary, however, did not contain the lessons, since the lessons were not read by the priest himself but by the lector or the deacon, who used for this the lectionary or simply a codex of the Bible. Neither did the sacramentary contain the chants (Introit, Gradual, Alleluia, Tract, Offertory and Communion); these, too, the celebrant did not have to read, because they were sung by the chanter or the singers, who had special texts for this purpose. No Roman lectionary, no book of songs for the Mass or for the hour prayers has been preserved to us from the time before Gregory the Great. Such texts must have been in existence, and they cannot have differed very much from those which have come down to us from the seventh century. The system of the lessons at the stational services towards the end of the fifth century must have been similar to that which we know from a later time, and which still stands in the Roman Missal, for it is at least a well-founded assumption that the stational services received their fixed order from Pope Hilary, the successor of Leo the Great. But it is hardly thinkable that at the same time the lessons should not have been fixed—those lessons, namely, which we find in the Roman Missal (for example, in Lent). For, as we shall see in the following chapter, some of these lessons must have been selected under conditions that obtained only during the period before Gregory the Great.

From the time before Gregory, however, only the sacramentary, the *Sacramentarium Leonianum,* has been handed down to us without intermediary.[12] It is preserved in one single manuscript of the seventh century and, unfortunately, this manuscript is incomplete; the canon itself is missing and the entire vernal section, with the Mass formularies for Lent and Easter, is lacking. Nevertheless, this sacramentary contains more than three hundred Mass formularies, chiefly for the various feasts of martyrs, some of which even have several formularies. Each Mass formulary consists of a preface and three or four orations; the orations are meant for

12. K. Mohlberg, *Sacramentarium Veronense* (Roma: Herder, 1956).

the same points in the Mass as today: one for the beginning before the lessons, one for the offertory (our *secreta*), a post-communion after communion and then fairly often an *oratio super populum* at the end.

The second sacramentary which comes under consideration, namely the *Sacramentarium Gelasianum,* or more correctly, the older *Gelasianum,* has a similar structure.[13] Although in the form in which it is extant it originated somewhere in France during the eighth century, the material added in France can in general be easily separated from the rest. The Roman material remaining is dated about the sixth century. The majority of the orations and prefaces in our missal in the *proprium de tempore* are already contained in these two old sacramentaries.

These two sacramentaries were discovered and first published in the seventeenth and eighteenth centuries, and were rather arbitrarily named after the two great liturgical Popes Leo and Gelasius. Subsequent study has led to the conclusion that these actual collections may not be Leonine or Gelasian, but that a great portion of the matter contained therein does indeed go back to these two Popes. Many Sunday orations and several prefaces which we still recite today contain terms and phrases strikingly in accord with Leo the Great's phraseology. Even the rhythm of the language is the same. Thus the assumption, that he is the author of many of the prayers in the Leonine Sacramentary is well founded.

Of Pope Gelasius I, who reigned some decades later (492–496) we have the explicit record that he composed *sacramentorum prefationes et orationes.*[14] It seems also that he introduced trenchant reforms in the liturgy of the Mass. The intercessions for the various needs and the various classes had previously been inserted after the lessons, as they still are on Good Friday. Gelasius, it seems, was the one who dropped these intercessions and instead introduced a litany at the beginning of the Mass, in the place where today we have the Kyrie. Such a litany is extant under the name of *deprecatio Gelasii.* To the canon of the Mass, also, he seems to have given its final form, for it cannot be a mere accident that in a later source this canon is called *canon papae Gelasii.*

Thus it seems that it was Leo the Great and Gelasius I who shaped the Latin liturgy of Rome in a most decisive manner. But their work was of a minor and incidental character, having to do mainly with arrangement and with the incorporation of suitable

13. ed. H. A. Wilson (Oxford, 1894).
14. *Liber pontificalis* (Duchesne, I, 255).

material. Even the canon of the Mass itself, in its substance, is of an earlier date; for it is quoted already by St. Ambrose about 390, and must have existed at least some decades earlier.

The last great reform of the Roman liturgy, especially of the Mass, is connected with the name of Pope Gregory the Great, but he belongs to a later period of the history of the liturgy, and therefore does not come within the compass of this book.

Section V

THE ROMAN LITURGY BEFORE GREGORY THE GREAT

CHAPTER NINETEEN

Baptism and Penance

IN THIS and the remaining chapters of this book, we shall try to sketch the liturgical life of the Roman Church as it was lived during the fifth and sixth centuries, in so far as our sources permit us to catch a glimpse of that life. It is a varied picture that these sources reveal, sometimes bright, sometimes less attractive. We could not, of course, present all the details of this varied life, even if our sources permitted. We must be satisfied, therefore, with considering those aspects that are of general interest—the sacraments, especially Baptism and Penance, the Divine Office and the Mass.

During the first centuries of the Church, it was, beyond question, Baptism that, of all the sacraments, occupied the foreground of ecclesiastical life. For the Church at large, it was Baptism that, year after year, brought in new crowds of believing confessors and professors of the faith. Baptism it was that gave Easter its special splendor and that enhanced its victorious rejoicing. And Baptism was the great event in the life of the individual Christian when, after years of eager preparation, he was deemed worthy of it; Baptism was his resurrection to a new life.

The Sacrament of Penance, also, was certainly familiar to the early Christians. They were aware that even within the Church there could be sinners; daily experience showed this only too clearly. They were aware also that the Church possesses powers to reconcile to God, through prayer and judicial sentence, the sinners among her children. Yet not much mention was made of these powers of the Church. Particularly in the instruction of the catechumens and neophytes, when the mysteries of the faith were explained to them, there was a certain reluctance about broaching the subject of Penance. The thinking was that the new converts should preserve their baptismal grace; they should not even bring to mind the possibility that they could ever again stand in need of a conversion. Hermas tells the Shepherd that he heard from some teachers "that there is no other repentance except the one when we went into the water and received the remission of our former sins." [1] The teachers (διδάσκαλοι) are obviously the catechists whose task it was to instruct the catechumens, and apparently they spoke only of the repentance connected with Baptism.

We can hear such a catechist actually speaking just a few decades later. Tertullian, while still a Catholic, wrote a special book on the subject of Penance, *De Poenitentia*. It is one of those writings of his that probably stemmed from his own activity as a catechist. In this work, he first deals with penance as conversion from sin in general. Then he speaks of Baptism, when the great change, the great conversion has to take place. In the seventh chapter, he goes on to say that he must treat of another penance, but he takes up the subject only hesitantly, reluctantly, because he is afraid that someone hearing that even after Baptism there is further occasion for doing penance and for finding forgiveness might take this as an incentive to carelessness and to sin. I am afraid, he says, to mention this second hope: *Piget secundae, imo iam ultimae spei subtexere mentionem.*[2] If somebody was once shipwrecked on the sea, he says, and was then saved, such a one as a rule does not think any longer of ships and of seafaring. So it must also be with one who, having sinned, has found forgiveness through God's mercy in Baptism. He should not think that he could perhaps be saved once more. So it is quite likely that in the early Church the majority of the faithful never made use of the Sacrament of Penance.

No Sacrament has undergone such great changes in the course of centuries as has the discipline concerning the Sacrament of Penance. Nowadays the Sacrament is administered in a comparatively short time and with the simplest of ceremonies. How different it was in ages past.

The Church has always exercised her penitential powers. As early as the first and second century, and then especially in Origen and Cyprian, we find sufficient proofs of this. But during all Christian antiquity the Church used this sacrament very sparingly, that

1. *Mand.* 4, 3.
2. c. 7.

is, only when it was necessary to forgive grave and public sins, sins "that barred a person from the Kingdom of heaven." [3] Especially during the early centuries Penance was given under conditions that grew ever stricter. One who committed so grave a sin that he had to do public penance was considered or even declared excommunicated, and from then on he had to travel a lengthy road before he could again find reconciliation with the Church and with God. For this public penance, a special penitential liturgy was now formed, with the outlines of which we shall now more closely acquaint ourselves. It is controverted by scholars whether in the fourth and fifth centuries there was also the possibility of sacramental penance in a less public form for less grave sins and especially for secret cases. For the rest, it may be noted here that even though the penance was public, there is no indication (except in isolated instances, which were condemned as abuses) that a public confession of individual sins was ever exacted. The confession was made to the bishop or his representative, and was the preliminary to the whole penitential ritual.

What, then, were the outlines of the penitential liturgy during this period—the fourth and fifth centuries? We are concerned particularly with the Roman Church; but as the data are quite scanty, we have to include also what we know of other western Churches, especially (through Augustine) that of North Africa. We may assume that the outlines of the penitential praxis and of the penitential liturgy were about the same all over the West.

In these outlines we can distinguish three components, three phases of the penitential process.

(1) The first one was that the sinner—be it of his own accord, or at the urging of others—after reporting to the bishop, had to confess his guilt to him. After this he was excommunicated at a public service, that is, he was declared excommunicated (it was, in our present technical terminology, a *sententia declaratoria*). This action was based on the viewpoint that the Church, taken in its fullest sense, is or should be a community of saints, a *communio sanctorum;* whoever by sin has lost the life of grace no longer belongs to the Church in this full sense. The sinner was, however, not completely rejected; for the Church wished to bring about his forgiveness. Hence, he was enrolled in the class of penitents.

In the Orient, the penitents who had lost baptismal grace were considered more or less like catechumens who are not yet baptised.

3. Cf. Gal. 5:19 ff.

Hence, like the catechumens, they were only allowed to be present at the Fore-Mass; after the lessons they were dismissed.

In the West, at any rate in the Roman Church, they were treated less strictly, on the grounds that even so the penitents are baptised and remain baptised. Hence they were permitted to be present during divine service at the back of the church, or perhaps in the atrium (exactly where we do not know); but they were forbidden not only to receive Holy Communion but also to bring their offerings to the altar; they remained excluded from active participation. One thing they were allowed, and this forms the second component of the penitential liturgy.

(2) They regularly received from the bishop a special blessing, and this, it seems, at every episcopal service. In the Orient, this blessing was given immediately after the lessons, for here they were dismissed after the lessons. In some churches, for instance in North Africa, it was given before the Communion; after that apparently they had to leave. Elsewhere, and at least for a time also at Rome, this blessing was given after the Communion; they were present at Communion, but as silent witnesses. The penitents had to present themselves for this blessing throughout the whole term of penance. This blessing, this intercession by the Church, was to assist the penitents to spend their time of penance more fruitfully and thus at last to obtain forgiveness from God.

(3) The third component of the penitential liturgy, the decisive act, came at the end of the term of penance; this was the reconciliation. The penitents were again received into the bosom of Holy Church; they were again introduced as members into the organism of the Body of Christ, the living Church, replete with the Holy Spirit. In this way they were given renewed life, and grace was bestowed upon them. The reconciliation, therefore, was not a mere act of ecclesiastical jurisdiction; it was not a mere annulment of the excommunication. The withdrawal of the excommunication, accompanied by prayer and imposition of hands, was at the same time meant as a sacramental act. For when the bishop, with the appropriate rite, declared to the penitent that he once more was to be a full member of Holy Church, he gave him the absolution from his sin. This reconciliation was, therefore, the sacramental act proper.

In the Roman church during the time of Pope Innocent I (at the beginning of the fifth century), this reconciliation took place on Maundy Thursday: *Quinta feria ante Pascha eis remittendum*

Romanae Ecclesiae consuetudo demonstrat.[4] Obviously the Church wanted the erring brethren to be able to celebrate a joyous Easter together with the whole community. Since the celebration of Easter began with Good Friday, the penitents were reintroduced into the Church on the day previous, i.e., on Maundy Thursday.

The exact rite of this reconciliation we learn from the *Sacramentarium Gelasianum,* the contents of which regarding this point go back probably to the sixth century or even earlier. We see from this sacramentary that the act of reconciliation was inserted into the Mass after the Gospel; for the penitents were again to be allowed to offer their gifts at the offertory. The act began with the deacon giving an address to the bishop wherein he stressed the significance of what was now to take place and wherein he requested the bishop in the name of the penitents to grant them the reconciliation. *Adest, o venerabilis pontifex, tempus acceptum, dies propitiationis divinae* —thus begins this address as recorded in the Gelasian sacramentary.[5] The bishop, in an admonitory speech, warned the penitents against any relapse into sin. The penitents prostrated themselves (just as the ordinands do before the reception of major orders) and a prayer was said over them. Then the bishop pronounced the reconciliation in deprecative form, or more accurately in supplicative form, in the form namely of the so-called *supplicationes;* these were orations in the ordinary style of the Roman oration, containing the petition directed to God (the *supplicatio*), that He forgive the sinner. In the Gelasian sacramentary three orations are given; the second, the shortest of them, runs: *Praesta, quaesumus Domine, huic famulo tuo dignum poenitentiae fructum, ut Ecclesiae tuae sanctae, a cuius integritate deviarat peccando, admissorum veniam consequendo reddatur innoxius. Per.*

After this, the penitent received the reconciliatory imposition of hands (again the process must have been quite similar to the laying on of hands at the ordination of priests and deacons). Then the bishop raised the penitent, who up to then had been on his knees. Apparently we have a reminiscence of this reconciliation in the chant which is still sung on Maundy Thursday at the offertory, hence directly after the place of the former reconciliatory ritual: *Dextera Domini fecit virtutem, dextera Domini exaltavit me.*

This is the description of the Sacrament of Penance during the first half of the fifth century, the period of Popes Innocent I and Leo the Great. But the penitential liturgy underwent a further

4. Ep. 25, 7.
5. Wilson (ed.), *The Gelasian Sacramentary,* 63 ff.

development, especially in connection with the question of *when* the penitential time was to begin.

At first no particular time appears to have been stipulated for admittance to the penitential status. But our liturgy still shows traces of a practice in vogue towards the end of the era of Christian antiquity, of beginning the period of penance right after Pentecost, that is, after the conclusion of the Easter season.

In the early Church it was a widespread principle that on Sundays and during the joyful Easter season (hence, during the seven weeks between Easter and Pentecost) no penance could be performed. During this time, as we read in Tertullian, one should not fast, nor should one pray kneeling, as the penitents had to do. If someone, therefore, reported for penance during this time, he could not be immediately enrolled amongst the penitents, but only after the lapse of these seven weeks, only after Pentecost, on Whitsun Monday; for in Christian antiquity Pentecost had no octave—it was simply the conclusion of the seven weeks of Eastertide. But directly after Whitsunday, penance could be resumed. For this reason, several Oriental liturgies (the Byzantine, the West-Syrian, the Coptic) have (even to the present) a special penitential devotion on Whitsunday afternoon: an *officium genuflexionis*. The Roman liturgy, too, has something of the sort.[6] Perhaps it has already struck some of our readers that the Gospels on Pentecost Monday and Pentecost Tuesday do not contain anything appropriate to the Pentecostal theme. Monday's Gospel deals with the judgment dealt out to the world and of the mercy of God: God did not send His Son into the world to judge the world, but that the world might be saved through Him. On Tuesday the topic is the Good Shepherd calling His sheep. These are indications that for the penitents the time of penance has been reopened; penance is a judgment, but a merciful judgment; the Good Shepherd is searching again for His sheep.

At a later period, but still within the fifth century, Lent began to be considered as the penitential time proper, as the time, namely, of strict penance. Hence a service, an *officium*, was created for the opening of penance at the beginning of Lent. Lent in those days began with the Sunday which today we call *Dominica I. in Quadragesima*. Sunday itself, however, was not a day of penance. Hence the start of the penitential period fell on the Monday following. If we again examine the lessons on that day as they are in our present-day missal, we find that the Gospel selected deals with the shepherd

6. J. A. Jungmann, "Pfingstoktav und Kirchenbusse in der römischen Liturgie," *Miscellanea Liturgica in honorem L. C. Mohlberg*, I (Rome, 1948), 169–182.

who separates the sheep from the goats; this is precisely the process supposed to take place in church on this day: the sinners, the penitents, were separated from the ranks of the faithful. But in the lesson from Ezechiel, the theme of the Good Shepherd appears again: *quod perierat requiram*. And as on the Tuesday after Pentecost, so we find also on this Tuesday the continuation: once more a scene appears in which evil is swept away from the sanctuary, for the Gospel topic is the cleansing of the temple. There is still one further proof that we are on the right road in the explanation we are making. The Mass formularies just spoken of are remnants of the stational services. For such a service, the stational church was frequently, at least on important days, chosen so as to fit in with the day's theme. And so we find in our missals both on the Monday after Pentecost and on the Monday after *Dominica I. in Quadragesima* the superscription: *statio ad s. Petrum ad vincula*. The divine service takes place at the church of St. Peter, who possesses the power of binding and loosing. On Tuesday, too, there is in both cases a stational church which was chosen only for these two days and which, therefore, was obviously connected with the penitential service: *ad s. Anastasiam*.

The starting of the penance later on was transferred once more, when the beginning of Lent was fixed on Ash Wednesday. And here once more—hence for the third time—an office for the opening of penance was created; but this third day for the opening of penance belongs to a later period which does not pertain to our theme.

The duration of the penance for each penitent appears to have depended on the judgment of the bishop, and we find a wide divergence in different ecclesiastical provinces and at different periods. Whereas in the Syrian Church of the third century as a rule a few weeks sufficed, in Gaul somewhat later the penance for abortion, for instance, lasted a whole lifetime.

From what we have already mentioned, we can readily see that it cannot have been easy to undertake such a public penance. And yet this was the only way in which the Church in those days granted absolution, at least in cases of grave transgressions which had somehow become public, like fornication, adultery, and the denial of the faith. Public penance was a public stigma. The works of penance, too, were heavy ones, for not only did they include strict fasting, but also a series of other obligations, including prayer on one's knees, the wearing of rough penitential garments, refraining from bathing and shaving and from the use of marital rights and even from doing one's ordinary secular work. And, in addition, some of the penitential obligations did not cease even after the reconciliation. For example, the penitent was obliged, if married, to make no use of matrimonial rights; in other words, any one who once had become a penitent, had henceforth to live like a monk. And should someone fail in this, he was considered a recidivist; and the Church in this case denied him any help whatsoever, for it was possible to do public penance once only. On this account a movement arose to postpone the penance, if it was required, to the end of one's life. And the Church did not seriously oppose this movement. Although the dangers of such a postponement were clearly indicated, yet about the fifth century a special rite of penance was created for the sick, as we find in the liturgical books of the period. Here the time of penance was compressed into a few days; after that, if possible at the very last moment, the reconciliation was given. Even today in the *Rituale Romanum,* in the prayers said at the last moments of life, namely the *commendatio animae,* we have a prayer which stems from this ancient penance of the sick: *Deus misericors, Deus clemens;* and its concluding words still make a pointed reference to the *sacramentum reconciliationis.*

Sinners thus continued to live in the state of sin until their dying days, till they received the penance of the sick. But, of course, they were admonished to penance, to interior conversion, to sorrow, and thus many a poor sinner will have found his reconciliation with God through perfect sorrow *cum desiderio sacramenti.* But it was not possible to grant him absolution.

What we must call a real crisis in the penitential praxis of the Church occurred during the period from about the fourth to the sixth century. On the one hand, there was the effort to cling to a conception of the Church that coincided more or less with the *communio sanctorum,* whose members remained in the life of grace and who could, therefore, without further ado receive Holy Communion as often as was common. On the other hand, there was the empirical actuality that sins were to be found even within the Church, such sins, in fact, which could not by any stretch of custom be fully included in the public ecclesiastical penance. It was not until after the sixth century that another form of penance gained prevalence in the Church, and the Sacrament of Penance was granted in a more private form without such heavy conditions. It is doubtful whether or not during the previous period there existed for secret cases something like a private (or, rather, semi-private) penance. Some authors uphold this view, and, indeed cases can be adduced where the sinner had only to receive the penitential blessing for a time without having been enrolled amongst the penitents. But this question is far from being clarified; at any rate, there remained great uncertainty and confusion, and it is obvious that the faithful themselves suffered from this difficulty and tried to escape its consequences.

Now the deferment of penance till the very end of life was not the only way out. For another phenomenon in the Church's life appears to be related to this critical state of affairs, a phenomenon that had already come to prominence at the beginning of the fourth century and which survived at least throughout the whole century. This was the postponement of *Baptism*.

People wanted to become Christians, but since one could pass for a Christian merely by becoming a catechumen, many preferred to enroll as catechumens and remain such as long as possible. For there were many advantages in not accepting Baptism at once. For one thing, the catechumen was still free from many of the obligations imposed on the baptised and did not have to live as strict a life. Baptism was still ahead, and with it the possibility of obtaining the remission of sins without undergoing the terrible conditions associated with ecclesiastical penance. People, therefore, remained catechumens till the dangerous years of youth were past and, if possible, till the very end of life. Even Constantine the Great did not have himself baptised until his deathbed. Many new Christians must have followed suit. But even older Christian families took up the example. St. Augustine had become a catechumen when a child. As a boy he once became dangerously ill and himself asked for Baptism. But his mother, St. Monica, delayed, since the danger of death had not become grave; her reason was very significant (Augustine himself mentions it in his *Confessions:* I, 11), namely, after that cleansing the defilements of sin would have been greater and therefore all the more dangerous. So Augustine was not baptised till the age of 33 after a stormy youth and manifold aberrations. St. Monica's family was not the only one that followed this practice. From the great Fathers of the Church of the fourth and fifth century, one after the other, we learn that they received Baptism not as children, but only at a mature age. Chrysostom was baptised when twenty-five years old, Basil was twenty-six, his friend Gregory Nazianzen, who came from a saintly family, was twenty-eight; Ambrose was not yet baptised when he was elected bishop at the age of thirty-four. But this deferring of the sacrament was considered an abuse. The bishops opposed the practice, even those who themselves had received Baptism at a later age. At the beginning of Lent, they addressed the catechumens who stood amongst the audience listening to their sermons: Easter is near, come and be enrolled for Baptism (*Ecce Pascha est, da nomen ad baptismum*).[7] It was not till the time of the Pelagian controversy, about 410/420, that we begin to notice that infant Baptism has again become the rule in North Africa. Even the Pelagians themselves acknowledged this as the normal order of things; for they, too, in general practised infant Baptism. The council of Carthage in the year 418 declared: *Quicumque parvulos recentes ab uteris matrum baptizandos negant, a.s.*[8] But in the meantime the Church had already begun to make provision for the great majority who put off Baptism by transforming the whole pattern and plan of the catechumenate.

As we learned from Hippolytus, the catechumenate in the third century had lasted for three years—three years which had to be spent according to definite regulations. Such a plan could not be maintained during the fourth and fifth centuries. A plan for the catechumenate was, therefore, devised whereby the most necessary spiritual equipment for those wishing to become Christians was supplied immediately at the beginning of the catechumenate. A preliminary catechesis was introduced, accompanied by certain ceremonies. Then the prospective convert was left to himself until some years later, even many years later, when at the beginning of Lent he reported for Baptism. During this Lent he underwent all the necessary preparation for Baptism and received complete instruction in the Christian religion. The entire preparation for Baptism was, therefore, condensed into two sessions: the opening catechesis and the catechesis in Lent.

The catechesis in Lent was what it had always been: a systematic introduction into the entire Christian doctrine, summed up in the *symbolum*. But the preliminary catechesis which accompanied the enrollment into the catechumenate was something new. The candidate received at once a rather thorough instruction in Christian conduct, as is still indicated in the present-day ritual of Baptism where the priest declares: "If it is life that you wish to enter, keep the commandments. . . ." The pattern followed in this preliminary or introductory catechesis we can learn from St. Augustine. A deacon, Deogratias of Carthage, had asked the bishop of Hippo for some hints on how to conduct this introductory catechesis. Augustine answered by writing the booklet: *De catechizandis rudibus*. (The *rudes* in the title refers to those who have not yet been in-

7. Augustine, *Serm.*, 132, 1.
8. Denz., n. 102.

structed; hence the title signifies: "The art of catechizing those who are to receive elementary instruction in Christian Doctrine.") According to Augustine, the catechist was to put before the candidate at the very start the most important facts of the Christian order of salvation by telling him the outlines of the history of the redemption both from the Old and the New Testament. Stress this essential idea, that everything in Scripture down to the coming of Christ is a figure of what is realized in Christ and His Church. Get the catechumen to understand that the Redemption was basically a work of love, and that human love should respond to divine love by a full and hearty obedience to the commandments of God. Such is the general method which Augustine advocates.

This new beginning had to have a corresponding liturgical setting. By means of symbolic acts, an indication was given of what was beginning to happen within the candidate's soul. There was the act of breathing upon the candidate—or rather, blowing *at* him (*exsufflatio:* the devil should disappear before the breath of the Holy Spirit). The sign of the cross was made on his forehead, hands were laid upon him; an exorcism was pronounced over him; blessed salt was given him (*sal sapientiae*—because it gives *sapor* to food) as a counterforce against the rottenness of sin. As everybody knows, all these rites are still to be found at the beginning of our rite of infant Baptism. Of *infant* Baptism—this is really striking! And it brings us to a new point for discussion.

As we have already seen, infant Baptism had been a practice in the Church from earliest times; the children could be brought to church for the sacrament at any season of the year and even at the Easter vigil to be baptised with the adults. But for children the rite began with the renunciation of Satan and either the parents or a *sponsor* gave the responses. The liturgy of infant Baptism was, therefore, comparatively simple.

But now, at the beginning of the Middle Ages, a change took place in the liturgy of Baptism. Adult Baptism had become less frequent, because in the countries adjoining the Mediterranean the entire population had gradually become Christian. Baptism was now administered almost exclusively as infant Baptism. Not wanting to drop altogether the various customs of the preparation for Baptism as they had evolved in connection with the catechumenate, the Church began to transfer these ceremonies to infant Baptism. Thus our rite of infant Baptism came into existence; we find in it the ceremonies of the opening catechesis: the *exsufflatio,* the sign of the cross, the imposition of hands and the presentation of the blessed salt. We find here, from the time of the catechumenate, an exorcism and oration; we find here especially those practices which had been created in Lent for the *electi* or *competentes:* the communication (*traditio*) and the repeating back (*redditio*) of the Creed and of the Our Father.

Adult Baptism, of course, had not entirely ceased even after the fifth century. New nations came knocking at the doors of the Church seeking admission. But the old order of the catechumenate was no longer applied to them; it did not seem to be suitable because the Germanic peoples had only an inferior culture and at the same time possessed strong tribal ties, so much so that if they were to become Christian the whole tribe had to become Christian. It was not possible for a whole tribe to undertake the rigorous discipline of the catechumenate, say for a whole year. Hence attempts were made first to convert the tribal princes and the leading nobles. A short term of catechumenate, lasting perhaps for a few weeks only, was deemed sufficient and then the whole tribe was baptised in so far as it was ready, with the hope that subsequent education and living in common under Christian law would complete what had been begun before Baptism.

Thus we hear of cases during the conversion of the ancient Germans in which the catechumenate lasted only forty days, in others where it lasted only twenty days, as Martin of Braga testifies with regard to the conversion of the Suevi. There were even cases where it lasted only eight days, as Socrates reports of a tribe of the Burgundians.[9]

With regard to the peoples of the Roman empire, the Church applied the principle that the conversion should take place from the inside to the outside, and from below to above; this certainly was one way to a thorough reformation of life. With regard to the new peoples, an opposite principle was applied: from the outside to the inside and from the top to the bottom; hence a more or less external change of adherence preceded firm conviction and inner reformation, and the people had to learn a new way of life from their converted leaders.

But when we consider the result, namely the Christian culture of the Middle Ages, we have to confess that this, too, was a good way. The goal was achieved much more slowly, but, surprisingly, not too slowly; among the Anglo-Saxons, for instance, the goal had

9. *H. E.*, III, 30.

been reached already in the second and third generation. For Baptism is a sacrament; it is a means of grace, a means whereby God works on the human mind and will to produce a complete "incorporation into Christ."

CHAPTER TWENTY

The Easter Cycle

As we have previously seen, Easter was already being celebrated during the first and second centuries of Christianity. Even then it was the feast of feasts and this it has remained during the following centuries. We shall now consider Easter and the Easter cycle in the condition it had attained in the liturgy of Rome during the fifth and sixth centuries. In our discussion, it is especially important that we keep in mind the correct idea about the Easter feast itself. This idea we have already indicated. Easter is not merely the feast of Christ's resurrection; it is the feast of the Redemption accomplished by Christ's death and resurrection, the redemption which is the very basis of the life of the Church and of Christendom.

Hence the Easter festival does not consist of Easter Sunday only; it comprises also the commemorative day of Christ's passion and death. Easter embraces the triduum from Good Friday till Easter Sunday, or as St. Augustine says: it is the *sacratissimum triduum crucifixi, sepulti, suscitati.*[1] This triduum was a development of the fourth century.

In our traditional Roman liturgy, this one triduum has become two: we include also Maundy Thursday, and consider Maundy Thursday, Good Friday and Holy Saturday as the triduum of the passion; and we add to Easter Sunday also Monday and Tuesday as feastdays of equal rank and consider these three days as the triduum of the resurrection. But to gain a proper understanding of the development of the festive cycle of Easter, we have to base our consideration on the old Easter triduum: the triduum from Good

1. Ep. 55, 24 (*PL,* 33, 215).

Friday to Easter Sunday. For this old triduum had an effect also on the arrangement of Lent.

Since the beginning of the fourth century, Lent had taken shape in the Church as the season of preparation for Easter; it is presupposed in the letters of St. Athanasius. And from Rome a series of sermons for Lent by Leo the Great is extant; Leo paraphrases the significance of this preparatory time with the words: it is a *quadraginta dierum exercitatio,* "a time of forty days' spiritual exercises," during which we are to cleanse ourselves from the dust of our daily lives, to reorder our conduct; hence it was meant to be a religious renewal, a kind of annual retreat.

This preparatory period was to last for forty days. A period of forty days had already become a favorite space of time for the penance imposed upon individual penitents. Forty days was, after all, a span hallowed by Holy Writ—Christ's fast, Moses on the mountain, the wandering of Elias. Thus for the preparation for Easter forty days were fixed. When should these forty days begin? The solution was very simple: if Easter started with Good Friday, forty days had to be counted backward from Maundy Thursday, and thus the Sunday which we call *Dominica (prima) in Quadragesima* was fixed as the starting-point. (Five days in Holy Week, in addition thirty-five days or five full weeks, totalling altogether forty days.) This First Sunday of Lent still indicates that once it was the first day in Lent. In the *Secreta* we offer the *sacrificium quadragesimalis initii.* In the Gospel of our Lord's forty days' fast, for the first time the number forty appears, as the program, so to say, for the period following. And it is not accidental that on this day for the first time we take up the *pars verna* of the Breviary; for it is only with this day that the Breviary begins the complete order of Lent. Also ecclesiastical penance quite logically began on the next day, as we saw in the previous chapter.

What, then, was the content of this *Quadragesima?* We can distinguish two components: war against sin through penance and fasting; and strengthening in virtue through an increased cultivation of the spiritual and liturgical life. Fasting, therefore, although constituting an important item, in the beginning did not constitute the dominant content of this season. Generally we think of Lent as including forty days of fast, but when it was first organized, it was thought of simply as forty days of preparation. In the beginning, only the ordinary fast of each week, on Wednesday, Friday and Saturday, seems to have been observed, but more strictly. Later, towards the end of the fourth century, a stricter fast of three weeks became customary at Rome. Socrates seems to indicate that these three weeks were simply the last three weeks before Easter. Duchesne, on the other hand, musters arguments and testimony tending to prove that the weeks chosen were the first week (which is now Ember week), the fourth week (which still has a third lesson on Wednesday), and the sixth week, or Holy Week.[2] Finally the fasting was extended to all the weekdays of this period; but the Sundays were not counted because on Sundays no fasting should be done. Hence the six Sundays dropped out of the count and only thirty-four fast days remained within the original forty days of preparation. About the sixth century, therefore, when fasting was increasingly emphasized, Lent was found to include only thirty-four fast days. Or if you include the two additional fast days in Holy Week, Good Friday and Holy Saturday (days which up to that time had been considered as belonging to the Easter cycle, since they were commemorative of the Passion) the number came to thirty-six. John Cassian found this number thirty-six quite suitable, for it was exactly a tenth of the days of the year (365) and so we were offering almighty God our tithe of fasting and penance. It was not until later that four more days were added at the beginning to bring the total to forty days—forty days not only of preparation but of fasting as well.

How was this fast observed? Was it of strict obligation? For it was a very strenuous fast; it entailed taking actually only one single meal—the *coena* in the evening, and abstaining absolutely from wine and meat.

It seems that in the beginning at least, the fasting was not taken as a strict obligation; there is no mention of a commandment of the Church making it obligatory. It was taken for granted as something which everyone observed, rather as civilized people realize the obligation of rules of politeness, although they are nowhere prescribed. In a sense, the fasting was prompted as much by philosophical as by religious motives at least with regard to the educated class, who had a very pessimistic conception of the body in line with the teachings of Plato. The body is merely the prison of the soul; hence, it has to be repressed as much as possible, in order to free the soul. Knowing this attitude of mind we understand more easily the great fervor and the rigor of the fasting. If this fervor declined considerably during the later centuries, if today fasting has

2. That Socrates is right, is supposed by A. Chavasse, "La structure du carême," *La Maison-Dieu,* 31 (1932, III), 82–84. But cf. J. A. Jungmann, "Die Quadragesima in den Forschungen von A. Chavasse," *Archiv für Liturgiewissenschaft,* 5 (1957), 84–95.

little importance in the Church's life, is this the fault only of an ever increasing lukewarmness? We can also point to the change in our ideas and our appreciation of the body and of physical life. The Scholastics have given us the knowledge that the body is more than the mere prison of the soul, that the body's senses form the necessary foundations for the life of the intellect; while the last centuries, with their advance in science and knowledge of nature, with their hygiene and physiology, have confirmed us still more in this view. Although we know that penance and fasting should never be lacking in a Christian's life, we also know that other factors are of even greater importance for the spiritual life.

Christian antiquity knew this also; hence another, and a more *positive* component, was included in the Lenten program: the increased cultivation of the spiritual life, above all in the form of communal worship. Whereas ordinarily a public community Mass was celebrated only on the Sundays, during Lent almost every day was provided with divine services; only the Thursdays for some time were excepted. This worship took the form mainly of stational services; that is, whereas as a rule each single parish had its own divine service every Sunday, during Lent (as at other times on certain great feasts) a common service was held by the Pope himself, for which deputations from all parts of the city came together. This service was held each time in a different church or "station."

This service was consciously conducted to further the *quadraginta dierum exercitatio,* the spiritual renewal and preparation for Easter. Of course the faithful who assembled offered their gifts at the offertory and all received Holy Communion. True, daily Communion, as well as the general reception of Holy Communion at each Mass, was no longer the absolute rule during the fifth and sixth centuries. But the old practice still survived during the Lenten season. This was true even much later, in the ninth century, as we can gather from an incident in the time of Pope Nicholas I; he was asked by the Bulgars, who had just embraced Christianity, whether one had to receive the Body and Blood of Christ every day; the Pope replied that such a practice would certainly be praiseworthy, granted the proper disposition of the soul, but that daily reception was customary in the Church only during Lent. Clearly then the custom existed all the more in the sixth century.

This service was a stational service. The word *statio* in this connection means merely "a fixed place," a place for assembling. This *statio* was now chosen purposely to fit in with the significance of the particular day. The Roman stational order, it seems, in the main had been fixed in the fifth century by Pope Leo the Great's successor, Pope Hilary.

We have already seen that the service for the opening of penance was appointed to take place *ad s. Petrum ad vincula.* Similarly we find a special service for the baptismal candidates fixed at St. John the Baptist: *ad s. Johannem in Laterano.* On the other important days of Lent, especially on Sundays, the divine services took place in one of the great basilicas: *ad s. Petrum, ad s. Paulum,* etc.

On certain days, when penance was to be particularly stressed, the divine service began with a penitential procession. During the period we are speaking of, this was the case only on a few days: probably only on Wednesday and Friday in the first week, on Wednesday in the fourth week, and on Wednesday in Holy Week. The people gathered in some church conveniently situated and not too far away from the stational church, and a short service was held; this service was the *collecta.* In the old sacramentaries, therefore, we see a heading on certain days regarding a *collecta;* e.g. *collecta ad s. Anastasiam;* then an oration is given, and only after this follows the stational Mass. On other days, when there was no penitential procession, no *collecta,* the people went from all directions straight to the stational church; the Pope, however, together with his suite, came on horseback from his *patriarchium* in the Lateran. In the services themselves, the lessons in particular were chosen in accordance with the significance of the feast and as circumstances demanded.

As we already mentioned, Lent was dedicated in a particular manner to the preparation of catechumens for Baptism and of penitents for reconciliation. And as everybody knows, the Masses in Lent refer to this preparation in many ways. Every commentary on the Lenten Masses makes mention of these facts. It is, however, hardly correct to take every passage that speaks of sin or conversion as referring to the penitents or candidates of Baptism. When, for example, the penitents are already said to be calling to God for mercy on Septuagesima, such a statement cannot be correct, because the penitents were segregated from the congregation only on the Monday of the first week in Lent, or later, on Ash Wednesday. It is therefore wrong to try to find references to the candidates for Baptism in each single Mass; first of all, because the candidates for Baptism were allowed to be present only at the Fore-Mass; and secondly, because their instructions as a rule were not connected with public services; for this purpose they had special gatherings, perhaps in a chapel or some other suitable place.

The catechumens attended the stational service only on certain days, on those days, namely, on which the preparation for Baptism was to reach a certain climax. This was the case when the *symbolum* was put before them for the first time, also when the text of the Our Father was communicated to them, and (according to the Roman custom) again when the Gospels were opened for the first time in front of them. These three acts seem to have been carried out on the third, fourth and fifth Sundays of Lent, because on these three Sundays the Mass in the Gelasian sacramentary is entitled: *Pro scrutiniis electorum;* these Masses, therefore, concern the catechumens in a special manner. The candidates for Baptism themselves could be present only at the Fore-Mass, at which the sacred formulas were told them for the first time: they had then to depart, but their sponsors remained. For in the same sacramentary we read on this day: In the canon at the *Memento vivorum,* the names of the sponsors are to be recited; for they are the ones of whom it can be said in a special way: *qui tibi offerunt hoc sacrificium laudis.* The candidates for Baptism themselves could not offer—*offerre*—because they were not baptised as yet. But at the *Hanc igitur* (as the above sacramentary says) their names could be read out, because they are those for whom the prayers and the sacrifice were offered up on this day. This took place on the third and fourth and fifth Sundays in Lent, hence on those Sundays which enclose the third and fourth weeks of Lent. If now we look more closely and examine the Mass formularies in the third and fourth weeks, we meet with allusions to Baptism at every turn, especially on those weekdays which from time immemorial had been preferred: on Wednesday, Friday and Saturday, and also on Monday.

On Monday of the third week in Lent, we still read the epistle of Naaman the Syrian, who was cleansed from leprosy through the sevenfold bath, and also in the Gospel mention of Naaman is made: he alone was healed in the days of the prophet Eliseus.

On Wednesday, in the epistle, the Ten Commandments, the Old Law, are proclaimed, and in the Gospel we are told with what spirit the children of the new people of God should keep the law: not as the Pharisees do, who give only lip service to God.

On Friday, reference is made to the water which Moses struck from the rock (the familiar and frequent picture in the catacombs) and the water which our Lord proferred to the Samaritan woman.

On Saturday, the bath of Susanna is mentioned, which as early as the third century had been taken as a figure of Baptism.

The traces of the catechumenate are even more conspicuous in the fourth week of Lent. On Wednesday of this week we have even today a Mass for the candidates for Baptism *ad s. Paulum,* beginning with the words: *cum sanctificatus fuero . . . effundam super vos aquam mundam.* The Gospel is about the healing of the man born blind, for Baptism was called the illumination, the enlightening: φωτισμός.

On Friday (and on Thursday, too, by the way) in both lessons, there is mention of the raising to life of some dead persons, for Baptism is a resurrection of the dead with Christ and through His power.

On Saturday, the Mass begins with the call: *Sitientes venite ad aquas,* and in the epistle the echo of this call resounds: *non esurient, neque sitient;* in the Gospel our Lord calls Himself the light of the world.

It is clear, therefore, that during these two weeks the theme of Baptism occupies the central place. Even though the individual lessons, as we have them today, can be traced only to the seventh century, there is no doubt that before Gregory the Great they had already been chosen in much the same way.

The first week of Lent, too, had its fixed theme, or rather two of them. One was the penance of the penitents, as we already pointed out. The other was the commencement of the forty days. For this reason, on the very first day, the Sunday, there is the Gospel of our Lord's forty days' fast. And on Wednesday, Moses is put before our eyes, who spent forty days with God on the holy mountain, and Elias wandering for forty days and forty nights on the strength of the food he was given till he reached Horeb, the mountain of God. On Sunday we find all three united: Christ on the mount of the transfiguration accompanied by Moses and Elias. The Friday of this first week, by the way, may also be drawn into the picture, for it contains the Gospel of the man sick for thirty-eight years, a sickness which Augustine explained by the fact that two years were lacking in the full number of forty.

From the fifth week onward, the theme is already fixed: Passion Week and then Holy Week. From the paschal theme of the Passion and the Resurrection, the theme first dealt with is the Passion. But the physical suffering which our Lord took upon Himself is not immediately touched upon; instead, the prelude of the Passion, the battle with the Pharisees as told with special clarity by St. John, is first presented. Hence the series of the lessons in Passion Week are taken from St. John. In Holy Week, however, the lessons treat of the Passion itself.

We have thus established a theme for all the weeks of Lent—a theme which was decisive for the choice of the texts of the stational services. Only for the second week were we unable to fix a theme; it really does not have a program of its own. Here, therefore, the stational service itself forms the theme. Each day a significant church was arbitrarily chosen for the *statio*. And the church itself, with its sacred objects, with its particular traditions, suggested the theme, the *leitmotif*, for the service. On Wednesday, for example, the *statio* is *ad s. Caeciliam;* the two brothers, Tiburtius and Valerian were her co-martyrs, hence the gospel of the two brothers James and John, to whom participation in the Lord's chalice had been prophesied. Or on Saturday: *ad s. Vitalem;* Vitalis had been thrown into a hole and covered with stones; hence the lessons of the Egyptian Joseph thrown into a well, and of the wicked husbandmen killing the son of the lord of the vineyard and throwing him out of the vineyard.[3]

If we survey this picture of Lent and compare it with the program drawn up by Leo the Great: *quadraginta dierum exercitatio,* we must admit that, relatively speaking, it was a magnificent solution. However, we miss the clear logical sequence, the strictly planned progress of thought that we would expect to find in a present-day popular mission or retreat; the ideas are knit together only very loosely. For other reasons, too, we could expect today only a moderate success from a mere revival of the ancient forms, unless their content was reorganized at the same time. Certain important prerequisites are not to be found in our present age; neither the penitential discipline (whose return we certainly do not wish) nor the catechumenate; and the stational churches mentioned in the missal are solely churches of the city of Rome. But we most certainly admire the idea of making use of Lent for the spiritual renewal of the entire congregation, and furnishing the liturgy of Lent with some form of "stational" worship adapted to modern conditions that would make its way to all the important churches of the city. The calling to mind of the benefits bestowed upon us by Baptism, the using of prayer and penance, the penitential processions and fasting along with the contemplation of Christ's Passion and Resurrection—these made up a program manifesting the Church's wisdom.

3. The influence of the stations on the Mass-formularies is studied in detail in H. Grisar, *Das Missale im Lichte römischer Stadtgeschichte* (Freiburg, 1925).

And now let us cast a hurried glance at Holy Week and the *tempus paschale.*

Holy Week, beginning with Palm Sunday, is an extension of the two first days of the old triduum; it is dedicated exclusively to the contemplation of the Passion. But the Roman liturgy did not follow the path taken, for example, by the liturgy of Jerusalem as given in the *Peregrinatio Aetheriae.*

At Jerusalem, the attempt was made to recall, on each day and at each hour, just the precise event which corresponded to the hour concerned beginning with the entry on Palm Sunday, from the prayer on the Mount of Olives on Thursday evening till that hour on Good Friday when our Lord bowed His head and died. Some churches, for example, the Mozarabic or old Spanish churches, in arranging the reading of the history of the Passion during this week, made use of a harmony of the gospels. This was then distributed among the different days, and thus the whole history of the Passion was read only once but at the appropriate time, beginning with the entry into Jerusalem on Palm Sunday. Rome never accepted such a method; the Roman liturgy considers the mystery of salvation and also the history of the Passion as one whole. Therefore on Palm Sunday the entire Passion according to Matthew has always been read.

Leo the Great gave sermons on the Passion on Palm Sunday, on Wednesday, on Good Friday and on Easter Sunday, apparently in connection with the reading of the *Passio* according to one of the four gospels. Probably even on Easter Sunday the *Passio* was read once more, using the narrative according to Mark, whose Easter gospel is still read on Easter Sunday. If this is true, then the *Passio* which we now read on Tuesday—a surprising thing indeed—would have been read instead on Easter Sunday.

The Roman liturgy always keeps before its eyes the entire drama of the Passion. Hence already on Palm Sunday we beg of the Lord in view of the cross: *ut et patientiae ipsius habere documenta et resurrectionis consortia mereamur.* And even on Good Friday, at the adoration of the Holy Cross, the hymns speak of the *sancta resurrectio;* while on Easter Sunday our attention is turned in the preface first to the cross and only then to the Resurrection: *qui mortem nostram moriendo destruxit, et vitam resurgendo reparavit.*

In this connection, we must note that in Rome the liturgy of Holy Week was very simple, particularly during the period we are dealing with here. It is probable that as late as the middle of the fifth century, before the almost daily stational worship was organized, services took place only on Wednesday and Friday and the services consisted solely of readings and prayers. At a later period, the old order was kept at least for Good Friday. Even during the sixth century, the Good Friday service consisted merely in reading and prayer: Osee, Exodus, and the *Passio secundum Johannem,* followed by the *orationes solemnes* (which at that time were also said on other days, in any case on Wednesday in Holy Week); with this the service came to a close. For the rest, the day was passed in silent mourning as a day of penance; and likewise Holy Saturday, which did not have any service of its own at all. Only the clergy said the office, the *officium tenebrarum,* probably pretty much as we do today. Thus, the worship of these two days was of the greatest simplicity.

When we consider the worship of Holy Week as we celebrate it today in the Office and according to the missal, we are struck by a series of peculiar customs which appear to give it the character of severity and mourning. In reality these practices were not introduced to give the services the character of mourning; they are very ancient practices preserved from a time when the liturgy was still very simple. The law: "Primitive conditions are maintained with greater tenacity in the more sacred seasons of the Liturgical Year," called Baumstark's law,[4] was operative here. For this reason, there are on these days no private Masses, but only a service at which all the clergy are present, con-celebrating (although today without form) and communicating, as formerly they did on all Sundays and feastdays. When the clergy approach the altar, they first prostrate themselves for silent prayer, as formerly they did at the beginning of every Mass. The altar is bare and not covered except for the service, as formerly also at other times. No bells are used, only clappers, as formerly when there were as yet no bells. In the Office, there is no introduction with *Deus in adjutorium,* no *Gloria* after the psalms, no prayer for the blessing before the lessons, no hymn—all this in conformity with ancient usage throughout the year. So the ancient practices in the services have been piously preserved through the centuries, and, therefore, it is on these days that we stand in a specially close relationship with the faithful of Christian antiquity.

This holds good also with regard to Easter itself; it had the form of a vigil or night-watch. During the sixth century, it is true, it was no longer kept throughout the whole night, but only in the

4. A. Baumstark, *Comparative Liturgy* (Westminster: Newman, 1958), 27.

late evening, so that it was surely finished by midnight. By the fifth century, adult Baptisms had become less frequent, and less time was required for them. The service being shorter, Mass was not postponed till dawn but appended to the vigil itself. And so in the sixth century, in contrast to the usage of the earlier centuries, another Mass was celebrated on Easter morning itself—our present Easter Mass.[5]

But the principal celebration was the vigil. Like any other vigil of the period, it consisted chiefly in the reading of long passages from Scripture, in this case the twelve lessons still to be found in the Roman missal before the renewal of the Holy Week liturgy in 1956. And the solemnity closed with the celebration of Holy Mass, the true *memoria passionis et resurrectionis*. In between the lessons and the Mass, the sacraments were administered, especially Baptism, for on this night the neophytes were to rise together with Christ. They were also confirmed and received their First Holy Communion. This night-watch was also a favorite time for ordination to the priesthood, for this too is a fruit of Christ's passion and victory.

However, the mystery of the day was given its most forceful expression in the twelve lessons. All of them revolve around the same subject: newness of life through the resurrection. Each prophetic type depicts a new aspect of this wondrous mystery. Here is a new creation; here is rescue from the great deluge; here is a promise of sonship greater than that of children of Abraham; here is deliverance from the bondage of Egypt and passage through the Red Sea; here is life for death-doomed mankind; here is resuscitation of limbs dead to grace; here, the Land of Promise. Christ's Resurrection—our Baptism: these were the thoughts that give this night its special character.

But there is another feature of Holy Saturday's service that has to be mentioned—the solemn candle service. Since this was a night service, lamps had to be lighted. And as was but natural, the lighting of the lamps was carried out ceremoniously, with a blessing. This occurred at any and every vigil service. But on this night the ceremony had special significance and was carried out with special solemnity. For in the light we have an apt symbol of the risen Christ, the Light of the world, from whom we in turn are to receive enlightenment, by whom we are to be illumined. At this pe-

5. H. Vorgrimler, "War die altchristliche Osternacht eine ununterbrochene Feier?" *Zeitschrift für kath. Theologie,* 74 (1952), 464–472.

riod, the consecration of the Easter light was carried out by the deacon, with the singing of the *Exsultet,* traces of which are already to be discovered in St. Jerome's writings.

About Eastertide not much need be said. All the seven weeks that followed were considered as one single festive time. Pentecost was from olden times the closing day of this period; in fact the whole season received the name *Pentecoste,* a name which designated not only the closing day ("the fiftieth") but the intervening time as well. But now Pentecost itself received greater prominence, and was celebrated as the commemoration of the descent of the Holy Spirit, through whom the work of our salvation was completed. A Pentecost octave did not as yet exist. And since Whitsunday was celebrated for its historical connotation as the day of the Holy Spirit's descent, another day of historical significance also received liturgical recognition; since the fourth century the feast of the Ascension also was celebrated.

But of the remaining days of the season only the first week, Easter week, gained any special prominence. In a particular way this was the week of the neophytes. All this week they wore their white garments. At the daily Mass they occupied a place of honor. And the lessons and songs used at the Masses continued to stress the theme of Baptism. Every afternoon the newly-baptized assembled at the baptistry and assisted at special devotions. The close of this festive week was the Sunday after Easter, *Dominica in albis,* "The Sunday of the White Garments," so called because the neophytes wore their white baptismal robes for the last time that day. Sometimes this title is explained as an abbreviation for *Dominica in albis depositis*—"white garments no longer worn." Such an explanation may be true for a later period, but not for the fifth or sixth century. Later, when Baptism was administered late in the afternoon of Holy Saturday, the octave of that solemnity was, of course, Easter Saturday, and so the white robes were set aside on Saturday. But as long as Baptism was administered during the night watch—morally one with the feast of Easter—the Sunday following still belonged to the Easter octave. In the oldest of the sacramentaries, Low Sunday is still marked with the special rites of Easter and the familiar changes in the canon. So during the sixth century this Sunday was really *Dominica in Albis.*

Originally, then, the Easter season closed with Whitsunday and the ordinary season with its weekly fasts was again inaugurated. In Rome, as Leo the Great witnesses, the week after Pentecost was an Ember week, as is still the case at present. It was not till after the sixth century that any attempt was made to make Pentecost a feast similar to Easter by assigning to it an octave, although this did not fit in well with the existing Ember days. Since then the Easter season, as our missal remarks, has closed with the Mass of the Saturday in Whitsun week.

CHAPTER TWENTY-ONE

The Christmas Cycle

AFTER having seen the form given to the Easter cycle in the Roman liturgy during the last centuries of Christian antiquity, we shall now study the parallel development of the Christmas cycle. In Christian antiquity, at least at Rome, Christmas did not occupy the same high rank as Easter. True, it was for a long time celebrated with all that love and perhaps with all that holy enthusiasm with which we today celebrate our feast of Christ the King, for if Arianism attempted to degrade the person of Christ, Christmas presented a favorable opportunity for extolling Christ's greatness and glory. For similar reasons, as we have seen, its companion feast, the feast of Epiphany, which was of Oriental origin, was adopted in the West, so that two feasts of identical theme were already being celebrated in the fifth century. But in the beginning these two feasts stood isolated; for a long time there was no question of a festal cycle, at any rate not of a preparatory time preceding the feast.

Very early, however, Christmas was given a nocturnal celebration, perhaps as early as the fifth century. But for a long time there was no thought of advancing it to a rank similar to that of Easter and the night of Easter. In those days if anyone had spoken of a Holy Night as we do today in German ("Heilige Nacht," "Weihnachten"), nobody would have understood it to refer to Christmas night, but rather to the *nox sancta,* which always was Easter night.

In the Oriental liturgies, and also in the Gallic liturgies, it was somewhat different. True, it was not Christmas but Epiphany which here was early advanced to a high rank, placing it almost on a par with the Easter feast. For Epiphany, like Easter, had become in the Orient a baptismal feast, and as such it had not only been given a vigil similar to the Easter-vigil, but also a corresponding time of preparation which soon evolved into a *Quadragesima*, as we shall see later. So out of the feast itself a festal cycle was easily developed.

But Rome in the fourth and fifth centuries was still far from following such a lead. However, stirred by these suggestions coming from outside, Rome also gradually came closer to adopting such a development. There were, for example, hints of a development in Jerusalem which had led to an increase in the festive celebration of Christmas day itself. The services at Jerusalem were, of course, well known in Rome. We need only remember Jerome and the Roman matrons of his circle living in the Holy Land.

Already in those days, around the year 400, the feast of Epiphany (which was really the Christmas feast of the Orient) was celebrated at Jerusalem with a solemn nocturnal service. This consisted in a pilgrimage to Bethlehem, as we learn from the *Peregrinatio Aetheriae*. Here at midnight, Mass was celebrated over the Grotto of the Nativity in the basilica built by Constantine, a church which still survives; it is the oldest church in the world. Then at dawn the procession returned to Jerusalem, where, after a short rest, a second Mass was said. This celebration was imitated in Rome. After the council of Ephesus (431), Pope Sixtus III reconstructed the ancient basilica of Liberius as a church of our Lady: *Ad Sanctam Mariam Maiorem;* later on a special side chapel was built in the basilica in imitation of the grotto of the nativity at Bethlehem and therefore called *ad Praesepe*—the crib chapel. It was here that the service was held the night before Christmas. Even our present-day missal still assigns the station here for the first Mass of Christmas: *Statio ad s. Mariam Maiorem ad Praesepe*. And even the song which was sung on the way from Bethlehem to Jerusalem is preserved in our Christmas liturgy in the *Graduale* of the second Christmas Mass: *Benedictus qui venit in nomine Domini; Deus Dominus et illuxit nobis.*[1]

This was the new service that was added to the Christmas Mass during the fifth century. The Christmas Mass itself, the old and principal service, still took place at the usual hour in the morning and it used the St. John's prologue as Gospel. *Et Verbum caro factum est* is the decisive statement in this Gospel. This phrase provides the theme which the celebration of Christmas in Rome had

1. Baumstark, *Comparative Liturgy*, 162 f.

possessed from the very beginning. Just as Easter was the feast of the Redemption, so was Christmas the feast of the Incarnation of the Son of God. The great mysteries of the faith, understood in their full theological depth, were, therefore, the proper and prime subjects of the great festivals. But because of the new midnight Mass, because of the representation of the crib and the celebration *ad praesepe,* the celebration was enriched and shaped in accordance with the popular tastes, and accordingly the Gospel at the midnight Mass was chosen to tell in a more realistic and concrete manner the historical events of the nativity, the angels, the shepherds, and the Child in the crib.

But we must not forget that the origin of the Roman Christmas feast is found in the idea of the *Sol Invictus,* of Christ as the new Sun, as the Light in the midst of the darkness of this world. And we may suppose that this very idea may for a long time also have been present in the celebrating of the midnight Mass. For there was a double application of the picture of Christ as the Rising Sun: His first appearance as the Sun was at His birth of the Virgin Mary, His entrance into this earthly life; for His second appearance, more glorious even than the rising Sun, was His Resurrection, His entrance into the life of glory.[2]

The third Mass to be added to the Christmas festival, the Mass *in aurora* (our *second* Christmas Mass), must belong to an era even before Gregory the Great, for in the sermon so familiar to us in which he tells us we are allowed to say Mass three times on this day (*Missarum sollemnia ter hodie celebraturi sumus*), he seems to speak of this privilege as of a custom existing already for some time. Of course he did not mean that every priest said Mass three times, but that three times a solemn stational service took place which the Pope himself had to celebrate.[3]

The significance of the second service *ad s. Anastasiam* is not quite clear. Its origin, however, seems to have been as follows: In the church of the *titulus Anastasiae* the feast of a holy martyr Eugenia was always celebrated on December 25. However, at the time of the Byzantine rule, in the second half of the sixth century, the government palace stood in the vicinity of this church, and the Byzantine officials made this church their court church; and on this day they venerated there a martyr who was already highly venerated in Byzantium, a St. Anastasia who, by a curious coin-

2. Cf. H. Rahner, "Die Gottesgeburt," *Zeitschrift für kath. Theologie,* 59 (1935), 333–418.

3. J. P. Kirsch, *Die Stationskirchen des Missale Romanum* (Freiburg, 1926), 237 f.

cidence, bore the same name as the foundress of the church (which consequently was called: *tit. sanctae Anastasiae,* for the martyr Anastasia). Obviously in order to honor the imperial court, the stational service was held here at the church of Anastasia. But because it was the great feast of Christmas, the service eventually took the form of a second Christmas Mass, with St. Anastasia reduced to a simple commemoration. Again we can see the operation of the Baumstark law which was mentioned in an earlier chapter, "That primitive conditions are maintained with greater tenacity in the more sacred seasons of the Liturgical Year."

Thus was Christmas celebrated in Rome about the middle of the sixth century. But along with Christmas there came, twelve days later, the feast of Epiphany, which also was celebrated with the rank of a high feast, as the eight festive sermons by Pope Leo the Great testify. The first beginnings of a festive cycle appeared when both these feasts received an *after-celebration.* Easter, too, had first acquired a fifty days' after-celebration, and only later a preparatory period. Christmas acquired an octave. True, there is direct evidence of this octave only since the seventh century, and then only in the form of a celebration of the eighth day itself, New Year's day; in the ancient sources it is called *octava Domini.* But at an earlier period, even before this day was expressly designated as the octave of Christmas, it was celebrated in Rome as a feast of our Lady, the oldest feast of our Lady in the Roman liturgy: *Natale s. Mariae.* We must certainly suppose that this feast of our Lady was meant as an after-celebration of Christmas. Eight days after Christmas a new aspect of the mystery of the Incarnation was celebrated by honoring our Lord's mother. For the veneration of Mary grows spontaneously from the contemplation of the Christmas-mystery. On Christmas day itself we say the beautiful responsorium: *Sancta et immaculata viginitas. . . .* Our admiration and glorification of the divine counsel realized in the Incarnation leads us spontaneously to praise Christ's Virgin Mother. The Mass formulary, as well as the Office, of January first still displays many strong Marian characteristics. For example, the oration of the day is *Deus, qui salutis aeternae, beatae Mariae virginitate fecunda, humano generi praemia praestitisti. . . .* The Post-Communion oration is even more pointed in its reference to our Lady's intervention. The psalms at Vespers are those of the Blessed Virgin's Office. And as the stational church, a church of Our Lady is still given: *ad s. Mariam trans Tiberim.* The present name for the Christmas octave, *festum Circumcisionis,* is not of Roman but of

Gallic origin; this name came to Rome after the tenth century when so many other institutions of the Franco-Germanic north were incorporated into the Roman liturgy. The Mass formulary, however, has not been substantially changed.

Epiphany, too, must have been given an after-celebration at a fairly early date. In the seventh century list of lessons, this after-celebration is already so formed that during the weeks following the feast not only the Sundays but also the Wednesdays, Fridays, and Saturdays have lessons founded on the Epiphany mystery; emphasizing in the Gospel lessons two sides, two aspects of the greatness of Christ: His power and His wisdom. His power is illustrated by His miracles; cf. the Offertory, *Dextera Domini fecit virtutem.* And His wisdom is illustrated by His parables; cf. the Communion verse, *Mirabantur omnes de his quae procedebant de ore Dei.* If this is true of the seventh century, we must suppose that also in the sixth century an after-celebration of a similar nature must surely have existed.

I said that Christmas did not immediately acquire a specially high rank and that in the beginning an octave of the feast was celebrated only on the eighth day. This, I believe, would explain to some extent why immediately after December 25 we celebrate feasts which have very little to do with Christmas: St. Stephen, St. John the Evangelist and other saints. How did this come about? Although the breviary on the feast of St. Stephen presents a sermon of St. Fulgentius in which he puts before our eyes a whole string of connections between Christ's birthday feast and the day of death of the first martyr, he probably has not convinced any of us that the Protomartyr's death really has such a close relationship to the Saviour's birth. Both these feast-days of December 26 and 27 were surely celebrated at a time when Christmas did not yet have a very high rank and when, therefore, these days were still free. The same two feasts were already celebrated in the Orient in the fourth century, at a time when Christmas was just gradually beginning to become known in the Orient. The feast of St. Stephen was celebrated in various churches of the Orient always on the same day, on December 26. But with regard to the days following there were differences; December 27 generally celebrated the memory of the two sons of Zebedee, John and James. It is probable, therefore, that the feast of St. Stephen had been already fixed in the Orient before Christmas was introduced, and that it was then also transferred to Rome. It is not impossible that, in fixing the date, some ancient tradition regarding the saint's day of death was consulted.

On the other hand, we have to take notice of another possibility; it was not unusual at the close of Christian antiquity to add one or more accompanying feasts to a feast of higher rank; it goes without saying, then, that during a time when the veneration of the martyrs was flourishing, the Protomartyr would be so distinguished.[4]

Now let us ask, when did the *preparation* for Christmas come into existence? In other words, how long has *Advent* existed? And what precisely is the significance of the Advent season? Here we must remark an important difference between the Roman and the Gallic liturgies. In Gaul as early as the end of the fourth century, we find an Advent lasting three weeks. And by the end of the fifth century this Advent has already developed into an Advent much more extensive and intensive than our present Advent—a second *Quadragesima.*

In Rome, on the contrary, there was at this time no question of an Advent. The first trace of anything like it comes from nearby Capua. In a Capua list of pericopes, of about the year 540, the four Sundays of Advent are mentioned. For Rome itself, the first account we have of an Advent is in the four sermons preached by Gregory the Great. Under him it assumes substantially the same shape it has today. However, this is beyond the period we are considering and so a discussion of it must here be omitted.[5] The only thing we can ascertain regarding Rome before the age of Gregory is a transformation of the Ember week that falls in the month of December, shortly before Christmas, into a sort of Christmas prelude.

Before we take up this matter, let us use the occasion to deal briefly with the Ember seasons. These are among the most ancient institutions of the Roman liturgy. We say *quattuor tempora,* but the most ancient sources of the Roman liturgy speak only of three such times. Three times a year a sort of retreat period was held; this was the *ieiunium IVi, VIIi, Xi mensis.* In other words, during the months of June, September, and December one week was especially devoted to prayer and fasting. Wednesday and Friday were kept as days of fast, with the fast continuing also on Saturday. And then on Saturday evening a vigil was held in much the same way as the Easter vigil, with twelve lessons and with corresponding songs and prayers. This vigil-service continued far into the night and, therefore, held good for the usual Sunday observance; hence in the

4. Baumstark, *op. cit.,* 184 f.

5. W. Croce, "Die Adventmessen des römischen Missale," *Zeitschrift für kath. Theologie,* 74 (1952), 227–317; *idem,* "Die Adventsliturgie," *ibid.,* 76 (1954), 257–296; 440–472.

sacramentaries we still find even at a later time in the formularies of the Ember days the title: *Sabbato in XII lectionibus*, and for the following Sunday the simple notation *Dominica vacat*, that is, there is no proper Sunday Mass, because the vigil takes its place. Those of us who recite the Breviary know the formula with which Pope Leo the Great announces the beginning of the Ember weeks: *Quarta igitur et sexta feria jejunemus; sabbato vero apud beatum Petrum Apostolum vigilias celebremus.*

These Ember weeks, as we already remarked, were spaced three months apart, in the summer, in autumn, and in winter. The fourth place, in spring, remained free, because there was already the great season of recollection, *Quadragesima*. That recollection and spiritual renewal were the purpose of these Ember days can be seen from the fact that not only the concluding day (Saturday) but also Wednesday and Friday had special Masses of their own. Outside of Lent, these are the only weekdays which are still provided with special Mass-formularies in the *Proprium de tempore*. In a secondary way the Ember days are also days of thanksgiving for the harvest—the three harvests that would come into question in Italy, namely wheat, wine and oil. And because the Ember seasons included a vigil fashioned after the Easter vigil, this was also an opportunity for the conferring of major orders, and it was so determined in 494 by Pope Gelasius I: ordinations are to be conferred *quarti mensis ieiunio, septimi et decimi*, as well as on the Saturday before what we now call Passion Sunday. It should be pointed out that there is a close connection between this third component of the Ember weeks and their primary purpose; the ordination dates were considered suitable because the preceding days represented days of preparation both for the ordinands and the people. In substance the same concept was operative here as is enshrined in Canon 1001 of our present legislation; namely, that the candidates for orders should spend some time before ordination in "spiritual exercises."

Opinions differ regarding the origin of the Ember seasons. Some authors advance the idea that they were founded on the harvest-feasts of ancient Rome. The objection that immediately comes to mind, namely that the early Christians were wary of imitating the forms of heathen worship, is not pertinent, since the early converts might well have continued to observe the same periods of prayer after their conversion that they observed before. Still this remains a mere conjecture. Perhaps Leo the Great was right in tracing the

Ember seasons to apostolic tradition, for there appears to be a kindred custom in pre-Christian Judaism. The Prophet Zacharias speaks mysteriously about "fasts you kept ever, when three months of the year, or four, six months or nine were gone" (8:19). And in the Hebrew scrolls discovered in 1947 near the Dead Sea, texts contemporary to Christ, special exercises of prayer are appointed for the three (or four) seasons of the year. In any case, as we have already seen, the Ember days were given a new character when the Roman Church adopted the practice.

Originally, as we mentioned, only three seasons were observed. It was not until some time in the fifth century that the fourth season, spring, was endowed with an Ember week; the first week in Lent. But in doing so apparently no new formulary was written for the vigil service of the Saturday; instead the December formulary was simply transferred to Lent. For December a new formulary was created not only for the Saturday vigil but for Wednesday and Friday as well, and these were written to serve as a prelude and preparation for Christmas. In other words, Ember week was given an Advent character. Thus we now read the Gospels of the Annunciation by the angel and of Mary's visit to Elizabeth and of the precursor John; and the other lessons are nearly all taken from Isaias, from the chapters predicting the Saviour's coming.

This is for the present only a hypothesis, but it is supported by considerable evidence. In the Breviary on the commemorative days of the earliest Popes, we often notice the statement: *habuit ordinationes . . . mense Decembri, quibus. . . .* These reports come from the *Liber Pontificalis,* a biographical sketch of the Popes, the oldest part of which was composed around the year 530. For the first centuries this book is not reliable, but for the period since the fifth and sixth centuries it is a good source. During the fifth century, therefore, according to the *Liber Pontificalis,* there were sacerdotal ordinations in Rome during December. But for the Popes who reigned about 500 or later, we no longer read of ordinations *mense Decembri;* only the month of February is mentioned. We must conclude, therefore, that towards the close of the fifth century the term for the ordinations was transferred in Rome from December to February. And probably the old liturgical framework, the Mass formulary of the Saturday in Ember week, was transferred with it; for in this Mass formulary now used on the Saturday of the first week in Lent there are several passages that speak in a striking manner of the people whom God chose as His portion (e.g. first reading: *Dominus elegit te hodie*) and of the *servi Domini*—passages, which could very well be understood of those selected for the priestly office.

The Ember week of the month of December, which was thus reformed towards the end of the fifth century, was the first step taken in Rome towards setting up a preparation for the Christmas feast. In the older *Sacramentarium Gelasianum* (a book now extant in only one manuscript, probably written at St. Denis about 750, but whose prototype was used at Rome at the latest in the sixth century) the orations of the Masses of the two Sundays before Christmas and the Ember days that lie between are like those we have today. But Rome allowed matters to remain at this stage for a whole century. It was not till the time of Gregory the Great that an Advent of four weeks' duration, much as we have it today, was introduced.

An entirely different development took place in Gaul. This we will now have to consider, because the Advent of the Gallic liturgy later on, in the course of the Middle Ages, exerted a strong influence on the Roman Advent and gave it its final shape. In Gaul, as already remarked, an Advent of three weeks is already traceable as early as the fourth century. Under Bishop Perpetuus of Tours (490), we then hear of a fast beginning on November 11th (the feast of St. Martin of Tours) and lasting till Christmas. This fast can be traced also in the following centuries under the name of *quadragesima s. Martini.* Thus in the Gallic liturgy the step was taken in the fifth century of assimilating the feast of Christ's nativity to the Easter feast by prefixing to it a forty-day fast starting with November 11. The liturgical books conform to this arrangement and give formulas for six or even seven Sundays of Advent. But there are certain puzzling features in this arrangement. Why forty days? and why this long stretch into early November? The answer is to be found in the fact that in Gaul, where the influence of the Orient was quite strong, Epiphany was introduced long before Christmas.[6] And since Epiphany was considered a baptismal day in the Orient, and therefore in Gaul, it was in many respects observed like Easter; in the *Missale Gothicum,* one of the most important witnesses of the Gallic liturgy, the feast of Epiphany has a vigil with a series of readings similar to the Easter night-watch. Epiphany, therefore, had to be preceded by a season of fast, and more precisely, a season of forty days' fast, reckoned strictly. But in Gaul

6. Jungmann, *Gewordene Liturgie* (Innsbruck, 1941), 240 ff.

not only Sundays but Saturdays as well were excluded from the fast—two days each week. Hence to finish the forty-day fasting period by January 5, it had to start on November 11, eight weeks before Epiphany ($20 + 31 + 5 = 56$ days, containing $8 \times 5 = 40$ fast-days).

Later this *quadragesima s. Martini* was considered a preparation for the feast of December 25, and then a different type of reckoning had to be employed. In fact, other systems were devised, with Advent starting twelve days earlier or, as in Spain, the forty days were simply counted back from Christmas and thus November 15 was made the first day of Advent. In some parts of the Carolingian area there was even a pre-Christmas period of three months, beginning on September 24, on which was celebrated—nine months before June 24—a feast of the *Conceptio sancti Johannis,* our Saviour's precursor.

All these developments occurred within the period we are dealing with, but in the area of the Gallic liturgy. They are of importance for our study of the Roman liturgy only because later on they were transferred on a surprisingly large scale to the Roman liturgy.

Even the former beginning of Advent on September the 25th seems to have exerted an influence upon the Roman liturgy. For a long time liturgists were struck by the unusual character which the 18th Sunday after Pentecost shows in our missal. This is seen, for example, in the Epistle, which interrupts the series of the other Sunday Epistles (which are read according to their order in the biblical canon). The Epistle for this Sunday is taken, not from Ephesians, as one might expect, but from I Corinthians, and concludes with the words: *qui et confirmabit vos sine crimine, in die adventus D.n.J.C.* This sounds like an allusion to Advent. And this seems to be the special intention: this 18th Sunday in the old documents is also the end of the Ember week of the month of September; in other words, it was so placed that it did not fall far from September 25. The Introits on this and succeeding Sundays are also different from those that precede, being taken from other books than the Psalms and disposed with reference to the pre-Advent *cursus.*[7]

Even more distinct is the influence of the Gallic conception of Advent on the Roman liturgy in the month of November. In the Breviary we start the first week of November with lessons from the Prophets, which are then continued until Christmas: first Ezechiel, Daniel and the lesser Prophets, then Isaias. The reading of the

7. Jungmann, *Mass of the Roman Rite,* I, 330.

prophets is the most appropriate reading for Advent. In this regard we must mention another item. Although the lessons and orations on the last Sundays after Pentecost (which fall within November) change from Sunday to Sunday, the songs of the *Proprium* are always the same from the 23rd Sunday onwards. They start in the Introit with the thought of Advent taken from Jeremias: *Dicit Dominus: ego . . . reducam capitivatem vestram de cunctis locis.* Finally, the last Sunday after Pentecost has a Gospel which also originated in the Gallic Advent traditions: the Gospel of the end of the world and of the second advent according to Matthew, exactly parallel to the Gospel we read on the first Sunday of Advent taken from Luke. Formerly it, too, had been an Advent Gospel.

We can say, therefore, that the last weeks of the ecclesiastical year preceding our present Advent represent a sort of pre-Advent. In this pre-Advent period, the idea of the final coming of Our Lord, of the *parousia,* is predominant, as it is in Advent itself. By remembering this second and glorious advent, we prepare ourselves to celebrate the remembrance of the first advent. And this idea is being emphasized once more in our own time. For not only is the feast of All Saints celebrated in this period, but the feast of Christ the King, who is *in gloria Dei Patris,* is added as background, showing the depths of our hope and expectation.

There is yet one more item of our present Roman Advent which we must trace to the Gallican tradition: its penitential character. According to the liturgical books of the early Middle Ages the Roman Advent was not a penitential season. It was simply a period of preparation for, and a joyful expectation of, Christmas. Therefore only the Sundays had the special characteristics of Advent. It was not until after the tenth century, when the Gallic Advent had exerted its influence on the Roman Advent, that it received its present penitential character. Now, however, the *Gloria* and the *Te Deum* are omitted on the Sundays in Advent, purple vestments are worn just as in Lent, and a restriction is placed on the use of flowers and the organ. However, it never became—except in passing—a period of fasting. These are the influences of the old Gallic liturgy, of the ancient *quadragesima s. Martini,* on the Roman liturgy; it gave to our Advent and to our preparation for Christmas its more serious character.

In closing this chapter let us summarize what we have said regarding the Christmas cycle as it appeared in the closing years of Christian antiquity, before Gregory the Great. There was a simple preparation during the December Ember week. Christmas itself already possessed its three Masses and a sort of octave on January 1. But the cycle also included the twin feast of Epiphany and the Sundays that followed, which were already stamped with the features of the Epiphany mystery.

CHAPTER TWENTY-TWO

The Daily Office

IN THIS and the following chapter, we shall inquire what the everyday public services of the occidental churches looked like at the end of the period of Christian antiquity, especially in Rome. How was the service conducted on Sundays and on week days throughout the year? What did the clergy do, and how far did the people take part in it? In the present chapter, we shall ask ourselves in particular, what did the canonical horary prayer look like in those days?

The over-all picture of divine worship bore little resemblance to that of our own times. The greatest difference, certainly, was the way in which use was made of Mass. It will come as a surprise to many, no doubt, to note that the Eucharistic celebration did not occupy the prominent place which it has at present. Today we are accustomed to finding in all our churches day after day as many Masses as there are priests on hand. And on Sundays Masses are said till noon; in fact Masses now are celebrated even in the evening. But during the period of Christian antiquity, Mass was said only sparingly; anyhow this holds true at least for public service.

Divine service for the whole community was conducted on Sunday. As far as possible, the entire community was expected to gather at one divine service; this was to represent the unity of the Church. This idea was so deep-seated and so widespread that recently writers have ventured the opinion that during the fourth and fifth centuries even in cities like Milan or Carthage only one divine service took place, namely the episcopal one. I do not believe that this opinion is correct.

In Rome, at any rate, Mass must have been celebrated regularly on Sundays not only in the twenty-five titular churches (we would call them parish churches) but also in the larger basilicas of the martyrs. A decision of Leo the Great has come down to us, in which he replies to a question from the Orient: it is allowed to conduct divine service twice in a church if otherwise part of the people would not have an opportunity to take part. But one service in each church on Sundays and feast days was the rule. We may assume that in the *Proprium de tempore* of our present *Missale Romanum* we possess the service calendar followed by the Roman churches of the fifth to the sixth century. Besides Sundays and feastdays of the Lord, therefore, Mass was celebrated everywhere perhaps only in Lent and on Ember days. As yet the feastdays of the martyrs were not celebrated with divine services in all churches, but only in the pertinent sepulchral church. A relic of this concept is still preserved in our Missal in which sometimes for one day two Mass formularies are given. Take, for example, August the 7th: there is first a Mass with the heading *S. Cajetani:* then a second one follows with the inscription: *Eadem die 7 Aug. pro S. Donato, Episcopo et Martyre.* This is a reminiscence of the ancient regulation. The festive Mass of a martyr was meant especially for his sepulchral church; and here apparently a stational service was often held on the commemorative day in question, even though it is not specially marked in the Missal; and often a solemn vigil was also held during the previous night.

But besides this public worship, there also existed a service of a more private character. In Rome towards the close of Christian antiquity there was a large number of small sanctuaries, chapels and oratories, most of which surely were connected with the memory of a martyr. We know that when St. Ambrose came to Rome, he celebrated Mass in the house of a noble Roman matron. Often, too, smaller chapels were connected with the larger churches (for example, the chapel *ad Praesepe* at S. Maria Maggiore); for the principle still held good: in the church itself there should be only one altar; if a second one was desired, a special chapel was built for it. (It was only in Gaul, it seems, that this principle was already abandoned as early as the sixth century.) In such more or less private oratories, whether they were permanently equipped as such or only for a time, private services must have taken place fairly frequently, for example, a divine service for a deceased member of the family in question, or a divine service for some special intention.

The third of the three parts of the Gelasian Sacramentary consists almost entirely of formularies for votive Masses and for Masses for the dead. There are Masses for somebody going on a journey, for rain, for good weather, for the warding off of a cattle disease; a Mass for a birthday, a Mass for a sick person, a Mass in thanksgiving for recovery from sickness, a Mass to obtain children, etc. Finally there are also various Masses for the dead. The majority of these Masses could not have been used, as a rule, in public churches or for public services. They served for the private devotion of some small circle.

But in the public churches day after day, a different type of service took place: the *canonical Hours*. Of course, not all the canonical Hours which we have today in our Breviary belonged to this public worship. We recall that during the third and fourth centuries, prayers at the various hours of the day and of the night were private exercises of individual Christians and of their families. During the centuries that followed, accounts of such exercises become more scanty, but on the whole the same order must have been retained. And the clergy, too, must have held these exercises just like the laity—as private exercises. For two of the Hours, however, an exception soon was made: for a morning hour—mostly called Matins, and today called Lauds: and for an evening hour—what we call Vespers. From the fourth century on, these two Hours began to be conducted publicly day after day in all larger churches. They were the ordinary daily services: the morning worship, for which many faithful came to the church, as at present they come to the Mass; and the evening worship, in which the people likewise took part.

So it was in the Orient. In the *Apostolic Constitutions* (VIII, 35) the bishop is exhorted to assemble the faithful every evening and recite the vesper psalm (that is, Psalm 140, with the words: *elevatio manuum mearum sacrificium vespertinum*). After this, there is a detailed mention of the intercessions for the various classes and intentions. In conclusion, the bishop summarized the prayer in the oration. Similarly he is to assemble the faithful in the morning (c. 37); here, besides other psalms, the morning psalm is said (that is, Psalm 62, *Deus, Deus meus, ad te de luce vigilo*) followed by prayers similar to the ones said at Vespers.

A similar order was followed elsewhere: in Spain, Gaul, Italy and also in Rome.[1]

In Rome there is extant in the *Liber diurnus*, the papal chancery book, a formulary probably of the sixth century; it is the so-called *Cautio Episcopi*, which the newly consecrated bishop had to sign

1. Some items are collected in *Brevierstudien* (Trier, 1958).

and in which the various duties were enumerated which were incumbent upon him. Amongst them there is also the obligation to celebrate the horary prayers (*vigilias in ecclesiis celebrare*) every morning in the church together with his entire clergy. Here the morning worship is already increased to some extent. The order is given: three or four lessons were to be read out each time, and an equal number of psalms were to be sung both antiphonally and responsorially.[2]

The communal horary prayers were much richer in those places where, since the fourth century, communities of *monks* had come into existence. Where monks lived in common (and similarly also virgins consecrated to God), the entire horary Office was said in common: hence not only the prayers in the morning and in the evening, Lauds and Vespers, but also the prayers during the Hours of the night and especially during the three Hours of the day. In these services they observed an order similar to that observed in public worship in the morning and evening hours, as noted above. There was reading from Sacred Scripture; psalms were sung; intercessions were recited, and in conclusion an oration was said. Such monasteries were generally erected in isolated places; a famous example is Monte Cassino. But it was precisely in Italy that such monasteries were also erected in towns, preferably in the vicinity of some famous martyr's grave. In Rome monasteries existed already in the fifth and sixth centuries at S. Sebastiano, at S. Agnese, at S. Lorenzo, and a convent even at St. Peter's.[3] These foundations had obiously arisen from the pious desire that the horary prayers, performed according to the manner of the monks, should never cease either day or night in the basilicas erected over the graves of the martyrs.

The order of worship followed in such institutions was already to be found in Jerusalem around the year 400. The pilgrim Aetheria describes how, day after day, very early in the morning (*ante pullorum cantum*), the monks and the virgins consecrated to God (*monazontes et parthenae ut hic dicunt*) appeared in the Church of the Holy Sepulchre and began their prayers; and how, during the day, they continued them. But the two Hours of the morning and the evening stand out in these monastic daily Offices, because they were celebrated with greater solemnity and more people were accustomed to assist at them.[4]

When, in the beginning of the sixth century, St. Benedict founded

2. n. 74; Sickel, 77 f.
3. H. Grisar, *Geschichte Roms u. der Päpste* (Freiburg, 1901), 257 f.
4. *Peregr. Aeth.*, c. 24.

his monasteries and wrote the rule for his Order, carefully arranging the daily Office, he already had well-tried models before his eyes for the arrangement of the daily office. Of the seventy-three chapters of his *Regula,* thirteen (ch. 8–20)—hence more than a sixth—deal with the arrangement of the Office: how many psalms and which psalms are to be said at each hour, what is to be done on Sundays and on weekdays, when the Alleluia is to be sung, how the single hours are to be concluded, etc. It is the first detailed description of the Office extant. And because St. Benedict, as he himself once expressly says (c. 13) and as he hints in another passage, had the practice of the *Ecclesia Romana* before his eyes, it is possible for us to make certain inferences from the data he gives us as to the essential form of the Roman Office as it was then performed.

Even at that date it was already remarkably similar to the Office we have today. It was essentially a monastic office; it even contained the two latest Hours to be included in the diurnal, Prime and Compline. These two Hours were, without doubt, an outgrowth of the exigencies of monastic life. Since the original morning Hour (Lauds) and the original evening Hour (Vespers) had become solemn Hours held in the church at a time when the people, too, were able to be present, the monasteries introduced two other periods of prayer immediately after rising and immediately before going to bed, a special morning and a special night prayer recited in the dormitory. John Cassian (d. 435), that much-traveled Oriental scholar, so well acquainted with eastern monastic practices, tells this anecdote regarding the development of these two Hours: In a certain monastery in Bethlehem some of the monks began to go back to bed after Lauds and to sleep till the time for Terce. To put a stop to this, a new Hour was introduced to mark the start of the work day. Similarly Compline was inserted just before bedtime. The more private character of these Hours can be seen from the fact that they were prayed not in the church or in an oratory but in the sleeping quarters (*ubi dormiunt*).[5] Such is the origin of Prime and Compline. And these two were then also incorporated into the cursus of the Hours.

In the Office of the Roman Church of the sixth century, the distribution of the psalms was already identical with the one which continued in use for fourteen centuries till the time of Pope Pius X. The whole psalter was said once a week; Psalm 118 was always used in the Little Hours. For Lauds, psalms were specially chosen

5. *De cursu diurno vel nocturno* (M. Andrieu, *Les Ordines Romani,* III [Louvain, 1951], 205 f.).

which included mention of the morning hour, or were directed to the divine praises (from which this hour received its name). Both kinds of psalms are extant also in our present Roman form of Lauds. Every day the second or third psalm in Lauds is one in which mention is made of the morning: not only on Sunday, with *Deus, deus meus ad te de luce vigilo;* but also on other days: on Monday (in Psalm 5): *Quoniam ad te orabo, mane exaudies vocem meam;* on Wednesday (in Psalm 64): *Timebunt qui habitant terminos a signis tuis, exitus matutini et vespere delectabis;* on Thursday (in Psalm 89): *Mane sicut herba transeat, mane floreat et transeat;* on Friday (in Psalm 142): *Auditam fac mihi mane misericordiam tuam;* and on Saturday (in Psalm 91): *Bonum est confiteri Domino . . . ad annuntiandum mane misericordiam tuam.* In the other hours, the psalms for the ferial office generally were simply taken in their successive order, as is still done today. All the psalms were concluded with *Gloria Patri.* Other details, too, and especially the structure of each hour were quite similar to what we have today.

Let us now consider in more detail the composition and structure of the Office and of the individual Hours. In this way we will obtain at the same time a general insight into the way in which the ancient Church understood and arranged the prayers. In the individual Hours, we have to distinguish between an older and a later component. The later component, which already existed in the beginning of the sixth century, consists of the Psalms, with which the Hours begin. The older component is made up of what follows, beginning with the lesson (the *capitulum,* and the lessons of Matins).

In those days, the chief principle guiding the arrangement of the daily Office was to provide considerable time and space for the readings, especially for the scriptural lesson. Today when we hold some evening devotion, the most important element is the blessing with the Blessed Sacrament; hence an evening service is generally called simply Benediction, although it may comprise some other devotion as well. In those days the Sacred Scriptures occupied the central position. The word of the Sacred Scriptures is an instrument by which God gives us His grace and blessing. Sacred Scripture stood in high esteem; the majority of the sermons, for instance, were simply an explanation of Sacred Scripture. Besides books were very rare and costly in those days. For this reason, the public reading of the Sacred Books was of much greater importance than it is today when anyone can acquire a Bible at a relatively small cost.

The canonical Hours, therefore, began regularly with a reading from the Sacred Scriptures.

A more profound theological reason, too, can be given for this order. If we assemble for the purpose of honoring God, for praying, for presenting our petitions, it is fitting that we first listen to what God wishes to tell us. In the Christian order of salvation, it is of primary importance to realize always that God is speaking to us, that God's grace is calling us. Then, and only then, can we turn to God with our own response. This concept was certainly a concurring principle in the original set-up of the Hours, where each Hour of prayer began with a lesson. And it is from this principle, too, that the further structure of each devotional hour derives. After the reading or lesson, came the answer which the assembled congregation gave to the word of God. In the canonical Hours this reply is a song, for the word which comes to us in the Christian revelation is a word of grace and of divine mercy. Hence this word evokes a holy joy in our hearts, and the expression of holy joy is song. Only after the song is there any praying in the stricter sense: the assembled congregation or community expresses its own intentions and petitions and the one presiding at the gathering, the priest, the abbot, the bishop, summarizes the prayer in the concluding oration, the collect. This prayer is, therefore, in principle a twofold one: first, the prayer of the community and then that of the priest. The community's prayer is often announced with the exhortation: *Flectamus genua:* let us kneel down for prayers, till the signal for rising is given again by the *Levate;* or perhaps actual petitions, *preces,* are inserted, to be recited alternately by all the assembly *flexis genibus,* unless it is a festive season; parts of a litany are used (*Kyrie eleison*) and psalm verses, short versicles, and the like. In either case, however, it is the officiating priest who summarizes the prayers with the concluding *collecta* or *collectio*—"gathering together."

This sequence occurs quite constantly in the ancient prayer services. We find it, for instance, in the description in the *Peregrinatio Aetheriae* (10, 7): When Aetheria arrived at one of the holy places on her pilgrimage, she said a short preparatory prayer and then had a pertinent passage from Holy Writ read. Then an appropriate psalm was recited, followed by the prayer proper. In the churches of Jerusalem, she found substantially the same order observed; special importance was attached to the requirement that, at the end of each canonical Hour, a cleric, priest or deacon, be there to recite the concluding prayer in the name of the Church. The same order is also met with in the monastic rules of southern Gaul in the sixth century. It is also to be found, in all its purity, in the oldest parts of the prayer-service of the Roman liturgy that we still possess, namely in the Fore-Mass on an Ember Saturday (which was originally a vigil) and also in the Easter Vigil, but with the difference that here the sequence is repeated several times in order to fill out the long hours of the night. In each instance, we have the sequence: lesson, song (in the form of a Gradual), and the double form of prayer (*preces* and *oratio*).

As already pointed out, this sequence is also to be found in our present Roman Breviary, in the second part of each of the Hours. In the Little Hours it is particularly clear, save that here everything is reduced to the shortest possible form. The second half of Terce (or Sext, or None) commences with a *capitulum* or short Lesson from Holy Writ. Then a psalm verse is sung in the form of a responsory (in this instance it is a *responsorium breve*). The conclusion is formed by the *oratio,* which, in the public recitation of the Office, is spoken by the officiant, the *officiator*. This order we find also in the solemn Hours, namely in Lauds and in Vespers. Here, too, the second part begins with the *capitulum*. Then follows a song in the form of a metric hymn, which is a later development enhancing the solemnity. In addition there is the *canticum* from the New Testament—the *Benedictus* and the *Magnificat*—a most appropriate musical insert. Lastly comes the oration.

Let us now consider some further details. Regarding the lesson, which was already discussed, we have only to add here that sometimes instead of a lesson from Sacred Scripture, a lesson from the Acts of the martyrs or from the writings of one of the famous Fathers could be used. About the oration we shall speak in the following chapter. There remains only the song to consider more particularly. The ordinary form of the song which followed the lesson was the responsory, as in our Breviary at present. This is a tradition from Christian antiquity that has continued to survive. The responsory is the oldest form of the ecclesiastical song employed in the Church. What does the essence of the responsory and of responsorial song as such consist in? We have already discussed this matter; in this context we have merely to summarize and supplement what we have already said. The responsorial song consists of a song built up of strophes or of verses sung by a soloist, and of a recurring refrain or *responsum* sung by the congregation or chorus after each strophe or verse. We still have such responsorial singing in its more complete form at the beginning of Matins: the singer begins, first singing the refrain or Invitatory (e.g. *Christus natus est nobis, venite adoremus*), and all repeat it. The singer begins the first verses of Psalm 94, *Venite exsultemus Domino,* and after each verse all repeat the refrain either in whole or in part. We have a short form of responsory in Compline. After the lesson (*Capitulum: Tu autem in nobis es*) there follows the responsory: *In manus tuas Domine commendo spiritum meum,* and all repeat: *In manus tuas . . .* ; then the chanter goes on: *Redemisti nos . . .* ; all answer: *Commendo spiritum meum* (the second half of the refrain), and finally the chanter adds the doxology, *Gloria Patri,* to which all respond with the full refrain.

The various responsories which we find in the Breviary and in the Missal (here under the name of Gradual) are all similarly constructed. We have only to remember that in Christian antiquity all these responsories were still sung in their full form, in the same way as we today sing the *Venite exsultemus.* Later on they were shortened; of an entire psalm only one single verse remains in the majority of cases, and sometimes even the repetition of the refrain has been omitted.

But besides the responsorial song, there already existed in Christian antiquity another type, namely the antiphonal song. This, too, was used for the singing of the psalms and is today the usual form in which we sing them. This is a more difficult form, and did not come into use in the Church till about the fourth century. For the antiphonal type of song, two choirs are necessary and both choirs must be able to alternate in chanting the psalm. They must, therefore, either know the psalms by heart, or have the text before them. The name *antiphon* originally signified merely the alternation of two voices or of two choirs. But at the beginning of the psalm a short verse was inserted to indicate the melody, to "intone" (because musical instruments were not used), and those verses were then artistically expanded, and thus finally this verse was given the name *antiphona.* This antiphonal method is a later way of singing the psalms; it became customary especially amongst the monks. In their daily Office they prefixed to the older second part of the Hours (where the responsorial singing was customary) a newer first part, where the psalms were sung antiphonally, as they could be by monks. These are the three psalms of the Little Hours and of the nocturns, and the five psalms (or in the monastic office, the four psalms) of Vespers and Lauds.

This first part of the canonical Hours is, therefore, the later part. It is also the secondary part. Except on great feasts, the psalms here are and were taken simply in the order in which they stand in the Bible. No special ideas were sought for; it was sufficient to spend the time in reciting psalms. Hence in some ancient documents concerning the liturgy of the daily Office, we find the remark that the clergy appeared only at the second part, beginning with the little Chapter; apparently what preceded was originally a recitation devised to fill out the time piously and prayerfully. For example in an Egyptian document, the *Canones Basilii,* it is expressly said that psalms should be read as long as the people keep filing into the church, and the service proper was not to begin till all had entered.

These are the most important details regarding the general order of worship and particularly of the daily Office at the close of Christian antiquity. Not everything is equally certain (the sources are very scanty), but at least we know the principles according to which the prayers were arranged and the basic outlines of that arrangement.

CHAPTER TWENTY-THREE

The Roman Mass Before Gregory the Great

I. General Prospect

The beginnings of the Latin Mass in Rome are wrapped in obscurity.[1] While we are fairly well informed about the shape of the Mass during the period when it was celebrated in Greek, thanks to the *Apostolic Tradition* of Hippolytus, it is only by a hypothetical reconstruction that we can arrive at any description of the Mass at the time that it was translated into Latin. This transition from Greek to Latin must have occurred some time during the third century, but our sources are for the most part from the sixth and seventh centuries. The sacramentaries give us first of all the variable prayers of the priest which change from feast to feast, from Sunday to Sunday throughout the year. They also contain the more or less unvarying principal part of the Mass, the canon, which corresponds to the *eucharistia* in the oldest accounts of the Mass. The canon found in the sacramentaries is almost identical with the present Roman canon. However, by a comparison of the traditional texts and by a study of other data to be found in writers of the period, like St. Ambrose (+ 397), we can obtain some details about its earlier development.

In the Fore-Mass, though it still fulfills St. Justin's description, great changes have been made since the fourth century. On the other hand, the core of our Roman canon must have existed by the

1. For details see Jungmann, *The Mass of the Roman Rite*, I, 49–60.

end of the fourth century. But it is quite probable that this canon was not the first version produced after the change from Greek to Latin. Many versions must have been produced before this text, with its genuinely Roman terseness and simplicity, was finally evolved.

But when we have sifted all the data—as we hope to do in this chapter—we can establish the fact that the framework of the Roman Mass must have been essentially fixed and determined by the turn of the fifth century. There were a few modifications under Gregory the Great, chiefly in the *Kyrie,* the preface, *Hanc igitur* and *Pater noster*. Other modifications and additions do not belong to our period; they come mainly from Frankish sources—such as the wholesale intrusion of private prayers by the priest at the beginning of the Mass, at the offertory and at the communion.

One other important addition was made during this period before Gregory the Great, namely, the introduction of singing by a special *schola cantorum* or choir at the beginning of Mass when the clergy entered the church, at the offertory when the faithful presented their gifts of bread and wine, and at the communion. In each instance a psalm was sung while the action was going on, the texts varying with the course of the church year. And in each instance the prayer of the celebrant formed the conclusion; these are the three prayers which at present are usually called the *Collecta, Secreta* and *Postcommunio*.

And now let us take up these questions in more detail.

II. The Fore-Mass

The *Missa catechumenorum,* as the Fore-Mass is so often miscalled, has a double function; in itself it is a service of readings and prayer not unlike the basic pattern of the canonical Hours described in the last chapter; at the same time it serves as a preparation for the celebration of the Eucharist. By the end of the sixth century, the Fore-Mass had undergone a very vigorous development, so that at a solemn papal or episcopal function it had much the same pattern that we find today. To understand and explain the lines of this development we have to distinguish two distinct strata, two patterns, if you will, laid one upon the other.

The first and older of these two strata begins with the lessons. This portion of the Mass we find described as early as the second century, in the writings of St. Justin.[2] And it is to be found, still

2. See *supra,* p. 40 ff.

unencumbered by any additions, in the fifth century, in the time of St. Augustine. St. Augustine himself narrates an incident that took place at the beginning of Mass, and in so doing he describes the way in which the Mass began: "I came into the church, greeted the people with the customary greeting, and the lector started the lesson"—that was the beginning of the Mass.[3] It is substantially the same beginning as the one we have in the arrangement of the service on Good Friday as preserved in the Roman Missal: the priest simply approaches the altar, prostrates himself for silent adoration, and then, after he has risen, the service begins abruptly with the lector reading the first lesson. (The initial prayer inserted in the new Holy Week service is in imitation of a later tradition.)

In accordance with Baumstark's law regarding the preservation or survival of ancient forms, two other vestiges of the ancient Christian Fore-Mass are still to be found in the Good Friday liturgy: (1) The first lesson is read by an ordinary lector; (2) The Gospel is preceded by not one but two readings or lessons not taken from the Gospels. By the sixth century, the lector was supplanted by some other cleric even in Rome itself, for about this time we hardly hear of lectors in the city. But in the country, the lector must still have been the common assistant of the priest. At the Synod of Vaison in Gaul (529), an ordinance was enacted directing that in each church young men should be received into the house and instructed as lectors, thus assuring the education of capable successors "as was done in Italy." [4]

As regards the number of the lessons, it is almost certain that according to the older Roman order there were regularly three. This we can conclude from the fact that on certain days (for example, on Ember Wednesdays) there are still three lessons, and other liturgies had—or even have—three (or more) lessons regularly. Another proof is to be found in the fact that the present-day epistle is followed by two chants, the Gradual and the Alleluia-song; originally each of these must have been preceded by a lesson. Now both of these chants surely existed in the period we are treating, for they are in general the most ancient chants we have; they are responsorial chants from the earliest years of the Church's existence. Of course they have been drastically shortened as to their texts (and the music, in turn, elaborated), but at least in the Alleluia we can still clearly trace the original pattern: the precentor first sings the Alleluia, the people repeat it; the chanter begins the psalm;

3. *Serm.* 325 (*PL*, 38, 1449).
4. Can. 1. (Mansi, VIII, 726).

the people again repeat the Alleluia. This is a primitive tradition. We should note that nearly all liturgies have such an Alleluia chant before the Gospel; it is a fragment from the common heritage of the ancient Church.

With regard to the selection of the lessons in this period, however, it is somewhat more difficult to say anything definite, for as far as Rome is concerned there are no complete lectionaries or lists of lessons extant before the seventh century. Yet certain lessons for certain days must already have been determined as regards the stational service—hence for the principal feasts and for Quadragesima. For certain feasts we also have the direct witness of the homilies of St. Leo the Great.[5] For the rest, no doubt, the principle of the *lectio continua* must still have held good.

As in the canonical Hours so also at Mass, prayer forms the conclusion of the readings or lessons. Even today we still find this prayer after the Gospel in most liturgies. It is only in the Roman Mass that it has nearly disappeared. It is known under the name *Oratio Communis* or *Oratio Fidelium*, although strictly speaking this latter name designates only the last part of the prayer. This prayer has been preserved in its entirety in the Good Friday service, namely, the *Orationes Solemnes* which follow the Gospel, that is, the *Passio*. It must have been recited in a similar form during the fourth and fifth centuries at every public celebration of the Mass, on Sundays and feast-days. But towards the end of the fifth century, an incisive change was made, apparently by Pope Gelasius I. Suddenly the *oratio communis* is abandoned in favor of a new formulation at the beginning of the Fore-Mass. A new stratum was constructed *before* the lessons, containing a prayer with similar contents. Meanwhile, too, prayers duplicating the contents of the *oratio communis* had been inserted into the canon. Both these factors undoubtedly led to the relinquishing of the ancient and traditional *oratio communis*.

It is now time to consider the second stratum of the Fore-Mass, a stratum which, in all essentials, was formed during the fifth century.

To understand this later development, we must call to mind the conditions that evolved in the era of Constantine the Great. Basilicas were built of such magnitude and magnificence that they almost compelled a similar embellishment of the services. This held true especially of the divine services conducted by the Pope himself, and

5. S. Beissel, *Entstehung der Perikopen des römischen Messbuches* (Freiburg, 1907), 60.

in particular of the stational service on feast-days. The Pope already had a considerable retinue, and it seemed only fitting that when he came to worship his coming should be distinguished with suitable formality. Thus arose the solemn entry or *introitus* at the beginning of the service. So a kind of introduction was placed in front of the service of readings and prayers—a kind of vestibule leading into the service. Other liturgies also have formed such "vestibules," often much more elaborate than that of the Roman liturgy. In the Oriental liturgies, this takes the form of a little canonical Hour. In the Byzantine liturgy, in addition, there is a preliminary known as the *proskomide*.

The Roman liturgy was content to elaborate the entrance of the clergy. This was done in a very dignified and religious fashion. In this development, two elements were made to cooperate: prayer and song. The first element to consider is song—antiphonal song, for which a special choir, the *schola cantorum,* was provided. We have already had occasion to discuss this type of singing. It suffices here to mention that the *schola* would sing an appropriate psalm in alternate choirs while the Pope and his cortège proceeded to the altar; when he arrived at the altar, they would conclude with the singing of the *Gloria Patri* and the repetition of the antiphon.

The second element is prayer, a prayer spoken by the celebrant. The significance of the solemn entry is to appear before God for worship; now it is through prayer that we appear before God. It was a further evolution at the beginning of the Middle Ages, derived from the ceremonial of the imperial court, to greet the Pope with acclamations as he arrived for the service, just as formerly the ruler was greeted. Of course the acclamations took a more religious turn: *Ad multos annos! S. Petre, tu illum adjuva!* In some episcopal cities, the bishop was greeted in this way even in the late Middle Ages. But this salutation did not take place until the bishop or the Pope had first, so to say, saluted God in an oration.

Two things, therefore, formed the entry: song and prayer. We still have the same order under different circumstances, namely, when the bishop comes to a church to conduct the visitation or to administer Confirmation. According to the *Pontificale Romanum,* the *Ecce Sacerdos* is sung when he enters the church; that is the *Introitus,* the entry song. Then the bishop kisses the altar and recites an oration. The beginning of the Mass was formed along the same lines. As regards the chant, there might be some doubt as to whether in the period we are dealing with, it existed outside the papal stational service, since most places would probably not have a *schola cantorum*. But the prayer to be recited by the celebrant before the lessons—this was certainly already in general use in the time we are discussing. It was part of the plan of the Roman liturgy in the fifth century, but here the plan was further elaborated.

As we have already seen in our consideration of the canonical Hours, prayer always forms the conclusion, but this prayer, in its original conception, is binary: first, the people pray; then the priest sums up their prayer in the oration. The same arrangement was made for the beginning of the Mass: first the people were to pray, then the priest was to summarize their prayer in the oration. In the last analysis, this is already presupposed in the very idea of the oration. The oration is always a prayer that the priest prays in the name of the people; he speaks for the congregation. This is why the oration is always in the plural: *We* pray Thee. And this is also why the oration is always preceded by the invitation to the congregation to pray: *Oremus,* let us pray. Indeed the priest exhorts the congregation to pray; not that he says: My dear brethren, we ought to pray; he does more than this; he turns to them with a greeting, a greeting they are expected to answer: The Lord be with you—And with you too.

This is what takes place before the oration both in the daily Office and in the Mass. In the Mass, at the very beginning, the *Oremus* is, in fact, anticipated by the actual common prayer of the people assembled. Sometimes, as, for example, on Ember days, this is carried out by inviting the congregation to kneel in silent prayer: *Flectamus genua*. In the ordinary Mass, this is carried out by means of the *Kyrie* only; and if we are thinking of the circumstances of the fifth and sixth century, this means a litany, with petitions to which the answer was given: *Kyrie eleison*.

Why is the *Kyrie eleison* spoken in Greek? It would surely seem to indicate a Greek liturgy which employed this form of prayer. We are sometimes told that the *Kyrie eleison* is a vestige of that period when the liturgy in Rome was still celebrated in Greek; hence, the third century. But that is not true. The *Kyrie eleison* does not appear until the fourth century, and then not in Rome but in the Greek Orient. In the *Apostolic Constitutions,* dated near the end of the fourth century, we find the arrangement as follows: regularly, before the bishop recites a prayer, there is a litany in which the people respond *κύριε ἐλέησον* to each invocation.[6] The pilgrim Aetheria, too, in narrating her visit to Jerusalem, tells how such a litany was recited at the end of Vespers just before the bishop's con-

6. *Const. Ap.* VIII, 6, 9; cf. 35, 2.

cluding prayer, and how, as the deacon pronounced the petitions, the children, the *pisinni,* especially shouted out: *Kyrie eleison,* and she adds, by way of explanation: *quod dicimus nos: miserere Domine, quorum voces sunt infinitae.*[7]

Of course Aetheria could hardly have been the only pilgrim to notice this practice in the East and make it known in the West; there must have been many others. At any rate, in the course of the sixth century it appears to have spread throughout the West. The Synod of Vaison in southern France, in the year 529, recommends the practice, and expressly refers to the fact that it was already in use in other places, especially in Rome.[8] Many churches in the Gallic area translated the people's response into Latin or even paraphrased it: *Domine, miserere; Praesta, Domine, praesta.* Rome, however, preserved it in its original Greek; with a short phrase like this there is no difficulty in retaining the original, since the meaning can easily be learned. The same thing is done in the case of the *Alleluia* and the *Amen;* in their original use these, too, were the people's responses. So the *Kyrie eleison* was left in its native form.

We have some idea of the exact way in which the *Kyrie* was performed. Dom Bernard Capelle, the great Belgian liturgist and abbot of Mont-César, has presented some good arguments to suggest that in the so-called *Deprecatio Gelasii* the old Roman *Kyrie*-litany is preserved.[9] Its title hints that it is the litany which Pope Gelasius I—in the last decade of the fifth century—appointed to be sung by the "universal Church." At any rate, it represents the type in structure and form. An idea of the original shape of the *Kyrie*-litany can be gained if we examine the following invocations from this document:

> *Pro immaculata Dei vivi ecclesia, per totum orbem constituta divinae bonitatis opulentiam deprecamur—Kyrie eleison.*
>
> *Pro sanctis Dei magni sacerdotibus et ministris sacri altaris cunctisque Deum verum colentibus populis Christum Dominum supplicamus—Kyrie eleison.*
>
> *Pro universis recte tractantibus verbum veritatis multiformem Verbi Dei sapientiam peculiariter obsecramus—Kyrie eleison.*[10]

In the same manner, prayer was offered for all the needs and wants of Christendom: for temporal rulers, for good weather, for the catechumens, for sinners, for those in distress, for the dead, etc.—eighteen petitions in all.

7. *Peregr. Æth.,* c. 24.
8. Can. 3 (Mansi, VIII, 725).
9. B. Capelle, "Le Kyrie de la Messe et le pape Gélase," *Revue Bénéd.,* 46 (1934), 126–144.
10. *op. cit.,* 136–138; also *PL,* 101, 560 f.

And now let us return for a moment to what we said earlier about the disappearance of the *oratio communis* after the Gospel—precisely in the time of Pope Gelasius I. The reason for its disappearance seems obvious. The same intentions—with a few added!—to be found in the old *oratio communis* are also contained in the *Kyrie*-litany, the *deprecatio*. The former was, therefore, simply dropped. Later, indeed, the *Kyrie*-litany itself was abbreviated in consequence of the formation of still other substitutes to enshrine the petitions and intentions of the congregation and the Church. The latest of these substitutes is the series of prayers ordered by Leo XIII to be said after private Masses.

However, in the period we are discussing, the *Kyrie*-litany was still in its original complete form, whatever that was; for (as already pointed out) we can determine that form only with a limited probability.

And what about the *Gloria?* Did the *Gloria* form part of the Mass during the period we are dealing with? Here we can speak with greater certainty.

The *Gloria* has been known throughout Christendom since the fourth century. St. Hilary had transplanted it from the Orient to the West. And that it was used in the Mass, in the very spot it occupies at present, is attested by the *Liber Pontificalis* about 530.[11] Its use, however, was very restricted. In Rome, only the Pope was permitted to intone it on ordinary feast-days; the rest of the clergy could use it only at Easter.

The *Gloria,* like the *Kyrie,* was a popular element of prayer; it was something that the people themselves could sing. The text was little more than a series of acclamations, and the melody—even at a much later date—was very simple. It was a sort of popular song inserted in the Mass. It was also used outside of the Mass, much as we use the *Te Deum.*

Some commentaries on the Mass seem to express a regret that the *Gloria* was introduced into the Mass and that at present it is employed not only on great feasts but even on the lesser feasts of saints. It interrupts the flow of prayer, they point out—prayer whose continuity is, in the oration, a prayer of petition. Is this criticism justified? I think not. At the beginning of Mass, what is to be expressed is the religious sentiment of the assembled community. As we appear before God we are certainly poor beggars. But when we are celebrating a feast, we are in a festive mood from the very beginning; the festive joy is, in fact, the occasion for bringing us together. On such days, then, we should start out not only by begging

11. Duchesne, *Lib. Pont.,* I, 56; cf. I, 129 f.

God but by praising and blessing Him. Even the oration itself is not always simply a prayer of petition. Precisely on feast-days, a clause is often inserted at the beginning of the prayer to indicate this mood of festive joy: *Deus, qui hodierna die . . . ; Deus, qui ecclesiam tuam. . . .* This is the so-called relative predication, a word of praise and blessing in the form of a relative clause. You will find that in the majority of Masses in which the people's part contains not only the *Kyrie* but the *Gloria,* the priest's summarizing oration also contains such a relative clause.

And so we come to a discussion of what constitutes the very climax of the second and later stratum in the Fore-Mass—the oration. The entrance of the celebrant and the clergy is concluded by prayer, and that prayer itself is concluded by the priest's oration.

The orations of the Roman liturgy have always evoked great admiration. Edmund Bishop's justly famous treatise, *The Genius of the Roman Rite,* is based substantially on a consideration of the Roman orations. The features of the Roman orations that he singles out are soberness and sense. By means of these two qualities at any rate, the Roman oration exhibits in an outstanding fashion the essence and significance of this prayer. The oration is essentially a summary; it is therefore called a *collecta or collectio* in the liturgies of the Gallic type. For this reason, the oration mentions only the larger and more general intentions, without dealing with the merely accidental or individual. Wide perspectives, matters eternal—these characterize it in all the liturgies. But the Roman oration is especially distinguished by its conciseness and brevity. One has only to compare a typical Roman oration with those of the Gallic type, some of which are to be found in our Roman Missal. Take, for instance, the last oration recited after the Litany of the Saints, *Omnipotens, sempiterne Deus, qui vivorum dominaris,* or the Post-communion which used to be added during the weekdays of Lent, *Purificent nos, quaesumus.* These Gallic orations set forth the contents of the petition in long paraphrases; the Roman oration is content with a word or two. A favorite device is the use of two terms. How often we observe the contents of the petition expressed by an antithesis: *corpus et anima; temporalia et aeterna; fides—effectus; confiteri—imitari.* Almost all these antitheses ultimately return to the one great thought: We are at present on a journey, which is a steady struggle, but we beg God to lead us through all perils to our eternal homeland.

Another device of the Roman oration deserves mention: the *cursus.* By *cursus* is meant the arrangement of the words at the end of phrases and clauses so that their accents produce a beautiful rhythm. This was one of the principles of ancient rhetoric. In the sermons of Leo the Great as well as in his letters, the law of the *cursus* was so strictly followed that the absence of the *cursus* could be used as a criterion of literary criticism. In the more ancient orations, the rules of the *cursus* have been regularly observed. And this is another reason why many of these orations are probably attributable to Leo the Great.

We cannot here consider the matter more in detail. But we can clearly illustrate the three main forms of the *cursus* in a familiar oration, which in its substance originates from Leo the Great:

Deus qui humanae substantiae dignitatem . . .
mirabílius rèformásti (cursus velox)
da nobis . . . eius divinitatis
ésse consórtes (cursus planus)
qui humanitatis nostrae fieri
dignátus est párticeps (cursus tardus)

It is more important for us to study briefly the theological character of the Roman oration. It is significant that all the orations which go back to old Roman tradition—those in the *Leonianum* and in the older *Gelasianum*—are addressed to God the Father and invariably conclude with the formula: *Per Dominum nostrum.* Naturally, even in ancient Christendom, prayer addressed to a holy martyr, to an angel, or at least to Christ was permissible; indeed in private prayer this was general practice. In official prayer, however, the rule was to address the prayer to God Himself, to God the Father. At a synod of Hippo (393) this was expressly enacted: *Cum altari assistitur, semper ad Patrem dirigatur oratio.*[12] This tended to emphasize the common validity of the oration, its universal and objective character. So, too, the oration was displayed as the classic form of prayer.

Similarly the conclusion, which corresponds to this address, is without exception a formula beginning with the word *Per,* and here and there the sources already mentioned give the formula in full, so that we can see it is the same one we are familiar with: *Per Dominum nostrum Jesum Christum. . . .* What is the precise meaning of this "through . . . Christ"? It is not an oath, an adjuration: Grant us this *by* Christ, for His sake, in His name. Much less is it intended to express the hope that God give us these gifts through Christ, through His hands, so to say; the formula is not concerned

12. Can. 21 (Mansi, III, 922); cf. Jungmann, *Die Stellung Christi im liturg. Gebet* (Muenster, 1925), 150, 198.

with the *coming down* of the gifts but with the *going up* of our prayer. Our prayer should come to God through Christ who, as our representative, as our head, as our High Priest, is already with God. Christ is, so to speak, the bridge over which our prayer can reach God. He is the Mediator between God and ourselves.

All this is aptly expressed in the formula by the addition to the name of our Savior of two qualifying phrases: *Dominus noster* and *Filius tuus.* He is our *Dominus;* we belong to Him, are bound to Him firmly since Baptism. At the same time he is *Filius tuus,* that beloved Son of Thine who is joined most intimately with Thee in the unity of divine nature. For that reason we can surely trust that our prayer is heard.

To the mention of Christ's name and of his office as Mediator a further addition is made; we could call it a relative predication—the clause: *Qui tecum vivit et regnat. . . .* Here we are not looking back to the Savior who once sojourned upon this earth of ours, who once died for us. We are looking up to Him who lives now and forever, who lives as a glorious King: *vivit et regnat.* Manifestly this is a reference to Christ as the God-man, and of Him it is said that He lives and reigns *in unitate Spiritus Sancti.* This is naturally not the same as saying *cum Sancto Spiritu.* The phrase *in unitate Spiritus Sancti* means that He lives and reigns in that *unity* which the Holy Spirit creates. He is the unity between Father and Son. But perhaps we may think also of the unity which the Holy Spirit creates in the redeemed; it is the Communion of the Saints of heaven. This is the kingdom where Christ lives and reigns.

However, because the Holy Spirit is named along with the Father and the Son, the prayer receives a grand and solemn finale; it overflows into the profoundest mystery of our faith; it dies away in the profession of belief in the Triune God.

III. The Canon Missae

By the end of the sixth century, the Mass proper, that is, the Mass exclusive of the Fore-Mass, had likewise evolved to a point where it definitely resembled the Mass of the present, if we except certain fringe developments. The only important differences were along the edges, at the offertory and at the communion. The *canon missae,* the main body of the Mass, was remarkably like our own present Mass. It will be our task in this final chapter not only to determine the differences between our present Mass and the Mass before the time of Gregory the Great, but more especially to try to explain how the Mass evolved as it did during the intervening years since Hippolytus.

In the beginning of the Mass, that is, at the offertory, the rite was still very simple. Only the essentials were there, but more clearly outlined than at present. The faithful either approached the altar to bring their gifts of bread and wine or else the clergy went down into the nave of the church and collected the gifts. The priest selected what was required for the Mass, arranged it on the altar, and then said only one prayer, the *oratio super oblata,* the oration which we call the *secreta,* only then it was not a *secreta* but, like all the prayers of the Mass, was spoken in a loud voice.

The same is repeated at the end of the Mass, at the communion. The faithful approach for communion or else, as we gather from a narrative in the life of St. Benedict, the communicants remain at their places and the deacon calls out: *Si quis non communicat, det locum;* whoever is not communicating make room (i.e., leave, or at least step aside); [13] then the celebrant and his assistants come and distribute Communion under both kinds to those who remain. After that, he again says just one prayer, and the people are dismissed.

At solemn services, or at least at the papal stational Masses, a psalm is sung at the offertory and at the communion just as was done at the introit. This singing at the offertory and at the communion is already mentioned by St. Augustine; it must, therefore, have been customary at Hippo as early as the end of the fourth or the start of the fifth century.[14] Even the Oriental liturgies have a chant during the communion. Outside the papal services, the chant of the communion was probably carried on in a simpler form, as a popular song, without the aid of a *schola cantorum.*

Otherwise the communion part of the Roman Mass at this period was still quite short and simple. First the consecrated loaves were broken. Then the *Pater noster* was said, with its introduction, *Praeceptis salutaribus,* and the embolism, *Libera nos, quaesumus.* Some doubts have been raised as to whether the Our Father belonged to the Roman Mass before Gregory the Great. To me it seems quite certain; one of the reasons to prove my contention is the fact that in one of the Mass formularies in the *Sacramentarium Leonianum* the *Libera nos* is expressly cited; this presupposes the

13. Greg. the Great, *Dial.,* II, 23 (*PL,* 66, 178 f.).
14. Augustine, *Retractationes,* II, 37 (*CSEL,* 36, 144).

Pater noster. After the *Pater noster* there followed the Kiss of Peace, given with the words *Pax Domini sit semper vobiscum*, and then Communion was received.

This leaves only the *canon missae* to discuss.

In the terminology of the period under discussion, the canon included also the preface. In the most ancient of the texts in which the canon is transmitted, the title in question stands *before* the preface. In the older *Gelasianum*, for instance, we find the words, *Incipit canon actionis*, and then follow *Sursum corda* and *Gratias agamus* and what we at present call the *praefatio communis*, and then, without any spacing or break, the continuation in the *Te igitur*.[15] We are momentarily surprised, for we have been taught—and it is still repeated in many commentaries on the Mass—that *praefatio* means "foreword, introduction," and that what follows is the main prayer, the canon, that which "always remains the same." Actually *canon* does not mean that at all, much less does *praefatio* mean foreword or introduction. Let me explain.

It is evident from the start that the position of the title, *Incipit canon actionis*, before the preface is an indication that the original conception of the structure of the Mass here still survived. We have seen that the Mass in the earliest centuries was a *eucharistia*, a grand prayer of thanksgiving into which the consecrating words were introduced. Now it is precisely that portion in which the thanksgiving is formally expressed that is retained in our preface. Besides we must correct the notion that *praefatio* is to be rendered as foreword or introduction; this is an arbitrary translation. *Praefatio* is indeed made up of the words *prae* and *fari*, to speak before. But it need not be taken only in a temporal sense, one speech before another. It can also be thought of in terms of space, speaking before an audience. The word was used in this sense in pre-Christian sacral language; it was the speech made before the divinity or else the speech made before the assembly. A public proclamation was also called a *praefatio*. This word was transferred to the liturgical language of Christendom and at least at Rome continued to be used in its original sense. *Praefatio* was therefore the solemn prayer and was part of the canon; in fact, for a time, the whole canon was, it would seem, called *praefatio*.

And now we come to the question, what was the appearance of the Roman canon before the time of Gregory the Great, that is, in the sixth century? To this question we can give a fairly definite

15. *Gelasianum*, III, 16 (Wilson, 234); cf. Jungmann, *Mass of the Roman Rite*, II, 103 ff.

answer, since the canon has been transmitted to us in several manuscripts which, though they are not of the sixth century, are, as is evident and generally admitted, traceable to models which do belong to the fifth and sixth centuries. These manuscripts agree among themselves almost perfectly. There are only insignificant variants, so that we can accordingly speak of an Irish or a Milanese or a Gregorian recension, but these variants have no bearing whatever on the question we are discussing. In all these traditions, the canon looks almost exactly as it does today. The *praefatio communis* is the same. It is followed by the *Sanctus* and *Benedictus*. Then come the *Te igitur* and all the other prayers down to the end, to the *Per ipsum et cum ipso*. Only the few differences that follow can be noted for certain.

The *praefatio communis* apparently served only as a skeleton, a framework. In the *Sacramentarium Leonianum*, practically every Mass has its own preface which was inserted into the framework-formula. The *Gelasianum* also has a considerable number of prefaces.

In regard to the prayers before the consecration, there is only one difference of any importance to mention; it concerns the *Hanc igitur*. The *Hanc igitur* was, indeed, already in existence, but it was not a prayer to be used at every Mass, and when it was inserted its wording varied. The purpose of the *Hanc igitur* was to express the particular intention of the Mass. The various votive Masses devoted to the many wants and needs of the faithful, therefore, had their own special *Hanc igitur* formula. On the other hand, the ordinary Sunday and feast-day Masses which served the community for their regular services as a rule had no *Hanc igitur*, unless there was some special occasion, like the Easter Mass when prayers were offered for the newly baptized.

After the consecration, too, there was one place, or rather two, where a similar difference was to be found. The *Memento* for the dead was already in existence; its very wording betrays the fact that it is an exceedingly ancient and venerable formula, for we find in it the same expressions that are found on the old epitaphs in the catacombs. But it did not belong to every Mass; in this period it was still excluded from the service on Sundays and feasts. Behind this fact is the same idea that even to the present excludes Masses for the dead on Sundays and holydays.

Then there is another place near the end of the canon where, on certain occasions, a formula was inserted, namely, before the *Per quem haec omnia*. Here, according to the occasion, the priest interpolated the blessing of natural gifts, the produce of the farms, foodstuffs and the like, just as at present on Maundy Thursday the blessing of the Oil of the Sick takes place at this position in the Mass.

This finishes our description of the Roman canon as it appeared in the sixth century. Now we must turn to our second task, that of explaining how all this came about. If we look back at the Roman Mass of the beginning of the third century as we found it in Hippolytus, we must confess that in three hundred years, from the third to the sixth century, many important changes took place. Let us now investigate these changes in the Roman canon more closely.

(1) In the first part of the ancient *eucharistia,* or prayer of thanksgiving, the principle was established that changes be made according to the Church year and particularly according to the occasion of the celebration. In the *Sacramentarium Leonianum* practically every Mass has its own special preface; it contains 267 prefaces in all, even though the sacramentary is not complete. The same principle of variation was operative in regard to the orations. But in the case of the preface, the principle involved the danger that the original theme of the eucharistic prayer might be lost. On feasts of our Lord the old theme could still be clearly traced, to offer thanks to God for what He has accomplished for us through Christ. But the feasts of martyrs also had to have their own special prayer of thanksgiving, and while the obvious theme was the victory of the martyrs, sometimes, for the sake of variety, this theme was combined with a description of the martyrdom. But this was a course fraught with peril. Instead of adhering strictly to the theme of every prayer of thanksgiving, man's salvation through Christ, more and more attention was paid to matters of much less importance. A reform was bound to come sooner or later. A certain improvement is already to be noticed in the older *Gelasianum,* where special prefaces are found only in the *proprium de tempore* and on a very few feasts of saints (there are fifty-four prefaces in all). Later the reform was extended to a point where, in place of excessive abundance, we have an excessive scarcity of prefaces.

(2) Again keeping in mind the *eucharistia* of Hippolytus, we find another change in the fact that the preface reaches a climax in the *Sanctus.* This was a very fortunate development. The community of the redeemed, the Church here on earth, joins with the angelic choirs in heaven to adore the eternal and all-holy God. We are thus made aware of the dignity to which we have been raised, we are made to realize that we are already *cives sanctorum et*

domestici Dei. It is, moreover, quite probable that the *Sanctus* was a part of the Mass from the very beginning, and that its absence in Hippolytus is an exception, perhaps because he wanted to make the prayer of thanksgiving run straight through to the words of consecration without a break.

(3) In the section between the *Sanctus* and the consecration, there is one very profound difference between the *eucharistia* and the canon of this later period; this is the insertion of the intercessions. Immediately after the *Sanctus,* the train of thought is again resumed; the word *igitur* indicates that: And so, most gracious Father, we humbly pray and beseech Thee—in the spirit of gratitude and adoration we have just manifested—to accept and bless these gifts we are offering Thee. Already, even before the consecration, the gift is offered to God. This is, after all, what was already done at the end of the offertory, in the *oratio super oblata.* Originally there would have followed a transition to the consecratory words, in a prayer similar to our *Quam oblationem.* But already as early as the fourth century a new element was interposed, namely, the intercessions. This brings us face to face with a phenomenon that occurred about this time in almost all the liturgies. Intercessions, bidding prayers, had long been connected with worship. We saw this already in Justin. But there, as we know, they were inserted immediately after the lessons. Now, however, people apparently discovered the possibility of connecting the intercessions more closely with the holy Sacrifice, the closer the better. All hesitation is put aside, and the heavenly Father is to be besieged with petitions and supplications in His innermost sanctuary where His throne can most closely be approached. Another idea may have been at work, the realization that we are not only offering a prayer of thanksgiving, an *eucharistia,* but also a sacrifice; we are offering Him a precious gift, and surely we can make this gift a security for expecting a gift in return.

These ideas were worked out in different ways in the various liturgies. In the Egyptian liturgies, the intercessions were interpolated before the *Sanctus.* In the Syrian liturgies and also in the Byzantine, the intercessions were inserted after the consecration. In the Roman liturgy, they were interposed between the *Sanctus* and the consecration, except the *Memento* for the dead which, for special reasons, was inserted after the consecration. It is possible for us to observe the process of insertion at close quarters. In the year 416, Pope Innocent I received a series of questions from Bishop Decentius of Gubbio, a little town near Rome. Among them was the question, whether it is better to read out the names of those who offered the gifts before the gifts were recommended to God, or only after. The Pope answered: It goes without saying, only afterwards.[16] First, therefore, the offering of the gifts should be pronounced, and only then the names; in other words, the names should not be read out nor petitions made for specified persons until the canon.

What is the form and construction of these intercessions in the Roman liturgy? We can distinguish two layers which, during the sixth century, were much more distinct than is now the case. The first layer consists of intercessions for persons, the second, of intercessions for intentions.

The formula of intercessions for persons already had the form it has now. First there was the offering for the entire Church and for its pastors: *in primis quae tibi offerimus pro. . . .* Next those were recommended to God who were present and co-offering the sacrifice. Some of these would be mentioned by name, but as a rule they would be few in number, chiefly the founders and great benefactors of the church or else those who were more prominent at a particular celebration. We have already seen that, on the day the *symbolum* was confided to the candidates for Baptism, the names of their godparents were mentioned here in the canon. The rest of the faithful were included in a general phrase: *et omnium circumadstantium*. But they were included as co-offerers: *qui tibi offerunt hoc sacrificium*. They were included with all their intentions: *pro se suisque omnibus*. And they were included as being in communion with the saints in heaven. This last notion is specially underscored by the wording of the text. In the text of the canon then in use, the words *tibi reddunt vota sua aeterno Deo vivo et vero* formed the start of a new sentence, with the phrase *communicantes . . .* intimately joined to it. They offer their prayers along with the saints of heaven.

So much for the intercessions for persons. Next followed the intercessions for intentions. The formula *Hanc igitur* served this purpose, as we already noted above. The two oldest sacramentaries contained dozens of these formulas designed for special intentions, e.g., for the sick, for bride and groom at a nuptial Mass, for the neophytes on the day of their Baptism—the only special formula still retained in our Missal—for a successful journey or undertaking, for a safe return, in thanksgiving for the priestly dignity on the anniversary of ordination, for the dead, etc.

(4) If we compare the *eucharistia* of Hippolytus with the sixth

16. Innocent I, *Ep*. 25 (*PL*, 20, 553 f.).

century canon, we will find still another insertion before the consecration, namely, the *Quam oblationem*. This formula is, in substance and form, as we have already seen, an *epiclesis;* we can call it the Roman *epiclesis*. It is extant in an older recension in the work of St. Ambrose entitled *De Sacramentis*.[17] There the wording makes it clear that it is meant to be a prayer for the transformation of the gift: *Fac nobis hanc oblationem scriptam, rationabilem, acceptabilem, quod est figura corporis et sanguinis Domini nostri Jesu Christi*. We find similar prayers on other occasions, for example, before the blessing of the baptismal water or before the administration of a sacrament: May God grant the power to effect the sacrament, or May God Himself grant the operation or effect. The *Quam oblationam* is, therefore, what is technically called a consecration-*epiclesis*.

(5) The account of institution, as compared to the third century text, shows a certain amount of embellishment. Phrases were extended to make them more symmetrical and more reverent, and phrases were added from the biblical account.

(6) After the consecration, if we except the *Memento* for the dead, we find in the sixth century canon the same train of thought that we already discovered in the third century text. However in the latter everything is put more succinctly and simply. Thus in the *anamnesis*, only the death and resurrection of Christ are mentioned; the new text adds the ascension. Again the earlier text says quite plainly: *offerimus tibi panem et calicem*. That phrase is short but impressive and fraught with meaning. It can be called the most important word in the whole Mass in that it specifies what the Church is doing: *offerimus*. For that reason it was soon elaborated. Already in the text of the canon which St. Ambrose presents in the treatise *De Sacramentis* essentially the same ideas and phrases are found as in our present text: *offerimus tibi hanc immaculatam hostiam, rationabilem hostiam, incruentam hostiam, hunc panem sanctum et calicem vitae aeternae*.[18] The text of the sixth century canon tallies with our present one. The prayer has become tripartite: *offerimus praeclarae majestati tuae. . . . Supra quae. . . . Supplices te rogamus. . . .* In the first part we say that we offer these holy gifts to the divine majesty; and in the second and third part this basic idea is described in greater detail: We cannot place these gifts directly in God's hands, for He is a pure spirit; we have therefore placed them on the altar and now pray that He will look upon them with gracious eyes; but so that they may belong entirely to God

17. Ambrose, *De sacramentis,* IV, 5, 21.
18. *ibid.*

we ask further that He may have them carried to the heavenly altar. This is highly figurative language; all in all what we are saying is: May God really accept what we are offering.

(7) Next, as in the third century text, there is a petition that God may grant that we may receive Communion worthily and so be filled with all heavenly blessings. This petition provided the occasion for still another insertion, namely, the *Memento etiam* for the dead. Various reasons have been suggested why the *Memento* for the dead was interpolated precisely at this spot (that is, on those days when it was so interpolated). Some have conjectured that its original place was immediately adjoining the *Memento* for the living. Even the *etiam* was interpreted as a conjunction linking it with the *Memento* for the living. However, a comparison with the almost exact parallels in the Oriental liturgies, especially in the Egyptian liturgy, results in an entirely different explanation. There, too, in the most ancient texts, the *Memento* for the dead is found in the same place, and the line of thought is quite clear; first we asked God for the graces and blessings He might grant us by our reception of Holy Communion, but since the dead no longer enjoy the opportunity of partaking of the holy Table, we therefore intercede in their behalf: Be mindful also of Thy servants who have gone before us, and grant them also Thy blessings and graces so that, so to speak, they too may have a share in our holy repast.

The prayer that follows, *Nobis quoqúe peccatoribus,* is a continuation of this *Memento* for the dead, in the sense that the celebrating clergy, at the very end, desire to commend themselves also in a special way to the divine clemency. It is attached to the *Memento* in the same way that the *Libera nos* is attached to the *Pater noster;* it is a sort of embolism. In itself it is not very important, it is only an appendage. Nevertheless it is surprising how soon this *Nobis quoque* became an independent element and is already found in those manuscripts that do not contain the *Memento* for the dead. Probably the mention of the saints gave rise to this. The parallel to the *Communicantes* and its series of saints,[19] should be retained; the saints in heaven should stand at our side both before the consecration and after.

(8) After this double interpolation, there followed in some cases the blessing of the gifts of nature, and then the canon closed with the grand and solemn doxology, a doxology that was expressed not only in words but in the very ceremony that accompanied it: priest and deacon grasp the host and chalice and raise them on high in token of homage and adoration.

19. Cf. supra 304.

When we examine the result of this development in the Roman canon of the sixth century, we must admit that it no longer possesses that strict compactness we observed in the *eucharistia* of the third century, but at the same time there is no break in the continuity of thought nor any confusion or disorder. What a waste of time and effort were those many theories and hypotheses that were concocted during the nineteenth and early twentieth century to explain the origin of its many parts! One prayer was supposed to have been imported from Alexandria, another from Antioch; a prayer now situated before the consecration was said to have originally stood after it, and *vice versa*. We can read a long account of these conjectures and speculations in Fortescue.[20] But they have long since gone with the wind. Ever since our discovery of the *eucharistia* of Hippolytus, we have come to realize that the sixth century canon is merely a logical and reasonable development of what was already in existence.

And looking at the sixth century Roman Mass as a whole, we must say it was indeed a worthy service. It was still, in the fullest sense, a community exercise, a rite in which the whole Christian people had a part. The members of the congregation were still conscious of their role as the *plebs sancta,* offering the Mass with the priest. They did not only bring their gifts to the altar. They could also still follow the lessons and the prayers because the language was as yet no barrier. They could join in the singing and make the proper responses. They could still participate actively.

The many magnificent churches and martyr shrines provided a dignified setting for this worship. The festive cycles, especially the two great feasts of Easter and Christmas, made the grand mysteries of redemption and grace come alive year after year; they drew attention to Him who for all times is the very center and focus of our religion, Christ our Lord. Thus we can say that this service was but an extension and a colorful unfolding of that which is, in the last analysis, the meaning of all liturgy, the glorification of the Triune God through Christ in His Church:

Per ipsum *et cum ipso* *et in ipso*
est tibi Deo Patri omnipotenti
in unitate Spiritus Sancti
omnis honor et gloria
Per omnia saecula saeculorum.

20. Adrian Fortescue, *The Mass. A Study of the Roman Liturgy* (London, 1912), 138–171; cf. *idem,* "Canon of the Mass," *Catholic Encyclopedia,* III, 255–267.

Index

Abitene, marytrs of 13
Advent, development of 268-275
Adversus Haereses 115
African liturgy 233-234
altar, development of 119-120
  versus populum 137-138
Amen 44
anamnesis 69
anaphora 217 *passim*
"Anaphora of the Apostles" 226
"Anaphora of Our Lady" 225-226
"Anaphora of St. Mark" 224-225
Anaphoricae Syriacae 224
Angelus, origin of 105
antiphonal chant 207, 284
Aphraat the Wise 203
Apostles' Creed, the 87-96
Apostolic Constitutions 5, 116, 191, 278, 291
Apostolic Tradition 6, 35, 41, 52-59, 98, 101-102, 139, 191
Aramaic, see Syro-Aramaic
Arianism 188 *passim*
  effects on liturgy 194 *passim*
Armenian liturgy 206
art, liturgical 127-128
Atchley, A. 132
Athanasian symbol 89-90

Bacchanalian mysteries 156
Baptism 74-86
  at beginning of Middle Ages 248
  by immersion 81
  by infusion 81-82
  formula of 82
  importance in life of early Church 85-86
  in Apostolic Constitutions 74-85
  in Lenten liturgy 256-257
  of infants 79-80
  postponment of 79-80, 246-247
Basil, St. 193
basilicas 123-124, 289-290
Benedict, St. 279-280
Bibliothek der Symbole und Glaubensregeln 88
Bianchini, Giuseppe 3
bishop, the 18
  consecration of 62-63
Bishop, Edmund 127
Blessing of food in Mass 299-300
"Breaking of Bread" 29-30
Bryennios, Philotheos 6
Burchard, John 64
burial customs 140-141
Byzantine liturgy 208, 222-223, 301

Cabrol, F. 4
Callistus, Pope 53, 58
Candlemas procession, origin of 145
canon missae, see Mass of the Roman Rite
Canones Hippolyti 55, 82
canonical Hours, origin of 105-106
Capelle, Dom B. 292
Casel, Dom Odo 153 *passim*
Catecheses of Theodore of Mopsuestia 6-7
catechumenate, in third century 74 *passim*
  in fourth and fifth centuries 247 *passim*
  at beginning of Middle Ages 249
cathedra of bishop 118

Cautio episcopi 278-279
cellae martyrum 179
Celtic liturgy 232
chaburah meal 31-32
chants of the Fore-Mass 288-289
Christian community in early Church 17-18
Christmas, feast of 147-149, 195, 265 *passim*
Christmas cycle 264 *passim*
Christmas Masses 265-267
church buildings, comp. with pagan temples and Jewish Temple 16
  influence of cult of martyrs 187
  orientation of 134, 137-138
church organization, early development 201-202
Church Order see *Apostolic Tradition*
Circumcision, feast of 267-268
Cirta, church of 15-16
Clement of Alexandria 155-156
"Clementine Liturgy" 55
clinici 79-80
Collecta 255
Collect prayer, see orations of Roman liturgy
Communion, Holy, decrease in reception 197-198
  in fourth and fifth centuries 170
Communion-rite of Roman Mass 297-298
confessores in *The Apostolic Tradition* 60-61
Confirmation 84
Connolly, Dom R. H. 54-56
Consecration, words of 37, 68-69, 220
Constantine 122-123
Constantinople, Second Ecumenical Council of 193
Constitutiones Apostolorum, see *Apostolic Constitutions*
conversion, methods of 249-250
Coptic liturgy 212-213
  anaphora 225
court ceremonial customs taken in liturgy 129 *passim*
Credo in Deum, significance 95-96
cursus 294-295
Cyprian, St. 116
Cyril of Jerusalem, St. 5

daily prayer in early Church 100 *passim*
deacon, in Oriental liturgies 215-216
  ordination of 63
"deaconesses" 62
dead, services in memory of 142 *passim*
De catechizandis rudibus 247-248
Decentius of Gubbio 84
De oratione of Tertullian 99-100
De poenitentia of Tertullian 239
De publicatione festorum 27
De sacramentis of St. Ambrose 6
De Spiritu Sancto of St. Basil 193
De virginitate of St. Athanasius 104
Deprecatio Gelasii 292
Dêr Balyzch, papyrus of 7
Dorsch, Emil 46
Didache 6, 35-36, 98
Die Kirchenordnung Hippolyts von Rom 54
Dionysian mysteries 156
disciplina arcani 85, 159
Divine Office 278 *passim*. See also "Hours"
Dix, Gregory 12, 33, 58, 68
Doelger, F. J. 128
Duchesne, L. 4, 233
Dura-Europos, church of 15

East-Syrian anaphora 223-224
East-Syrian liturgy, see Syrian liturgies
Easter, date of 25-27
  in fifth and sixth centuries 251 *passim*
  in primitive Church 25-28
Easter cycle 251 *passim*
Easter Mass after Baptism 35, 40-42
Easter triduum 251-252
Easter vigil 260-262
ecclesia, nature of 16-17
"Edict of Toleration" 122 *passim*
Egyptian Church Order 54-55
Egyptian liturgies 209, 224-225, 301
Ehrhard, Albert 109
Elfers, H. 54
Eleusinian mysteries 156-157
Ember Days 269-272
Engberding, H. 56
enemies of Christianity in first three centuries 109 *passim*
Entrance-Rite of Roman Mass 290 *passim*
Ephesus, Council of 196
Ephrem, St. 203-204, 205
epiclesis 70, 218-220, 303
Epiphany, feast of 149-151, 195, 267, 268, 272
Epiphany cycle in Oriental liturgies 264-265
Epistola Apostolorum 89

Epitome 55
Ethiopian liturgy 209, 225-226
Eucharist, the, and meal ritual 32-33, 34-35, 37-38
 as "Breaking of Bread" 29-30
 as sacrifice 45-49, 69, 117-118, 120
 as thanksgiving 44-49
 celebration in second century 40-44
 primitive form of celebration 30-38
 significance of term 38-40
Eucharistia, see Eucharistic Prayer, the
Eucharistic Prayer, the
 in the *Apostolic Tradition* 64-71
 in second century 43-44
Euchologion of Serapion 6, 192
exorcist 59

fasting 252-254
First Apology of St. Justin 5, 40-44
Florilegium Patristicum 7
Fore-Mass 42-43, 66, 287 *passim*
Forty Hours, origin of 28

Gallic liturgies 225-229
Gallic liturgy, the 231-233
Gallican sacramentaries 3
Gelasian sacramentary 235, 237, 242, 272, 299, 300
Gelasius, Pope 270
Germanic languages and liturgy 206, 207
Germano-Roman Pontifical 64
Gloria, the 293-294
Gloria Patri 193, 204
Gnosticism 110-114
 reactions in the liturgy 114 *passim*
graves, orientation of 138-139
Greek as liturgical language 205-206
Greek elements in liturgical prayer 125-126
growth of Church in third century 75

Hanc igitur 297
Hahn, A. 88
Hanssens, J. M. 32
Harnack, A. 75
Hippolytus of Rome 6, 52-53, 57-58, 91. See also *Apostolic Tradition*
Historia Lausiaca 56
History of the Use of Incense in Divine Worship, A 132
Holy Week in fifth and sixth centuries 259 *passim*
"Hours" 98 *passim,* 282-283. See also Divine Office.
Hour-books 104-105

Ignatius of Antioch, St. 12
Incarnation, the, and Gnosticism 112 *passim*
incense, use in liturgy 132-133
Innocent I, Pope 84, 301
Innocent VIII 64
intercessory prayers in canon 301 *passim*
Introit 290
Irenaeus, St. 115 ff.
Ite, missa est 129

Justin, St. 5, 40

Kiss, use in liturgy 128-129
Kiss of peace 66, 91
Kyrie eleison 291-292
Kyrios, as title of Christ 20-21

language of liturgy 125 *passim,* 211-214
 as factor in development of different rites 202 *passim*
Last Supper, the 12, 29-30, 31, 37
Latin as liturgical language 205-206
Lauds 106-107, 278-279
lectio continua 42
lector 288
Les origines liturgiques 4
Les origines du culte chrétien 4
Lessons of Mass 287-288
 in Oriental liturgies 221
Le Nourry 82
Lent, as preparation for Baptism 255 *passim*
 development 252 *passim*
 origin 243 *passim*
 themes of weeks of 256-258
Leo the Great, St. 236
Leonine Sacramentary 234-237, 299-300
libelli pacis 60
Lietzman, H. 69
lights, use in liturgy 132-133
litania major 145
liturgical worship, established by Christ 11-12
 importance in early Christianity 12-13
 in life of Oriental Christians 210 *passim*
liturgy, history of 1-3
liturgy in fourth and fifth centuries, characteristics of 169 *passim*
liturgy and pagan "mysteries," see "mysteries"

"Liturgy of St. John Chrysostom" 222-223
"Liturgy of St. Basil" 222-223
Lützler, Heinrich 124

Manual of Discipline 100
Maria-Laach 153
Marian devotion, early developments of 196
  oldest feast of Mary 267
Maronite liturgy 209
marriage-wreath 140
Martin of Tours, St. 181
martyr, the 175
Martyrium Polycarpi, see Polycarp, St.
Martyrs, cult of 175 *passim*
  early development 176 *passim*
  insertion of names in canon 181-182
  origin 176
  popular features 182 *passim*
  veneration of relics 184 *passim*
  vigils at graves 180 *passim*
Mass celebration, frequency of 276-278
"Mass of the Apostles" 66
"Mass of the Apostles Addai and Mari" 69
Mass of the Roman Rite
  before Gregory the Great 286 *passim*
  canon in sixth century 298 *passim*
  development of "private" form 277-278
  transition from Greek to Latin 286 to 287. See also, Entrance-rite, Fore-Mass, etc.
Mediator Dei 1, 98, 161
Melkites 209
Memento of the dead 304
Memento of the living 293
memoriae martyrum 178
metropolitan centres as factors in devel. of different rites 201-202, 207-209
Milan, liturgy of 232
milk and honey at Easter Mass 35, 139
Minucius Felix 17, 45, 119, 128
Missale Gothicum 272
Monophysitism 208-209
Montanism 110
Monumenta eucharistica et liturgica vetustissima 7
mother-tongue, in liturgy of early Church 166-167
  in Oriental liturgies 211-214
Mozarabic liturgy 229-230
music in early Christian worship 124-125
Mystagogic Catecheses of Jerusalem 5-6
"mysteries," pagan, and the Fathers of the Church 155-156, 158
  extent of influence on liturgy 157 *passim*
  initiation into 153-154
  origin 154
  relation to liturgy in Casel's theory 160 *passim*
  use of terminology by Christians 158-159
mystery, use of word by St. Paul 158

Newman, Cardinal 2
Nicea, Council of 189, 192

Occidental liturgies, origin 200 *passim*
  early development 227 *passim*
offering of gifts, in Apostolic Tradition 66-67
  in second century 41
  in Oriental rites 216-217
Offertory-rite, development of 116-118
  of Roman Mass 297
Offertory procession 171-172
Old Slavonic 213
oratio communis (*fidelium*) 41, 288, 293
orations of Roman liturgy 294-296
Orders, major, in *Apostolic Tradition* 62-64
Orders, minor, in *Apostolic Tradition* 59-60
Ordines Romani 3
orientation, during prayer 134 *passim*
  of churches 134, 137-138
  of graves 138-139
Origen 44, 57
Oriental liturgies, anaphora 217 *passim*
  early development 210 *passim*
  formularies 222 *passim*
  general characteristics 210-217
  lessons 221
  origins 200
  preparation of gifts 216-217

pagan religious customs taken into liturgy 132 *passim*

pagan state vs. Christianity 109-110
parousia 103, 135-136
participation of people in early liturgy 169 *passim*
Pastor Hermae 135
Pater noster in the Mass 297-298
Penance, in early Church 238-240
in fourth and fifth centuries 240 *passim*
per Christum . . . 43, 189 *passim*
Peregrinatio Aetheriae 6, 208, 259, 282, 291-292
Perpetua and Felicity, Sts. 177
Peter and Paul, Sts., origin of feasts 146-147
Philosophumena of Hippolytus 54
Piccolomini, A. P. 64
Pius XII 1
Polycarp, St. 177, 181, 190, 200
pompa diaboli 80
Pontificale Romanum and *Apostolic Tradition* 63-64
popular character of early liturgy 166
prayer, at midnight 100, 102-103, 104
at third, sixth and ninth hours 98-100, 101-102, 104
morning and night 100, 102, 104
orientation during 170
posture during 170
private 96-106
Prayer-service, basic structure of 282, 291
pre-Advent 273-274
Preface of the Mass 298-299, 300
presbyter, ordination of 63
priest, history of Christian use of term 17-18
priestly character of whole church 17-18
primitive liturgy, study of, first period 2-3
modern developments 3-5
sources 5-7
Probst, F. 5, 7
Psalms, in Divine Office 280, 281, 284-285
in liturgy of 4th and 5th centuries 167-168
de Puniet, Dom 82

Quadragesima s. Martini 272-273
Quasten, J. 7

Redemption as viewed in Christian antiquity 71-73
Reformation, the, and liturgical research 3
refrigerium 140-141, 183-184
relics, veneration of 184 *passim*
renunciation of Satan 80-81
responsorial chant 283-284
rites, Eastern and Western, early development of 200 *passim*
Roman canon of sixth century 300 *passim*
Roman elements in liturgical prayers 126 *passim*
Roman Mass, see Mass of the Roman Rite, etc.
Romano-African liturgies 227, 233-234
Roman sacramentaries 3
Rossi, G. B. 4

Sacramentarium Gelasianum 235, 237, 242, 272, 299, 300
Sacramentarium Leonianum 235-237, 299-300
sacramentaries 235
sacrifice, Christian and pagan 47-48. See also Eucharist as sacrifice
St. Maur, Benedictines of 3
Sanctus, 71, 300-301
Schwartz, E. 54
Scripture, Holy, familiarity with 167-169
in Divine Office 281, 283
in Oriental liturgies 221
see also Fore-Mass, lessons
Serapion 6
Shape of the Liturgy, The 12, 68
Söhngen, Gottlieb 162
Sol invictus 136, 148, 266
Sol salutis 136
songs of the Mass 221, 222. See also, Entrance-Rite, Introit, etc.
Spanish liturgy, see Mozarabic liturgy
stational services 254-255
Statuta Ecclesiae Antiquae 64
Stephen, St., feast of 268-269
Strauss, David Friedrich 3
Sun, as title of Christ 136-137
Sunday 19-25
as day of the resurrection 21-22
as the eighth day 22-23
as the Lord's day 20-21
origin of word 23-24
Sunday Mass 42, 276-277
obligation 173-174

Symbolum Apostolorum see Apostles' Creed
Symbol, oldest Roman 90-91
Syrian liturgies 204-205, 301
Syro-Aramaic, as early liturgical language 203-204

task of Church in pagan world 141-142
Tertullian 99-101, 116, 239
Testamentum Domini 7, 55, 173
thanksgiving, as primary attitude of liturgy 49. See also Eucharist
Theodore of Mopsuestia 6-7
Traditio Apostolica, see *Apostolic Tradition*

Valla, Laurenius 88
Vespers 106-107, 278-279
viduae in early Church 61-62
vigil, at martyrs' grave 179-180
see Easter vigil, Ember Days
virgines, in *Apostolic Tradition* 61, 62

week, the Christian 24-25, 72-73
West-Syrian liturgy 209, 224
Wieland, Franz 45
worship in the Old Testament and the New 10-11

Zepherinus, Pope 53